To those who have helped shape my work:

The Free Southern Theater
The New Orleans Group
The Performance Group
East Coast Artists

THE APPLAUSE ACTING SERIES

ENVIRONMENTAL THEATER

An Expanded New Edition including "Six Axioms For Environmental Theater"

Richard Schechner

APPLAUSE
NEW YORK • LONDON

AN APPLAUSE ORIGINAL

ENVIRONMENTAL THEATER

By Richard Schechner

Library of Congress Cataloging-in-Publication Data

Schechner, Richard, 1934-
      Environmental theater / Richard Schechner. --New, expanded ed.
            p.   cm. -- (The Applause acting series)
      Includes bibliographical references and index.
      ISBN 1-55783-178-5
      1. Performance Group. 2. Theater--Psychological aspects.
I. Title. II. Series.
PN2297.P4S3   1994
792--dc20   94-4199
                                                            CIP

British Library Cataloging-in-Publication Data

A catalogue record of this book is available from the British Library

APPLAUSE BOOKS

211 W. 71ST STREET, NEW YORK, NY 10023
PHONE: 212-595-4735 FAX: 212-721-2856

406 VALE ROAD, TONBRIDGE KENT TN9 1XR
PHONE: 0732 357755 FAX: 0732 770219

First Applause Printing: 1994

Contents

About the Author

Richard Schechner is the artistic director of East Coast Artists. He is University Professor and Professor of Performance Studies at New York University's Tisch School of the Arts. Schechner is the author of many books, including *Between Theater and Anthropology*, *Performance Theory*, and *The Future of Ritual*. Schechner is the editor of *TDR* and has directed performances and led performance workshops in North and South America, Asia, Europe, and Africa.

A Note on Names

All names used are real names. Where I felt that actual names should not be used, I substituted initials, although not the initials of the people whose anonymity I felt ought to be preserved. People may recognize themselves, and friends may recognize friends. This book is a lot about groups and group work. I did not want to invent names or create any more fiction than an author always does simply by putting into words what once were acts.

Re-Introducing
Environmental Theater

This book is back in print because the ideas in it are current. I wrote *Environmental Theater* in 1971-72 in order to put into writing what could be said about the practice of environmental theater as I played it with The New Orleans Group and The Performance Group (1967-80). Since then, environmental theater has gone big time, has been used in various popular entertainments, and even, among the art-conscious, earned a new name: "site specific" performances. Of course, the word "environment" doesn't mean in the 1990s what it meant in the early 1970s. I got the term from Allan Kaprow whose 1966 book, *Assemblages, Environments, & Happenings* had a big impact on me. Kaprow drew "environment" from the painter's world. To telescope Kaprow's argument: First there were paintings in solid frames; next artists began pasting stuff from the "real world" onto those paintings in order to make what were called "collages." Then these collages began to spill over the frames, eliminating the frames. "Assemblages," three dimensions (but not sculpture), began to protrude from what used to be canvases. Next the assemblages moved onto the gallery floor as artists began to energize all the space available to them. Paintings no longer hung tamely on walls (as they do, mostly, once again). Whole "environments" were created through which spectators travelled. Soon enough, events happened in these constructed spaces. Happenings are one parent of "performance art" (political performance & audience participation are others). Later on, in the late '70s or '80s, "environment" acquired its popular ecological meaning.

The theatrical and the ecological meanings of environment are not antithetical. An environment is what surrounds, sustains, envelops, contains, nests. But it is also participatory and active, a concantination of living systems. In terms of the planet earth, the environment is where life happens. The earth's environment is affected by living beings (as well as by non-living natural events such as volcanic eruptions, storms, floods, sunspots, etc.). There is a complex relationship between the so-called natural and the so-called human. Human agency may not affect volcanic eruptions or earthquakes, but human actions do affect the weather and the severity of its impact, the extent of and severity of floods (through deforestation and dams), and many other apparently "natural" events. Probably, we shall discover more and finer links between human agency, the agency of other living beings, and what was not so long ago believed to be a separate and dumbly operating nature. Rain forests not only sustain life far beyond the canopies of the Amazon or Malaysia, they are created by the plants, insects, fungi, and animals living in the forests. In terms of performance, an environment is where the action takes place. But theorists recognize that this action is not localized to the "stage" nor limited to what happens to the actors. The action is also where the audience is, where the actors dress and makeup, where the theater does its business (lobby, box office, administrative offices). Even the toilets and the transportation systems conveying people to and from the theater are part of the "performance environment." All these interlocked systems—those of the performers, those of the spectators, those of the people who run the theater business, those who get people to and from the theater, those who feed the spectators before, during, or after a show: all this, and more, comprise the "performance environment."

In a word, environments ecological or theatrical can be imagined not only as spaces but as active players in complex systems of transformation. Neither ecological nor performance environments are passive. They are interactants in events organically taking place throughout vivified spaces. A performance environment is a "position" in the political sense, a "body of knowledge" in the scholarly sense, a "real place" in the theatrical sense. Thus, to stage a performance "environmentally" means more than simply to move it off of the proscenium or out of the arena. An environmental performance is one in which *all the elements or parts* making up the performance are recognized as alive. To "be alive" is to change, develop, transform; to have needs and desires; even, potentially, to acquire, express, and use consciousness.

Some of these ideas I knew about when I wrote *Environmental Theater*. Some were implicit in the text. Others are plain to me now though I didn't have an inkling about them when I was writing in the early 1970s. But I believe that texts—like performances, people, places, planets, star systems, and thinking machines have or can develop lives of their own. That is, to speak only of texts, these exist only as relational nodes in constantly emergent systems. To put it plainly: a book is a relation between what is on the page and what is going on in and among its readers: a book is many simultaneous dialogs. How many depends on how many readers there are. Thus as I re-read *Environmental Theater* I get new and different things from it than when I composed it. Such a changing set of meanings and significances is what keeps a particular text alive. Great texts—whether of literature, visual arts, performances, architecture, or even "natural beauty" (such as the Grand Canyon of the Colorado or the range of stupendous Himalayan mountains visible from Darjeeling in West Bengal, India, or the Atlantic Ocean in hurricane where it meets the New Jersey shore)—are forever repositioning themselves as they are newly received and interpreted by different readers who are actually players in ongoing, historically grounded performances. I mean: each new "reading" or "experience" is a change in the relationship between players. Obviously, because I am a *homosapiens* I know more about, and can investigate more thoroughly, *my own* and *my species* position in the relationship. As a *homosapiens* of a particular culture and historical period, I am "specified" but by no means unable to communicate, and give-and-take, with and from other people of other cultures and historical periods. But even more—and this is what biologists, zoologists, and ethologists try to do—I can attempt to understand non-human species. And even beyond this, though I am not exactly sure what I am saying, I want to investigate and communicate with geographical formations, sub-atomic particles and waves, and many other non-biologic entities. I do not consider myself a mystic or a believer. Yet I suspect that the totality of the universe, and each of its uncountable constituent parts, is/are alive; and therefore can be understood and experienced as "partners" or co-consciousnesses. At least, this is some of what *Environmental Theater* now says to me, localized in and expressed through the world of theatrical performance as practiced in America during the last third of the 20th century.

To come back to earth: *Environmental Theater* is a history book detailing my experiences first with The New Orleans Group (1964-67) and then in New York, where I moved in 1967, with The Performance Group during the first two stages of its development (1967-69, 1970-72). *Environmental Theater* is also a performer training manual outlining practices and the theories underlying them that I developed in my work with TPG. These methods of training—based on whole body work, yogic breathing, sound-making, and the release of feelings (connecting these feelings, sooner or later, to social or political circumstances: "the personal is the political")—I used, and still use, in the many performer workshops I've led in the Americas, Europe, Asia, and, briefly, South Africa. Many of the same exercises form the basis of training with East Coast Artists, a company I founded in 1991 and am presently artistic director of. People who have seen ECA's first production, *Faust/gastronome* (1993), often ask me how have we accomplished such precision in performing along with such a strong mix of highly energized acting, singing, moving, and narrating. The answer, or that part of it that goes beyond working with very talented people, is in *Environmental Theater*.

But *Environmental Theater* is about more than performer training. It is also about directing, composing performances, designing spaces, site specific performances, and the formation (and destruction) of groups. In forming East Coast Artists I am attempting again to make an environmental theater. But the 1990s are very different from the 1960s. Regarding ECA, I do not foresee a theater staging only live performances, taking months for workshops and rehearsals, presenting shows in small theaters, ever providing "a living" for its member artists. The ECA model is: make movies or TV, or do whatever is necessary (and hopefully pleasant) to bake your daily bread; then work in ECA as you would in a club or religious organization, as a "volunteer." Think of ECA as life-long training, a place where theater art can be practiced. But don't think of it as a stepping stone to a "better" career in the theater. ECA is the better career. Don't expect ECA to provide you with "a living" in the monetary sense, but rather work together so that it can give you "a life" in the spiritual sense.

Environmental Theater specifies a way of working, putting this way in its definite historical and theoretical place. The book also projects a theoretical position regarding this way of working. The practice of environmental theater is alive, if different than what I thought it would be when I wrote the book. As for the theory, it continues to challenge more orthodox approaches to theater. Individual chapters in *Environmental Theater* locate nodes of particular importance for the construction of what I felt in the early 1970s would be a "new theater." Since writing *Environmental Theater*, much has changed in the theater and in American culture. What were hot issues have cooled off. Certain practices—such as nakedness onstage or in film—that were so disturbing and controversial have become commonplace (and too often exploitative). Other practices—such as audience participation—are now rare in "legitimate" theater but a staple of dinner theater, game parks, and interactive telecommunications. Environmental spatial configurations for performance are not frequent in mainstream theater. The construction in the regional theater or in New York, Chicago, Los Angeles, or San Francisco of many flexible-spaced theaters did not occur. Many flexible space theaters were built at colleges, hundreds of

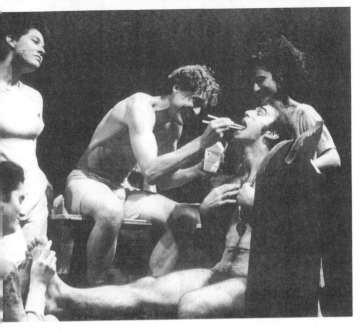

Faust is fed his last supper in East Coast Artists' *Faust/gastronome* (1993) at La Mama ETC, New York.

which boast of a "black box theater." But almost all of sometimes magnificent facilities are used orthodoxly, bleachers screwed to the floor, the staging drearily slapped up against a wall in a tired mimicry of the proscenium. Spatial experimentation has escaped mainstream theater, belonging instead to theme parks, "living museums" (such as Plimoth Plantation or Colonial Williamsburg) and enterprises specifically focused on environmental staging such as En Garde Arts in New York. But even En Garde Arts usually sits its spectators down facing a performance emanating from one side of the space only. For the most part, since 1980 I have also staged plays in a more sedentary manner than I did when composing *Environmental Theater*. Both *Faust/gastronome* and *The Prometheus Project* (1985)—my most recent New York productions—were endstaged. Environmental theater scenography is expensive and time-consuming because whole spaces have to be redesigned and constructed. Ironically, I've been able to experiment with environmental theater design in less-than-rich countries whose theater artists are avidly interested in environmental theater design and whose producers are willing to invest in it: Chekhov's *The Cherry Orchard* (1983) in Hindi in New Delhi and August Wilson's *Ma Rainey's Black Bottom* (1992) at the Grahamstown Festival in South Africa.

Some other concerns in *Environmental Theater*, in the background during the 1980s, are re-emerging these days. In the chapters on shamanism and on therapy, I discuss not only specific experiments conducted by The Performance Group, but an expanded view of what constitutes performance. I relate Western theater to performances in other cultures; and to "sources" (if not "origins") of performance in practices of healing, small-group interactions, exorcism, journeys through mystical time-space, and other such practices. I point out that theater goes far beyond rational and logocentric ("dramatic text") operations. I remind readers that performance consists of four great realms: entertainment, ritual, healing, and education. That modern Western orthodox theater emphasizes entertainment and education (political theater) over ritual and healing. But this does not foreclose the emergence, or rediscovery, of many performances that foreground healing and ritual. These affirmations of an expanded understanding of what performance is, became the basis of "performance studies," an academic discipline I have been engaged in for many years. The ideas in these chapters may also be of concern to scholars and practitioners of "new age shamanism" and others engaged in studying, inventing, or refurbishing ritual performances of all kinds.

As noted earlier, much of what is discussed in *Environmental Theater* can be found as practice in popular entertainments, theme parks, and site specific performances. It is in these places—removed from the regional theater, Broadway and its offshoots, and other kinds of orthodox theater—that environmental theater has flourished. In fact, newspaper critics and even more than a few scholarly journal writers regard the orthodox theater as "serious art," while marginalizing or dismissing both the avant-garde and popular entertainments. The orthodox theater is shrinking while alternative kinds of performance (from the avant-garde and new community-based theaters to a wide range of environmental and interactive popular entertainments) are definitely on the rise. This "new mainstream" ranges across the gamut of performance from the educational to the avant-garde, from crass commercialism to experimentation, from small-scale operations to vast enterprises. I am talking about the Disney theme parks and their imitators; the hundreds of "restored villages" and "living museums" that entertain and educate millions; re-enactments of the Civil War and other "real life" events; renaissance pleasure fairs, processions, and street carnivals celebrating an incredible diversity of cultural practices from Roman Catholic saints to Caribbean Carnival to cross dressing and gay pride; hunt-and-kill games played indoors and out, in real and in virtual spaces; "whodunit" dinner theater, boat trips, and train rides; site specific theater such as *Tamara* and *Tony and Tina's Wedding*; innumerable performance art pieces, both large and small scale, in galleries, on the streets, in the countryside; and an even larger number of religious and ritual performances; street entertainers now found in many parks and avenues across America. Academicians have not yet really got the message: but this diversity of performance *is* the American theater; and as such, the American theater is very much part of the diversity of world performance.

Of course, many of these events preceded *Environmental Theater.* As Arnold Aronson showed in *The History and Theory of Environmental Scenography* (1981, Ann Arbor: UMI Research Press) staging performances in found spaces or spaces especially constructed for a specific performance, involving the whole audience in the performance, processional performances, performances in multiple spaces, and so on is traditional in many cultures, including Western culture. In fact, the indoor theater in which every play is fitted into the same space modified on its surface by means of scene design and lighting is the minor tradition. Environmental theater is the major tradition. What *Environmental Theater* does is to specify the ways in which the minor and major traditions interact. When I began my practical experiments in environmental theater, I was making theater for audiences who went to "ordinary" theaters. Even if some of these same people enjoyed Disneyland or Plimoth; even if they participated in religious services by standing and sitting on cue, singing and reciting; even if they delighted in street fairs, carnivals, and Mardi Gras, most of them rarely made the connection between what they did and saw at these popular entertainments, religious observances, and festivals and "mainstream theater." What *Environmental Theater* does is make these connections clear; to say how the mainstream might be livened by reconnecting it to the major tradition. Once this possibility was made manifest, lots of things happened. Not that *Environmental Theater* was the only or the most decisive catalyst of change. Kaprow's works and writings, the theories and practice of John Cage, the swelling army of performance artists, practitioners of "new dance" (later called "postmodern dance"), the performance education of so many youths by rock concerts from Woodstock to thousands of smaller but also mind-bending events, and the mainstreaming of Christian evangelists via TV, the effervescence of many religious sects—often African based—who heal, prophesy, sing, dance, and play out their experiences, the widespread practice of new age shamanism, the opening up of formerly stodgy museums to playful, interactive, and participatory exhibits—all this and more formed the still emerging world of environmental theater.

What do I think about all this "qualitatively"? In other words, do I like some of what's happening even as I detest or am troubled by other practices? Should people's education about history and cultures depend so strongly on the interactive and participatory exhibits of living museums? Do I believe that new age shamans or those who invent rituals are tapping in to "truths" or are they shysters conning people? What do I feel about the gender values implicit in rock or rap? Where do I stand in relation to TV evangelists? What about the nihilism, violence, and rage spewed out by much of popular culture? My own world view, for those who are interested, is skeptical, ironic, and distrusting. My work habits are fierce, my workplaces orderly. I think that most of what people accept as "truth" is a projection of desire, neither more nor less. Because so many people's daily lives are full of danger, sickness, uncertainty, desperation, ignorance, poverty, and general unhappiness, there is always (and not only in America) a big market for performances that make people feel good, that answer their questions and settle doubts, that stimulate and satisfy sexual drives, that offer panaceas and various messiahs, that encourage the formation of cults, that feed xenophobia, and that provide escapist entertainment. Most of these performances from the viewpoint of "values" is crap; and some of the ideologies are socially corrosive, racist, and sexist. But the "legitimate theater" is even worse: pretentious, politically unexamined, badly done, and boring. Measuring one against the other,

I prefer the effervescence of popular culture and the risk-taking of experimental performance to the Nyquil of so-called mainstream theater.

Five years before finishing *Environmental Theater*, I wrote "Six Axioms for Environmental Theater." It was the first time I explored in writing what I meant by "environmental theater." The axioms provide the underlying theoretical basis for environmental theater. The axioms came out of historical research and my practical work with the New Orleans Group, co-directed by visual artist Franklin Adams, composer and musician Paul Epstein, and me. The New Orleans Group mounted two main productions: *4/66* (1966, in a large two floor artist's studio) and Eugene Ionesco's *Victims of Duty* (1967, at New Orleans' Le Petit Theatre du Vieux Carré). The axioms are important because they are my first full statement regarding environmental theater. What is developed in *Environmental Theater* is outlined and made plain theoretically in the axioms. And although many of the specific examples in the axioms are time-bound, the basic theory is, I believe, current even today. Therefore, I have included "Six Axioms" in this book.

—Richard Schechner
New York, 1994

SIX AXIOMS FOR ENVIRONMENTAL THEATER

1967, revised 1987

1: THE THEATRICAL EVENT IS A SET OF RELATED TRANSACTIONS

The theatrical event includes audience, performers, scenario or dramatic text (in most cases), performance text, sensory stimuli, architectural enclosure or some kind of spatial demarcation, production equipment, technicians, and house personnel (when used). It ranges from non-matrixed performances[1] to orthodox mainstream theater, from chance events and intermedia to "the production of plays." A continuum of theatrical events blends one form into the next:

"Impure," life   "Pure," art

public events, ⟷ intermedia ⟷ environmental ⟷ orthodox
demonstrations   happenings   theater   theater

It is because I wish to include this entire range in my definition of theater that traditional distinctions between art and life no longer apply. All along the continuum there are overlaps; and within it—say between an orthodox production of *Hamlet* and the October 1966 March on the Pentagon or Allan Kaprow's *Self-Service*[2]—there are contradictions. Aesthetics is built on systems of interaction and transformation, on the ability of coherent wholes to include contradictory parts. In the words of New York city planner Richard Weinstein, "competing independent systems within the same aesthetic frame." Kaprow might even take a more radical position, doing away altogether with the frame (see his "The Real Experiment," 1983), or accepting a variety of frames depending on the perspectives of the performers and spectators.

Surely the frames may change during a single performance, transforming an event into something unlike what it started out being. The end of *Iphegenia Transformed* (1966) at the Firehouse Theatre had Euripides' *dea ex machina* lowered onto stage bringing with her four cases of beer. The marriage ceremony that concludes *Iphegenia at Aulis* was followed by a celebration that included the entire audience— the party lasted several hours. Years later, in his production of *The Trojan Women*, Suzuki Tadashi, the Japanese director of experimental theater, ended the play with an onstage actors-only supper of Big Macs. In my 1973 production with The Performance Group of Brecht's *Mother Courage*, scene 3—the death of Swiss Cheese—was followed immediately by a supper served to the spectators.

The theatrical event is a complex social interweave, a network of expectations and obligations.[3] The exchange of stimuli—either sensory or cognitive or both—is the root of theater. What it is that separates theater from more ordinary exchanges—say a simple conversation or a party—is difficult to pinpoint formally. One might say that theater is more regulated, following a script or a scenario; that it has been rehearsed. Kirby would probably argue that theater presents the self in a more defined way than usual social encounters. Grotowski has said that the theater is a meeting place between a traditional text and a troupe of performers.

> I didn't do Wyspianski's *Akropolis*, I met it. [...] One structures the montage so that this confrontation can take place. We eliminate those parts of the text which have no importance for us, those parts with which we can neither agree nor disagree. [...] We did not want to write a new play, we wished to confront ourselves (1968a: 44).

Indeed, confrontation is what makes current American political activity theatrical. To meet Bull Connor's dogs in Birmingham or LBJ's troops at the Pentagon is more than a showdown in the Wild West tradition. In the movies, everything would be settled by the showdown. In the political demonstrations, contrasts are heightened, nothing resolved. A long series of confrontations is necessary to actuate change. The streets of Birmingham and the steps of the Pentagon are visible boundaries, special places of special turbulence, where sharply opposed styles are acted out by both sides. At the Pentagon, stiff ranks and files of troops confronted snake-dancing protesters; in Birmingham hand-holding civil rights activists marched peaceably into the snarling dogs and twisting fire-hoses barely held under control by the police. Grotowski's personal confrontation is converted into a social confrontation. Out of such situations, slowly and unevenly, guerrilla and street theater emerge, just as out of the confrontation between medieval ceremony and Renaissance tumult emerged the Elizabethan theater.

John Cage has offered an inclusive definition of theater:

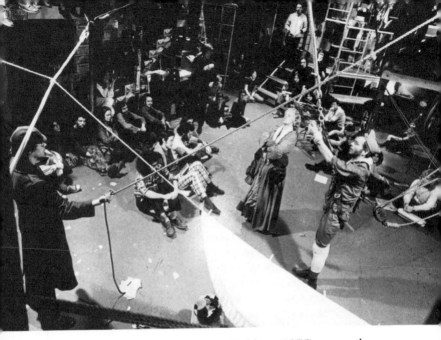

Bertolt Brecht's *Mother Courage and Her Children* (1975), scene three. Courage says she doesn't know Swiss Cheese who is under arrest. Note how the spectators are scattered around The Performing Garage environment, designed by James Clayburgh. (*Richard Schechner*)

Bertolt Brecht's *Mother Courage and Her Children* (1975), scene three, in The Performing Garage. As Courage watches, Swiss Cheese is hoisted aloft, where he will remain until executed. (*Richard Schechner*)

I would simply say that theater is something which engages both the eye and the ear. The two public senses are seeing and hearing; the senses of taste, touch, and odor are more proper to intimate, non-public, situations. The reason I want to make my definition of theater that simple is so that one could view everyday life itself as theater. [...] I think of theater as an occasion involving any number of people, but not just one (1965: 50-51).

Cage's definition is probably too restrictive. Performance artists have made pieces involving the "intimate senses." And there are performances involving only one person. In the New Orleans Group's 1967 production of Eugene Ionesco's *Victims of Duty,* three "private" senses were stimulated. During a seduction scene perfume was released in the room; frequently the performers communicated to the spectators by means of touch. At the very end of the show, chunks of bread were forcefully administered to the audience by the performers, expanding the final cruel gesture of Ionesco's play. Of course, the Bread and Puppet Theatre concludes all its performances with the sharing of home-baked bread.

In situations where descriptive definitions are so open as to be inoperative as excluding criteria, one must seek *relational* definitions. Taking a relational view makes it possible to understand theater as something more inclusive than the staging of literature, acting, and directing. It is possible to integrate into a single system works as diverse as *Self-Service* and Tyrone Guthrie's *Oresteia.* Goffman's assertions regarding social organization are broader even than Cage's and go right to the heart of the theatrical event:

[...] any [...] element of social life [...] exhibits sanctioned orderliness arising from obligations fulfilled and expectations realized (1961: 19).

Briefly, a social order may be defined as the consequence of any set of moral norms [rules] that regulate the way in which persons pursue objectives (1963: 8).

The nature of the expectation-obligation network and specific sets of rules vary widely depending on the particular performance.

Returning to the continuum, at the left end are loosely organized street events—the 1966 March on the Pentagon, activities of the Amsterdam and New York Provos [4]; toward that end of the continuum are Kaprow's kind of happenings. In the center of the continuum are highly organized intermedia events—some of Kirby's and Robert

Whitman's work, and "conventional" environmental theater such as the NOG's *Victims of Duty* or Richard Brown's 1967 production of *The Investigation* at Wayne State University. At the far right of the continuum is the orthodox staging of dramatic texts. The analysis of dramatic texts is possible only from the middle of the continuum to the right end; performance analysis is possible along the entire range.

What related transactions Comprise the theatrical event? There are three primary ones:

> Among performers.
> Among members of the audience.
> Between performers and audience.

The first begins during rehearsals and continues through all performances. In Stanislavski-oriented training the heaviest emphasis is given to performer-performer transactions. They are, in fact, identified with "the play." The theory is that if the interactions among the performers are perfected—even to the exclusion of the audience from the performers' attention both during rehearsals, which are closed, and during production when the audience is "hidden" on the other side of the proscenium arch—the production will be artistically successful. When this method works the spectators feel they are watching through a fourth wall, "visitors to the Prozorov household," as Stanislavski put it. But there are many examples showing that this method rarely works. It is simply not enough for the performers to be a self-enclosed ensemble.

The second transaction—among members of the audience—is usually overlooked. The decorum of orthodox theater-going is such that the audience obeys strict rules of behavior. They arrive more or less on time, they do not leave their seats except for intermission or at the end of the show, they display approval or disapproval within well-regulated patterns of applause, silence, laughter, tears, and so on. In events on the far left of the performance continuum, it is difficult to distinguish spectators from performers. A street demonstration or sit-in is made up of shifting groups of performers and spectators. And in confrontations between demonstrators and police both groups fill both roles alternately and, frequently, simultaneously. A particularly rich example of this occurred during the March on the Pentagon. The demonstrators had broken through the military lines and were sitting-in in the Pentagon parking lot. Those in the front lines sat against the row of troops and frequent small actions—nudging, exchange of conversation—turned these front lines into focal points. Every half-hour or so, both the front-line troops and front-line demonstrators were relieved of their posts. Demonstrators who were watching the action became part of it; the same for the troops. Elements of the Pentagon leadership stood on the steps in front of the building's main entrance watching the procedure. For someone at home, the entire confrontation was a performance and everyone—from Defense Secretary Robert McNamara at his window and the ad-hoc demonstration leaders with their bullhorns down to individual soldiers and protesters—was acting according to role.

Very little hard work has been done researching the behavior of audiences and the possible exchange of roles between audience members and performers.[5] Unlike the performers, the spectators attend theater unrehearsed; they bring to the theater adherence to decorum learned previously but nevertheless scrupulously applied now. Usually the audience is an impromptu group, meeting at the time/place of the performance but never again meeting as a defined group. Thus uncohesive and unprepared, they are difficult to collectivize and mobilize but, once mobilized, even more difficult to control.

The third primary transaction—between performers and spectators—is a traditional one. An action onstage evokes an empathetic reaction in the audience which is not an imitation but a harmonic variation. Thus sadness on stage may evoke tears in the audience or put into play personal associations which, on the surface, seem unrelated to sadness. Conversely, as any performer will eagerly testify, audiences "good" and "bad" affect the performance. Good and bad are sliding terms depending the kind of performance and who is making the value judgment. An active, boisterous audience may be good for farce but bad for serious plays. The "best" audiences are those who respond harmonically up to but not beyond the point where the performers become distracted. Orthodox theater in the West uses a thin fraction of the enormous range of audience-performer interactions. Other cultures are much more adventurous in this regard.

The three primary interactions are supplemented by four secondary ones:

Among production elements.
Between production elements and performers.
Between production elements and spectators.
Between the total production and the space(s) where it takes place.

These are secondary now, but they could become primary.[6] By production elements I mean scenery, costumes, lighting, sound, make-up, and so on. With the full-scale use of film, TV, taped sound, projected still images and the powerful impact of "style"[7]—production elements need no longer "support" a performance. These elements are more important than the performers. The Polyvision and Diapolyecran rooms at the Czech Pavilion at Montreal's Expo '67 introduced new kinds of film and still-image environments that can serve either as background for performers or as independent performing elements.[8]

Briefly the Polyvision was a total conversion of a medium-size, rather high ceilinged room into a film and slide environment. Mirrors, moving cubes and prisms, projections both from outside the space and from within the cubes, images which seemed to move through space as well as cover the walls, ceilings, and floors all built the feeling of a full space of great pictorial flexibility. The nine-minute presentation, programmed on a ten-track computer tape used eleven film projectors and twenty-eight slide projectors. The material itself was banal—an account of Czech industry. But of course more "artistic" or "meaningful" material could be used in the system. No live performers participated.

The Diapolyecran was not actually an environment; it was restricted to one wall and the audience sat on the floor watching the fourteen-minute show. Only slide projectors were used. According to the "Brief Description":

> The Diapolyecran is technical equipment which enables a simultaneous projection of slides on a mosaic projection screen consisting of 112 projection surfaces. The surfaces are projected on from behind and they may be shifted singly, in groups, or all at once. This enables one to obtain with still images pictures of motion, and the picture groups thus obtained are best characterized as "mosaic projection."

Each of the 112 slide projectors was mounted on a steel frame that had three positions: back, middle, forward. The images could be thrust out toward the audience or moved back from it. The mosaic was achieved by complex programming—there were 5.5 million bits of information memorized on tape; 19,600 impulses were emitted per second. By the mid-70s this or similar techniques had become commonplace in museums, business, music TV, and rock concerts. The theater, however, restricted its electronic research to computerizing lighting controls (still using old-fashioned fresnel and ellipsoidal instruments). Little attempt has been made to tap the resources suggested by the Czechs.

But the key to making technical elements part of the creative process is not simply to apply the latest research to theatrical productions. The technicians themselves must become an active part of the performance. This does not necessarily mean the use of more sophisticated equipment, but rather the more sophisticated use of the human beings who run whatever equipment is available. The technicians' role is not limited to perfecting during rehearsals the use of their machines. During all phases of workshop and rehearsals the technicians should participate. And during performances the technicians should be as free to improvise as the performers, modulating the uses of their equipment night-to-night. Light boards locked into pre-sets do not foster the kind of experimentation I'm talking about. The experience of discos is instructive. The rhythm and content of some light-shows are modulated to accompany and sometimes lead or dominate the activity of the spectator-dancers. During many intermedia performances, the technicians are free to chose where they will project images, how they will organize sound contexts. There is nothing sacred about setting technical elements. If human performance is variable (as it most certainly is), then a unified whole—if one is looking for that—will be better assured by a nightly variation of technical means.

Thus, possibilities exist for "performing technicians" whose language is the film-strip or the electronic sound, and whose range of action includes significant variations in where and what is to be done. The same goes for other technical elements. The separation between performers and technicians is erodable because the new accompany can be used not only to completely program all the material (as at the Czech Pavilion) but also to permit the nearly total flexibility of bits that can be organized on the spot, during the performance. The performing group is expanding to include technicians as well as actors and dancers.

Once this is granted, the creative technician will demand fuller participation in performances and in the workshops and rehearsals that generate performances. At many times during a performance actors and dancers will support the technician, whose activated equipment will be "center stage." A wide-ranging mix is possible where the complexity of images and sounds—with or without the participation of "unarmed" performers—is all but endless.

To achieve this mix of technical and live performers nothing less than the whole space is needed. The kind of work I'm talking about can't happen if one territory belongs to the audience and another to the performers. The bifurcation of space must be ended. The final exchange between performers and audience is the exchange of space, spectators as scene-makers as well as scene-watchers. This will not result in chaos: rules are not done away with, they are simply changed.

The Director talks to Marilyn in David Gaard's *The Marilyn Project* (1975), in the upstairs studio space of The Performing Garage. Note in the background the exact scene duplicated.

The final scene of David Gaard's *The Marilyn Project* (1975), in the upstairs studio space of The Performing Garage. Two men take the famous "calendar girl" pose of Marilyn Monroe as Marilyn photographs them with a polaroid camera.

2: ALL THE SPACE IS USED FOR THE PERFORMANCE

From the Greeks to the present a "special place" within the theater, the stage, has been marked off for the performance. Even in the medieval theater which moved from place to place on wagons the performers generally stayed on the wagons and the spectators in the streets. Most classical Asian theater agrees with the West in this convention. And even village folk-plays are acted out in marked-off areas established for the performance, removed when the show is over.

To find examples of the continuous systematic exchange of space between performers and spectators we must look into ethnographic reports of rituals. There, two circumstances deserve attention. First, the performing group is sometimes the entire population of a village. Or, perhaps, a definite subset of the population such as adult, initiated males. In these cases frequently the uninitiated—women and children—are not permitted to watch; either the uninitiated are kept away or the performances take place in secluded areas. Secondly, these performances are not isolated "shows" but part of ongoing cycles that may extended for months or longer (see chapter 5). Of course, such rituals are entertainments, and prized as such by the people doing them, even as they are something else too. The ritual performances are an integral part of community life, knitted into the ecology of the society—for example, the Hevehe cycle of the Orokolo of Papua New Guinea which recapitulates the life experiences of each individual performer.[10]

During these kinds of performances, the village, or places near it, is co-opted for the performance. But the performance does not stand still. It ranges over a defined territory. If there are spectators they follow the performance, yielding to it when it approaches, pressing in on it as it recedes. *Dance and Trance in Bali* (1938) filmed by Margaret Mead and Gregory Bateson shows this spatial give-and-take as well as the full use of a spatial domain that continuously modulates its boundaries. The dancers are highly organized in their movements. But for parts of the performance they and other performers do not feel called on to stay in one spot. Children playing demons race around the village; entranced followers of the lion Barong chase Rangda (the "witch" in Mead's narration) and, as she turns, flee from her. The performance moves in and out of the temple and all across the open areas at the center of the village. The space of the performance is defined organically by the action. Spectators watch from a variety of perspectives, some paying close attention, some ignoring the goings-on (see chapter 7). Unlike orthodox Western theater where the action is trimmed to a fixed space, this Balinese dance-theater creates its own space as it is being performed. That is not to say that the performers can go anywhere. By the time Mead and Bateson filmed, the Rangda-Barong dance had developed its own mise-en-scene.

Once fixed seating and the automatic bifurcation of space are no longer preset, entirely new relationships are possible. Body contact can occur between performers and spectators; voice levels and acting intensities can be varied widely; a sense of shared experience can be engendered. Most important, each scene can create its own space, either contracting to a central or a remote area or expanding to fill all available space. The action "breathes" and the audience itself becomes a major scenic element. During NOG's *Victims of Duty* we found that the audience pressed in during intense scenes and moved away when the action became broad or violent; usually they willingly gave way to the performers[11] and reoccupied areas after the action passed through. During the final scene, Nicolas chased the Detective all around the periphery of the large room that was both stage and house, stumbling over spectators, searching in the audience for his victim. Nicolas' obstacles were real—the living bodies of the spectators—and the scene ended when he caught and killed the Detective. Had someone in the audience chosen to shelter and protect the Detective an unpredictable complication would have been added, but one that could've been dealt with. At several points in the performance, a member of the audience did not want to give up a place where an action was staged. The performers in character dealt with these people, sometimes forcibly moving them out of the area.[12]

These extra tensions may not seem to be a legitimate part of the performance. Surely they are not part of "the play." But the exchange of place implies possibilities of conflicts over space; such conflicts have to be dealt with in terms of the performance. They can be turned to advantage if one believes that the interaction between performers and spectators is a real and valuable one. In many intermedia performances and happenings spectators actively participate. Often the entire space is performing space—no one is "just watching."

The exchange of space between performers and spectators, and the exploration of the total space by both groups, has not been introduced into our theater by ethnographers turned directors. The model influencing theater is closer to home: the streets. Everyday life is marked by movement and the exchange of space. Street demonstrations are a special form of street life involving keen theatrical sense. A march for civil liberties or against the Vietnam War is a performance using the streets as stages and playing to spectators both on the spot and watching at home on TV or reading about it in the newspapers. People march with or without permits. Having a permit means that the marchers are obeying one set of conventions, to demonstrate without a permit defines the event as guerrilla theater. In either case, the march—or is it the parade?—is defined by rules of the genre; as one set of rules are obeyed another set may be broken. This ever-increasing use of outdoor public space for rehearsed activities—ranging from demonstrations to street entertainers—is having an impact on indoor theater.

3. THE THEATRICAL EVENT CAN TAKE PLACE EITHER IN A TOTALLY TRANSFORMED SPACE OR IN "FOUND SPACE"

Theatrically, environment can be understood in two different ways. First, there is what one can do with and in a space. Secondly, there is the acceptance of a given space. In the first case one *creates* an environment by transforming a space; in the second case, one *negotiates* with an environment, engaging in a scenic dialog with a space.[13] In the created environment the performance in some sense engineers the arrangement and behavior of the spectators; in a negotiated environment a more fluid situation leads sometimes to the performance being controlled by the spectators.

In the orthodox theater, scenery is segregated; it exists only in that part of the space where the performance is played. The construction of scenery is guided by sight-lines; even when "the theater" is exposed—bare walls of the building, curtains removed—as in some Brechtian scenography—the equipment is looked at as an indication that "this is a theater your are seeing, our workplace"; the place where the spectators are is the viewing place, the house. In short, mainstream attitudes toward scenography is naive and compromised.

In environmental theater, if scenery is used at all, it is used all the way, to the limits of its possibilities. There is no bifurcation of space, no segregation of scenery. If equipment is exposed it is there because it must be there, even if it is in the way.

The sources of this extreme position are not easy specify.[14] The Bauhaus[15] group was not really interested in ordinary scenery. Members of the Bauhaus wanted to build new organic spaces where the action surrounded the spectators or where the action could move freely through the space. Their scenic program was close to Artaud's. Most of the Bauhaus projects were never built. But persons wishing to make theater in the environmental tradition learned from the Bauhaus of new audience-performer relationships.

Although not a member of the Bauhaus, Frederick Kiesler (1896-1966) shared many of their ideas. Between 1916 and 1924 he designed, but never built, the Endless Theatre, seating 100,000 people. Kiesler foresaw new functions for theater:

> The elements of the new dramatic style are still to be worked out. They are not yet classified. Drama, poetry, and scenic formation have no natural milieu. Public, space, and players are artificially assembled. The new aesthetic has not yet attained a unity of expression. Communication lasts two hours; the pauses are the social event. We have no contemporary theater. No agitators' theater, no tribunal, no force which does not merely comment on life, but shapes it (1932).

These words were written in 1932. In 1930, Kiesler described his Endless Theatre:

> The whole structure is encased in double shells of steel and opaque welded glass. The stage is an endless spiral. The various levels are connected with elevators and platforms. Seating platforms, stage and elevator platforms are suspended and spanned above each other in space. The structure is an elastic building system of cables and platforms developed from bridge building. The drama can expand and develop freely in space.[16]

With some modification, Kiesler could be describing that great environmental theater of middle American consumerism, the shopping mall: vast enclosed spaces where people meet, play, eat, see various organized entertainments, peer through store windows and open doors as if each were a small proscenium, entering whatever particular space entices them. The object of all this desire certainly revolves around buying but is not limited to buying. It also includes numerous rituals of strolling, browsing, mixing, displaying, greeting, and festivity.

From the Bauhaus and people like Kiesler, the environmental theater learned to reject the orthodox use of space and to seek in the events to be performed organic and dynamic definitions of space. Naturally, such ideas are incompatible with mainstream scenic practice.

Kaprow suggests an altogether different source of environmental theater:

> With the breakdown of the classical harmonies following the introduction of "irrational" or nonharmonic juxtapositions, the Cubists tacitly opened the path to infinity. Once foreign matter was introduced into the picture in the form of paper, it was only a matter of time before everything else foreign to paint and canvas would be allowed to get into the creative act, including real space. Simplifying the history of the enduing evolution into a flashback, this is what

happened: the pieces of paper curled up off the canvas, were removed from the surface to exist on their own, became more solid as they grew into other materials and, reaching out further into the room, finally filled it entirely. Suddenly there were jungles, crowded streets, littered alleys, dream spaces of science fiction, rooms of madness, and junk-filled attics of the mind.

Inasmuch as people visiting such Environments are moving, colored shapes too, and were counted "in," mechanically moving parts could be added, and parts of the created surroundings could then be rearranged like furniture at the artist's and visitors' discretion. And, logically, since the visitor could and did speak, sound and speech, mechanical and recorded, were also soon to be in order. Odors followed (1960: 165-66).[17]

Many intermedia pieces are environmental. Only recently have happeners "discovered" the proscenium stage; a paradoxical cross-over is starting in which the theater is becoming more environmental while happenings and intermedia (and later Performance Art) are becoming more orthodox scenically.

Kaprow says that his own route to happenings (a usage he coined) was through "action collage"—not the making of pictures but the creation of a pictorial event. In his 1952 essay, "The American Action Painters," Harold Rosenberg described what it means to "get inside the canvas":

[...] the canvas began to appear to one American painter after another as an arena in which to act—rather than as a space in which to reproduce, redesign, analyze or "express" an object, actual or imagined. What was to go on the canvas was not a picture but an event (1965: 25).[18]

It is only a small step from action painting and collage to intermedia and happenings and from there to environmental theater. My own interest in environmental theater developed from my work in intermedia. My partners in the New Orleans Group—painter Franklin Adams and composer Paul Epstein—followed the same path. Our first definition of environmental theater was "the application of intermedia techniques to the staging of scripted dramas." A painter's and a composer's aesthetics were melded with that of a theater person's. Traditional biases—theatrical, painterly, musical—fell by the wayside. We were not interested in sightlines or in focusing people's attention onto this or that restricted area. The audience entered a room in which *all* the space was "designed," in which the environment was an organic transformation of one space—the raw rooms in which we put our performances—into another, the finished environments. In *Victims of*

Duty there were "ridges" and "valleys" of carpeted platforms. For those who sat in the valleys vision beyond was difficult. Either they did not see all the action or they stood or they moved. Some of the action took plays in the valleys, and then only spectators very close to the action could see it.

For *Victims* a large room, about a 75' x 75' space, at New Orleans' Le Petit Theatre de Vieux Carré was transformed into the Chouberts' living-room. But it was not a living-room in the ordinary sense. Not all the elements had a clear or usual function. It was, rather, the "idea of a living-room most useful to this production of *Victims of Duty.*" In one corner, chairs spiraled to the ceiling; at another place there was a psychoanalyst's couch; on a high isolated platform a wooden chair sat under a bright overhead light; a small proscenium stage was built against one wall for the play-within-the-play; trap-doors allowed the performers to play underneath the audience; a trapeze permitted them to play overhead; certain scenes took place in the street outside the theater or in other rooms adjoining or over the theater—not all of these scenes could be seen by spectators; stairways led to nowhere; technical equipment was plainly visible, mounted on platforms against two walls; the walls themselves were covered with flats and lightly overpainted so that scenes from previous proscenium productions faintly showed through; on these same walls graffiti was painted: quotations from *Victims of Duty.* The scenic idea was to render visible Ionesco's formulation that the play was a "naturalistic drama," a parody of theater, and a surrealistic-psychedelic-psychoanalytic-detective story.

We did not foreplan the set. The directors, performers, technicians, and production crews had been working for about a month in the space where the play was to be performed. We had, by the time we moved into the space at Le Petit, been rehearsing for four months. One Saturday afternoon we decided to build the environment. We lugged whatever flats, platforms, stairways, and carpets we could find and worked for ten hours straight. Out of that scenic improvisation came the environment. Very few changes were made during the ensuing weeks of rehearsal. The changes that we did make amounted to tuning up the environment that had been brewing for months but which came into concrete existence during one day. I do not want to make out of this experience a general principle. But I would observe that the close work on the production by more than twenty people led to a felt knowledge of what the environment should be. By not planning at all, by working, we understood very well what was needed.

The very opposite of such a total transformation of space is "found space." The principles here are very simple: (1) the given elements of a

A view of the circular theatre, designed by Jim Clayburgh, erected inside The Performing Garage for Seneca's *Oedipus* (1977). The playing space is filled with tons of earth to the depth of three feet. (*Jim Clayburgh*)

space—its architecture, textural qualities, acoustics, and so on—are to be explored and used, not disguised; (2) the random ordering of space or spaces is valid; (3) the function of scenery, if it is used at all, is to understand, not disguise or transform, the space; (4) the spectators may suddenly and unexpectedly create new spatial possibilities.

Most found space is found outdoors or in public buildings that can't be transformed.[19] Here, the challenge is to acknowledge the environment at hand and cope with it creatively. The American prototype for this kind of performance is the protest march or demonstration—for civil rights, women's rights, anti-war, labor, special interest groups, etc. The politics of these marches and confrontations have been discussed elsewhere. Their aesthetics deserves more than passing attention. Take the black freedom movement of the 1950s and 1960s, for example. The streets were dangerous for black people, the highways were not free, and local and state governments inhospitable. The sit-ins explored small indoor spaces; the freedom rides had claimed the interior of buses as they passed through the interstate countryside. But the ultimate gesture was the march of thousands in the streets and across miles of highway. The and was proclaimed open, and if there are those who disagree let them make themselves known. The aesthetic fallout of that grand gesture was that the streets were no longer places used only to get from here to there. They were public arenas, testing grounds, theaters over which morality plays were acted out.

Many demonstrations against the Vietnam War modeled themselves on the civil rights marches. The American-Roman facade of the Pentagon was the proper backdrop for a confrontation between anti-war youth and the troops deployed/displayed by the military-industrial complex. Draft centers and campuses were other natural focal points. What happened at these places is not properly described as political action only. Ceremonies were being performed, morality plays enacted not only for the benefit of the thousands directly involved but for many more people watching on TV. Adapting a phrase from Goffman, these were the places where parts of the public acted out their reality in the expectation that other parts of the public would attend the drama.

One step more conventionally theatrical than the street demonstration or march is guerrilla theater. I helped plan and direct a series of events called *Guerrilla Warfare* which was staged at twenty-three locations throughout New York City on 28 October 1967.[20] Two of the twenty-three performances were worth recounting here. One was the 2 p.m. performance at the Main Recruiting Center in Times Square and the other the 6 p.m. performance at the Port Authority Bus Terminal at Eighth Avenue and Forty-Second Street. The Recruiting Center is a place where demonstrations occurred frequently. The police were familiar with the routine. However, our anti-war play attracted a large hostile crowd who closed in on the performers, not threateningly, but aggressively. Some people shouted, many mumbled their disapproval. Because the play was intentionally ambivalent—the "plot" was the public execution of a Vietcong: a super-super patriot might think we were for the war—several teenage kids thought we were American Nazis and from that point of view began to question their own support of the war. The performance went swiftly, some of the dialog was lost in the open air. The performers were not comfortable. We found that the narrow triangular sidewalk, surrounded on all sides by the noise and rush of automotive traffic, and further abbreviated by the pressing crowd, added up to a performance that was brief and staccato.

The opposite happened at the Port Authority. Here, the large, vaulting interior space was suited for sound. We began the performance with performers scattered in space who hummed and then sang "The Star-Spangled Banner." Responding to a sight cue, the performers converged on a central area singing louder as they got closer together. In the Terminal the swelling anthem seemed to come from everywhere. Because the commuter crowds were not expecting a performance, at first they didn't seem to believe one was taking place. A West Point cadet walked through the performance, paused, and walked away only to return shortly, scratch his head, and stay. Finally when he realized what was being said, he walked off in disgust. A large crowd gathered; they were curious rather than hostile; their remarks were made quietly, questioning each other about what was going on. Standing as we were in front of the Greyhound ticket booths, just next to the escalators, and alongside a display Ford car, the performance took on a strange surreality without becoming esoteric or arty. The police were not expecting a performance and acted confused; finally they stopped the show seconds away from completion. More than in the other locations, the Terminal performance of *Kill Vietcong* was direct and meaningful. Here, where people passed through on the way to somewhere else, in the bland but massive institutional architecture our culture specializes in, was the place where a symbolic confrontation of values could be clearly demonstrated.

It is possible to combine the principles of transformed and found space. Every space has its own given character. This particularity ought to be lived-in, felt, and respected. An environmental theater design should not be blindly imposed on a site. Also it is possible sometimes to make just a few modifications to a found space so that a performance may more effectively "take place" there. Once a performance "takes shape" in a space, either transformed or found, spectators correspondingly take their places. A definite reciprocity occurs. Frequently, because there is no fixed seating and little indication of how they should receive the performance, spectators arrange themselves in unexpected patterns; and during the performance these patterns change, "breathing" with the action just as the performers do. Audiences can make even the most cunningly transformed space into found space. In environmental theater it is not advisable to block all the stage action with same rigidity as can be done in orthodox theaters. The actions develop more as in a sports match where certain rules govern how the physical action unfolds as moves by one person or group opens opportunities for responses. Performers need to take advantage of the audience's mobility, considering it a flexible part of the performance environment.

4. FOCUS IS FLEXIBLE AND VARIABLE

Single-focus is the trademark of orthodox theater. Even when actions are simultaneous and spread across a large stage, such as at the

200-foot proscenium of the Palais de Chaillot in Paris, the audience is looking in one direction. A single glance or a simple scan can take in all the action, even the most panoramic. And within these panoramic scenes, there are centers of attention, usually a single focal point around which everything else is organized. Correspondingly, there is a "best place" from which to observe the stage. Traditionally, the king's seat offered the proper vantage; the further one was from this place, the worse the viewing.

Environmental theater does not eliminate these practices, they are useful. But added to it are two other kinds of focus, or lack of focus.

In *multi-focus,* more than one event—several of the same kind, or mixed-media—happens simultaneously, distributed throughout the space. Each independent event competes with the other for the audience's attention. The space is organized so that no spectator can see everything. Spectators move or refocus their attention or select. Some of the qualities not only of multi-compartmented happenings but also of street-markets, side-shows, and amusement parks are employed. I mean more than the three-ring circus. In multi-focus, events happen behind, above, below, around, as well as in front of the spectator. The spectator is surrounded by a variety of sights and sounds. However, it is not necessary that the density of events be "thick." Multi-focus and sensory overload are not equivalent terms though at times they are coincident. Sparse, scattered, low-key and diverse events may be offered simultaneously. Sensory overload leads to a feeling of a small space exploding because it is so full. Sparse events evoke the feeling of space that is large, barely populated, with most of its volume still unexplored. The range of multi-focus extends from one extreme to the other including all intermediate points.

A performance using multi-focus will not reach every spectator in the same way. There is no king's seat. Reactions may be affectively and cognitively incompatible with one another because one spectator puts events together in a different way, or sees different events, than a person sitting close by or at a distance. In multi-focus, the director's role is not to organize a single coherent "statement." Coherence is left to the spectators to assemble. The director carefully organizes the symphony of events so that various reactions are possible. The goal is neither anarchy nor rigidity, but extreme flexibility yielding harmonious combinations—a kind of intellectual-sensory kaleidoscope. The technicians and performers control the sensory input (and one works painstakingly on this), but the reception of various mixes of elements is left to the audience.

In *local-focus,* events are staged so that only a fraction of the audience can see and hear them. During *Victims,* Choubert went into the audience and spoke quietly to three or four persons. He was saying lines from the play, intimate speeches that asked for a small circle of witnesses and a very low vocal level. At the same time as he was speaking to these few people, another action—on a larger scale—was happening elsewhere. Later, during the bread-stuffing sequence, Nicolas left the central action—which was staged single-focus—and went into the audience where he picked a young woman at random and began kissing and fondling her. He went as far as she would allow—on several evenings Nicolas found a very permissive partner. He spoke into her ear private words of lovemaking. He was also listening for his cue, a line by the Detective who continued the central action of stuffing bread down Coubert's throat. When Nicolas heard his cue, he said to the woman he was kissing, "I'm glad you agree with me." If the woman had not been cooperative, Nicolas would say, "I'm sorry you don't agree with me." In either case, spectators nearby this local scene laughed. Then Nicolas left the woman and rejoined the central action.

Local-focus has the advantage of bringing certain scenes very directly to some members of the audience. A commitment on the part of the performer is possible that cannot be got any other way. But what about the other spectators, those who can't hear or see what's happening? One may offer them their own local actions or a central action. Or—and NOG used this successfully several times in *Victims* —nothing else is going on. Spectators out of the range of sight and sound will be aware that something is happening "over there." A few people will move to that place, but most spectators are too timid, too locked into orthodox theater decorum, to move. Some people will begin to look around the environment, see it and other spectators. For those who are neither participating nor trying to participate, the moments of local-focus are breaks in the action when they can recapitulate what has gone on before or simply think their own thoughts. These open moments allow for "selective inattention." Why should an intermission occur all at once? I have found that these pauses—these pools of inattention—surprisingly draw spectators further into the world of the performance.

Local-focus may of course be used as part of multi-focus. In this case, certain activities are potentially viewable by all, while other activities are not. In fact, all focus possibilities can be used alone or in combination with each other.

It is very hard to get performers to accept local-focus. They are hooked on projecting to everyone in the theater even the most intimate situations and language. They do not understand why the entire audience should not share these intimacies, these private moments. Or they play local-focus scenes as if they were single-focus, with stereotyped intensity and stage mannerisms. But once a performer accepts the startling premise that privacy (of a kind) is possible and proper in the theater and that the close relation between a performer and a very few spectators or even one, is valid artistically, wide possibilities open. In *Dionysus in 69* while Pentheus was being made love to by his mother (a double mother played by two actresses), members of the Chorus were circulating among the spectators whispering into their ears, "In ten minutes we're going to tear him limb-from-limb, will you help us?" In *Commune* performers moved among the spectators "borrowing" clothes and jewelry that became their costumes for the climactic murder scene. A wide range of subtle actions played out at low volume and intensity can be used. Real body contact and whispered communication is possible between performer and spectator on a one-to-one basis. Local whirlpools of action make the theatrical line more complex and varied than in performances relying on single-focus. The environmental theater space becomes like a city where lights are going on and off, traffic is moving, parts of conversations faintly heard.

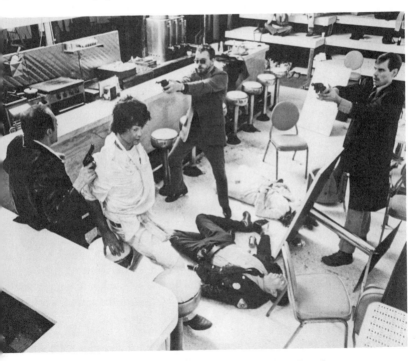

Jim Clayburgh's hyperreal environment for The Envelope, a small theater next to The Performing Garage for Terry Curtis Fox's *Cops* (1978). (*David Behl*)

5. ALL PRODUCTION ELEMENTS SPEAK THEIR OWN LANGUAGE

This axiom is implicit in the others. Why should the performer be any more important than other production elements? Because she/he is human? But the other elements were made by people and are operated by them. While discussing the first axiom, I pointed out that technicians should be a creative part of the performance. In environmental theater one element is not submerged for the sake of others. It is even possible that elements will be rehearsed separately, making the performance itself as the arena where cooperating or competing elements meet for the first time.[21]

Either all or portions of the performance can be organized so that production elements function "operatically," all joining to make one unified artwork. When this happens, a pyramid of supporting elements may lift the performers to the apex. But there are other times when the performers may find themselves at the base of the pyramid; and times when there is no pyramid at all but distinct and sometimes contradictory elements. Many multi-focus scenes are structured this way.

The long dialog between the Detective as father and Choubert as son in *Victims* was played in near-darkness with the Detective reading from an almost hidden lectern at the side of a projection booth and Choubert seated among the spectators, his head in his hands. Their dialog supported two films which were projected alternately and sometimes simultaneously on opposite walls. The dialog which held the audience's attention was the one between the films. At other points in the production the performers were treated as mass and volume, color, texture, and movement. Although they were the only performers there, they were not "actors" but parts of the environment.

The principle of autonomous channels each speaking its own concrete performative language underlies many multimedia shows and some rock-music concerts. The same principle has been important in the development of postmodern dance. Its roots go back to Artaud at least, and have been powerfully expressed in the work of John Cage and Merce Cunningham. Cage's music is heard while Cunningham's dancers dance. But the dancers aren't dancing to the music, nor is the music supporting the dance.

Grotowski has carried to the extreme the idea of competing elements, contradictory statements. "There must be theatrical contrast," he says. "This can be between any two elements: music and the actor, the actor and the text, actor and costume, two or more parts of the body (the hands say yes, the legs say no), etc." (Barba 1965: 163).

6. THE TEXT NEED BE NEITHER THE STARTING POINT NOR THE GOAL OF A PRODUCTION. THERE MAY BE NO VERBAL TEXT AT ALL.

One of theater's most enduring clichés is that the play comes first and from it flows all consequent productions. The playwright is the first creator (the author = the authority) and her/his intentions serve as production guidelines. One may stretch these intentions to the limits of "interpretation" but no further.

But things aren't that way. Even in the orthodox theater the play doesn't usually come first.

Plays are produced for all kinds of reasons, rarely because a play exists that "must be done." A producer has or finds money—or needs to take a tax loss; a group of actors want a vehicle; a slot in a season needs to be filled; a theater is available whose size and equipment are suited to certain productions; cultural, national, or social occasions demand performances. One thing is sure—the play is not the thing. Shakespeare's famous sentence ought to be quoted in full: "The play's the thing/ Wherein I'll catch the conscience of the king." Certainly Hamlet didn't serve the playwright's intentions, but his own pressing motives.

Sanctimonious attitudes toward the text and rehearsals that follow the writer's intentions—where these can be known, which is not very often—yield little in terms of satisfying productions. The repertory as performed in most of our theaters most of the time—from Aeschylus to Brecht and beyond—clogs rather than releases creativity. That repertory will not go away. But need it be preserved, expressed, or interpreted? Cage puts it well:

> Our situation as artists is that we have all this work that was done before we came along. We have the opportunity to do work now. I would not present things from the past, but I would approach them as materials available, to something else which we are going to do now. One extremely interesting thing that hasn't been done is a collage made from various plays.

> Let me explain to you why I think of past literature as material rather than as art. There are oodles of people who are going to think of the past as a museum and be faithful to it, but that's not my attitude. Now as material it can be put together with other things. They could be things that don't connect with art as we conventionally understand it. Ordinary occurrences in a city, or ordinary occurrences in the country, or technological occurrences—things that are now practical simply because techniques have changed. This is altering the nature of music and I'm sure it's altering your theater, say through the

employment of colored television, or multiple movie projectors, photo-electric devices that will set off relays when an actor moves through a certain area. I would have to analyze theater to see what are the things that make it up in order, when we later make a synthesis, to let those things come in (1965: 53-54).

Cage's attitude—treat the repertory as materials not models—is tied to his high regard for advanced technology. But such a link is not necessary. Grotowski shares many of Cage's views regarding classic texts, while taking an altogether different position on technology. A radical new treatment (some will call it mistreatment) of texts does not depend upon one's attitude toward technology. Grotowski's "poor theater" is precisely a theater without technological help, one stripped of everything but the performer-spectator relationship.

> By gradually eliminating whatever proved superfluous, we found that theater can exist without make-up, without a separate performance area (stage), without lighting and sound effects, etc. It cannot exist without the actor-spectator relationship of perceptual, direct, "live" communion. This is an ancient theoretical truth, of course, but when rigorously tested in practice it undermines most of our usual ideas about theater. [...] No matter how theater expands and exploits its mechanical resources, it will remain technologically inferior to film and television (1967: 62).

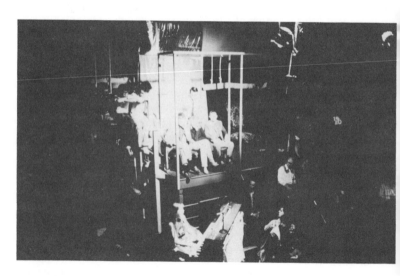

The opening scene of Jean Genet's *The Balcony* (1979), designed by Jerry Rojo for The Performing Garage. (*David Behl*)

The final scene of Jean Genet's *The Balcony* (1979), designed by Jerry Rojo for The Performing Garage. The floor of the theater slid open to reveal a basement mausoleum. The spectators crowd around the edge peering in. (*David Behl*)

Choosing between Cage and Grotowski is not necessary. Each production contains its own possibilities, some productions want to be "poor" others "rich." What is striking is that men with such diverse attitudes toward technology should stand so close in their understanding of the text's function. Cage says the repertory is material, Grotowski practices montage: rearranging, extrapolating, collating, eliminating, combining texts.

These practices flow from the premises of Axiom 1. If the theatrical event is a set of related transactions, then the text—once rehearsals begin—will participate in these transactions. It is no more reasonable to expect that the text will remain unchanged than that performers will not develop their roles. These changes are what rehearsals are for. In the orthodox theater these changes often are minor adjustments or they may be rewrites by the author. In environmental theater there may be no principle author, or the texts may be a collage of classics, or a mix from many sources and periods. In such a situation "change" does not precisely describe what happens. Grotowski's *confrontation* is a more accurate word.

> [The actor] must not illustrate Hamlet, he must meet Hamlet. The actor must give his cue within the context of his own experience. And the same for the director. [...] One structures the montage so that this confrontation can take place. We eliminate those parts of the text which have no importance for us, those parts with which we can neither agree nor disagree. Within the montage one finds certain words that function vis-a-vis our own experiences (1968a: 44).

The text is a map with many possible routes; it is also a map that can be redrawn.[22] You push, pull, explore, exploit. You decide where you want to go. Workshops and rehearsals may take you elsewhere. Almost surely you will not go where the playwright intended. Michael Smith, writing in the *Village Voice*, said this of NOG's *Victims:*

> I don't in short, think this was a good production of *Victims of Duty*. It might be described as a very good happening on the same themes as Ionesco's play, using Ionesco's words and structure of action; or as an environment in which *Victims of Duty* was the dominant element. The play was there somewhere [...] but it was subservient to, and generally obscured by, the formal enterprise of the production. Several episodes were brilliantly staged, but what came across finally was not the play but the production (1967: 28).

Smith's reaction is correct given his attitude. Later in the same review he said, "I do think the text of the play [...] is 'the first thing, the original impulse, and the final arbiter.'" For environmental theater the play is not necessarily first, there is no original, and those at hand making the production are the final arbiters. This "making of the production" can be reserved for a single auteur, belong to a collective, or shared with the spectators. The New Orleans Group did not "do" Ionesco's play; we "did with it." We confronted it, searched among its words and themes, built around and through it. And we came out with our own thing.

This is the heart of environmental theater.

Notes

1. Michael Kirby, 1965 and 1972, discusses the distinctions between non-matrixed and matrixed performances. See also Kaprow 1968.

2. For a description of *Self-Service* see Kaprow 1968b.

3. In two books—*Encounters* (1961) and *Behavior in Public Places* (1963), Erving Goffman discussed the expectation-obligation network.

4. A Provo event organized by Abbie Hoffman and James Fourrat was described by John Kifner in *The New York Times* of 25 August 1967. "Dollar bills thrown by a band of hippies fluttered down on the floor of the New York Stock Exchange yesterday, disrupting the normal hectic trading place. Stockbrokers, clerks, and runners turned and stared at the visitors' gallery. [...] Some clerks ran to pick up the bills. [...] James Fourrat, who led the demonstration along with Abbie Hoffman, explained in a hushed voice 'It's the death of money.'" To forestall any repetition, the officers of the Exchange enclosed the visitors' gallery in bullet-proof glass.

5. Since the writing of "Six Axioms" considerable work has been done in the area of "reception theory"—how audiences and readers respond to and construct the works presented to them. For an overview of these studies see Holub 1984. For particular investigations of audiences at performances see Hanna 1983, de Marinis 1987, and Schechner 1985: 117-50.

6. Robert Wilson, Richard Foreman, and many performance artists as well as the high-tech of pop music in the MTV era, demonstrate the potentialities of these "secondary interactions." It could be said that the period from the mid-70s through the '80s was one dominated by scenography and technical effects. This is true for theater, pop music, TV, and movies. It is less true for dance where the body as such commands attention.

7. See Hebdige 1979.

8. A complete outline of these techniques can be found in Jaroslav Fric's pamphlet, "Brief Description of the Technical Equipment of the Czechoslovak Pavilion at the Expo '67 World Exhibition." In

1967 Fric was chief of research and engineering for the Prague Scenic Institute. Both the Polyvision and the Diapolyecran were developed from ideas of scenic designer Josef Svoboda. For further examples of Svoboda's work see Svoboda 1966: 141-49 and Bablet 1970. I do not know what happened to this line of work, or these people, after the Soviet invasion of Czechoslovakia in 1968.

An interesting extension of this idea happened during the NOG *Victims of Duty*. There, for Several scenes, performers ran slide projectors and tape decks. During these scenes the actors were both technicians and role-playing performers. They modulated the technical environment in which they were performing.

The Hevehe cycle takes from six to twenty years. I discuss it more extensively in "Actuals" (1988: 35-67). See F. E. Williams 1940 for a full account. Williams believes that the cycle has been abbreviated since the intrusion of Western culture in the Papuan Gulf. It seems to me that the cycle is meant to incorporate the life-stages of each initiated Orokolo male. During a lifetime each Orokolo male plays, literally, many roles each of them embodied in the cycle.

On two occasions spectators came to *Victims* intent on disrupting the performance. These attempts were in bad faith: using a mask of spontaneity to conceal planned-in-advance participation. One of these occasions led to a fist fight between a disrupter and another member of the audience who was a friend of mine. The disrupter was thrown out and the show continued with most of the audience unaware that anything unusual had happened. The disrupter's actions and my friend's reactions both seemed to the rest of the audience to be part of the show. The disrupter was a newspaper critic. Such are the small but real pleasures of environmental theater.

"Axioms" was written more than a year before I staged *Dionysus in 69*. *Victims* was my first attempt to stage a scripted drama according to the principles of environmental theater. "Axioms" came out of that experience plus my other work with the New Orleans Group and my scholarly research. *Dionysus* was a continuation of work in the same direction. In it the audience participation was more varied and extreme, the use of space more radical. I have always tried to keep a lively dialog going between my practical and theoretical persons. Much of this dialog relating to environmental theater is discussed in *Environmental Theater*. Beyond that, of *Victims* there is little documentary evidence in existence except a few photos and a short film used in the production. A sizable library exists concerning *Dionysus*, including a full-length film made by Brian de Palma, Robert Fiore, and Bruce Rubin, a book edited by me (Schechner 1970), and William Hunter Shephard's *The Dionysus Group*, 1991.

13. See my "Negotiations with Environment" in *Public Domain* (1969: 145-56).

14. Arnold Aronson (1981) traced one possible line of development of environmental scenography. In Aronson's view "the word *environmental* is applied to staging that is non-frontal. Proscenium, end, thrust, alley, and arena stages are all frontal [...]. Any performance of which this is not true—in which the complete *mise-en-scene* cannot be totally apprehended by a spectator maintaining a single frontal relationship to the performance—must be considered non-frontal or environmental" (1-2). Aronson then goes on to trace "the environmental tradition" from medieval Europe to contemporary Ramlilas performed in northern India, from mumming to the avant-garde, from fairs to amusement parks.

15. For a full account of Bauhaus theater works see Schlemmer, Moholy-Nagy, and Molnar 1961.

16. *Architectural Record*, May 1930. Ideal theaters are a hobby of architects. See, for example, *The Ideal Theatre: Eight Concepts* (1962). When it comes time to build, the visions are scratched and "community" or "cultural" interests take over. The results are lamentable compromises. What most architects and community planners usually ignore are the needs of actors, designers, writers, and directors. Money talks. See A. H. Reiss's "Who Builds Theatres and Why" (1968).

17. For more detailed discussions elaborating on the historical roots of happenings see Kirby 1965 and Kaprow 1966.

18. The quest for sources can become, in composer Morton Feldman's term, "Mayflowering." As such it is an intriguing but not very useful game. However, since I've begun playing the game let me add the Russian Constructivists, the Italian Futurists, Dada, and

Surrealism as all important predecessors to modern environmental theater. Traditional performances all around the world have for millennia used environmental theater.

19. In this regard it's sad to think about the New York Shakespeare Festival or the Avignon Festival. For the first, a stage has been built in Central Park which does its best to make an outdoor space function like an indoor theater. Central Park itself is all but blotted out. When the Festival moves around New York it lugs its incongruent stages and equipment with it rather than negotiating in each locale. At Avignon, the stages built around town are imposed on the architecture and natural environment rather than making productive uses of them. Negotiations have not been attempted between the large environments—natural or people-made—and the stages set in or alongside of. The Greeks—see Epidaurus—knew how, as do those who stage the Ramlila of Ramnagar in India (see Schechner 1985, 151-212). Lee Breuer (*The Tempest*) and Peter Brook (*Mahabharata*) have tried to make creative use of the New York Shakespeare Festival and Avignon spaces.

20. The scenario for *Guerrilla Warfare* was printed in the *Village Voice* on 7 September 1967, prior to the staging of any of the events. The scenario is reprinted in my *Public Domain* (1969: 201-8). Accounts of the events themselves appeared in the *Voice*, 2 November 1967, *The New York Times*, 29 October 1967, and the March 1968 *Evergreen*. The play I used as the root of *Guerrilla Warfare* was Hed's (Robert Head) *Kill Vietcong* (1966).

21. Noh drama uses this principle. A noh performance consists in the meeting of several groups of people each of whom train and rehearse independently. The shite (principle actor), chorus, and koken (non performing performer) work as a unit; the waki (second actor), the kyogen (comic actor), the shoulder drummers, hip drummers, stick drummers, and the flutist each work apart from all the others. If noh is done according to tradition, the shite notifies the others that on X date he plans to do such-and-such a play; they each prepare separately. Several days before the performance the shire assembles the ensemble. He outlines his basic interpretation, maybe there is a low-key run-through of certain key scenes of dances, but there is nothing like a full-scale rehearsal. Only at the performance itself does everything come together. This same approach of unity in immediacy arising out of tension applies to other aspects of noh such as basic play structure,

organization of a day's program of noh dramas, stage architecture, etc. Kunio Komparu calls this "an aesthetic of discord" (1983: 21-29).

22. When I wrote "Axioms" in 1967 I was still several years away from enunciating a clear distinction between dramatic texts and performance texts. Here I am speaking of dramatic texts, and especially of how the NOG treated Ionesco's *Victims of Duty*. The pushing, pulling, exploring, and exploiting referred to is the emergence during rehearsals of a performance text.

References

American Federation of Arts
  1962   *The Ideal Theatre: Eight Concepts*. New York: The American Federation of Arts.

Aronson, Arnold
  1981   *The History and Theory of Environmental Scenography*. Ann Arbor: UMI Research Press.

Bablet, Denis
  1970   *Svoboda*. Paris: La Cite.

Goffman, Erving
  1961   *Encounters*. Indianapolis: Bobbs-Merrill.
  1963   *Behavior in Public Places*. Glencoe: The Free Press.

Hanna, Judith Lynne
  1983   *The Performer-Audience Connection*. Austin: University of Texas Press.

Hebdige, Dick
  1979   *Subculture: The Meaning of Style*. London: Methuen.

Holub, Robert C.
  1984   *Reception Theory*. London: Methuen.

Kaprow, Allan
  1966   *Assemblages, Environments, and Happenings*. New York: Abrams.

1968a   "Extensions in Time and Space," interview with Richard Schechner, TDR 12, 3: 153-59.

1968b   *Self-Service*, TDR 12, 3: 160-4.

1983   "The Real Expiriment," *ArtForum* 22, 4 (December): 36-43.

Kirby, Michael

1965   "The New Theatre," TDR 10, 2: 23-43.

1972   "On Acting and Not-Acting," TDR 16, 1: 3-15.

Komparu, Kunio

1983   *The Noh Theater*. New York: Weatherhill; Kyoto: Tankosha.

Marinis, Marco de

1987   "Dramaturgy of the Spectator," TDR 31, 2: 100-14.

Reiss, Alvin H.

1968   "Who Builds Theatres and Why," TDR 12, 3: 75-92.

Schechner, Richard

1969   *Public Domain*. Indianapolis: Bobbs-Merrill.

1970   ed. *Dionysus in 69 by The Performance Group*. New York: Farrar, Straus, & Giroux.

1973   *Environmental Theater*. New York: Hawthorn.

1985   *Between Theater and Anthropology*. Philadelphia: University of Pennsylvania Press.

1988   *Performance Theory*. New York and London: Routledge.

Shephard, William Hunter

1991   *The Dionysus Group*. New York: Peter Lang.

Svoboda, Josef

1966   "Laterna Magika" TDR 11, 1: 141-9.

Williams, F. E.

1940   *The Drama of the Orokolo*. Oxford: Oxford University Press.

Ranevskaya's house in act one of Anton Chekhov's *The Cherry Orchard* (1983) in the outdoor theater on the National School of Drama Repertory, India. The production environment was designed by Nissar Allana. (*Nissar Allana*)

Strolling through the orchard in act two of Anton Chekhov's *The Cherry Orchard* (1983). The orchard was planted several hundred feet from the house. The production environment was designed by Nissar Allana. (*Nissar Allana*)

This earth is my body. The sky is my body.
The seasons are my body. The water is my
body too. The world is just as big as my body.
Do not think I am just in the east, west,
south, or north. I am all over.
Killer-of-Enemies, Apache Hero

Not every place was good to sit or be on.
Within the confines of the porch there was one
spot that was unique, a post where I could
be at my very best. It was my task to
distinguish it from all the other places. The
general pattern was that I had to "feel" all the
possible spots that were accessible until
I could determine without doubt which was
the right one.
Carlos Castaneda

1 Space

In June, 1970, I spent nearly three hours in the anechoic chamber
at the Massachusetts Institute of Technology. After a period of
very deep sleep, I awoke with no sense of how big the room was.
I could see the walls, the floor, and the ceiling, but that wasn't
enough to fix distance, and therefore size. How big was I? How
big were the things in the room? When I spoke or shouted, there
was no echo. I discovered how much I depended on echo to fix
distance and how much I depended on distance to fix size. I
crawled across the floor. It was like a big inner-spring mattress
with no cloth covering. I measured the space with my body, but
I had no assurance that, like Alice in Wonderland, I hadn't
changed size. Then I lay still, and I heard gurglings in my stomach,
my heartbeat, and an incredibly loud whirring and ringing in my
ears. I felt my body try to expand to fill the space of the chamber,
and I experienced my skin as a thin bag containing bones and a
lot of sloshing fluid.

The fullness of space, the endless ways space can be transformed, articulated, animated—that is the basis of environmental
theater design. It is also the source of environmental theater
performer training. If the audience is one medium in which the

performance takes place, the living space is another. The living space includes all the space in the theater, not just what is called the stage. I believe there are actual relationships between the body and the spaces the body moves through. Much of workshop and rehearsal is devoted to discovering these relationships, which are subtle and ever-shifting.

The first scenic principle of environmental theater is to create and use whole spaces. Literally spheres of spaces, spaces within spaces, spaces which contain, or envelop, or relate, or touch all the areas where the audience is and/or the performers perform. All the spaces are actively involved in all the aspects of the performance. If some spaces are used just for performing, this is not due to a predetermination of convention or architecture but because the particular production being worked on needs space organized that way. And the theater itself is part of larger environments outside the theater. These larger out-of-the-theater spaces are the life of the city and also temporal-historical spaces—modalities of time/space. At the start of the Open Theater's *Terminal:*

> "We come upon the dying to call upon the dead." We tried many routes to call up the dead: we invented some, and we studied procedures used by people who believe in invocation. What we chose finally was to knock on the door of the dead by tapping with the feet on the floor, the door of the dead. There is no ground where underfoot—below the wood, below the stone—are not the bones of someone who once lived. The guides invited the dead below the stage floor to come through and speak through the dying.[1]

There is no dead space, nor any end to space.

The Performing Garage is roughly fifty feet by thirty-five feet, with a height of twenty feet. Photograph 1 shows the environment for *Dionysus in 69* during the preperformance warmups. One of the two dominant towers is partially visible. The space is organized around a central area marked by black rubber mats. The audience sits on the platforms or on the carpeted floor. The only concentration of audience is a five-tier vertical structure on the north wall, which seats about one hundred persons. The lower levels of this tier can be seen in the upper left corner of the photo. Photograph 2 shows one of the dominant towers of the *Dionysus* environment. Pentheus, with his foot on the rail, is at the top of the

[1] Chaikin (1972), 30.

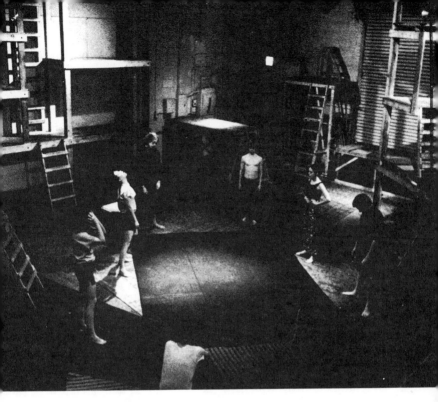

Photograph 1. Preperformance warmups for *Dionysus in 69.* Performers stretch out on their backs for breathing exercises. Warmups take about one half hour. (*Frederick Eberstadt*)

Photograph 2. Pentheus addressing the citizens from the top of one of the towers (*Raeanne Rubenstein*)

tower addressing the audience and the performers. Spectators sit all around Pentheus. Diagonally across from this tower is its twin, separated by the black mats; about fifteen feet separate the towers.

The action of *Dionysus* occurs in several areas and in several ways. Dominant actions such as the birth of Dionysus, the seduction of Pentheus, and the death of Pentheus take place on the black mats. Choric actions such as the taunting of Pentheus by the chorus, the planning of Pentheus' murder by the chorus, and the soliciting of help from the audience take place in various areas around the periphery, mostly among the spectators. Some actions such as the sexual relations between Dionysus and Pentheus and the initial meeting between Cadmus and Tiresias take place entirely out of sight of the audience, privately. Underneath the visible environment is a pit 35' by 8' by 8'; two trapdoors allow access to the pit. There are good hiding places underneath some of the platforms back close to the walls. These "secret" places were used as well as the public places.

Most of the action is single-focus, but significant actions take place simultaneously. While Pentheus is trying to make love with a person from the audience, the chorus is whispering to other spectators: "Will you help us kill him in ten minutes?" After Pentheus is killed, all the women in the company rush into the audience and simultaneously tell about their part in the murder. At the end of the play, weather permitting, the large overhead garage door—just visible in the upper right hand corner of Photograph 1—is opened, and all the performers march out into Wooster Street, often followed by spectators.[2]

Photograph 3 shows the same space reconstructed for *Makbeth* (1969). Here a series of tightly connected rectangles rise from a central table. On this table much of the major action of the play takes place. But scenes are also acted high in the ramparts, back in corners out of sight of most spectators, and in the pit, which is wholly open, making a trench down the north side of the Garage. The rugs of *Dionysus* are gone, and the bare wood rises from a cement floor. Unlike the open feeling of the *Dionysus* environment, *Makbeth* suggested closed-in spaces, "cabin'd, cribb'd, and confin'd." Photograph 4 shows Lady Makbeth at the opening of the play sitting in her place reciting quietly to herself the text of Makbeth's fateful letter.

In *Dionysus* the audience is free to sit anywhere and invited

[2] For a complete account of *Dionysus in 69* see The Performance Group, 1970. A film of the play taken in the Garage is also available.

Photograph 3. *Makbeth* environment, looking across the table to the stairway down which the audience comes entering the theater from the second floor (*Frederick Eberstadt*)

Photograph 4. Lady Makbeth as she appears while the audience is entering. Quietly she is reciting the text of Makbeth's letter to her. (*Frederick Eberstadt*)

to move around the environment. One scene is a dance with the audience. Spectators frequently join in the action at various times during a night's performance. In *Makbeth* the audience is restricted to a thirty-inch rim at the edges of the platforms. Action takes place in front and behind the audience, but not with them. On only one occasion during the run were spectators invited to participate. I told the audience of about fifty who were gathered upstairs before the performance that they should feel free to move around the space, following the action, exploring the complexities of the environment. I warned them that most of the actions were clustered in bunches performed simultaneously, so that following one action meant missing others. I asked them to remove their shoes so that their movements would not unduly disturb the performers. Nevertheless most of the performers felt that the movement of the audience was a distraction, and the experiment was not repeated. Audience movement is used extensively in *The Tooth of Crime*.

Photograph 5 is of *Commune*. Here "pueblos" are built in two corners of the Garage; these are connected by a four-foot-wide "road" elevated to eleven feet. The center area is dominated by a gentle Wave that rises, falls, rises, and falls again. Next to the Wave is a tub three feet deep and six feet in diameter. The Wave and tub are used during the performance as many things: boat, sea, land, house, blood, village, beach, yard. The audience sat mostly high in the environment, though on crowded nights a number of persons sat on the floor. There was some audience movement through the space. For one scene all the audience was asked to sit on the Wave, and most did so. The action shown in Photo 5 is of Clementine leaping off a promontory into the arms of the other performers who then "fly" her around the space.

Photograph 6 is a view of the *Commune* environment from a height of about five feet and looking out through the legs of a spectator sitting above. Most of the views are not obstructed. But more than in *Commune* or *Dionysus* spectators have the choice of sitting at the edge of a platform, deep in a pueblo, with other persons, or alone. The spectator can choose his own mode of involving himself within the performance, or remaining detached from it. The audience was offered real choices and the chance to exercise these choices several times throughout the performance. The spectator can change his perspective (high, low, near, far); his relationship to the performance (on top of it, in it, a middle distance from it, far away from it); his relationship to other spectators (alone, with a few others, with a bunch

Photograph 5. *Commune,* looking toward the west *pueblos.* In the foreground is the Wave, and at the rear right is the tub. (*Frederick Eberstadt*)

Photograph 6. *Commune,* from back in a *pueblo.* (*Elizabeth Le-Compte*)

of others); whether to be in an open space or in an enclosed space. Surprisingly few spectators took advantage of the opportunities to change places. Even when the performers encouraged moves—such as saying to the audience when everyone was assembled on the Wave, "When you return to your places, perhaps you want to go to a new place to get a different view of the events"—only a small proportion of the spectators went back to places different from where they'd come.

Photograph 7 shows a group of spectators assembled in the center of the Wave during the play's final scene. The spectators had previously been invited into the center of the Wave to represent the villagers of My Lai. (This scene has undergone many changes over the years *Commune* has been in TPG repertory; the play is still being performed and still being changed.) The scene photographed is of an interview between Spalding and several reporters. The character is being asked about his reactions to the murder of his pregnant wife.

Photograph 8 is of the *The Tooth of Crime*. The view is from a gallery above the playing areas which are in and around a large houselike structure built entirely from plywood modules. For the first time TPG used a structure that blocks vision and has no single arenalike central playing space. Spectators move around the viewing gallery or on the floor in order to follow the action of the play. Also there are windows cut in the environment so that scenes can be seen framed in the environment—giving a filmlike shifting focus to the action. The patterns of movement in *Tooth* are irregular circles on the floor, with a lot of climbing into the modules. Each of the characters has a station in the environment; the characters move but often return to their stations. Some of the feel of *Tooth's* action is of a medieval play.

The *Tooth* environment is modular. Each of the plywood sides is perforated so that it can be joined to other sides in a variety of ways. Squares, rectangles, polygons, and near-circles can be built. Low, medium, and high platforms or towers rising to sixteen feet as in *Tooth* are possible. The modules can be reconstructed in numberless variations. The entire system is nonmechanical: It can be entirely reconstructed by hand. Jerry N. Rojo designed this modular system because TPG needed flexibility in order to stage a number of works in repertory. I will not be discussing *The Tooth of Crime* except in Chapter 7, because we are still in an early stage of working on it.

Rojo, in collaboration with the Group, designed all the environments for TPG discussed in this book. He is, in my opinion, the

Photograph 7. Spectators and performers together in the final scene of *Commune* (*Frederick Eberstadt*)

Photograph 8. *The Tooth of Crime* environment, looking from the gallery to the center structure. Performers on four levels. The audience follows the action on foot around the theater from scene to scene. (*Frederick Eberstadt*)

world's leading environmentalist. A large portion of his genius is in solving all the formidable artistic-technical problems we put to him in requiring a flexible, transformational space without the encumbrance of heavy or expensive machinery.

I met Rojo at Tulane University where he came in September, 1966, on a leave of absence from the University of Connecticut. He had his master's from Tulane and came back to work for his doctorate. The New Orleans Group was working on *Victims of Duty*. I was teaching a seminar in performance theory. Paul Epstein, Arthur Wagner, and Rojo were among those who attended the seminar. We had before us some of the work of Jerzy Grotowski, Happenings, examples of ritual theater, and game theory—of both the mathematical kind and Eric Berne's. Wagner was teaching acting, Epstein was a musician, Rojo a designer. I recall nothing specific about the seminar, but I know it acted on my ideas strongly. I remember that Rojo said little. Over the year we got to be friends. He was the one "technical person" at Tulane who was interested in my ideas. Then when we were finishing rehearsals for *Victims,* we ran into some technical problems. We wanted a pile of chairs spiraling from the floor to the ceiling strong enough for Choubert to climb on. I asked Rojo to come down to the studio theater of Le Petit Théâtre de Vieux Carré where *Victims* was being staged.

He liked the environment very much. He solved the problem of the chairs by building an armature of very strong plastic-coated wires from which the chairs blossomed like tree leaves. The next year in New York TPG was in the middle stages of *Dionysus* rehearsals. Mike Kirby had drawn some towers that I thought would be a good central image for the environment. But Mike wanted towers of a certain shape placed in a certain way; and I wanted something else. I phoned Rojo at Connecticut, and he said he'd help. He made new designs for the towers. I liked them immensely. He went ahead and built the towers.

So that is Rojo with hammer and saw. I think my deepest respect for him comes because he knows that environmental design = construction. The ideas are okay, the renderings beautiful, the models exciting—but it all comes down to hammers, nails, materials, and making the space into the shapes you need.

I think it's the same with performing. The daily physical commitment is what counts. The spirit is the body at work.

After *Dionysus* I invited Rojo to design *Makbeth*. I also asked Brooks McNamara who, like Rojo, had been a student at Tulane.

During the winter of 1968–1969 they both worked on designs that ranged from Ziggurats to mazes to cattle runs. Finally, both Rojo's and McNamara's ideas were used. Then I asked Rojo to design *Commune*. Then he designed *The Tooth of Crime*.

These eight photographs give some indication of the flexibility possible in a small space such as the Garage. Each environment has a different feel, though all are made from simple wood structures. The audience is arranged in different ways and the action flows through the spaces differently for each production. In *Dionysus* there are many circular movements centered around the black mats; the flow is basically uninterrupted and with few turbulent eddies. In *Makbeth* the moves are angular, there are many private actions, much simultaneity, sharp, disjointed gestures, and harsh sounds coming from several directions at once. Heights were used much more than in *Dionysus*. *Commune* returns to some of the circularity of *Dionysus,* but the circles are incomplete, broken off. Most of the action takes place in the center area, on or near the Wave. *Tooth* flows in tight eddies, circles, and figure eights, and the characters often spy on each other from heights or hidden vantage points.

Each environment grew from detailed work with the performers. Work with Rojo begins after the work with the performers is well under way. I try to make the environment a function of the actions discovered by the performers. Of course a reciprocity develops between space and idea, movement and characterization. In the case of *Makbeth* the fact that so much of the rehearsing was done in Yugoslavia far from the Garage led to a production style that hampered the performance.

Environmental design comes from daily work on the play. The environment develops from workshops, discussions, drawings, and models. Models are important because no two-dimensional rendering can give an accurate feel of space. Rehearsals are held in partially finished environments because the performers' work will revise the plans even during the construction phase. After opening, the environment changes as new aspects of the work are uncovered. The Performance Group's work with both the *Dionysus* and *Commune* environments was superior to work with the *Makbeth* environment because many rehearsals, open and closed, were held in the partially completed environments. The space and the performance developed together. On the other hand, the Group returned from Yugoslavia to a totally finished, extraordinarily strong *Makbeth* environment—a marriage between the environment and the performance was never consummated.

Work on an environment may begin long before a play has been selected or a script assembled. The basic work of TPG is with space: finding it, relating to it, negotiating with it, articulating it.[3] Whenever the Group arrives somewhere to perform, the first exercises put people in touch with the space.

> Move through the space, explore it in different ways. Feel it, look at it, speak to it, rub it, listen to it, make sounds with it, play music with it, embrace it, smell it, lick it, etc.
> Let the space do things to you: embrace you, hold you, move you, push you around, lift you up, crush you, etc.
> Let sounds come out of you in relation to the space—to its volumes, rhythms, textures, materials.
> Walk through the space, run, roll, somersault, swim, fly.[4]
> Call to another person with words, with names, with un-worded sounds, with unsounded breathing. Listen to the calls, try them from different places.
> Then find a place where you feel most safe. Examine this place carefully, make it your home. Call from this place, this home, this nest. Then find a place where you feel most threatened. Call from there. Move from the bad place to the good place while singing softly.

I believe there is an actual, living relationship between the spaces of the body and the spaces the body moves through; that human living tissue does not abruptly stop at the skin. Exercises with space are built on the assumption that human beings and space are both alive. The exercises offer means by which people communicate with space and with each other through space, ways of locating centers of energy and boundaries, areas of inter penetration, exchange, and isolation, "auras" and "lines of energy."[5]

---

[3] Articulating a space means letting the space have *its* say. Looking at a space and exploring it not as a means of doing what you want to do in it but of uncovering what the space is, how it is constructed, what its various rhythms are. Maybe staying still in it, as in the spaces of some cathedrals.

[4] When an action is literally impossible—such as swimming or flying—the performer does it sonically, or in action with the help of others. If a person cannot fly by himself, he can be carried in such a way that he gets a sense of flying. If he cannot swim through air, he can make his breath find the rhythms of swimming.

[5] Much work needs to be done in pinpointing the exact relationships between the human body and space. Many apparently mystical concepts will

An exercise based on these assumptions was developed by the Group at the start of a summer residency at the University of Rhode Island in 1971.

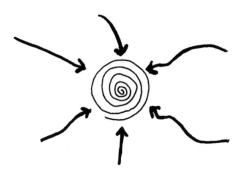

1. Performers move slowly toward each other until they are compressed into a living ball. They pack themselves together more and more tightly until there is no room. They collapse toward no space, toward infinite inward pressure.

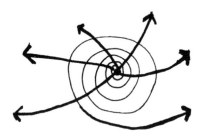

2. Then, an explosion of the primal mass into the space; an explosion with sound. Ideally the primal mass is at the center of the

---

I think, be found to have roots in fact. Just as the blind bat sees with high-frequency sound, so the human being has many ways of locating himself in space; means other than seeing and sounding. I believe that energy is broadcast and received very precisely and that we are at the threshold of understanding what and how. Also we are on the verge of conceding that there is no such thing as dead space or empty space.

space, equidistant from walls, ceiling, and floor—so that the explosion goes in all directions.

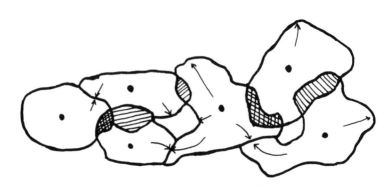

3. Each person comes to rest in a place where he feels safe, centered, defined in relation to space and the others. From this center each person marks out his boundaries, finds the points where he confronts others, where there are contested spaces, where he harmoniously shares space. The space is structured by fields of personal energies.

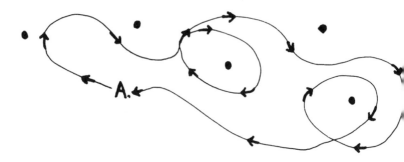

4. Each performer determines for himself a route through the space. He keeps this map to himself, and once it is set, it cannot be changed. The reason for this rigidity is so that the experience of one performer does not cause another performer to later alter his route, his own experience. Of course the exercise can be done with people choosing maps on the moment. The map of performer *A* is shown above.

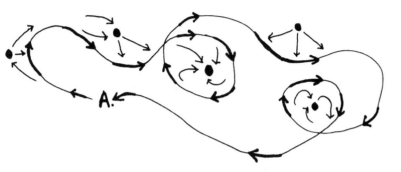

5. Performer *A* passes through many different energy fields. Sometimes he is drawn in, sometimes pushed away, sometimes torn between two or more currents. As *A* makes his way, the others react with sounds, movements (without displacing the feet), and breathing rhythms. *A* moves either fast or slow, depending on the energies he feels; he makes sounds or remains silent.

This exercise with its allusions to the "big bang" theory of universal creation and to the voyage home of Ulysses through seas of temptations, dangers, and pleasures gives performers a sense of *how full space is*. The problem is identifying the constantly changing patterns of energy that radiate through spaces—energy that comes from people, from things, from the shapes of the space.

Exercises like the two described help performers make space-maps—read space in many different ways. Western thought accustoms us to treat space visually. But acoustic, thermal, tactile, olfactory, and brain-wave maps can also be drawn. An olfactory map, for example, will not have the sharp edges of a visual map—it will be fluid, always changing, literally drifting on the wind, with eddies and intense centers shading off toward ill-defined edges.

In the spring of 1969 TPG explored the relationship between the snout—the nose and mouth, the cavities of the sinuses and throat—the gut, and the larger spaces in the theater to the large gut spaces in the body. The work culminated with an exercise in June:

away. The basket is full of peaches, strawberries, bananas, cherries, grapes, and blueberries.

Everyone concentrate on the fruit. Imagine biting into it, tasting it, smelling it. Then, one at a time, performers go to the basket and using only the snout take one grape or berry. Roll it around your mouth, under your tongue; play with it as long as you can. Then bite into it, feel its juices and flavor, chew it as slowly as you can. Swallow.

One performer goes back to the basket, takes a berry or grape with his snout. This piece of fruit is passed around the circle from mouth to mouth.

Everyone goes to the basket and with your snouts, making as many trips as necessary, bring back a pile of fruit for yourself. Then put as many berries and grapes in your mouth as you can keep count of. When you lose count of how many you have, bite. Let the juices run down your chin. Sit quietly.

Look at the basket. Everyone at once, animal-like, making sounds, using only snouts, rush to the basket and take the fruit. Carry it to a safe place and eat.

Find each other. Clean each other with your tongues, cat-style. Relax, make sounds, take each other in. Take in the whole scene: empty basket, white cloth, stained clothing, scatterings of fruit-leavings.

This exercise took about three hours. The lighting in the Garage was a spotlight on the basket of fruit and scattered low-intensity lights elsewhere. The *Dionysus* environment was standing, and the soft rugs helped the exercise. I recall the fierceness with which people took the fruit and devoured it. Then they rushed from the center of the theater to dens, perches, nests, lairs. Only after a long while did they return to the open.

Through a process I don't understand but accept, the *insides of the body perceive space directly*. This visceral space-sense is activated by exercises like the fruit-eating. Exercises in smelling also activate the visceral space-sense. Visceral perception is related to the actual wash of the guts inside the body. To get at this you have to let go of sight, hearing, and touching with the skin. Things must be tasted and smelled, touched with the nostrils, mouth, lips, tongue, anus, and genitals: those places where the viscera is on or close to the surface. Visceral space-sense is not about edges, boundaries, outlines; it is about volumes, mass, and rhythm. The exercise in which a performer moves through spaces energized by others is about boundaries. "Fruit-eating" is about rhythm.

I can't draw all this material into a neat bundle because I don't have a theory that can handle it. But let me throw a few more things at you. Richard Gould says that Australian aborigines perceive landmarks as "nothing less than the bodies of the totemic beings, or items connected with them, transformed . . . into individual waterholes, trees, sandhills, ridges, and other physiographic features, as well as into rock alignments and sacred rock-piles." [6] This is very much like what S. Giedion finds in the prehistoric art of the caves:

> One could give an almost endless list of instances showing how forms of animals, imbued with mystic significance, were born out of the rock: the bison in La Mouth (Dordogne), where the whole outline of the back, and to a certain extent even of the head, had been formed by the natural rock; the bison of the cavern of El Castillo (Santander), where major parts of the body had been seen in a stalactite and only a few lines were necessary to bring out the image; the group of polychrome bison on the ceiling of the cavern of Alta ira, whose unusual recumbent positions stem from the for of the rock protuberances. . . . Rock, animal, and outline form an inseparable unit. [7]

Or the things Antonin Artaud saw in Mexico:

> Nature has wished to express itself over a race's entire geographic compass. . . . I was able to grasp that I was not dealing with sculpted forms but with a specific play of light, which *combined* itself with the outline of the rocks. . . . And I saw that all the rocks had the shape of women's busts on which two breasts were perfectly outlined. [8]

Artaud also saw heads, torsos in agony, crucifixions, men on horses, huge phalluses, and other images impressed on the rocks or rising from them. "I saw all these forms became reality, little by little, in accordance with their rule."

In all these cases not only is the separation between man and his environment transcended, but each is the image of the other. A recurrent claim of shamans is that they can take their guts out, wash them, and replace them; or that they have had their corruptible human guts replaced by eternally durable ones of stone.

[6] Gould (1969), 128.
[7] Giedion (1962, Vol. 1), 22.
[8] Artaud (1965), 94–96.

The visceral space-sense is elusive, even for those who have experienced it. It is a communication from within the spaces of the body to within the spaces of the place one is in. You become aware of your body as a system of volumes, areas, and rhythms as a coordinated collection of chambers, channels, solids, fluids and gases; as a combination of resilient, hard, inner skeleton covered and held together by supple, tensile muscles and membranes—all this supporting and surrounding central, pulsating life-source bays, gulfs, and bundles of mobile guts.

Donald M. Kaplan has carried these ideas to the point where he believes all theater architecture is an expression of infant body-states. He thinks that the proscenium is a perfected form wherein the digestive guts seated in the darkened auditorium hungrily await the "food" chewed and fed from the brilliantly illuminated stage (mouth). "The interface of stage and auditorium is not a celebration of a maturational achievement, as certain other architectural forms are. A theater reminds us of a dynamic condition." [9] This condition is the digestive tract from mouth to stomach.

> Thus, as the theatre fills up and the performers prepare to go on, a voracity in the auditorium is about to be shaped and regulated from the stage by an active exercise of some kind of prescribed skill. At this point, we can begin to answer the question of what a theatre does kinesthetically, by observing that its geometrics and functions favor a juxtaposition of a *visceral* and *executive* experience.[10]

The visceral audience awaits satisfaction from the actors who feed the performance to them.

By putting everyone on stage, so to speak, the environmental theater does away with the dichotomy Kaplan identifies. The audience in environmental theater must look to itself, as well as to the performers, for satisfaction of visceral needs. This less sharply delineated division of roles, actions, and spaces leads *not* to deeper involvement, not to a feeling of being swept away by the action—the bottomless empathy enhanced by darkness, distance, solitude-in-a-crowd, and regressive, cushioned comfort of a proscenium theater—but to a kind of in-and-out experience; a sometimes dizzyingly rapid alternation of empathy and distance.

The orthodox theater-goer is snuggled. He can keep his reac-

[9] Kaplan (1968), 113.
[10] Kaplan (1968), 117–108.

tions to himself, and he is more likely to get utterly wrapped up in the experience on stage. This is even truer in the movies, where there is absolutely no responsibility to respond, because the actors in a film are not present at the theater. In the environmental theater the lighting and arrangement of space make it impossible to look at an action without seeing other spectators who visually, at least, are part of the performance. Nor is it possible to avoid a knowledge that for the others you are part of the performance. And insofar as performing means taking on the executive function, every spectator is forced into that to some degree by the architecture of environmental theater.

Spectators experience great extremes—of deep, perhaps active involvement and participation; then critical distancing, looking at the performance, the theater, the other spectators as if from very far away. Sometimes a spectator will freak out, go so far into the experience that he is lost inside it. More than a few times I have talked someone back from very far places. But the other extreme also occurs. I have spent many hours watching performances from a detached, disinterested point of view; and I have seen others do likewise. This is not a question of boredom, but of focusing on aspects of the performance other than the narrative, or the feelings of the performers. These aspects—technical, environmental, spectator behavior—are masked in the orthodox theater. You couldn't focus on them if you wanted to. In environmental theater there are endless degrees of attention, subtle gradations of involvement. The experience of being a spectator, if you let yourself get into it, is not smooth but roller-coaster.

Many people, trained in the rigid reaction program of orthodox theater, are embarrassed by what they feel at environmental theater. They think that the in-and-out reaction is "wrong" or an indication that the play "doesn't work." People come up to me and say, "I couldn't keep my attention focused on the play." Or, "I was moved by some of it, but I kept thinking my own thoughts. Sometimes I lost track of what was going on." Or, "Sometimes I felt good, but at other times I felt threatened." Or, "You know, I watched the audience so much I lost part of the play." Or even, "I fell asleep." I think all of these responses are splendid.

If the body is one source of environmental theater design, there are also historical and cultural sources. The body gives data for space-senses while historical or cultural studies give data for *space-fields*. Modern European-American culture is prejudiced in favor of rectangular, hard-edged spaces with clear boundaries and definite senses of right and left, up and down. There is only a blurry idea of what happens inside these boundaries. We fight wars to preserve boundaries, while letting the life inside our nations deteriorate.

Space may be organized without a single axis, as among the Eskimo where figures in the same field are "upside down" relative to each other. Give an Eskimo child a paper to draw on and he will fill up one side and continue to draw on the other side with no more thought of discontinuity than you have when you follow a sentence in this book from one page to the next. Space may be organized with a distorted or permutated axis as in surrealist art or topographic mathematics. Or it may be organized according to the X-ray technique of the Northwest Coast Indians who see the inside and outside of an object with equal clarity—a cow with her unborn calf in her belly, a fish with a hook lodged in its throat, a man with his heart beating in his chest.

Space can be organized according to time, so that sequence in space = progression in time, as in Egyptian panels, medieval tryptichs, and the settings for morality plays in which the progress of history from the Creation to the Fall to the Crucifixion to Salvation or Hell was plain to all who had eyes to see. Space can be organized so that size, not distance, indicates importance. In Egyptian art the gods are biggest, the pharaohs next, and so on through many classes until we reach tiny slaves. Examples are without limit. Space can be shaped to suit any need.

The concept of *space-field* may be easier to grasp if I briefly present five kinds of performance space-fields: Egyptian, Greek, Balinese, Mexican, and New Guinean. The first two are historical and the last three exist today.

The Egyptians staged periodic ceremonial spectacles. For these they built entire cities and floated great, ornate barges down the Nile. The river was not only the liquid, flowing stage for much of the Heb-Sed; it was itself the source of all Egyptian life, a living participant in the great drama of renewal. Time itself was stopped for the Heb-Sed festival. (We retain this idea of a holiday being time out.) The days of the Heb-Sed were not part of the calendar. The function of the mighty festival was to renew all of Egypt starting with the pharaoh. He himself played the major role in the drama. "It was not a mere commemoration of the

:ing's accession. It was a true renewal of kingly potency." [11] The
heater event was performed in a special place that existed in a
special time. But through this specialness flowed the eternal
Nile which was both sacred and profane. And like the Nile, everyday Egyptian life was transformed by the Heb-Sed and renewed.

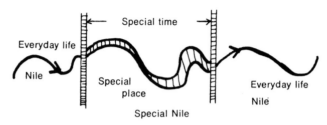

Via Crete and other Mediterranean stepping-stones the Greeks
took much from the Egyptians including the idea that the
theater is a festival: something that exists at a special time in a
special place. But the Greeks were also influenced by prehistoric
shamanistic ceremonies coming down from central Asia and
Europe. Animism, nature worship, and landscape were very important to the Greeks who, in this regard, were not so far from
today's aborigines. The Greek theater raised its audience in a
semicircle around a full-circle dancing area. The audience area
was made from a natural hill, and every Greek theater gives
a beautiful view over the skene to the landscape beyond. Thus
the Greek arrangement included elements of holiday (= time out)
and continuity with the landscape and the gods who dwelt therein.

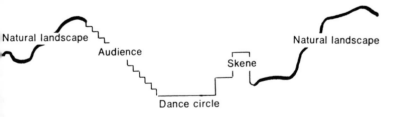

Furthermore, the Greeks liked watching the dances not as discreet
moves but as completed sequences, finished figures—a kind of
stepped-out destiny in movement. In some surviving Greek
theaters there are pavements of different-colored stones tracing
the dance routes: architectural scripts. These pavements help the
memories of dancers and spectators alike. At any given moment

[11] Frankfort (1948), 79.

the whole dance is known, and the dancers are seen as figures somewhere on the course. We tried for something like this in the *Commune* environment where different maps, figures, routes, and writing were marked on the floor and other parts of the environment. We used masking tape because that suggests the police reconstructing a crime and a stage manager marking the floor of a theater.

Nothing could be further from the Egyptian and Greek uses of space than the Balinese. The Balinese build nothing special for theater. They do no seasonal plays. They perform in the village square, on temple steps, in courtyards, or on temporary stages thrown up for the occasion. And the occasion may be a marriage, a birth, a stroke of good fortune, a Hindu holiday, a need to placate the gods, or the means by which a rich man shows how rich he is. The performers are magnificently costumed and trained; they are professional in every sense except the commercial. But there is little formality surrounding a performance. Dogs eat some of the ceremonial food signaling the gods' acceptance of the offering, children play in the street in the midst of the trance-dancers, old men doze on their porches, women market, and those who want to watch the play do.

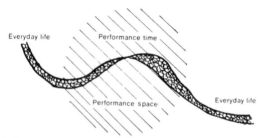

Theater in Bali accompanies everyday life. There is no time out for theater. To the Balinese theater happens anytime, anywhere, and its gestures are continuous with the rest of living.

This integration of ceremonial and everyday is present in many Oriental cultures. M. C. Richards describes the Japanese Raku Ware where a person makes a teacup, fires it, and drinks out of it "all in a single rhythm." [12] The high formality of Japanese theater is a refinement of daily, courtly, and military gestures. There is no break between theater and the rest of life—only increasingly delicate stages of refinement. The Japanese theater seems alien even to Japanese, because its gestures have been

[12] Richards (1970), 29.

frozen in time. But at the beginning these gestures were not strange.

Sometimes a ritual drama can absorb the whole attention and energies of a town without calling for any special construction. The existing village remains intact, but it is transformed by the drama into another time and place. Recently such a drama has been uncovered in coastal mountains of western Mexico. The Cora of Mesa del Nayar were converted to Catholicism by the Jesuits in the sixteenth century. Then in 1767 the Jesuits were expelled from Mexico. No priest appeared on the Mesa until 1969. During the two hundred years without contact these Cora maintained many Roman Catholic rites, among them a Holy Week passion play.

> But they had made them uniquely their own. For example, they had come to identify Our Lord Jesus Christ with their ancient deity Tayau, the sun god. . . . They took elements from the story of Christ's Passion, death, and Resurrection and made them into a ceremony apparently designed to ensure the renewal and continuity of their communal life.[13]

In the Cora play a boy of about seven plays Christ. There is no Pilate, no Judas. The villains are called *borrados,* which means "erased ones" in Spanish. The borrados are the Judeans responsible for the crucifixion. For the three days of the festival "all authority, civil and religious, passes to a man called the Captain of the Judeans. He and his borrados—young men of the region—darken themselves with soot and mud and thus 'erase' their own personalities and their personal responsibility for whatever they do." Fortified with peyote, the borrados hold forth for three days and nights. The crucifixion is preceded by a chase through the town with the boy-Christ doing his best to get away from the borrados. He is helped by a wooden cross that he brandishes. "Three times —in the name of the Father, the Son, and the Holy Ghost—the borrados chased the boy, and three times they fell writhing to the ground at the sight of the cross." Then they catch him, tie him, and bring him to the church. There women groom him, and he sleeps overnight. The next morning he is brought out by the borrados and made to stand in front of a cross in the churchyard. This is the crucifixion. The next day at noon

---

[13] Guillermo E. Aldana's extraordinary *National Geographic* article (June, 1971), "Mesa del Nayar's Strange Holy Week," has many unforgettable photographs. All quotations are from Aldana's article.

the village governor arrives on horseback. He plays the role of the
centurion. He rides among the borrados and breaks their bamboo
spears. They fall dead to the ground and then get up, go to the
stream, and take a purifying bath. "Near the church all was
mirth and happiness." Many things are interesting about the Cora
play: how it is integrated into the life of the village, the changes
made in the traditional Christ story, the double quality of drama
and initiation ritual.

The Central Highlands of New Guinea provides the fifth mode
of using space. Catherine Berndt observed an all-night ceremony
and noted the changes that occurred in a large open field.[14] "At
first there were district clusters of dancers, although the edges
of the clusters blur as people greet kin, attend to ovens, or rest
on the sidelines." The blurring continues leading to wholesale
intermingling "until it becomes impossible to distinguish groups.
Nevertheless, a certain nucleus is likely to resist this tendency
to disperse." Finally, as the time to set off for home approaches
"the various units reform (though less compactly then before)
and set off."

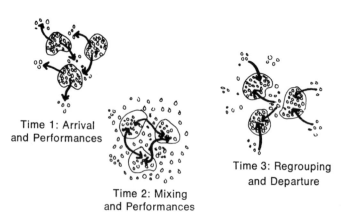

Time 1: Arrival
and Performances

Time 2: Mixing
and Performances

Time 3: Regrouping
and Departure

This is not unlike what happens at party—except that in New
Guinea the gathering is the occasion for performances of farces,
dances, and songs. These are ornately costumed and often carefully staged.

Is the New Guinea use of space more "primitive" than the
Egyptian? The New Guinea use suits New Guinea ceremonial
events which are also informal social gatherings like parties.

[14] Quotations and drawings from Berndt (1959).

The Egyptian use suits the great formality and impressive scale of the Heb-Sed. What the environmentalist learns in studying these examples—and many others—is that space-time-action is a single, flexible unit. The first obstacle to environmental design is preconception. The great enemy of preconception is a knowledge of cultures and periods other than one's own.

Thus far I've spoken of environmental design abstractly. I've said that it is related to body spaces, space-senses, and space-fields, but I have not been concrete in showing how. For one thing environmental design practice is ahead of theory. This is true partly because there are so many extraordinary examples of environmental design if we simply open our eyes to see. Whether the environmentalist looks at American Indian, Asian, Oceanic, African, Siberian, or Eskimo societies, he finds many models that may stimulate his creativity. Also he can look back in history as far as he can—to Altamira and the other caves; and then forward to Egypt, the Near and Middle East, Asia, and medieval Europe. In our own day he can study productions like Ludovico Ronconi's *Orlando Furioso*, Gilbert Moses' and Archie Shepp's *Slave Ship* (designed by Eugene Lee), Peter Brook's *Tempest* and *Orghast*, the work of Jerzy Grotowski, and the extraordinary work of Peter Schumann and the Bread and Puppet Theater.

What all of these works past and present, dramatic and ritual, in industrial and nonindustrial societies have in common is that they each create or use whole space. Whether it is *Orghast* or Robert Wilson's *KA MOUNTAIN and GUARDenia TERRACE* set amid the ruins of Persepolis and the mountains near Shiraz, or the Heb-Sed on the Nile, or an initiation rite that starts in a village, moves to a road leading to the river, climaxes along the riverbanks, and concludes back in the village, or *Akropolis* with its environment being built out of stovepipes during the performance, or a pig-kill and dance at Kurumugl in New Guinea—each example is of an event whose expression in space is a complete statement of what the event is.

Sometimes the space is broken into many spaces. Sometimes the audience is given a special place to watch from. Sometimes the space is treated fluidly, changing during the performance. Sometimes nothing is done to the space. The thing about environmental theater space is not just a matter of how you end up using space. It is an attitude. *Start with all the space there is and then decide what to use, what not to use, and how to use what you use.*

Work on *Makbeth* began in October, 1968, with workshops exploring Shakespeare's *Macbeth*. We did a lot of exercises about prophesy, laying on hands, witchcraft. We took the text apart and reassembled it in funny ways. We tried to find the main threads of action from both an individual and a group point of view. In December we had Rojo and McNamara down to the Garage. Both of them sat in on workshops and talk. Many models of the environment were proposed. We selected, finally, Rojo's —but did not discard McNamara's. After modification it became the Makbeth Maze: the way into the theater from the second floor of the Garage. The Maze was a bit of Madame Toussaud, a bit of fun house, scraps of theater history, mirrors, and information about the performance. It ended at an open hole in the floor, a narrow descent into Makbeth's hell.[15]

The mise-en-scène for *Makbeth* was worked out in six phases, the environment in five.

Mise-en-scène

1. October, 1968–February, 1969. Improvisations without keeping to Shakespeare's text. Search for basic actions, basic movement patterns. First determination of space-field as "cabin'd, cribb'd, and confin'd."

2. March–June, 1969. Making of scenes not in Shakespeare. These expressed some actual situations in the Group. Using Shakespeare's text as raw material. Demystifying Shakespeare. First character groupings: Dark Powers, Founders, Doers, Avengers.

3. July–August, 1969. Cast assignments. Decisions about the shape of the space, the nature of the music. Much work with Rojo and Epstein. End of group workshops. I worked alone assembling what we had into a coherent script.

4. September, 1969. Rehearsals in Baocic, Yugoslavia, while Rojo built the environment in the Garage. Composition of music by Epstein in Philadelphia.

5. October–November, 1969. Rehearsals in the Garage.

---

[15] The New Orleans Group had something similar in the lobby for *Victims of Duty* in 1967. The exhibit was mounted on billboards and contained hundreds of photos, newspaper articles, letters, birth certificates, and other personal crap dealing with the private lives of the performers and directors—a takeoff on the trivia in theater programs. Also there was a short film, slides, and taped music counterpointing the Tulane NROTC band with Hitler marches. During the performance the exhibit was changed so that when the audience left, people were forced to duck under a sheet on which was written the famous Eichmann quotation: "I am a victim of the actions of others and obedience to duty." From the ceiling hung pictures of Eichmann all neat in his uniform.

Revision of script. Integration of music into the production. Opening.

    6. December, 1969–January, 1970. Run. Few changes except tightening. Closing.

The second phase of work didn't yield an acceptable performance text, but it gave performers a handle on the language. The work overcame the scared feelings people have when first approaching sacred Shakespeare. Also the second phase made it clear how to organize the story and divide the roles.

Environment

    1. October, 1968–February, 1969. Rojo, McNamara, and I discussed the themes of the play and possibilities for the environment. They came to a few workshops.

    2. March–May, 1969. Rojo and McNamara attended Wednesday night workshops devoted to text construction and environment. Drawings and models, many rejected ideas including ziggurats, corrals, and wire fences. Finally, Rojo's design is accepted, and McNamara's is transformed into the Maze.

    3. June–August, 1969. Construction of working models. Decision to move Maze upstairs and use it as the way into the environment downstairs. Approval of final building plans before my departure for Yugoslavia in August. Also approval of costumes.

    4. September, 1969. Construction of about 90 percent of the environment while the Group rehearsed in Yugoslavia.

    5. October, 1969. Completion of environment, lighting, costumes.

The big mistake with *Makbeth* was that we rehearsed it in Baocic, and the space-field of that outdoor meadow stayed with us. It was impossible to work effectively in the Garage environment. The Yugoslavian rehearsals broke in two our work on the play; and yet the rehearsals in Yugoslavia gave us the fundamental scenic actions. The production could not survive the contradiction. Ultimately the magnificent Garage environment was alien to a mise-en-scène worked out in Yugoslavia.

The Baocic meadow was large; performers looked across at adversaries who could be seen but not heard. There was a limitless ceiling of sky, the play of natural light, the sweet smell of clean air. In the meadow the Dark Powers transformed into birds hiding in the trees or woodchucks in the underbrush. The Makbeths lived atop a knoll near a large tree. Malcolm and

Macduff, after the murder of their father, Duncan, took a long semicircular route through forests and shrubs to get at the Makbeths. I directed by running from one side of the meadow to another, ducking behind trees or rocks, flattened on my belly in the grass, watching, yelling directions, just keeping up with the action. I saw Banquo, trapped by the Dark Powers in a blind alley of shrubbery, vainly struggle before they bashed her head in with a rock. I hid nearby as the Dark Powers lured Makbeth into a dusky gully cut by a brook and whispered to him that he would never be slain by a man of woman born. I watched as Malcolm and Macduff, assisted by the Dark Powers, camouflaged themselves with grass and branches and advanced on Dunsinane. Only a few of these scenes were translatable into the Garage environment. The long, deep pit against the north wall served well as the gully-home of the Dark Powers; Banquo was trapped amid the wood columns supporting the environment; the advancing Malcolm and Macduff darted from column to column as in a forest as they approached Dunsinane. But the amplitude of the Baocic meadow could not be stuffed into Rojo's magnificent Garage environment. Furthermore, this amplitude did not suit the play we started the previous winter in New York.

What happened during the month's rehearsals in Baocic was that the performers developed the action according to the space-field there while Rojo built from what he perceived from work-shops. The space-field of Baocic contradicted the space-field of Rojo's environment. Disunity within the Group made it impossible to overcome or live with this contradiction. We could not use it creatively. I remember William Finley saying, when he first saw the Garage, "It's great, really marvelous, but how do we work in it?" I panicked and resorted to blocking. Instead of taking the time to let the performers feel their way around, through, and into the space, I imposed actions and rhythms. Throughout its run *Makbeth* never felt at home in the Garage. I hope I've learned the lesson: *Text, action, and environment must develop together.*

Rojo's environment had one supreme quality: It incorporated the tensions he sensed in the Group, conflicts that led to the dissolution of TPG early in 1970. The rehearsals of *Makbeth* coincided with the undoing of the Group. Daily, heavy personal things came down, and although no one said so out loud, I think we each knew that *Makbeth* was our last play together. Because of the way TPG works, our conflicts fed into the structure of *Makbeth*. It became an angry play of blood, power struggles, betrayals, fleeting contacts, brief flashes of quiet punctuated by screams. All of this is in Shakespeare's script. It also characterized the environment. Gone were the soft carpets and suffused lighting of *Dionysus* replaced by a concrete floor, bare wood platforms framed by iron piping, lighting that came in fitful bursts. The bare feet of *Dionysus* gave way to boxing shoes, nakedness to unisex costumes of crushed corduroy.

It was better with *Commune*. Rojo and I met during the spring of 1970 to talk over the play while it was in its very early stages. He visited New Paltz several times during the summer to watch workshops and present and revise his drawings and models. Sculptor Robert Adzema made several models that were helpful in getting the environment together. Everyone in the Group went over the models and made suggestions. At the end of July the Wave was built in New Paltz, and we rehearsed with it for the rest of the summer. We appropriated scaffolding and built an approximation of the environment Rojo was designing. He saw enough rehearsals to change his plans according to what was happening to the play. There were weekly open rehearsals to see how the audience reacted to the environment. By the end of August a plan was agreed on, and during September while TPG and Wave were in residence at Goddard, Rojo built about one third of the environment in the Garage. In October we did a few open rehearsals in the Garage working in the partially finished environment. Rojo learned from watching us work. He completed the environment in October while the Group was on tour—still with the Wave, our cumbersome environmental security blanket. When the Group returned to New York in November, everyone pitched in to paint the Garage. We painted the ceiling sky blue and the walls desert red-brown. The environment was finished. Later, during performances, spectators—given chalk—added much interesting graffiti.

Some of the graffiti is still on the ceiling, even for *The Tooth of Crime*. And lumber, fittings, scraps of every environment ever built in the Garage comprise part of whatever is most current. This is not only a matter of economy. Like new cities built on the rubble and from the rubble of older ones, the present recapitulates and transforms the past: There is a tangible tradition in the Garage.

There is no such thing as a standard environmental design. A standard design mocks the basic principle: *The event, the performers, the environmentalist, the director, and the audience interacting with each other in a space (or spaces) determine the environment.* Having said that, I offer a "standard environmental design." A theater ought to offer to each spectator the chance to find his own place. There ought to be *jumping-off places* where spectators can physically enter the performance; there ought to be *regular places* where spectators can arrange themselves more or less as they would in an orthodox theater—this helps relieve the anxieties some people feel when entering an environmental theater; there ought to be *vantage points* where people can get out of the way of the main action and look at it with detachment; there ought to be *pinnacles, dens, and hutches:* extreme places far up, far back, and deep down where spectators can dangle or burrow or vanish. At most levels there ought to be places where people can be alone, be together with one or two others, or be with a fairly large group. Spaces ought to be open enough so that in most of them people can stand, sit, lean, or lie down as the mood directs. Spaces ought to open to each other so that spectators can see each other and move from one place to another. The overall feel of the theater ought to be of a place where choices can be made. The feel I get from a sucecssful environment is that of a *global space,* a microcosm, with flow, contact, and interaction.

This long list of "ought to be's" is obliterated by the specific needs of a production. None of the TPG environments meets all of these "requirements."

As the environmentalist works, particularly if he is new at the game, he should ask himself questions. These questions are implicit in the work, different from questions an orthodox designer might ask.

1. Does the mass, volume, and rhythm of the whole environment express the play? Not the play as I abstractly conceive it, but as I have watched it develop in rehearsals?

2. Does the material out of which the environment is built—texture, weight, color, density, feel—express the play?

3. Can spectators see each other? Can they hide from each other? Can they stand, sit, lean, lie down? Can they be alone, in small groups, in larger groups?

4. Are there places to look down on most of the action, to look across at it, to look up to it?

5. Where are the places for performing? How are they connected to each other? How many places are used both by the audience and by the performers?

6. Are there efficient ways of moving up and down as well as in all horizontal directions?

7. What does the environment sound like? How does it
smell?

8. Can every surface and supporting member safely hold
as many people as can crowd onto it? Are there at least two
ways in and out of every space?

The thing about safety is that nothing should be disguised. If
a ladder is hard to climb, make it look like it's hard to climb.
In five years working in the Garage there have been no major
accidents and only a few scrapes and sprains. The worst that's
happened has been a broken foot that occurred to William
Shephard when he made a spectacular leap changing his course in
midair to avoid demolishing a spectator.

The environmentalist is not trying to create the illusion of a
place; he wants to create a functioning space. This space will
be used by many different kinds of people, not only the performers. The stage designer is often concerned with effect: how
does it *look* from the house? The environmentalist is concerned
with structure and use: how does it *work?* Often the stage
designer's set is used from a distance—don't touch this, don't
stand on that—but everything the environmentalist builds must
work. Stage designing is two-dimensional, a kind of propped-up
painting. Environmental design is strictly three-dimensional. If
it's there, it's got to work. This leads to sparseness.

Have you ever thought how *stupid* the proscenium theater
is architecturally? Start with the auditorium, the "house." A silly
name for row after row of regularly arranged seats—little properties that spectators rent for a few hours. Nothing here of the
freedom of arrangement in a house where people live—and can
push the furniture around. And most of the places in the "house"
are disadvantageous for seeing or hearing. The first few rows
are so close that the actors—in their effort to project to the
back and up to the balconies—spit all over you; the seats to the
side give a fun-house mirror view of the stage, all pulled out
of proportion; the seats at the back of the orchestra under the
balcony are claustrophobic and acoustically murder; the view
from the second balcony makes the stage look like a flea circus.
Only a few seats in the orchestra, mezzanine, and first balcony
offer anything like a pleasing view of the stage. But this is no
surprise. The proscenium theater was originally designed to emphasize differences in class and wealth. It was meant to have
very good seats, medium seats, poor seats, and very bad seats.

When people come late or leave early, they all but step on you, push their asses in your face, and disrupt whole rows of spectators. There is no chance to readjust your body, take a seventh-inning stretch, or extend your arms. During intermission everyone runs to the lobby to gobble food, drink, smoke, talk. Intermission is just about the only human thing going on. Also, of course, to see who's here—which undeniably is one of theater's chiefest and oldest joys. Not just to look at or for famous people—but to look over the crowd, see who's out with you this evening. This looking is impossible in the darkened house that cruelly makes you focus straight ahead, as in church or at school, at a performance that, finally, may not interest you at all.

The worst thing about the "house" is that it imprisons you away from the stage where there are many interesting things to see if you were only allowed. What's visible of the stage from the house is only a fraction of its total area and volume. For me the wonderful direction is up. To gaze up into the flies through rods and curtains and lights and ropes and catwalks and galleries into the immense space! Whenever TPG is asked to perform in a proscenium, I accept with enthusiasm. "Bring everyone on stage," I say, "and turn a few lights upward so that people can see how high the flies are." Also in newer theaters there are vast chambers to the left and right of the playing stage, and often behind the playing area, too. These are for "wagons," a term as old as medieval theater, meaning rolling platforms on which whole sets are built and then brought into place. And sometimes there is a turntable—a device Brecht loved. Usually there are trapdoors leading to a cellar under the stage, and doors going to the backstage, the shop, the dressing rooms, the greenroom. So the proscenium stage is a focused space surrounded on every side by other spaces attending on the stage like an old queen. How mean that audiences should be exiled from this royal realm of magic. Such exclusion is pitiable, cheap, unfair, and unnecessary.

My own preference is to do away with most of the machinery. It makes the theater worker like a soldier trapped inside his burning tank. But I would keep the spaces—the overs, unders, and arounds.

Some new theaters designed by people who want to keep up to date try to keep "the best" from previous ages. These theaters are like old trees weighted down by so many branches that they break. Such a theater is the brand-new job at the University of Rhode Island, where TPG was in residence in the summer of

1971. The theater wasn't even open to the public when I saw it. In the semicircular arrangement of seats in the house is the Greek amphitheater, in the vomitoria leading from the house to the foot of the orchestra pit is the Roman stadium, in the space for wagons are the medieval moralities and pageants, in the fly system are the Italian scenic conventions of the Renaissance, in the slightly thrust stage is the Elizabethan theater, in the proscenium posts is the eighteenth-century theater, in the orchestra pit is the nineteenth-century opera, in the turntable is the early twentieth-century, in the bank after bank of computerized lighting controls are contemporary electronics. Pity the poor student actor!

When the Group took one look at this monster, we decided to work in the scene shop—an honest, large, irregular space that could be made into anything. Not by building scenery or pushing buttons, but by putting down a plywood floor we could dance and run and jump on, some scaffolds to climb over, a few velours to soak up extra noise, and fewer than twenty lights to make it bright enough to see. The rest is performing.

The simple fact that in most theaters actors enter through their own door at one time and audience enters through another door at a later time architecturally expresses a strong aesthetic and class consciousness. The separate doors are entrances literally to different worlds. The stage door leads to all the equipment and facilities backstage. This stuff is not at all dressed up. Layers of paint, raw pipes, old scenery, costume racks, lights, wires, tools, are all laid out in ways that facilitate use and accessibility. Except on the stage things are arranged according to systems that make for easy indexing and use. On the stage, of course, things are arranged for the audience's eyes. The audience enters the theater door into a plush, often ornate, and stylish lobby. This is so even off off-Broadway where, in their own way, the lobbies are modish. The house itself is as plush as the producers can afford to make it. From the house the audience views the stage where an illusion has been created. From the front the stage presents its false but pretty face. From backstage the scenery is ugly (if you like illusions) but working—supports, nails, ropes, and wires are visible—and the view of the stage from behind or the sides reminds me of nothing so much as a ship: a lot of equipment focused in a small space.

What if the audience and the actors were to enter through the

Photographs 9 and 10. Taking *Dionysus* out into Wooster Street— exploding the space of the theater (*Frederick Eberstadt*)

same door at the same time? What if all the equipment of the theater, however arranged, were available to public view at all times? What if we eliminated the distinctions between backstage and onstage, house and stage, stage door and theater door? No theater that I know of has done this, not absolutely. Once in Vancouver in August, 1972, TPG experimented with a "real-time" performance of *Commune*. I announced to our workshop and to some university classes that anyone would be welcome to come to the theater at 6 P.M.—at the time of the performers' call. About ten students showed up, and they entered the theater together with the performers. The visitors were free to go wherever they pleased. They watched warmups, listened to notes, helped the tech director check the lights, set the props, fill the tub, clean up the theater. They watched the performers put on their costumes and saw the regular audience arrive at 7:45. Then the performance. After, the routine of closing up the theater for the night: removing costumes and putting them in the laundry bag for washing, re-collecting props, emptying the tub, and all the other routines of ending. Out of the ten students only two or three stuck for the whole process that was over about 10:30. (*Commune* itself takes only about ninety minutes.) The performers were a little uneasy at their presence for warmups and notes. After the performance no one minded who was there. I felt funny, too, and performed a little for the "real-time" audience. I wanted them to have a good time. Removing the "magic" from theater won't be easy.

A further experiment in this line is part of *The Tooth of Crime* production. Performers man the box office, greet spectators as they enter the theater, explain aspects of the production: particularly the fact that spectators can get as close to a scene as they wish by moving throughout the theater during the entire performance. At intermission performers prepare and sell coffee, talk to spectators, socialize, and let everyone know when the second act is beginning. The difference between show time and intermission is clear, but there is no attempt made at hiding the non-performing life performers lead even in the midst of a night at theater. Strikingly enough, I find that the performers' concentration on their work and the audience's interest in the story is not at all diminished by the socializing. If anything, the playing of the play is enhanced. Roles are seen as emerging from a full constellation of activities that include economics, logistics, hostings, and one-to-one relationships. The performers are seen not as the magic people *of* the story but as the people who *play* the story.

When I design an environment, I try to take into account the space-senses of the performers, of the text-action, and of the space we're working in. These make an irregular circle, an interconnected system that is always changing.

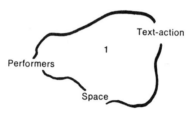

In time the space gets set as the environment is built. Or doesn't get set. The finest thing about *Orlando Furioso* was the way the environment itself kept changing because the environment was the audience. As the big set pieces crawled or hurtled across the floor, the audience scattered or followed. I climbed a lighting tower and looked down from about twenty feet. Not knowing Italian helped me concentrate on the changing figures of movement. I thought I detected a pattern. For gentle, quiet scenes the audience pressed in, heads and shoulders forward. Running away from a careening platform, they seemed to run in front of it instead of to the sides as one might expect. In other words, they challenged the platform to run them down—they played a game with the platform. They stood back from declamations, with hips thrust forward, head and shoulders back.

Once the audience is let into the environment, the basic relationship is changed. There are four points on the circle.

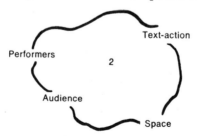

This is as simple as ABC except that in orthodox theater the audience is outside the circle. Fixed seating, lighting design, architecture: Everything is clearly meant to exclude the audience from any kind of participation in the action. Even their watching is meant to be ignored. The spectators are put into the semi-fetal prison of a chair, and no matter what they feel, it will be hard to physicalize and express those feelings.

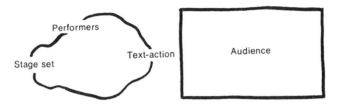

I don't see any middle ground. Either the audience is in it or they are out of it. Either there is potential for *contact* or there is not. I don't deny that the spectator in the orthodox theater feels something. Sure he does. *But he cannot easily, naturally, unconsciously, and without embarrassment express those feelings except within idiotically limited limits.*

When we say of a great performer that he or she has *presence,* that we are *moved* by the performance, that we have been *touched,* we are not speaking nonsense or entirely metaphorically. Many times I've seen an audience collectively catch its breath, shift position, become very still, change their points of contact and orientation to each other, or to the performers, quite unconsciously, without thought or intention. These changes in body positions, in expressive poses—the way a person fronts himself (or sidles, or turns his shoulder, or his back) on another—on an action is a delightful part of every performance in an environmental theater. The theater ought architecturally to offer a rich field for this kind of communication—not only to occur but to be observed by whoever has eyes for it. The orthodox theater lets the audience see the actors making this kind of movement. But what about letting spectators see spectators and performers see spectators? Such open architecture encourages a contact that is continuous, subtle, fluid, pervasive, and unconscious. Lovely.

Three major tendencies of contemporary Western theater are exemplified by the ways audiences are arranged and treated. In the orthodox theater, including so-called open stages, such as arenas, thrust stages, and calipter stages, the stage is brightly lit and active; from it information flows into the darkened auditorium where the audience is arranged in regular seats. Feedback from the house to the stage is limited.

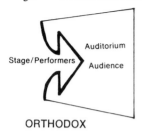

ORTHODOX

Stage	Auditorium
bright	dark
active	passive
giving	taking
noisy	quiet
irregular arrangement	regular arrangement
costumed	everyday dress
magic space	plain space

Confrontation theater, as in the Living Theatre's *Paradise Now,* uses orthodox theater space for unorthodox ends. Many local scenes or confrontations take place both on the stage and in the auditorium. The traditional uses of stage and house are frequently inverted. The aim of confrontation theater is to provoke the audience into participating or at least to make people feel very uncomfortable about not participating. Confrontational theater is a transitional form depending heavily on an *épater le bourgeois* attitude and the need among the bourgeois to experience suffering as a relief of guilt.

Stage	Auditorium
bright	alternately bright and dark
active	forced into activity
giving-taking	taking-giving
noisy	noisy
irregular arrangement	regular arrangement changed by attempts to use the whole space
usually in street clothes, sometimes naked	usually in street clothes, but sometimes provoked to nakedness or exchange of clothes
magic space made plain	plain space made magic

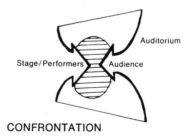

CONFRONTATION

Environmental theater encourages give-and-take throughout a globally organized space in which the areas occupied by the audience are a kind of sea through which the performers swim; and the performance areas are kinds of islands or continents in the midst of the audience. The audience does not sit in regularly arranged rows; there is one whole space rather than two opposing spaces. The environmental use of space is fundamentally *collaborative;* the action flows in many directions sustained only by the cooperation of performers and spectators. Environmental theater design is a reflection of the communal nature of this kind of theater. The design encourages participation; it is also a reflection of the wish for participation. There are no settled sides automatically dividing the audience off against the performers.

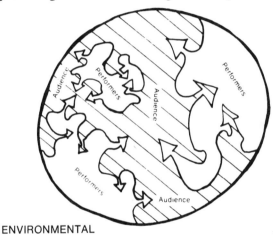

ENVIRONMENTAL

I end this chapter by proposing a few principles of environmental design. These have all been discussed. I gather them as a way of easy reference and summary.

1. For each production the whole space is designed.

2. The design takes into account space-senses and space-fields.

3. Every part of the environment is functional.

4. The environment evolves along with the play it embodies.

5. The performer is included in all phases of planning and building.

People are frightened of theatre because it is the nearest thing to talking and touching each other, which is the deepest flash: In the ladder of artificiality, theatre is on the lowest rung.
Heathcote Williams

To imitate another successfully requires a cooperative audience; the actor establishes an agreement with his audience to attend to certain aspects of a performance. That agreement is seldom open and explicit. In fact, it is often so embedded in the conventionalized context as to be as difficult to analyze as the signal behavior itself.
Ray L. Birdwhistell

2 Participation

What happens to a performance when the usual agreements between performer and spectator are broken? What happens when performers and spectators actually make contact? When they talk to each other and touch? Crossing the boundaries between theater and politics, art and life, performance event and social event, stage and auditorium? Audience participation expands the field of what a performance is, because *audience participation takes place precisely at the point where the performance breaks down and becomes a social event.* In other words, participation is incompatible with the idea of a self-contained, autonomous, beginning-middle-and-end artwork.

The Performance Group didn't talk much about audience participation while preparing *Dionysus in 69*. As we worked, more scenes needed the active collaboration of the audience, and soon nearly all of the play was open to the audience. In any given night we could expect spectators to join in the performance at one point or another. The most extraordinary participatory moments happened when people came to the theater in groups, or when individuals gave over to the performance so fully that for the duration of the performance they joined the Group as if they were members.

One night a bunch of students from Queens College kidnapped Pentheus, preventing his sacrifice to Dionysus. As they seized him, William Shephard, playing Pentheus, went limp, and Jason Bosseau, playing Dionysus, jumped between the students and the theater door. A fierce argument raged between Bosseau/Dionysus and the students.

"You came here with a plan all worked out!" he shouted.

They agreed and said, "Why not?"

Arguments broke out among many spectators not a few of whom thought the whole thing was rigged by the Group. This contingent cynically whined, "Come on now, we've had enough of this, get on with the play we paid money to see!" Finally Pentheus was carried from the theater and unceremoniously dumped on Grand Street. He refused to come back and resume his performance. "I was taken out of it and that's that." Bosseau went upstairs and only returned when he was assured that the play was ready to go on. The disruption was mended when I asked for a volunteer Pentheus from the audience. A sixteen-year-old boy who had seen the play five times took the role of Pentheus. He was instructed by the performers and me concerning his tasks, and he improvised his lines.

For some performers and spectators the conclusion of the play that night had a rare poignancy; for others there was the bitter taste of a double betrayal; first by Shephard/Pentheus for letting himself be carried out of the theater and then by me for yielding to my impulse to finish the show "by any means necessary." I remember my confusion after the performance. The Group was upstairs scrubbing off stage blood and arguing with spectators, including the Queens College "kidnappers." I was elated that something "real" had happened. I didn't think it was wrong that the students planned their actions. After all, if the performers rehearse, why shouldn't the audience? And I was excited by the aftermath: the discussions, the confrontations, the meeting between performers and spectators on new ground. At that time I didn't know the depth of hurt and anger that some performers felt.

Most participations in *Dionysus* were not the result of well-laid plans. Not infrequently spectators spontaneously stripped and took part in the Death Ritual. These people already knew what was expected of them from seeing the Birth Ritual; and they identified strongly with Pentheus, or his murderers. Spectators always allowed themselves to be caressed in the scene that precedes the Death Ritual. More than once a spectator responded

Photograph 11. Participation in the Caress scene of *Dionysus*. The performers are the women in panties and halters. Everyone else is audience. After three months the scene was dropped. Too often performers—especially the women—felt used, prostituted. (*Raeanne Rubenstein*)

with more ardor than a performer bargained for. (The entire problem of sexuality and participation will be discussed later.) Parts of the play—such as the Tag Chorus and the Ecstasy Dance following the birth of Dionysus—were easy to participate in simply by singing, clapping, or dancing, and each night nearly everyone took part in one or both of these scenes.

Underlying much participation in *Dionysus* was the wish of spectators to get closer to the Group as a group. Many spectators thought TPG was a community, even a religious community. Audiences did not want to think of *Dionysus in 69* as "just a play." And in many of its techniques *Dionysus* was not only different from an orthodox play, but *more* than an orthodox play. However, in retrospect, I know that often people were projecting —they wanted to find a community, so they found one in us. But there's more to it than that. The opportunity for authentic interaction with the performers made it true that *Dionysus* was not an orthodox play (that is, a finished thing, a self-contained event) but life (an organic, unfinished thing, an open event). The audience brought their old aesthetics to *Dionysus*. When they saw these did not fit, they didn't formulate a new aesthetics —instead they concluded that the play was not a play but life.

Many who saw *Dionysus* thought it was a celebration of our own religion and that the symbolic events of the play—the birth, taunting, orgies, torture, and killing—were a kind of new Mass; participating in *Dionysus in 69* was a way of performing an arcane ritual in the catacombs of Wooster Street. The audience was not altogether wrong. Members of the Group shared the needs of the audience. What the audience projected onto the play was matched by what the players projected back onto the audience. We all assumed a religion, if we had none.

The performance was often trans-theatrical in a way that could not last, because American society in 1969 was not actually communal. *Dionysus* was overwhelming to the degree that audiences believed it was not a play and found that belief confirmed by the Group. This belief in the play's actuality was corroborated by its participatory elements. Joining in *Dionysus* —like declaring for Christ at a revival meeting—was an act of the body publicly signaling one's faith. Participation and belief supported each other—on any given night the strength of feeling created by joining participation to belief could be such that everything else was swept away.

But, as Euripides himself reminds us in *The Bacchae,* "we are not gods, but men." The great Dionysian circle was an evasion of the circumstances in the streets of New York. It was an evasion of the circumstances within the Group. Arguments flamed concerning whether the Group was a theater or a community. Looking back from three years' distance, I see now that the arguments were beside the point. The real question was: Would we acquiesce in being a function of the audience's fantasies? Were we to become one of the first theaters to reverse the old arrangement—no longer would the illusion originate on stage and be sustained by the audience; the illusion was now originating with the audience and enhanced by the performers.

TPG was not then to become a community. And the basis for audience participation changed because the Group could not survive intact as a function of the audience's fantasies. During the winter of 1968–1969 the Group began weekly encounter therapy sessions guided by professional therapists. These sessions helped members recognize that the Group was not a community, nor did it seem headed in that direction. Certain irresolvable conflicts surfaced, and irreconcilable differences emerged. One member called these therapy sessions the "weekly tear and mucous meetings." As members got deeper into group therapy, the therapeutic scenes in *Dionysus* were modified and finally dropped. Participation grew tamer and more predictable. Performers began to resent participation especially when it broke the rhythms of what had been carefully rehearsed. By the time *Dionysus in 69* closed at the end of July, 1969, most of the performers had had it with participation.

Two points should be made clear regarding the participation in *Dionysus*. First, participation occurred at those points where the play stopped being a play and became a social event—when spectators felt that they were free to enter the performance as equals. At these times the themes of the play—its "literary values"—were advanced not textually but wholly through action; or the themes were not advanced at all but set aside so that something else could happen. And just about everything did happen at one time or another—from a young male model dancing in his jockstrap around the Birth Ritual distributing business cards with his name and phone number, to passionate denunciations of the Vietnam war. For spectators who participated, performers were no longer actors but people doing what they believed in, "spontaneously." It was impossible for most people to acknowledge that the attributes of "actor" and "person" were not mutually exclusive. The second point is that most of the participation in *Dionysus* was according to the democratic model: letting people into the play to do as the performers were doing, to "join the story." This was all the easier in *Dionysus* because the story is clear and simple and because the performers did not display skills popularly identified with acting. The Group did not try to impersonate, or speak in fancy tones. (Fully trained bodies were not identified with acting by most spectators, and so the superb body work of the performers didn't put anyone off.) In short, participation in *Dionysus* didn't mean acting-like-actors-do but believing-in-what-The-Performance-Group-believes, and "acting spontaneously" from those beliefs.

Before going ahead, let me review. I began by asserting that participation takes place at the precise point where the performance breaks down—is broken down. It is hard to talk about participation because participation is not about "doing a play" but *undoing* it, transforming an aesthetic event into a social event —or shifting the focus from art-and-illusion to the potential or actual solidarity among everyone in the theater, performers and spectators alike. The orthodox view of aesthetics insists on an autonomous, self-contained (separate) drama performed by one group of people who are watched by another group. The architecture and conventions of the orthodox theater strongly enforces these aesthetics. However, I also said that participation is such a powerful intrusion into this orthodox scheme, that in the face of participation we must reconsider the very foundations of orthodox aesthetics: illusion, mimesis, the physical separation of audience and performers, the creation of a symbolic time and place.

Why has audience participation appeared at this moment in Western theater history, reintroducing methods that have been dormant since medieval times? Because participation is extra-aesthetic (according to orthodox aesthetics), the answer cannot be found in aesthetics. The theater is a particularly sensitive measurement of social feeling and action. It is also a holdout, technologically speaking: the last of the hand-crafted entertainments. In society in general, and in entertainment in particular the movement is to self-contained, electronically processed, unresponsive systems—closed systems on which the individual can have little effect. Shout as you will at the TV set, Johnny Carson does not hear you. And even the phone-in programs have the famous "five-second delay," giving the broadcaster absolute control over what goes out over the air. Closed, one-way systems are inherently oppressive. They are even more maliciously so when they wear the costume of openness, as so much of "media programming" does. Orthodox theater is much more open than TV or films but much more closed than environmental theater. Environmental theater's attempts at audience participation are both last-ditch stands, and tentative first-tries at creating and enhancing entertainment, art, and actual situations by opening the system, making feedback not only possible but delightful.

Opening the closed circle occurs by democratizing the performance, as in *Dionysus,* or by making sure that continuous change and indeterminacy is part of the whole process of theater-making, as TPG tried to do in *Commune*. There are scenes in *Commune* that *need* the audience in order to be played. No one is let into the theater unless he/she takes off his/her shoes. The first action of the play (in one of its versions) is a police line-up in which performers stand amid spectators who are selected for the line-up randomly. Standing on the Wave, the fifteen people look more or less alike. Then Lizzie steps from the line-up, stands on the edge of the Tub, and picks out the performers. As she identifies each one, he/she takes a step forward. When all have been identified, Lizzie says: "They're the ones, they did it." Next is the March to Death Valley—a circle dance around the whole theater that can end only when the circle has been made, and to make a circle, at least fifteen or more spectators must join the dance. There have been times, when the house is small, that everyone joins the dance, and the circle is small. Throughout *Commune* there are moments—some seen by everyone and some rather private—in which individual spectators, or groups, are needed to further the action of the play.

The inflexible rule that everyone remove their shoes upon entering the theater has stirred every feeling from indifferent compliance to delight to bitter anger and cynicism. Critics can't understand how this gesture "liberates" them—so simple-minded is their cliché identification of the new theater with "liberation," that every gesture must be instantly translated into some signal of "freedom." Libertarians protest against the "fascistic" demand of giving up one's *private* property. Few of these same people protest that TPG charges an admission price, making our whole performances private, limited property. Some people say that because they have paid for their tickets, they should not have to take their shoes off. The fastidious have assured me that the indelicate odors of bare and stockinged feet are all that has prevented them from seeing *Commune*. For me, the significance of taking off shoes is multiple. It is an actual gesture of collaboration focusing on an item of personal property; it is a mild initiatory ordeal; it makes everyone in the theater alike in at least one way; it has some metaphorical references to the victims of Auschwitz and My Lai; and because the performers wear the shoes while depicting the Sharon Tate murders, there is the suggestion of audience involvement—group responsibility—in that act. Removing one's shoes is a way of accepting hospitality; in Asia guests always leave their shoes at the door.

The most difficult, paradigmatic, and unsettling scene of

audience participation in *Commune* is the My Lai sequence. Up till now the Group has tried four solutions to this scene, none of them definitive. The action of the scene is a re-presentation of an interview relating the killing of Vietnamese civilians at My Lai by American trops. The data was taken from newspaper and television reports. The one constant throughout all the versions is the stationing of the three performers taking part in the interview in a triangular relationship to each other overlooking whoever or whatever represents the people of My Lai assembled between, among, or below them.

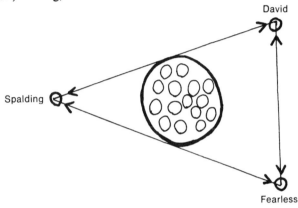

There is little physical action in the scene until the very end when Spalding asks, "How do you shoot babies?" and David answers, "I don't know. It's just one of them things. It seemed like it was the natural thing to do at the time." Then Fearless begins a song-and-dance which the other two men join.

> The little pigs they roast themselves
> And trot about this lovely land
> With knives and forks stuck in their backs
> Inquiring if you'd like some ham.[1]

Throughout the scene Lizzie, blindfolded, is finding her way through the environment by locating road signs reading "El Dorado."

The first solution is to have the audience represent the villagers

---

[1] This is a verse from a popular nineteenth-century song of American utopia, *Oleana!* The well-known chorus of the song is sung early in *Commune.*

Photograph 12. Eleven spectators in the Circle during the My Lai scene of *Commune*. They are waiting to see if four other spectators will join them or if the play will stop. (*Frederick Eberstadt*)

at My Lai. Fearless herds spectators into the circle. He plays cowhand and kicks spectators with his feet and shouts, "Get a move on, move along now!" until he gets about fifteen people inside the ten-foot-diameter circle. The interview is played as soon as the audience is settled. They are not told why they are brought into the circle or what to do after the scene is over. Some people stay in the circle until the end of the play; some sheepishly slink back to their places. Many people are confused about what is expected of them. Clearly this first solution is obscure and manipulative. Sometimes people play "doggie" games with Fearless; often they giggle.

The second solution is that Fearless selects fifteen persons at random from the audience and says to them, "I want you fifteen people to come into the center of this circle to represent the villagers at My Lai." Usually the fifteen persons come in. But sometimes there are holdouts. Then James Griffiths (Fearless) takes off his shirt and says: "I am taking off my shirt to signify that the performance is now stopped. You people have the following choices. First, you can come into the circle, and the performance will continue; second, you can go to anyone else in the room and ask them to take your place, and, if they do, the performance will continue; third, you can stay where you are, and the performance will remain stopped; or fourth, you can go home, and the performance will continue in your absence."

Whenever Griffiths recites these conditions, there is a shock wave in the theater. The "real world" penetrates the "theater world" interrupting a performance. As Griffiths speaks, the other performers relax, go to the toilet or take water, sit down, talk. Soon the audience understands that the play really has stopped. Usually the break is brief because in the face of an interrupted performance pressure builds fast for resumption, and the recalcitrant spectators either come into the circle or select substitutes. But for the duration of the break one point is made absolutely clear: What is at stake is not the themes of the play —not the people of My Lai—but the immediate question of whether or not the show will go on. The longer the break, the more urgently this question asserts itself.

On Sunday, February 28, 1971, the break lasted more than three hours. Two days later I wrote out my impressions in my notebook. I think it is worth quoting that entry at length.

From My Notebook

The performance went along splendidly. There was an audience of about forty, including two small student groups—eight from the Columbia Players' Club and about five from an English class at Long Island University. The march to Death Valley showed that the audience was warm to us. Upstairs, before sending them into the theater, I made the following announcement: "There is some participation. If you want to be left alone, sit up high."

When My Lai came, Fearless selected his fifteen people. It was almost a random choice. He passed over Loren from Norman Taffel's theater next door *(Little Trips),* because last time she was at *Commune* she was disruptive. He included three very straight looking fortyish people sitting protectively deep back on the carpeted overhang above Freedom Circle. One of them not only took his shoes with him to his place, but stuffed them into the pockets of his overcoat for double safekeeping. The other man had a funny, short nose and something wrong with his teeth. He kept quiet most of the time. The lady was tough, but not in an attractive way. She was hard, up-tight, dressed all in black, a middle-aged social-worker type.

Four persons refused to come into the My Lai circle—the three on the overhang and a Frenchman named Jean. At first I thought that the three on the overhang were French, too, and didn't understand what was happening. The waiting began. As usual, there was some consternation as people became aware that the performance was stopped. Were we serious? Was the play really stopped? The toilets were in use. People strolled and explored. One spectator later told me that it was "the first *real* intermission I ever took part in." Conversations began; people looked at each other and at the theater. The Three settled back deeper. Jean smiled and said in a nicely French way, "Yes, yes, I understand. Oh, no, I won't go in." The people in the circle, mostly students from Columbia, were giggly. They taunted those who wouldn't go in.

Soon some spectators began to chant, "We want the show, we want the show!" The actors held their places pretty well, though Bruce and Lizzie went into the alcove where the lighting board was. Then T. W. [former general manager of the Group] began a tirade. In a very loud and sneering voice he attacked Griffiths and the Three. He accused Griffiths of not choosing people randomly but in order to stop the performance. He called the Three up-tight, unhip, old, not tuned in; he disparaged them for dressing in ties and jackets. T. W. got louder and more abusive; he was angry, giggling, and breathing hard. Still talking, he put on his coat, grabbed his date by her wrist, and stalked out of the theater, shoes in hand.

It was about 9:45—the show had stopped at about 9:15. People went over to talk to the Three, who were very angry: "We came here to see a play! We were told we didn't have to participate! We do not want to participate! Get on with the play!" Then they said they were enjoying the play until the interruption.

Then they asked if they could have their money back. Someone told them they could pick substitutes to go into the circle. "That would be participating! We were told upstairs we would not be forced to participate!"

The man with the small nose motioned me to him. He whispered, "Get on with the show!" These people were afraid and angry. But as time went on, some of their anger drained, and they grew to enjoy the attention heaped on them; they hoarded those gratifications. It seemed that for the first time in a long while they were the center of attention in a matter concerning their ability to make a decision. They were not in the spotlight because of some sudden accident or disease. There were no lawyers or doctors to serve as intermediaries. They were in control —able to keep the play stopped or to license its resumption.

At one point the man with the pipe and the lady—probably man and wife—threatened to sue the theater for "forced participation." But they soon withdrew their threat, assuring me that they would not give the Group the "satisfaction of so much publicity." They were convinced that they were picked for the circle because Fearless knew they were people of substance who would seek redress in the law. But they were not going to fall into the trap.

About ten people gathered around the Three, and the mood got warmer. The woman in black said she'd already raised her share of adolescents and didn't choose to go through the process a second time with us. The man with the pipe kept insisting he wanted to see the play. "It's very good, and I want to know how it ends." He draped his arm around my shoulder and confided, "Now tell them to start again, will you?" He didn't believe the matter was out of my hands. People came and left the overhang as if it were a place where critical negotiations were going on. After Griffiths left the overhang, the man with the pipe told me that they had "discussed the issues meaningfully." He offered to let anyone in the room volunteer to take his place in the circle, but he would not select people. The lady in black wouldn't even let anyone take her place. It was 11 P.M.

Meanwhile, throughout the theater, among performers and audience alike, new situations developed. The small audience got to know not only each other but the performers, too. Names were exchanged. Wine and cheese were suggested, but it was Sunday and stores were closed. The coffeepot was put to use. One performer asked if she could go home. I said I was not in charge. Several people talked with Jean, who assured them that no matter what the Three did, he wouldn't go into the circle. A performer put on his coat and said: "Rich, there ain't gonna be any more play tonight." Another performer was anxious because several of her friends had come to the play that night, and left.

Finally it was decided that performers could go home if they picked spectators to take their roles. The logic was that if the performance had stopped, then it had stopped for performers as well as audience. Shortly thereafter Patricia Bower left, picking Wendy, Jean's wife, to play Lizzie. So here was a locked situation: Jean would not go into the circle, and Wendy—who wanted to play Lizzie—would not go home. A little while later, Jayme Daniel, playing Jayson, left after picking Nancy Walter [one of the writers of the Firehouse Theater] as his replacement. No one knew how Wendy and Nancy would play their roles if the play resumed.

After the performers playing Lizzie and Jayson left, a crisis was confronted: *the crisis of the absolutely prepared performance.* Everyone knew that when/if the play resumed, it would not rest on the same aesthetic basis as before.

Steadily people left the theater. By around 11:30 there were only twenty-five people there. Griffiths proposed a vote. "Here are the alternatives. We go home or we continue as we are." The vote was overwhelmingly to continue. The man with the pipe proposed a vote on continuing the play without getting the holdouts to participate. About seven people voted for this, five abstained. The rest—except Spalding who voted for both sides—voted to continue as we were: to play out the new scenario wherever it might lead, however long it took. Someone asked Spalding how come he voted twice. He answered, "I voted twice, but not for the same candidate."

The vote broke the back of the Three's resistance. They were visibly upset by the outcome of the "democratic process." I don't remember precisely when—I think before the voting—the group from Columbia staged an improvisation. It was not clear what it was about. It began with seven of them lying on their stomachs in the center of the My Lai circle. Then they roamed the space, whispering and shouting, and finally they surrounded a girl and pulled at her clothing. It ended sheepishly, subsiding back into the room.

I began singing. We sang "America the Beautiful" and, for Jean, "La Marseillaise." The performers threw the I Ching and got Hexagram 7, *The Army:* "The army needs perseverance and a strong man. Good fortune without blame." The hexagram was interpreted as putting full faith in Griffiths/Fearless. I was told not to interfere in any way. The singing continued, and when we began "Do, a deer, a female deer" from *The Sound of Music,* everyone in the theater picked it up and aimed it at the Three. It was too much; they picked up their coats and moved toward the door. A feeling of excitement and triumph shot through me. Even the Three seemed happy. Not just about leaving (at last!) but also because something had happened, somehow the night hadn't been wasted. As they got to the door, I embraced the lady in black. She responded. They left.

The room was unified, and only Jean stood between everyone and a resumed performance. He said he wouldn't go into the circle because he didn't know what going in meant. I explained to him: "You are asked to represent the villagers who were killed randomly at My Lai." Suddenly Jean said, "Okay, I go in." It was 12:15.

I volunteered to read Lizzie's and Jayson's lines, and Wendy and Nancy would repeat the lines after me giving them any expression they felt appropriate. We began. The room was very quiet. There were nineteen spectators, including me and Elizabeth Le Compte, the play's codirector, and nine performers, including the two from the audience.

The performance was *without aesthetics.* There were no questions of good or bad; all did as well as they could; naturally the performers worked more skillfully than the newcomers. But this skill was not overbearing—it didn't shut out the feelings of Wendy and Nancy. The skills of the Group were no more in question than eye color. The play was ritualized and demimeticized. *The performance itself was what was important.* The audience remained not to find out what happened in the play but to witness the play completing itself. The play, of course, had its references to events outside the room, but essentially the performance was an event inside the room. The event that had been in question for more than three hours was now completing itself. Everyone was collaborating in that, just as everyone had collaborated in the interruption.

The next day Spalding Gray told me that the lights seemed brighter to him when the play resumed. At first he attributed it to his exhaustion. But then he thought it was because so many barriers had come down. There were fewer things between him and the audience. They saw him *as he was*—not as a magician-performer, but as a person *out of whom* the performance arose, just as the Commarque Horse arises out of the stone of its cave.

Seeing him thus—as the performer and not as the role the performer was playing—when he resumed the actions of his role, there was no need to pretend that those actions took place anywhere else than in this theater at this time.

When Wendy speaking Lizzie's lines confessed crimes, I had the sense of *objective crimes* needing to be listed, finding their reality in the telling. The play ended with the usual dialogue between Clementine and Spalding:

> What would you describe as the role of the artist in today's society?
> The role of the artist?
> Yes.
> Yes, yes, of course.

Slowly the theater emptied. People stuck around as we pumped out the tub. Water = blood = water. I was giddy. Steve and I had an overwhelming desire for milk shakes—breasts, come—and we bought milk, ice cream, chocolate syrup, and mixed some rich stuff at my apartment.

Analysis

Most of what I feel about the long interruption of February 28 I got down in my notebook entry a few days later. But I wish to emphasize a few points. *Commune* that night had three parts, only one of them dramatic in the orthodox sense. The first, until the stoppage, was "just a play." The second—from the stoppage until the Three left the theater and Jean agreed to go into the circle—was the struggle of a community-in-formation against those who prevented this community from organizing itself. However, the struggle itself was what made solidarity inevitable. The Three were as necessary to the building of a community as an antagonist is to traditional drama. The building of the community had two parts: first, breaking down barriers so that the majority could act together against the Three. This part culminated in the votes. Secondly, the increasing pressure against the Three so that their leaving was actually a moment of supreme triumph.

The third part of the night began when Jean entered the circle and the play resumed. Doing the play was a confirmation of the power of those who expelled the Three and a demonstration of the community's ability to carry out a positive program. Doing the play was an authentic celebration. This celebration couldn't have happened—indeed it never occurred before or since—without the long stoppage and struggle. The solidarity between the audience and the performers (even those who left knowing that they were not betraying the others) did away with *Commune*-as-play and replaced it with *Commune*-as-ritual.

I do not want to overvalue the experience of February 28. It reached such extraordinary levels because it was unrehearsable. Were the Group to repeat such events with regularity, I am sure they would be drained of meaning. Also the community that was formed in the Garage that night didn't last. A few weeks later the Group went to Wendy's for a party; but most of the people present at the Garage on February 28 never saw each other again (the exceptions being the student groups who were together for reasons other than TPG). Also I am not at all convinced that nights like February 28 can take place with a large audience, say more than seventy-five people. But insofar as the long stoppage was what it was, it was a model of participation in which individuals were free to use their own judgments in a generally nonmanipulative situation.

The third solution. On April 24, 1971—the day of a mass demonstration in Washington against the Vietnam War—the Group decided to donate the night's box office to the antiwar movement. As part of the benefit performance members wanted somehow to involve the entire audience in the My Lai scene. Also the random selection of fifteen persons was wearing the performers down; some people detested the unpredictable interruption of the play, the inability to know whether or not the prepared rhythms would complete themselves as rehearsed.

It was decided that Spalding would say, "I want everyone in the theater to come down to the center here to represent the villagers at My Lai." There was a moment's hesitation, and then a few people began moving. Soon just about everyone in the theater was on the move. The floor was covered with people. The performers took positions high in the ramparts. When the scene was over, Lizzie shouted, "You're all disgusting." (It's never clear exactly to whom she is saying this, performers-as-soldiers, spectators-as-citizens, performers-as-members-of-the-commune, spectators-as-My-Lai-villagers.) Spalding then says, "The scene is over. You can go back to where you were, or maybe you'd like to find another place in the environment from which you can watch the play. And we'd like a few people to stay in the center circle." Again there was general movement.

Then the play resumed—not from where it leaves off but back a few beats. Spalding, David, and Fearless take their places on the Wave (as in the first two solutions to the My Lai scene) and do the "Little Pigs" song-and-dance. This time Lizzie's line is unambiguously directed at the men. Except for the ten or so people who remain in the circle the rest of the audience sees the My Lai scene from two perspectives: under the gun and outside the action; they are able to apprize the action from two opposing points of view, that of the victim and that of the soldier.

The fourth solution. In December, 1971, the Group began doing the My Lai scene without any direct participation of the audience at all. As people enter the theater, they deposit their shoes on a large cloth laid out like a blanket. At the start of the My Lai scene Fearless and Clementine drag the sack up the Wave and dump it in the circle. Spalding, David, and Fearless take their places on the Wave and play the scene across the footwear of the audience. People sometimes react strongly to seeing their shoes. Gasps, giggles, pointing. Just about everyone connects the image to the concentration camps, and the scene's meaning is clear. Occasionally, someone retrieves his/her shoes at once.

Each of the solutions to the My Lai scene is an attempt to find non-manipulative participatory actions. Herding the audience is manipulative because people didn't know what was expected of them. But even the second solution is manipulative because it casts the audience as "villagers" and forces them into playing roles they may not be prepared to play. It only becomes non-manipulative when someone refuses to enter and the play stops. Then performers and spectators have the chance to meet on equal terms. But the second solution was not dropped because it was manipulative. It was dropped because the performers didn't enjoy the uncertainty introduced nightly into the play. The performance became aimed at the moment Jim/Fearless selected the fifteen. The question was: Would we get *through it,* or would the play be *disrupted?* It is hard to keep prepared rhythms when threatened by the chance that the play might not be completed. And when the play is stopped, the focus shifts from the performance to the entire theatrical event, from the performers to the spectators. This is where participation hurts. Performers are trained to perform, they resist events that disrupt prepared rhythms. It is not easy to balance the need for "scored roles" with the uncertainties of participation. Performers, like anyone else, do not like to appear clumsy, off-balance, or ineffectual. Once someone refuses to come into the Circle, the illusion of theatrical inevitability is shattered, and with it goes the

Photograph 13. The third solution to the My Lai scene: Bruce dries himself near the end of *Commune,* standing amid the spectators' shoes. (*Frederick Eberstadt*)

Photographs 14, 15, and 16. Some subtle participations in *Commune* by spectators. In Photos 14 and 15 Spalding gestures during the Shoot Out. He is straddling the shoulders of a spectator who points his own gun and shoots twice, once while Spalding is there and once as Spalding leaves. In Photo 16 a young woman reaches out to comfort Clementine who has just experienced orgasm, exhaustion, and death during the Father Jesus gang-bang scene. (*Frederick Eberstadt*)

performer's magic powers. However satisfactory this may be from a director's point of view, it is dismaying and sometimes humiliating to the performers.

The third solution is all-inclusive and generally non-manipulative. Most of the time a few people don't come to the center of the floor, but this does not detract from the overall effect of the scene. The stay-behinds are somewhat like combat photographers or professional witnesses. They usually huddle back out of sight. For the rest of the audience the trip to the floor enables them to change perspective, meet their neighbors, and be included in the drama. Although the third solution interrupts the play, the interruption is known in advance, and it lasts a regular thirty seconds to a minute. Therefore it doesn't destroy the performers' scores—in fact, it can be made part of their scores. My objection to the third solution is that it is innocuous. It is too easy, makes no real point, and waters down the My Lai scene.

The fourth solution is not participatory. It uses the audience's shoes as props. It is extremely effective theatrically.

The riskiest participation is the second solution, the one that resulted in the long stoppage of February 28. This is the solution that most interests me because it permits the spectators to enter the performance on their own terms—or to leave it altogether. It wasn't very exciting when the fifteen people immediately came into the Circle, sheepishly accepting whatever roles they were asked to play. But with the slightest resistance or hesitation a shock of recognition, surprise, power, and possibilities runs through the theater. The performance itself is in doubt, open to revision, questionable, human, here and now. The performers are seen as people playing roles, telling a story and not just as characters. Theatrical structure is revealed starkly, and choices are out in the open.

Reviewing the history of the My Lai scene there appears to be a kind of entropy operating. Participation is risky, both for the spectators and for the performers. In a way as director I have the easiest position. I am not manipulated as the audience might be; and I am not out front risking my well-prepared score as the performers are. I monitor the experiments and tell the performers during the next night's notes what I saw. Over the long run what I have seen is that participation decreases as a play runs—this is true of *Dionysus* as well as of *Commune*. I think the participation decreases because scores are built, either consciously or unconsciously, and disruptions become increasingly annoying and finally intolerable. Also because there is a scant tradition of participation the audience also feels more comfortable when left alone. I think both the problem of scoring and of building a tradition of participation are solvable. But in doing so the means of participation will change.

In *The Tooth of Crime* TPG is for the first time mainly telling a story and playing characters in order to tell a story. But we do not want the production to be fundamentally mimetic or illusionistic. Among the things we are doing are certain new kinds of participation. First off, we consider the Garage as the TPG's home. Instead of hiring a box-office person and a technical crew, the performers (and me) are doing that work. So that when a spectator comes to buy a ticket before the play, he deals with a performer or the director. On the walls of the lobby upstairs over the theater are pictures of the performers—displayed in a style like that of Broadway. (*The Tooth of Crime* is all about image-makers, stars, and performing styles.) But underneath the pictures are the performers themselves, doing jobs. When the audience enters the theater, some performers are cleaning up the space, others are arranging the props, checking the lights and the environment. If a performer sees someone he/she knows, there are greetings, maybe a discussion. The performance begins where it actually is rooted: in the ongoing lives of the performers and spectators. As curtain time nears, the performers will begin to put on their costumes, make final preparations, actually "get into character." Again during intermission the performers divest themselves of their roles and relate to the audience on a person-to-person basis. And again after the play is over, instead of vanishing with the audience's applause, the performers begin to put on their costumes, making final prepara- for the night. Within *The Tooth of Crime* as well as around it are participatory moments, but of a different kind than we have tried before. There is much direct address to spectators, soliloquies, and movement of the audience around the space. More then ever each spectator chooses how he is to place himself in relation to the action. The environment allows everyone three clear choices and many gradations. A spectator can stand, sit, or walk on a gallery eleven feet above the floor surrounding half the space, or he/she can sit, stand, or walk around the floor and surround each scene as it occurs as if it were being played in the street, or the spectator can sit or stand on the large house-like construction of platforms, towers, and bridges that fills the center of the theater to a height of sixteen feet. There is no way to stay in one place and see everything.

The more I examine the questions that audience participation raises, the more I see that these penetrate to the heart of the audience-performer relationship. What does the performer "owe" to the spectator, and vice-versa? If a spectator "finds out" that a character is not "real," does this diminish his enjoyment of the play? How does this knowledge change his experience of the play? To what degree is the performer a story-teller and not a story-actor? How deeply do performers need spectators to support the illusion of character and situation? Can this support suddenly be removed, a new situation created, and then transformed back into the support? Why does a performer feel threatened when a spectator "moves into" the performance space? Why does a spectator feel threatened when directly addressed by a performer? What is clear is that the relationship between the performers and the spectators needs to be straightened out by being painstakingly scrutinized—examined not in theoretical discussions but by means of many, many experiments in participation. On both sides are great reservoirs of doubt and distrust. There are many causes for this, but not the least are the conventions of the orthodox theater that separate audience from performers and which make the performers into sellers of pleasure-services, depriving them of self-respect. Although much has been said about spectators feeling manipulated by performers, as much can be said on the other side. Performers are used by producers, directors, and writers. And by audiences who want only to get off on the show.

Participation is a way of trying to humanize relationships between performers and spectators. This process far transcends what goes on in a theater. But there is no better laboratory for trying out ways of responsivity than in the intense, microcosmic space of a theater. If my recent experiments in audience participation seem hesitant, even timid, it is because I recognize the size and depth of the problems revealed by participation. Each big jump is followed by exploratory probes in various directions. Each apparent halting is only temporary. There is no technique more important to the development of contemporary theater than participation.

Some TPG experiments in participation have come from ideas first tried out by John Cage and later by Allan Kaprow. The impact of new music and Happenings on participatory theater cannot be overestimated. It was from the direction of music and painting that theater was revolutionized, and no one has had more effect than Cage and Kaprow.[2] In 1966 Kaprow published an essay on the theory of Happenings. In it he lays down the following seven axioms:

(A) *The line between art and life should be kept as fluid, and perhaps as indistinct, as possible. . . .* Something will always happen at this juncture, which, if it is not revelatory, will not be merely bad art—for no one can easily compare it with this or that accepted masterpiece.

(B) *Therefore, the source of themes, materials, actions, and the relationships between them are to be derived from any place or period* except *from the arts, their derivatives, and their milieu. . . .* Freedom to accept all kinds of subject matter will probably be possible in the Happenings of the future, but I think not for now.

(C) *The performance of a Happening should take place over several widely spaced, sometimes moving and changing locales.*

(D) *Time, which follows closely on space considerations, should be variable and discontinuous. . . .* Above all this is "real" or "experienced" time as distinct from conceptual time. . . . Real time is always connected with doing something, with an event of some kind, and so is bound with things and spaces.

(E) *Happenings should be performed once only. . . .* There is a special instance of where more than one performance is entirely justified. This is the score or scenario which is designed to make every performance significantly different from the previous one.

(F) *It follows that audiences should be eliminated entirely.* All the elements—people, space, the particular materials and character of the environment, time—can in this way be integrated.

(G) *The composition of a Happening proceeds exactly as in Assemblage and Environments, that is, it is evolved as a collage of events in certain spans of time and in certain spaces.*[3]

[2] A bibliography of Cage's and Kaprow's writing is no substitute for an experience of their work in performance. And the relationship between them is more than coincidence: Kaprow was a member of a class taught by Cage during the 1950's at the New School. See Cage's *Silence* (1961), *A Year from Monday* (1967), and Notations (1969). And Kaprow's *Assemblages, Environments, and Happenings* (1966), *Some Recent Happenings* (1966b), *Untitled Essay and Other Works* (1967), and *Days Off* (1970). Also Michael Kirby's *Happenings* (1965) and the TDR special issue on Happenings, Vol. 10, No. 2 (1965).

[3] All Kaprow quotations from *Assemblages, Environments, and Happenings* (1966), 188 ff.

Kaprow's view of participation is sophisticated and humane —more humane than mine has been on some occasions.

> To assemble people unprepared for an event and say that they are "participating" if apples are thrown at them or if they are herded about is to ask very little of the whole notion of participation. . . . I think it is a mark of mutual respect that all persons involved in a Happening be willing and committed participants who have a clear idea of what they are to do. This is simply accomplished by writing out the scenario or score for all and discussing it thoroughly with them beforehand. In this respect it is not different from the preparations for a parade, a football match, a wedding, or a religious service. It is not even different from a play. The one big difference is that while knowledge of the scheme is necessary, professional talent is not; the situations in a Happening are lifelike or, if they are unusual, are so rudimentary that professionalism is actually uncalled for. . . . The best participants have been persons not normally engaged in art or performance, but who are moved to take part in an activity that is at once meaningful to them in its ideas yet natural in its methods.

I have directed two participatory pieces somewhat according to Kaprow's model. One, *Clothes,* is discussed in Chapter 3. The other, *Government Anarchy,* was invented on invitation from Ted Becker of the American Civil Liberties Union who commissioned TPG in May, 1970, to do a participatory event for an ACLU meeting at the Electric Circus in Manhattan. The scenario for *Government Anarchy* collected political ideas that were in the air and focused them through a set of questions I took from Ralph Ortiz's event *The Sky Is Falling,* "a destruction ritual" written in 1969 and which I saw in Philadelphia in early 1970. The *Government Anarchy* scenario:

> Each A.C.L.U. member or guest was stopped at a desk at the front door of the Electric Circus. I sat at the desk, and behind me with an accordion file was Paul Epstein. I asked the name of each person and repeated it very loud to Epstein who pretended to look for a dossier of the named person. To each name Epstein replies with a color code: "Red," "Green," "White," or "Gray." His designations are random. One out of every nine or ten people is designated Gray. Gray is asked to step to one side and wait. All the others are let through. Upstairs there is a show staged by various other theater groups.

(I intentionally asked Ted Becker who commissioned TPG's part in the overall event not to tell me anything about the show upstairs.)

Gray is assured of his or her safety and then taken to a side room and put behind police barriers inside an empty, badly lit room. Several performers stand guard, refusing to answer any questions. As Grays are collected, some are blindfolded and led from the room to interrogation rooms upstairs. Other Grays are simply made to wait in the holding room. After about three hours they are released. The blindfolded Grays are led upstairs one at a time. The process of moving Grays from the holding room to the interrogation rooms begins about one half hour after the first person is stopped at the front door.

Interrogation rooms are on the third floor of the Circus. One is a storeroom, the other a toilet. In each there is a table, two chairs, a tape recorder and operator, a photographer, an interrogator. As soon as Gray is brought in he is photographed (by Polaroid process), and the tape is turned on. He is asked to sit, and then he is unblindfolded. Gray is asked a long series of questions (standardized) about his personal life, family, political affiliations, connection to the A.C.L.U., reading habits. Some questions are abusive and sexual. After each of these, Gray is asked to take off some of his/her clothes, and his photo is taken.

The interrogation takes about thirty minutes. If Gray refuses to answer a question, the interrogator repeats it. Like a broken record the question is repeated again and again until Gray answers or the time allotted for the interrogation is exhausted. After the questioning, Gray is politely thanked for his "cooperation," handed his clothes, and shown out of the room. Often Gray did not know where he was or how to get back to his friends. Some people remained lost for fifteen minutes or more.

The tapes and photos of Gray are delivered to the main floor of the Circus where in an alcove off the large ballroom the tapes are played over a speaker system and the photos projected on the wall by means of an opaque projector.

When the last person is processed at the front door—about two hours after we began, a long line formed outside the Circus—Epstein and I are free to go. When the last Gray is released after interrogation, about three hours after starting, the remaining Grays in the holding room are released, and the performers playing interrogators and guards are free. Those showing photos and playing tapes continue their tasks until the entire program is over—about three and a half hours afer the start.

Government Anarchy is participation by means of manipulation —manipulation raised to an extreme and cruel intensity. The audience is used as material; they are processed. This, of course, is a main part of the point we were trying to make: how the "legal system" uses people as material for its own perpetuation, not in order to "do justice," and how this system is maintained largely by the active, willing collaboration of those who are being processed. *Government Anarchy* is many "plays"—different for each participant. To those who enter without being detained, the play is just another waiting in line; to those who are detained but not interrogated, it is a bother, perhaps infuriating because they miss what's going on upstairs; to those who are interrogated, the play may be amusing, stupid, frightening: It was all of this, and more, to some of the Grays. One rule TPG followed was that no one was detained by force. If a Gray simply got up and left, either the holding room or the interrogation, he was not stopped —he was just *told* he could not go, that he *must* sit down. Grays collaborated because they thought it was all a game or because they were intimidated.

The play is what happens to each participator and performer, and what happens to them all collectively, but no one, not even members of TPG, can see everything. *Government Anarchy* extends over time and spaces and is much like what Kaprow envisions (in structure, not effect). The politics of *Anarchy* is clear—we put some A.C.L.U. people through what the A.C.L.U. is supposed to prevent—but with enough distance and lack of fear (everyone knew *Anarchy* was "just a play") to get a handle on the experience. Those who were not Grays would hear about the play from the Grays. Other pieces have been built the same way—Megan Terry's *Changes* at La Mama in 1968, for example. In this kind of participation audiences do not take part in a play —moving in and out of the drama. Instead the audience is the stuff from which the drama is made. The structure of *Anarchy* is close to that of an initiation ordeal/ritual. After the play is over, some people in the audience (Grays) are "different" from the others by virtue of having undergone an experience. From the perspective of a visiting anthropologist, *Government Anarchy* is a kind of ritual that induces separations. From inside the experience, each Gray had a different, somewhat fragmentary hold on the play. I feel uncomfortable calling *Anarchy* a "play." But when things got rough, more than one Gray protested, "Hey, this is only a play, remember?"

At that moment the performer bears down, trying his best to

convince Gray and himself that *Anarchy* isn't a play at all—if play means make-believe following a set script. One Gray was so rattled that he asked a friend outside the holding room to call the police. When two cops arrived, I told them that the Circus was private property and that TPG was hired to screen out "undesirables." I reminded the police that the neighborhood was unsavory. "If the gentleman objects," I said, "he is free to get out and stay out." Gray decided to stay, and the perplexed cops left. Now, what can one say of a scene like that? Where is the dividing line between make-believe and "reality"? The mixture of "game" and "reality" is difficult to analyze. Some of the fabric of expectations and obligations binding performers to spectators is ripped apart, but some remains. A basic agreement remains intact: No physical force is used, and even Gray knows somewhere that TPG are actors. One of the points of *Anarchy* is that in "real life" people collaborate with their oppressors not from fear but from the belief that the authorities will "play by the rules" and that these rules are based on "fair play." Cruelly, and too late, victims discover that the rules are bent to favor the powerful; if fair play means one set of rules for all, then it does not exist—except perhaps in the theater.

Anarchy attempts to teach these lessons—not by precept, but through experience. Anytime Gray removes himself from the performance, the performance is over for him. Some people left the holding room; a few would not answer questions. I felt that these learned as much as those who stayed to the bitter end, cooperating in every abuse.

A Brief Look at My Early Experiences in Participation

Moving South when I was drafted in 1958 was the most important single event in my artistic life. I was born in Newark, New Jersey, and lived there in the Jewish middle-class ghetto called Weequahic until I was fourteen. I was very close to my mother's father; we lived in his house, which was spacious. When he died a few weeks after my bar mitzvah, something definitely ended for me. Later my parents sold the big house, and we moved to South Orange where I went to high school. Then I went away to Cornell for college. None of these living places prepared me for rural Louisiana, and, later, New Orleans.

I lived in New Orleans from 1960 until 1967. There life goes on in the streets—especially the streets of the French Quarter where I lived. I took part in the street life from time to time, but I spent a great number of hours on my second-floor balcony watching the streets. Also I became part of the freedom movement and the antiwar movement, both of which took place in the streets in sit-ins, sit-downs, marches, demonstrations. I learned about dramas made by people in order to communicate a point of view, a feeling. I learned about exemplary actions.

My arrival in New Orleans coincided exactly with the school riots of September, 1960. I got involved, and committed to the ethos of participatory democracy. Participatory democracy is clumsy, inefficient, often stupid, and very frustrating to a person who sees the "right way" and wants to "get it done." But participatory democracy is a beautiful method of getting people to relate to each other on the basis of mutual desires, and of learning about power: how to get it, use it, abuse it. Over the years 1960–1963 I fused participatory democracy, New Orleans street life, and my own developing ideas about what theater could be. In 1964 I began an association with the Free Southern Theater that took me into rural Louisiana, Mississippi, and Alabama. I directed *Purlie Victorious* for the FST, I went to some black church services and funerals, I got deeply involved in FST affairs.[4]

The FST became, step by step, an all-black company, and my involvement declined. But what I had learned I kept. Along with Paul Epstein and Franklin Adams I founded the New Orleans Group in 1965. This work had roots in painting, music, Happenings. My contract with the Tulane Theater Department prevented me from directing plays there, so I worked outside the academic structure. While preparing the TDR special issue on Happenings I met John Cage in the summer of 1965. That four-hour meeting was very important because Cage focused for me much of what I was feeling but couldn't express. Cage spoke about his 1952 Black Mountain College concert.

> The structure we should think about is that of each person in the audience. In other words, his consciousness is structuring the experience differently from anybody else's in the audience. So the less we structure the theatrical occasion and the more it is unstructured daily life, the greater will be the stimulus to the structuring faculty of each person in the audience. If we have done nothing he then will have everything to do.[5]

[4] See *The Free Southern Theater by The Free Southern Theater*, ed. by Thomas C. Dent, Gilbert Moses, and Richard Schechner (1969).
[5] Kirby and Schechner (1965), 55.

After I left Cage, I chewed over what he had said. I sat on my balcony and looked at the busyness of the streets with new eyes. Was what was going on at the intersection of Toulouse and Dauphine theater? I could accept it theoretically, but it wasn't enough—after all, as a "theater person" I didn't want to "do nothing." Kaprow's applications and transformations of Cage's ideas were closer to my needs. Under the impact of these ideas, plus things that were happening in classes at Tulane, NOG prepared *4/66,* a Happening-like event shown twice in April, 1966. *4/66* was a mixed salad of games, chance music, performed bits (played by nonactors who were, nevertheless, rehearsed painstakingly), and "rituals"—all staged in an organic arrangement of a large open space. The events were loosely connected in a progression leading to the selection of a hero/victim spectator who was stripped and bathed in a sudsy bath the bottom of which was mud—so that the white, warm, sensuous softness gave way to the gritty, heavy, brown mudness. *4/66* had a scenario that was meticulously drawn by painter Adams on a seven-foot-long scroll. Each event had its allotted time and place; even "free play" had a beginning and end. *4/66* was latticelike in its structure—a form I like even now.

Mostly there was no free play. There were routines for the performers and options for the audience. For example, during one sequence, spectators could watch, play musical instruments, push a large pâpier-maché ball across the room, compete in one of several games. Busy and un-Cageian as *4/66* was, it taught me a lot. I worked collaboratively with two other directors. I worked in an open space that was frequently changing shapes to keep up with events. The piece had no plot, but instead was held together by a progression of actual events. Like a game, what went on in *4/66* had no one-to-one relation to life outside the room. No Hedda Gabler being impersonated. Whatever meaning the events had was metaphoric, structural, by analogy; or in the events themselves which were not secondary, not reflections, not mimetic, but actual.

4/66 was staged on the second floor of a large studio—a big open L-shaped space roughly forty feet square with a ceiling sloping from a crest of about twenty feet to about eight feet at the edges. The audience started out sitting on bridge chairs or standing. The chairs were arranged in many different configurations. I remember clearly being proud of setting up an S-shaped row of chairs, and a circle. But by the time *4/66* was a half hour old the chairs were swept aside or totally rearranged.

4/66 was the first time I had ever asked a spectator to do anything in the theater except buy a ticket, sit still, laugh in the middle, and applaud at the end.

NOG decided to try next an "environmental theater" production of a "regular play." I took the term "environmental theater" from Kaprow, who never used it as such but implied it in his writings. We selected Ionesco's *Victims of Duty* as the play—because no matter how "regular" it was, *Victims* was about identity-shifting, fantasies, transformations. It needed only a small cast and seemed to offer great possibilities for invention. We worked on *Victims* for most of an academic year and opened it for a run of twelve performances near the end of May, 1967. (*Victims* was my New Orleans farewell: The day after it closed I was on my way to New York for good. I and five other Tulane theater faculty members resigned after a long, grinding dispute with the administration.) Audience participation was only an incidental part of the NOG *Victims*. The most innovative thing was the use of whole spaces—the entire theater was converted into the Chouberts' living room.[6]

The action was staged so that some scenes overlapped others. Not every spectator could see or hear everything that was happening. In one scene Nicolas d'Eau picks at random a woman in the audience and begins making out with her. He stops as abruptly as he starts—when his cue is heard. There is no reason for him to begin, no reason for him to stop. During the run the actor playing Nicolas took ill, and I substituted for two performances. The participatory bit was fun, and I was surprised to discover how far I could get with a total stranger in a public situation. Maybe each of the women felt that giving in to me/Nicolas was what one should do to help the play along. During another scene the lights are very dim, and Choubert blindly gropes his way through the audience searching for his wife, Madeleine. He touches many spectators and asks them to help him find Madeleine.

Staging *Victims* helped clarify my ideas about environmental theater, but it did not much advance my thinking about audience participation. I felt that participating was a good thing—but I didn't know why, or even how. So it was blindly that I introduced participation into *Dionysus in 69* when I staged it the next year. People in the Group didn't talk much about participation while

[6] For descriptions of *Victims* see Schechner (1969a), "Six Axioms for Environmental Theatre."

Photograph 17. The New Orleans Group environment for *Victims of Duty*. Franklin Adams was the environmentalist who worked with me and Paul Epstein on this design. Rojo constructed the spiral of chairs seen at the right. The audience sat everywhere. The view is of the moment before the audience is admitted to the theater. The Chouberts and their friends are seated around the table eating supper—really. (*Matt Herron*)

planning *Dionysus*. Participation grew to a central place in the production in a very natural way: More and more scenes seemed to need the active collaboration of the audience. In April and May, 1968, about six weeks before the play opened, we began open rehearsals on Saturday afternoons. At one of these we worked on a scene we later called the Caress. The scene is an adaptation of a workshop exercise. Performers go in groups of three or four into the audience and select a spectator at random and begin caressing him/her. The caressing spreads out so that ultimately a number of spectators are caressing each other. The scene parallels Pentheus' visit to Cithaeron to spy on the women making love. Other participatory scenes—such as dancing with Dionysus, singing to taunt Pentheus, and marching out of the theater with the performers at the end of the play—were tested during open rehearsals.

I believe participation should generally be in the service of disillusion. It should not be to build an unreal world or a fantasy projection. I see a function of theater as helping people to *work through* their fantasies. I think that the only way to do this is to raise fantasies to full consciousness—to get them out front. D. W. Winnicott's ideas are very helpful:

> The important part of this concept [relating art, religion, and philosophy] is that whereas inner psychic reality has a kind of location in the mind or in the belly or in the head or somewhere within the bounds of the individual's personality, and whereas what is called external reality is located outside these bounds, playing and cultural experience can be given a location if one uses the concept of the potential space between the mother and the baby.[7]

This potential space is neither inside nor outside—it is an evanescent, temporary space *agreed on unconsciously* by all those participating in an event such as a performance. The first example of this kind of event in each individual life is the space between the mother and the baby: the very close relationship that is neither inside nor outside but, in Winnicott's suggestive term. "transitional."

> I am here staking a claim for an intermediate state between a baby's inability and his growing ability to recognize and accept reality. I am therefore studying the substance of *illusion,* that which is allowed to the infant, and which in adult life is inherent in art and religion.[8]

Now, if you'll permit me to explain, this illusion (= art) can be enlisted in the service of disillusion (= unmasking). It is a question of whether the illusion is allowed to stand unchallenged as the whole truth of a situation. Brecht understood this exactly. His *V-effekt* was not meant to eliminate "feeling" from theater, but to emphasize the performer's double role, his difficult function in the transitional space of the theater. "This principle—that the actor appears on the stage in a double role, as Laughton and as Galileo; that the showman Laughton does not disappear in the Galileo whom he is showing . . . comes to mean simply that the tangible, matter-of-fact process is no longer hidden behind a veil; that Laughton is actually there, standing on the

[7] Winnicott (1971), 53.
[8] Winnicott (1971), 3.

stage and showing us what he imagines Galileo to have been." [9]
The illusion is immediately disillusioned. To understand this
process one has to be clear about the difference between "acting
out" and "working through." Acting out is repeating obsessive
acts in different variations, not understanding why or even what
you are doing. Some kinds of acting methods encourage the
actor to be a professional actor-outer. Working through is
ripping an obsessive act up by its roots, examining it, talking
about it, demystifying it. One is not permitted the luxury of
"not knowing what I am doing."

Brecht's *V-effekt* is a way of transforming acting out into
working through. To work something through you need the help
of others. You need the chance to stop, reflect, repeat, see the
event with fresh insight—perhaps through the eyes of another—
test variations, follow associations. You need the chance to change
—to not do today what you did yesterday. The mechanics of
theater—practice, emphasis on collective working, use of the
director as an outside eye—are ways of working through if they
are consciously used as such. Otherwise there is no more powerful
mother of illusion than the theater.

Once a fantasy has been worked through, it is no longer
acted out. The theater that does the job of disillusioning its
workers and audiences is committing itself to perpetual change.

Winnicott locates the space where play takes place—a "transitional space"—as "the potential space between mother and baby."
That is, "the place where cultural experience is located." This
place is a mirror-place, a situation where all participants give
back what they get, not mechanically, but in subtle variations
and distortions. Winnicott's ideas have been confirmed by
researches such as those of Ray Birdwhistell who demonstrates
that "human beings are constantly engaged in adjustments to the
presence and activities of other human beings. As sensitive
organisms, they utilize their full sensory equipment in this
adjustment." [10] The performance space is living—messages are
being sent continuously through many channels. These channels
do not necessarily operate symphonically. What my face says is
not necessarily what my hands say, and what my body motion
says is not necessarily what I am saying with words; and so
on through the vast range and complexity of human communications.

[9] Brecht (1964 [1948]), 194. See all of Brecht's "A Short Organum for
the Theatre."
[10] Birdwhistell (1970), 48.

In orthodox theater the creative circle is closed. As many channels as possible except for words and the prearranged gestures of the performers are shut off, hidden, truncated, sidetracked, demolished. Although the audience is present at an orthodox theater performance, "presence" is a way of saying "as absent as can possibly be arranged." Feedback is kept to a minimum. As the narrator of *An Actor Prepares* confesses: "I felt that until we learned how to overcome the effect of that black hole we should never go forward in our work." The "black hole" is the audience as seen from the stage of a proscenium theater. Or not seen. It never occurred to Konstantin Stanislavski to transform the black hole into a living space. He devised instead his method of "circles of attention" so that actors could learn how to systematically exclude the audience and the fear that attends knowing that so many anonymous, hidden viewers are hungrily watching.

The orthodox theater is a closed system discouraging feedback. It is closed not only because the audience is excluded from it but also because whatever happens on stage is already known by the actors, and nothing is supposed to change this prearranged "score." If art and play are related to each other, then orthodox theater excludes one of art's most precious elements: getting back from the other player a version of oneself. Now, this is taken care of if one believes that only the other performers are players. And indeed the architecture and ideology of the orthodox theater are designed to propagate this myth. But obviously the spectators are there. Even in the most ingeniously designed proscenium theater there are hints once in a while that something lives in the black hole. And there is a need to relate to these people not on a mechanical basis, but on a person-to-person basis of exchanging sensory data and experience: playing. The organic mirror of biofeedback cannot take place if any of the partners is frozen, stereotyped, or systematically hidden. Play takes place when the players get back versions of themselves from each other player. This exchange is frozen out of the orthodox theater, with bad consequences. Actors are familiar with the effects of a long run—they lose touch with each other, with the performance. Then they resort to tricks to keep the performance fluid, alive. But the best remedy is to open the creative circle to include the audience who is always changing; to transform the closed system of orthodox theater into an open system of environmental theater.

For about a month starting in January, 1971, Friday's performance of *Commune* was followed by discussions. The performers, and Tom Driver, Dan Newman, John Lahr, Andre Gregory, and Dan Isaac, and audiences participated in these talks. The topic narrowed itself to participation and the relationship between audiences and performers. Newman and Driver returned each week to lead the discussions which, more often than not, moved from the theater to a restaurant in Chinatown and went on to early morning. The same questions returned, unanswered; questions that seem impossible because they make necessary the restructuring of the entire society.

1. How can we get *villagelike* responses from urban Western audiences?
2. How can there be solidarity in the theater when there is none in the streets?
3. Isn't the animosity between performers and spectators a function of the general reification of human relationships in modern, urban society?
4. How can the theater serve as a model, an example?
5. Ought spectators to play roles?
6. What is manipulation? Can it be avoided? Should it?
7. What is the relationship between *moving the body,* participation, and "moving an audience"?
8. Why does the performer fear the spectator? Why does the spectator fear the performer?
9. Why do we think stopping the performance in order to allow/incorporate participation is a disruption? Can it not be an integral part of the event?

From these discussions some practicals came: the My Lai second solution; the direct inclusion of the audience in the revival-meeting scene; the development of the march to Death Valley as a dance that needed the audience in order to complete the circle. Some participatory elements were dropped, others tried and dropped: picking someone from the audience and "killing" them during the murder scene; throwing and reading the I Ching with someone in the audience.

Commune became to a degree an ongoing experiment in audience-performer interaction. Newman devised a class at Livingston College in which the assignment was to come to the Garage on Friday afternoons to be the audience during workshop and then to stay on for Friday evening's performance and discussion. The Group made no formal plans for the class but let them watch rehearsals and talked with them about the various techniques of participation. It was the Livingstons who made me fully aware of the manipulation problem. They told the Group that the second My Lai solution troubled them because once they came into the center, they didn't know what was expected of them. The Livingstons suggested that if breaks in the performance took place, they should not be part of the thematics of the performance but real-time breaks; this way spectators would not spend time figuring out the style of their movements. We never did more than rehearse these breaks-and-now-you-move. The Livingstons told us that being told to move during the breaks was too much like grade school.

But the idea of breaks in the performance eventually became part of the performance. The Freedom Circle included an exchange of names between performers (who gave either their play or their actual names) and spectators. This sometimes branched out into the whole room until almost everyone was involved in an "active intermission." Often food was found and shared. When the performers wanted to start the play again, they said so. It resumed with Clementine's line, "I went to the ranch, it was a loving scene." The intermission was an analogy to Clementine's memories of her first day at the ranch. The second break ended the third solution to the My Lai scene.

All these experiments were Band-Aids on gaping gut wounds. The wounds were the real fears and hostility performers had for audiences and audiences had for performers. The performers felt that, given a choice, audiences wouldn't want the play to resume. The Livingstons, as audience, felt that the performers were manipulating them, showing them up. Driver felt that the fears and hostility were related to deep insecurities in each performer regarding his body, his abilities, and his worth. Driver didn't think that these were special problems of TPG but something generally true.

To search out these fears, to exorcise them if possible, I invited Driver to run a workshop on Friday, April 30. That afternoon there were six Livingstons at the Garage. Both the performers and the students felt the other side capable of manipulation and tyrannical control. One performer spoke of his fantasy that one night a spectator would come to the theater with a gun, and use it. Another feared the "deadness" of the audience: "No matter what I do, they will not respond."

Driver began the workshop by sending the Livingstons to high perches. He treated them brusquely. "Get out of the way and stay there." He then asked the performers to lie on the floor on their backs with their heads together, like a wheel with six heads at the hub. He asked them to speak simultaneously about their fears, feelings, and fantasies concerning the audience. A stream of words, laughs, some tears, and nonverbal sounds came from the performers. I couldn't pick up exactly what they were saying, but some barrier had begun to lower, and the effects of the "black hole" in the consciousness where Stanislavski locates the actor's perception of the audience began to come to light. Some fragments:

> I tripped last night, and I thought I broke their bones. I gave them elbows in the eye, knees in the groin. I loved it.
>
> First thing I do is take in the audience. Until I do that I think they are hostile. Then I look at them, and I see they want to be here.
>
> I was so disappointed in the motel after our performance in Baltimore. The show was so good—and then all these people showing their droopy personalities! Why didn't they take off their clothes and fuck with us?

After more than twenty minutes of fantasizing Driver invited the Livingstons down to where the performers were. After a while talk began between the two groups. Some fragments:

> PERF. I have fears the audience is on a power trip. I'm completely in your hands.
>
> LIV. I'm on the other side hoping you like me. But I'm afraid your ability as an actor will manipulate me.
>
> LIV. You know what's going to happen, and I don't. That makes me afraid—paranoia. I don't want to be made a fool of.
>
> PERF. The Hog Farm has each person be King for a Day. Everyone takes off from there, plays the roles the King wants them to play.
>
> LIV. I want you to act out your feelings—not alone—but while I act out mine.
>
> PERF. I want the audience to act out in reaction to me. I want them to be completely submissive to the situation.
>
> LIV. There are no feelings you have that I don't have.
>
> LIV. I want you to enjoy what you're doing.
>
> LIV. I feel like a piece of wood.
>
> PERF. Why do you expect to be more alive here than in another theater?
>
> LIV. The expectancy of it all makes me feel numb.
>
> PERF. I want to take you with me.

Talk came around to "support" and "sitting in judgment." Driver saw a clear relationship between the two. People who literally sit watching are always sitting in judgment; but to support someone means to move to them, to touch them. Certain body states do not permit sitting in judgment. I thought there was an equation that read: quantity and intensity of rehearsal = support wanted from the audience by the performers. Joan looked at the Livingstons and asked them to support her. Driver suggested that she do something that needed suport. She did the Clementine basket case, and three of the Livingstons lifted her off the floor and rocked her. She liked that, and they did, too. Driver said that when "the audience sits tight on its ass, its feelings are blocked, and there is nothing left for them to do but judge." Once the audience moves, its energies feed into the performance.

Jim Griffiths did a yoga tree, and no one helped him. He said he was glad no one helped him because helping him would have destroyed what he was trying to do. He asked how the audience could know when they were needed and when they weren't. Another performer spoke of how spectators felt betrayed by participation. "It's all right if you do something good one minute, but then you do something bad and no one knows how to signal the audience which is which." The Livingstons agreed.

I thought of *Commune* at Goucher College where students literally cradled the performer's heads in their hands during difficult moments and literally carried them through some scenes. When Lizzie was blindfolded looking for the El Dorado signs, spectators took her and led her from sign to sign. After the Father Jesus scene Clementine lies exhausted on the floor. Fearless asks that the audience touch her, and many of them do with extraordinary tenderness.

During most of the afternoon I was sitting on the overhang taking notes. A performer got very angry at me. "What really drops me out of performance is when Richard gets up"—the performer began dancing a parody of me—"and says, 'Go on, move, you can do it, we're pioneers, this is the new theater!' That really drops me out!" I was angry but stuffed it. A few minutes later Jim and Steve began talking to me about how I forced the issue of participation but didn't take any of the risks. Jim told me to come down from my perch and sit with the rest of them. Suddenly I got very angry at Steve (I don't remember what triggered it). He got angry back, and we shouted at each other.

At the height of our rage Driver told us to switch roles. I put on Steve's T-shirt, and he took my notebook. Trading roles was amazing. For a few minutes I saw from his eyes, from the point of view of a performer who felt pushed, abandoned, and betrayed. I realized that the director has no right to make the performer do anything, no less "be open" to an audience. The whole problem took on a new, big dimension. I think Steve saw me from a new vantage, too, and recognized that I didn't have things all planned out in advance—I wasn't a general running his war games.

Nothing was resolved by Driver's workshop which began at 1:30 and ended at 5:00. For a few hours defenses were lowered, and we glimpsed something of what theater might be like with lessened hostility between audience and performers. But I also knew how long and difficult the road would be. Once again I was face to face not with the problems of theater alone, but with the problems of society.

Participation is legitimate only if it influences the tone and possibly the outcome of the performance; only if it changes the rhythms of the performance. Without this potential for change participation is just one more ornamental, illusionistic device: a treachery perpetrated on the audience while disguised as being on behalf of the audience.

Those who oppose participation or are threatened by it feel manipulated. "I don't want to be *forced against my will!*" is the interesting redundancy I've heard often. Being forced works directly on the body; "against my will" has a more subversive tone to it. Even those who oppose participation acknowledge its seductive qualities. According to Walter Kerr, for example:

> The god Dionysus has appeared to his worshippers (all so like Euripides) to snap finger symbols and lift his skinny legs in rhythm beneath bushy hair, eyeglasses, and seedy mustache (not exactly like Euripides). The beat gets faster, some of the girls go topless, the garage spins, customers are cooed at: "Will you dance with me?"
>
> I do not dance divinely. When it comes to dancing I am an up-tight person. . . . Obviously I need a breakthrough. But I am something of a realist and I am not wholly convinced that darting into the melee is going to make a dancer of me.[11]

Kerr's description of the dancing in *Dionysus in 69* is of a seduction he has successfully not succumbed to. A forbidden

[11] Kerr's review of *Dionysus in 69*, New York Times, July 16, 1968, p. 1 ff.

sexual temptation is foresworn; the critic's honor is preserved. A critic's honor is proportionate to the distance he keeps between himself and the performance he is evaluating—is paid to evaluate.

What is it about participation that gives it such seductive and dangerous charm? Theater is traditionally the interplay of destinies, the actualizing of stories already completed by the author and rehearsed by the performers.[12] The performance is less dangerous than the processes that lead up to it. The logic of the play-in-performance is the "destiny" of tragedy and the "fortune" of comedy. Participation voids destiny and fortune, throwing drama back into its original theatrical uncertainty: re-introducing elements of the unrehearsed into the smooth ground of the performance. Things happen that are not "in the story" or "in the script." The audience is invited to put aside the role of witness and assume other, more active, roles. The characters of the story face the contingencies of the audience. The audience encounters the personalities of the performers unmediated by characterization. Thus on both sides the masks—the *personae*—are set aside. Participation doesn't eliminate the formalities of theater—it goes behind them to fetch private elements into the play. These two systems—the formal and the private—coexist, affecting each other. Illusions cherished, and needed, by orthodox theater-goers and practitioners are stripped away when the spectator and performer stand and say to each other, "I am, I do."

In 1969, toward the end of the *Dionysus* run, I formulated three rules of participation:

1. The audience is in a living space and a living situation. Things may happen to and with them as well as "in front" of them.
2. When a performer invites participation, he must be prepared to accept and deal with the spectator's reactions.
3. Participation should not be gratuitous.

In participatory situations game structure replaces aesthetics. Instead of events being worked out beforehand, there is a "game plan," a set of objectives, moves, and rules that are generally known or explained. The game plan is flexible, adapting to changing situations.

[12] Ponder the etymology of "rehearsal." It comes from the Old French *herce,* a harrow used to go over plowed land and break up clods, level the surface, and root up weeds: to smooth things out.

Several Greek tragedies, among them *Oedipus Tyrannus,* end with the banal choric injunction, "Count no man happy until the day of his death." Only when a life is over can others determine how it was lived: Destiny is applicable only to completed projects. Look at Oedipus, who thought himself the happiest of men. Oedipus uncovers his past, and in so doing, his present is changed. None of the events are secret; only the connections linking them are new. Jocasta is still Jocasta-wife, but she is now also Jocasta-mother. The man Oedipus murdered at the cross-roads is still a stubborn fellow, but he is now Laius-father. Antigone, Ismene, Polyneikes, Eteokles, are still Oedipus' children, but now they are also half-sisters and half-brothers. The curse on Oedipus is not simply that of murder and incest but of ignorance; and knowledge does not liberate him. His blindness is the ultimate ecstasy: a proper finish to a man doomed by self-knowledge. So, too, Lear's wheel of fire, Hamlet's flights of angels, and even Didi's:

> Was I sleeping, while the others suffered? Am I sleeping now? [. . .] Astride of a grave and a difficult birth. Down in the hole, lingeringly, the grave-digger puts on the forceps. We have time to grow old. The air is full of our cries. (*He listens.*) But habit is a great deadener. (*He looks again at Estragon.*) At me too someone is looking, of me too someone is saying, He is sleeping, he knows nothing, let him sleep on.

The heroes of drama are always gaining self-consciousness at the expense of everything else. Comic heroes celebrate a brief triumph over death. Participation injects these ancient themes directly into the structure of the performance. *The contingencies of life that are the traditional subjects of drama suddenly become its object.* Will the play go on? How? Will it complete itself? How? What is my place in it?

When there is participation, everyone in the theater tests destiny and gambles with fortune.

What is at stake is not the story being told but the telling of the story. In our mechanized theater this fundamental question has been pushed out of consciousness. Participation brings it back in. The play can stop, go on, go on in a new way. The performance is penetrated so that everyone can see it as a collaboration between performers and spectators, not a mechanical inevitability. In our days, when universal religious belief is gone and community solidarity rare, the wholeness of an Athenian or medieval audience is unattainable. A personal stake in one night's performance is not to be snickered at. Many attend "new theater" in the hope of taking part in a temporary community, in being invited to use responsivity instead of having to suppress it. To inject destiny, no matter how apparently trivial, back into theater restores danger, excitement, and vitality.

Sometimes participation doesn't need gross physical movement or role-playing. The Organism in *Commune* is a group of performers moving across the floor, up the Wave, and past a line on its crest marked INSIDE. They are enacting the approach of the Manson family to the Tate house. As they move, Spalding speaks from a pinnacle:

> Did you ever see a coyote in the desert, tuned in, watching, completely aware? Christ on the Cross, the coyote in the desert, it's the same thing. The coyote's beautiful. He walks through the desert delicately. He smells every smell, he hears every sound, he sees everything. You see, he's always in a state of total paranoia, and total paranoia is total awareness.

As Spalding speaks of Christ, Bruce extends his body from the tub in a crucifixion pose: The Jesus People will take as one of their victims the image of Him they adore. But Bruce is also a jet-setter, a playboy lounging in his Hollywood bathtub-as-large-as-a-pool. While moving up the Wave, the Organism responds to every sound in the room. The Organism is the embodiment of "total paranoia = total awareness." Each sound elicits a move from the Organism. Loud sounds bring it to a frozen halt; a barrage of sounds and the Organism collapses in a heap. Only in silence will the Organism rise again and go on its way. Audiences learn that the Organism is negatively responsive to sound. Most people are quiet. But some spectators play with the Organism, testing the performers or intentionally stopping the play. People tap the floor, clap, cough, make rhythmic noises, whistle. The Organism collapses into its huddle. Some spectators urgently "shhhhh!" the others, who as often as not respond with more noise. Several waves of interaction ensue before the theater is finally quiet enough for the Organism to get over the line marked INSIDE. This silence is not the "natural" silence of an attentive audience; it is the earned, conscious silence of participation.

Photographs 18 and 19.
The Organism of *Commune*
begins to move up the Wave.
At its crest they see a vic-
tim: Bruce, the Playboy–
Christ lounging in his
Hollywood–baptismal pool.
(*Frederick Eberstadt*)

When *Commune* was performed in France during autumn, 1972, the play was restructured so that the murders occurred at the beginning; and then they are repeated again at the end. When the Organism began up the Wave the second time, at the end of the play, the audience knew what was going to happen. Twice the spectators made such insistent noise with such clarity of purpose, that the play was stopped, the murders not re-enacted. In this way the audience chose to change how *Commune* ended.

Objections and obstacles to audience participation can be summarized:

1. The rhythm of the performnce is thrown off, maybe destroyed.
2. All participation is manipulative because the performers know things the audience does not.
3. A free-for-all such as what happened frequently at *Paradise Now* is neither art nor a party but a mess; and not in any way liberating.
4. Once the question "Who is boss?" is raised between performers and audience, nothing but hostility follows.
5. The audience comes to see a play and has the right to see a play. There can be no mixture of dramatic and participatory structures without confusion.
6. Neither the actor nor the spectator is trained to deal with participation.

Probably more objections could be added. They indicate that the root problem is with an aesthetics and the social system that are not built to accommodate participatory arts (or participatory politics, economics, education, or religion). To encourage participation is to demand changes in the social order—radical changes. From a strictly theatrical point of view these changes include:

1. Accepting random as well as prepared rhythms as artistically valid.
2. Finding times in the performance when the performers do not know any more than the audience. These are not improvised moments—where performers work freely from a set of objectives or rules—but truly open moments when all the people in the room acting either individually, in small groups, or in concert move the action forward. This "action"

is not necessarily known beforehand and may have nothing to do with the dramatic action of the play. This is the situation that developed on February 28.

3. Adaptation of a latticelike structure in which highly organized actions exist side by side with more open structures.

4. No forcing either the performers or the spectators. Some simple guides: Yield space and time; do not compete; if the play stops, let it stop, find out why, then decide whether it ought to resume, and how.

5. Do not mix dramatic and participatory structures but let them coexist in space and time.

6. Begin training performers to their additional jobs as "guide" and "host," and the spectators to their newly opened possibilities as people who can move, speak, act in the theater.

To accept these changes is to break the monopoly performers and directors hold over the means of production, particularly a monopoly on knowing what is going to happen next. Participation means openly acknowledging that the audience is the water in which the performers swim. Most of the time the audience is taken for granted. But when a spectator, or a group of spectators, makes a move, the performers ought to fall back, give over the space to the spectators: Let the majority rule. After all, the performance arises from the world of the spectators, it continues because of agreements made between spectators and performers, and when the play is over, the performance subsides back into the world of the spectators. A performance is a peak experience, not a separate experience.

Orthodox theater is mimetic: a reflection of prior experiences and an attempt to recreate them or give the illusion of recreating them. Psychodrama is entirely actual: the creation of circumstances in which the participants relive in the present troubling moments from their past. Environmental theater is neither mimetic nor psychodramatic. *The fundamental logic of environmental theater is not the logic of the story but the logic of story-telling.* Two groups of people agree to meet at a certain time and place. One group comes to witness a story, the other to tell a story. The story is of importance to both groups. For most of the performance time the agenda of story-telling is adhered to. But at any time the story can be set aside or advanced (told) in a different way. For most of the time the group witnessing the story plays the bass line of the performance while the story-telling group plays the melody line. But these roles may be shared or reversed. The sharing and reversing is possible because of an assumption everyone makes: *Anything that happens in the theater during the performance time is part of the performance.* At Skidmore College in 1971, during a performance of *Commune,* some people burst into the room demanding that they be given the chance to sell their radical newspaper. The demand was agreed to—after an argument. The apparent interruption sheds light on what *Commune* is about. But even if the interruption has no identifiable link to the themes of the play, the interruption itself is wholesome: It shatters the authoritarian fix of orthodox theater.

To facilitate these changes it is necessary for the performer to be "himself" and not his "character" when he deals with a participating spectator. This opens up a wide range of possibilities. The performer may be angry, distressed, pleased by the interruption. The performer is a host, not a guardian; he is not responsible for the play's going on: That is a shared responsibility. This kind of participation through inclusion and giving over to circumstances is different from, but not incompatible with, the kind of participation known from Grotowski's early works, or from plays like *Dionysus in 69.*

Peter Schumann's Bread and Puppet Theater specializes in another kind of participation, closely related to what Kaprow has done. The B&P arrives at a place, and a general invitation is issued for people to help build the puppets and perform. Around a core of professionals Schumann arranges each performance with the assistance of many volunteers. These volunteers are, in a true sense, spectators who agree to participate in the show—they are spectators recruited into the performance. Instead of entering the performance while it is going on, they enter during a preparation phase. Usually these volunteers do not prolong their work with the B&P, they are not would-be professionals. Nor is the use of people in this way a version of amateur dramatics that is more accurately described as a hobby using the same people over and over again, many of whom harbor ambitions to become professionals. Schumann's practice is more like medieval theatrical celebrations. The skills of people in the community are called on to mount a spectacle for the benefit of the entire community. Again like medieval pageants and plays, Schumann's work is often the celebration of a specific holiday, Christmas or Easter, or the response to a particular occasion: a peace march, protest, demonstration, or vigil.

In September, 1970, at Goddard College I saw an early version of the B&P's *Domestic Resurrection*. Many things about this outdoor spectacle were pleasing: the use of the quarter-mile-square meadow where the big B&P tent was raised; the slowness of the development of the action so that I could move around the big puppets, examine them from different angles, discover how they work. (Much recent experimenting by Robert Wilson and Richard Foreman has picked up on Schumann's work, attenuating the action in order to slow down time. The idea goes back at least to Andy Warhol's long, static movies; and to Cage's music. It is expressed in another field in Birdwhistell's analysis of movement made in frame by frame studies of films and in Alan Lomax's worldwide, cross-cultural study of movement. Film technology—the ability to speed up or slow down human movement, to come close to isolating phonemes and morphemes of gesture—has penetrated to the heart of theater. Speeding up and slowing down movement is characteristic of dreams, psychedelic experience, and dissociated states of consciousness. Thus the entire question of "pacing" now touches on mythological thought, psychosis, dreams, psychedelics, and various body poetries.)

For me the most effective scene of *Domestic Resurrection* was when B&P performers erected a twenty-five foot wooden mast, letting billow from it a vast blue and white sail. Then they unwound many yards of blue and white cloth, about three feet wide. With this band about fifteen of them formed the outline of a boat. The sail caught the brisk Vermont wind, and this veritable ark sailed across the meadow as the crowd of spectators parted like the waters to let it pass. The players chanted, "The storm is here! The storm is here!" They invited the audience to come aboard. Soon most of the several hundred spectators ducked under the bands of cloth and sailed along within the ark.

I admire the simplicity, strength, meaningfulness, and non-manipulative qualities of the scene. Each spectator is given a choice between staying outside or moving inside, between watching or doing, between the society that is going down or those who save themselves in order to start a new kind of world. No one is asked to "act" or do anything more extraordinary than play a little make-believe. And even if the point escapes you, it is fun to play along. That, finally, is the point.

I wonder if Schumann is aware of the parallel between the ark of *Domestic Resurrection* and a Tibetan festival play: "A boat is a wide band of brilliantly coloured cloth around a rectangular framework held up at the front and rear by oarsmen whose legs propel the boat in spurts while they paddle with long poles. The passengers walk in between the oarsmen." [13]

[13] Duncan (1955), quoted in Southern (1961), 93–94.

I am interested in a theatre where everything
is experienced for the first time, and I have
stripped away all ties with conventional dance
form. . . . I have come back to the ritualistic
beginnings of art as a sharpened expression
of life, extending every kind of perception.
I want to participate in events of extreme
authenticity, to involve people with their
environment so that life is lived as a whole.
Ann Halprin

People want to know: Why do you worry about
taking your clothes off when we have to
wipe out imperialism?
Julian Beck

3 Nakedness

Nakedness = turning the inside out, or projecting onto the
surfaces of the body events of the depths. Physiologically "interior
events" of muscular, visceral, and mental significance are always
altering the body's topography—from the slope of the shoulders
to the rhythms of breath to the look in the eyes to the movement
of the fingers or the curl of the lips: the body's surfaces are
always changing in relation to interior body events. And vice
versa, for the difference between *surface* and *depth* is not so
easy to discern. From a simplistic point of view we know the
inside from the outside. But from a dynamic point of view
the two are interchangeable: The surfaces are the outermost
aspects of the depths, and the depths are the hidden aspects
of the surfaces. It is not as if two different realms were in
communication but as if one realm were continually rearranging
itself. The body lives in the midst of fluidity, movement, changes:
surface to depth to skin to viscera to seen to hidden. . . .

Nakedness reverberates in apparently contradictory directions.
A naked baby, a naked corpse, a naked person asleep. A naked
prisoner running a gauntlet of truncheon-wielding concentration-
camp guards. Dreams of being naked alone among a crowd of

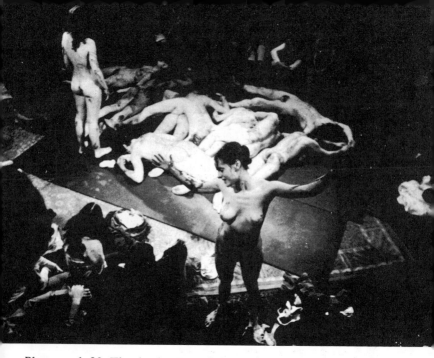

Photograph 20. The death scene of *Dionysus in 69*. Of the nine bodies on the floor, three are of spectators who voluntarily joined in the Death Ritual. (*Frederick Eberstadt*)

the dressed. Naked and seductive; hundreds of naked people sunning on a Vancouver beach; films of naked lovers; pornography. Medical films. From innocence and helplessness to vulnerability and the inability to defend oneself to confusing images combining vulnerability and sadomasochism. From eroticism to clinical detachment. Also nakedness implies a public event: To be naked with no one watching is to adumbrate a process that needs another's acknowledgment. Nakedness is a social condition.

If nakedness indicates vulnerability, it also can indicate imperviousness:

The Gaulish Gaesatae or "spearmen" went to war entirely naked, carrying only a spear. . . . This was not from sheer bravado, as the Romans thought, but was rather an invocation for magic protection, a practice that in fact had also been widespread in Greece and Italy in earlier times. In the Great Plains, Blackfoot warriors commonly rode into battle entirely nude, except perhaps for warpaint. Nakedness to frighten off demons is of course very common in various contexts in folk Europe.[1]

Hindu sadhus sometimes walk the roads of India naked. This inspires awe and terror, not embarrassment, among the people. Some paranoiacs use "nakedness as a means of inspiring terror." [2] When performers in *Dionysus in 69* rushed naked into the crowd of spectators, individuals often fled in sheer fright. The idea of a theater full of voyeurs is a too-easy cliché.

In parts of the world children run naked until puberty. Total nakedness by adults in everyday situations (except bathing) is rare. However, in our society "nudism" is everywhere. Nakedness is a time-honored way of showing the body's grace and beauty, as in the ancient Olympic Games or in the artistic tradition of "the nude." [3] But alongside this tame aesthetic tradition is another of fertility worship, orgies, cults of the vulva and phallus, and pornography.[4] From prehistoric times nakedness has been associated with generativity; the sexual organs have been represented triumphantly in exaggerated displays of sexual excitement.

Early cave art is especially interesting. Many of the greatest masterpieces are literally inaccessible, hidden in galleries hundreds of feet underground approachable only along the most difficult routes. It is as if these early men hid generative mysteries among the bowels of the earth, literally *mother earth,* so that going to participate in the dances was in itself an entry into that primeval female earth from whose deeps all life comes.

Nevertheless, we are not to suppose that these straightforward representations of animal and human sexuality are deep in the caves for any reason of prurience or cultural repression. On the contrary, every indication is that sexuality was

[1] La Barre (1972), 310.

[2] Ferenczi (1926), 329–332.

[3] See Kenneth Clark's study of *The Nude* (1953).

[4] A growing literature of and on pornography is available. Interestingly, many if not most great artists did work considered "pornographic" and until recently suppressed.

approached reverently as the central mystery of life; and any salacity is contributed by latter-day viewers, influenced by a religion long in rivalry and conflict with the old religion. The scenes are deep in the caves only to symbolize mysteries deep in the body of the earth, and the only complexity comes from the symbolic implication of coitus with the hunt and from the assimilation of human and animal sexuality.[5]

In truth, Paleolithic ritual-breeding caves are the first theaters. Still in the hardened clay of the cave floor we can see the footprints of the dancers; and in the drawings we can glimpse their spectacular costumes: The "Dancing Sorcerer" or "Reindeer Shaman" of Trois Frères "wears the antlers of a stag, an owl mask, wolf ears, bear paws and a horse-tail, but is otherwise a nude human male dancing, perhaps wearing streaks of body paint." [6]

The first performances concerned fertility-hunting magic. Early man hunted animals and knew, more strongly than we, he had to assure the replenishment of hunted species. His rituals were intended to forge links between the killed prey and replacements through birth. And man conceived of himself as continuous with the animal world. The masks and costumes—the whole complex called "totemism"—foster an identity of the human and the animal realms. At the very dawn of human culture the association between conflict-death-sexuality-birth was made absolutely clear. "For magic art in caves is clearly a supernatural, quasi-sexual, creative act of the shaman-artist to promote the increase of animals in the womb of the earth." [7] What we have left are the drawings, sculptings, and footprints: Shadows of ceremonies, dramas, dances, and song. Contemporary parallels exist—for example in the Kalahari desert where hunters perform magical acts after killing a prey because the death of "so large a spirit" must be immediately repaired. These ceremonies involve marking, painting, and scarifying the naked human body.

It is impossible to reduce to a single organizing factor the multitude of associations the naked human body stirs. The account of my work and thought in this vast, troubling area is indication mostly that much more work needs to be done.

I have explored nakedness in training and performance from the limited perspective of the middle phase of the cycle:

[5] La Barre (1972), 398.
[6] La Barre (1972), 410.
[7] La Barre (1972), 397.

undressing-naked-dressing. No TPG exercise or theater piece has ever presented all the performers naked throughout. So nakedness in the TPG context means undressing, doing something, and dressing. I admit a fascination for the exchange of clothes, for disrobing and rerobing again as another. When a person puts on someone else's clothes, a change occurs. I want to explore the ways people display themselves. The cycle undressing-naked-dressing has reverberations that range from peeling the psychic onion—unmasking, showing, revealing, confessing; getting down to the skinny, the nitty-gritty, the core—to striptease. Of this last Eric Bentley has noted that in the American theater of the sixties the progression has been "from strip-tease to cock-tease . . . the main reason for American theatregoing in the late sixties has been to see the penis." [8] Although performing is not exhibitionism *per se,* there is in theater a strong will to display and to see: A show is, among everything else, a showing of the body.

Earlier I said that the environment is in some ways an extension of the body. It is just as true that the body is experienced as an introjection of the surrounding geography. The human being doesn't end at the skin; and the outer world is not fenced out by the skin. Fields of energy radiate from the person and penetrate into the person. Instead of imagining the human being as a silhouette, one ought to visualize a dense convergence of energy fields, a breathing pulsar. I am not talking mysticism. Each person is in continuous commerce with the outer world. Each person is incandescent, and a vessel through which outside forces focus and flow. When we speak of a performer with *presence,* we mean someone with a highly developed sense of radiance and convergence. To a degree yet little known, clothes govern the influx and outgo of energy to and from the body. Naked, we each tumble from the womb, but life is lived in costume amid a myriad of costume changes, and the dead are especially sumptuously dressed.

Nakedness itself is a costume. Standing naked in front of others brings people face to face with their own body fantasies. Some of these are positive, but many are not. "I know you don't like me because . . . " is the unspoken refrain. It can be translated into, "I don't like myself because . . . " This in turn can be translated into, "I don't like what's going on around-and-in me because . . ." Even under the most encouraging auspices I have seen people dissolve in terror, disappointment, rage, and shame

[8] Bentley (1972), 375.

while experiencing their bodies naked in a room with other naked people. Women, especially, are prone to defenseless humiliation, the feeling of being transformed into a worthless object. This feeling mobilizes whatever character armor a person can muster. Hostile stares, looking away, blank looks. "Please don't look at me, as I am not looking at you." Or bold stares. "You see, I can do it. Can't you?" In circumstances where many people are naked—as on a beach—or among people who know each other very well the situation relaxes somewhat. But I have never experienced total easiness among naked people. One begins naked exercises in the context of a raw self-consciousness.

Before taking up any of the theoretical questions I want to cite some exercises. "Display" can be done naked or dressed. It deals with judgments.

> Sit in a circle. Someone says to another, "I want to see you." The other may decline, or he may come to the center of the circle. Once in the center he moves so that everyone may see him; he responds to requests to show this or that part of the body, assume different poses, and so on. When the person who made the initial request is satisfied, he says so, and the person in the center returns to the periphery. The exercise continues until there are no more requests or acceptances.

When this exercise is done naked, it is cruelly direct. But when it is done with dressing and undressing, with a person wearing the clothes of one or more other people, it can become farcical. "Display" is close to Robert Ashley's *Orange Dessert,* which I saw in New Orleans in 1966. In *Orange Dessert* a woman in an orange dress is given directions by an unseen man speaking over a speaker system. The directions are very simple body moves. "Walk across the stage. Sit. Cross your left leg over your right. Uncross. Lean back. Stand up. Turn around. Walk toward the audience. Walk away from the audience." And so on. After about ten minutes the woman leaves the stage, and a movie is shown in which an orange is slowly peeled and cut into sections. It is a very sensuous movie. Ashley's piece is related to other works of New Dance where the body is treated simply and objectively.[9] Such an objective treatment of the body does not desexualize it. The New Dance attempts to "remove the 'danceness' from dance.

[9] See the New Dance feature in TDR, Vol. 16, No. 3 (September, 1972), 115–150.

. . . It emphasizes the structure and organization of movement rather than its special style, difficulty of accomplishment, emotional expressiveness, and so forth." [10]

Of exercises like "Display" Joan MacIntosh comments:

> To be able to stand still, naked, and experience your feelings about your body is a fantastic way to learn to give up the mask. When you are no longer "what you would like to be" but unmistakably "who you are." Very often until a performer can really allow herself to let go, surrender, and experience her physical nakedness vis-à-vis others—that is, her shame, or whatever positive and negative things she feels—she can *never* understand psychic nakedness, but will put some sort of psychic clothing between herself and the expression of her feelings.

In "Display" it is not necessary to ask those around the circle what they feel about the person on display; or to ask the person displayed how he feels. These are obvious and important questions—but best unanswered in words publicly. "Display" is sometimes shameful and sometimes playful. Forcing the expression of feelings can make people cut off at an irreclaimable level. Body fantasies are deep, and they develop early. Often they are violent, destructive. They connect to hunting magic, wounding, and oedipal fantasies. The important thing for a director to do is to help people acknowledge that they have fantasies concerning their bodies; that people do think of their own bodies and the bodies of others as objects. There is no "cure" for such attitudes; they are part of the human condition. Pushing too hard to make people articulate what they are feeling—as some encounter groups do—scares people, freezes fantasies that might otherwise yield to more flexible attitudes. A director who pushes is probably projecting his own fantasies onto others.

"Display" is an exercise that acknowledges a curiosity and objectivity that people feel in relation to their own and others' bodies. The same end can be served simply by encouraging performers to do their basic psychophysical association exercises naked. These exercises will be described in Chapter 4. They are the basic preparation for all TPG work. Therefore to do this daily work naked means that the performers will begin to get accustomed to their own and the others' bodies. However, in my experience, things don't work out so simply. I never require

[10] M. Kirby (1972), 115.

nakedness. I suggest it. Members of the Group have been working together from two to five years. Several people routinely do the psychophysical work naked. Others rarely do. Everyone on many occasions has. There are two cycles regulating nakedness in the basic exercises. The first is seasonal, but is not related to room temperature which may be warmer in winter than summer. People are most prone to do their work naked in the early spring and then again in the early summer. They are least likely to work naked in February and March. There is a much greater likelihood of naked work in a sunlit room than in artificial light. The second cycle is related to our overall work. After weeks in which there has not been a crisis or enthusiasm, a film builds up between people. There is little likelihood of working naked. But after an explosive release—either through crisis or discovery in the work (and these often go together)—the amount of naked work increases.

"Display" tests the limits of taste, the degree to which one person allows himself to be the object of another's looking. "Animal" is an exercise that helps a performer experience his own body, and the bodies of others, on a direct, physical plane.

> The performer walks on his hands and feet (not hands and knees). The head is held high, the tail up or down. As the performer moves, he gets into different rhythms, and makes sounds accordingly. He walks, canters, lopes, gallops, slinks, stealths, struts, prances, skitters. When he meets another, he sniffs, nuzzles, joins with, combats, plays, runs, follows, displays, races.

The genuine animality of "Animal" comes out when it is done naked. Because of the relatively long legs of the human species, the sexual organs are elevated and displayed. If the performer keeps his head high and lets his body find its own rhythms of moving, breathing, and sounding, he will begin experiencing the world from all fours: a horizontal rather than a vertical world. Even a small room appears large and especially high. The performer discovers how important his nuzzle is, how he leads with his face not his hands, how keen his sense of smell, how limited his sight. With his snout close to the ground he comes face-to-body with his colleagues. The elevation of their genitals is an invitation to look and sniff. Some people are embarrassed. Men are more apt to do "Animal" naked than women.

The aim of these exercises is not to make people more comfortable or easier in their nakedness. The goal is to raise consciousness regarding the body.

While in residence at Goddard College in September, 1970, I led a student workshop. I explained, as I usually do, that the work is done best in a minimum of clothes, and I recommended leotards for the women and shorts for the men. A student asked me if he could work naked. I said yes, and about half the workshop of twenty people stripped. Frankly, I was shocked. Like so much else at Goddard, it struck me as natural and a put-on at the same time. Three workshops later I decided to lead an exercise that would bring out into the open whatever latent sexuality there was in the casual nakedness of the Goddard students. This exercise I call "Choices 2" because it is a variation of an exercise I devised in 1969 with TPG and the Firehouse Theater in Minneapolis.

> After finishing the association exercises everyone lies on the floor. The director marks out the following areas in the room:
>
> 1. A corner where people must be dressed and from which they can watch what's happening.
>
> 2. A corner where people must be naked and can interact in any positive way they like.
>
> 3. A corner where people may be dressed or naked and can interact only verbally.
>
> 4. A corner where people may be dressed or naked and can interact only through ritual combats.
>
> 5. A center area where people must pass on their way to or from any of the corners.
>
> Very dim illumination.

I participated in the exercise. For this reason I decided that the exercise would be over when the people from the next section of the workshop arrived and tried to enter the locked door. That gave us about ninety minutes.

Obviously I couldn't see all that happened. I divided my time between the observation corner and the naked, positive-interaction corner. As far as I could tell most people did not go to all four corners. Some stayed in the verbal corner, and although people could be naked there, no one was. Some remained in the ritual-combat corner fighting battle after battle. The largest number stayed in the observation corner. It was hard to see because of the dim lighting. As time went on, more people ventured out. In the naked, positive-interaction corner we fondled and kissed.

However, it was not an orgy. There were always at least three people there, and sometimes four or five, and everyone was timid; mostly we stroked each other's thighs, backs, stomachs, and faces. I did not get an erection. I felt funny: like an adolescent at the stage of games like Spin the Bottle or Pony Express. Also I felt afraid. It was a fear I located from (I think) early adolescence—like being afraid my mother or my brothers would discover me masturbating.

At the next workshop we discussed the exercise. People felt guilty about it. "There was something coercive, something *dirty,* about it," a woman said. "If you want to make it with someone, you should just say so and do it. You don't need an exercise to justify what you want to do!" A man answered her. "This wasn't just 'making it' with someone. No one made it with anyone. This was an exercise—something done in a formal way, like a game, with a lot of people around, during a workshop. And we're talking about it afterward. That makes all the difference." Someone added: "Yeah, that takes all the fun away!" There the discussion stopped, as if the fun could be saved if everyone shut up.

I wondered whether it was wrong to "use" an exercise to (as someone said) "get your rocks off."

The next week I devised another exercise for the Goddard students. I call it "groupings."

> People are dressed or naked. The room is well lit. A person arranges the other people in any way he wishes. This arrangement may be static—a *tableau vivant*—or it may be an event, something dynamic. Sounds, but no words.

"Groupings" took on many shapes, including a procession in which a man from the Group was carried away by six women, sexually fondled, and then borne in a slow procession that was illuminated with candlelight and accompanied by a dirgelike chant. Other "Groupings" were extremely erotic, including *tableaus* of fondling, embracing, and simulated cunnilingus and fellatio. "Groupings" was less playful than "Choices 2," and at least one woman was very disturbed by the exercise, breaking down into tears. If "Groupings" was not exactly an exercise in the primal scene,[11] it often approached it. It was also very much like the exercise "Witness" (see Chapter 4).

[11] Freud's term for children observing or fantasizing their parents copulating.

Exercises like those at Goddard point to a special kind of excitation associated with adolescence. Adolescent fantasies of sexuality, grandiosity, obscenity, farce, profanity, violent death, morbidity, competition against high odds, heroism, and romanticism are the very essence of "the dramatic." It is in adolescent fantasies, and the rites surrounding and incarnating these fantasies, that I think we can find the sources of drama both ontogenetically and historically. The prototypes of drama are extremely ancient hunting, fertility, and initiation rites; all closely associated with adolescence.

> Notable about shamanistic power, and "supernatural" power in general, is the association with adolescence, though far predominantly that of males, and among hunting peoples the first acquisition as the boy becomes a man. Psychologically, supernatural power is an answer to the *need* of the boy approaching manhood. It is a fusion of male aggression and sexuality—a north African drawing leaves no doubt of this, since a line connects the hunter's weapon with his wife's pubic region; a wife's behavior at home affects the hunter's luck in a magic way; and the Indian hunter aims an arrow at a legendary deer only to find her turning into a beautiful woman. Sexual aggression and hunting, body image and weapon, are very early fused in the human-animal coition and hunt scenes of the ancient caves.[12]

Theater is a peculiar art form because of its universal and exclusive preoccupation with themes of sex and violence. There are no plays in any culture that are wholly pastoral, peaceful, lyrical, tranquil; none lacking direct conflict and overt sexuality. Even in cultures such as the Japanese, where the style of production is refined, the themes of the plays are violent and passionate. Nowhere do we find theatrical equivalents to landscape or portrait painting, lyric poetry, pastoral or soothing music. Plays that include tranquil scenes also include violence, conflict, and sexuality. Always and everywhere theater tends toward the explosive, the bloody, the sexy. Yet despite the apparently partial nature of theater, people do not consider it incomplete; there are no cries raised in behalf of drama without conflict. Theater is a way of perceiving life from the point of view of conflict.

Also, and uniquely, the grossest farces are mixed with or closely associated with serious subjects, even high tragedy. This mixed style is not only characteristic of the age of Shakespeare. It is

[12] La Barre (1972), 169–170.

true also of medieval theater, the theater of the absurd, and the ritual theaters of many peoples. The association of sacred subjects with farce and obscenity is common in Africa, Oceania, New Guinea, and Australia. It is common, too, among Siberian and American shamans who are noted not only for their great curative powers and contacts with the spirit world but also for their tricks. The trickster is one of the major heroes of the world. Weston La Barre sees in this ancient "clown, culture hero, and demi-god" intimations of proto-drama:

> We must not forget the element of *entertainment* in Old World shamanism: were tales of the erotic escapades of eagle-Zeus once told in the same tone of voice as those of Sibero-American Raven? And did not shamanistic rivalry develop into both the Dionysian bard-contests of Greek drama in the Old World and into *midewewin* medicine-shows in the New? As for that, have modern medicine-men entirely lost the old shamanic self-dramatization? [13]

Among the Greeks it was established practice to show one brutal, farcical, obscene satyr-play along with a group of three tragedies during each day of the drama festivals. Of the satyr-play relatively little is known, but what information we have supports my thesis:

> In point of origins the satyr-play, like both comedy and tragedy, was closely bound up with Dionysiac fertility ritual. Even in the fifth century satyr-drama in its frequent obscenity, its conventional use of Silenus as "nurse" and companion of Dionysus, and its chorus of satyrs with their *phalloi* preserves more vividly than tragedy the memory of its origins. [14]

Farce, fertility, aggression, conflict, tragedy, adolescence: these are many faces of identical or intimately associated phenomena.

Furthermore, dramas are composed and performed mostly by men. This is not a Western bias but, if anything, more generally true of non-Western theater. Women's ceremonies, though often ribald, joyous, enthusiastic, lack the intensity, brutality, aggression, and storylike structure of men's ceremonies. In a word, women's ceremonies are less dramatic. With few exceptions the heroes of drama are young men, or old men who dream and scheme

[13] La Barre (1972), 196–197. See also Radin (1956).
[14] Arrowsmith (1956), 3.

of becoming young again either directly through miraculous rejuvenation or by using that great aphrodisiac, wealth. When confronted by women like Clytemnestra or Hedda Gabler, an audience reacts by classifying these women as "masculine." Another strong theme in drama is the struggle among men for the possession of women. Women are treated as chattel, albeit sometimes beautiful and eloquent chattel.

In our days we think of adolescence as an extension of childhood. Our life-span approaches seventy-five years, and a person of twenty is still very young. But in almost every other period of human history a boy became a man in every sense by the time he was thirteen to fifteen years of age. But, of course, there was no fundamental biological difference between these boy/men and adolescents of our own day; except that adolescents of an earlier age actually exercised authority and put their stamp strongly on cultures. Pentheus is in his early teens, Hamlet still a youth; when Oedipus confronted his father, Laius, and killed him, he could not have been more than twenty; Juliet is barely thirteen and Romeo not much older. Drama has its old men —Lear, Solness, and Oedipus at Colonus—but these ancient heroes yearn for the juices of youth, and fall in foolish attempts to rejuvenate themselves. And when we think of Faust or Don Juan, we speak of men who through magic or relentless striving make themselves young again.

The prototypes of drama are hunting, fertility, and initiation rituals. Often these are fused into one celebration. The celebratory marriage feast that caps the round of tragedies and satyr-play of the Athenian festivals is a rebirth of the god, an affirmation of community life, and an acknowledgment of the fertile life-force of youth. Rites are staged by older men for the benefit of adolescent boys who frequently are pressed into the leading roles. In each part of the world initiation rites have unique, culturally determined qualities. But a true composite can be drawn because the life-crisis of puberty and the enculturation of the violently aggressive young male are relatively universal occurrences. The boys are made to live through the sexual-social crisis. In the rites they find their identities as individuals, as adult members of their society, and as males. The rites are enactments of some of the cruelest and most exaggerated fantasies of adolescence. Boys are kidnapped, bodily punished, starved, buried alive, taunted, scarred, and generally tormented. Often the culminating ceremony is circumcision or subincision or some other painful and irremediable body mark. Then the boys are adorned in warriors' costumes, the dress of full-fledged males, and assembled in front of the whole community, women included, to dance. Obscene farces go hand in hand with more solemn ceremonies. Sometimes there is a mock battle between men and women.[15] Ithyphallic figures are displayed, and "venuses" with pendant breasts and swollen vulvas. The ordeals and ultimately triumphant conclusion to the rites are versions of the titanic struggles experienced by classic heroes. They are also versions of every boy's dream of torture, contest, and victory. The details and excesses of initiation rites are too well known to need elaboration.[16]

In these rituals we discern every basic structure and theme of drama: separation, ordeal, sacrifice, triumph; dismemberment and resurrection; birth, death, rebirth; mistaken identity; perilous journey; men versus women; young versus old; luck, fortune, fate, destiny. Here are the sources not only of tragedy but of farce. The father-king-god is overcome/replaced by the son-hero-savior who attains mastery over the family-state-cosmos. The young hero may meet death in his attempt to attain his goal. But if so, there is another young hero ready to take the dead one's place.

Whatever their themes, the rituals are themselves elaborate public performances. They need no further "development" into the familiar forms of drama to justify their existence. The rites are complete. They use body paints and/or costumes, environments and/or stage settings, conflicts and/or stories, dances, songs, feasting, and general celebration. It is the imagination of the adolescent boy that is the core of theater. It is the celebration of his achieving the status of manhood that is the subject of theater.

In these times of rising women's consciousness I feel I must make absolutely clear my assertions regarding the male domination of theater. The rites from which theater derives are aggressive —hunting, for example. When women hunt, the rites will still be about hunting—but the hunters will include women. Insofar as women free themselves from spending most of their lives child-bearing, child-raising, and man-keeping, exactly so far will women be enabled to enter areas once restricted to men, including theater.

[15] See Read (1965), 136–137.
[16] For examples see Bateson (1958), Berndt (1962), Eliade (1958), Firth (1967), Gould (1969), Lévi-Strauss (1966 and 1969), Malinowski (1954 and 1961), Read (1965), and Williams (1940). Each of these is loaded with further references. The data is universal and conclusive.

The struggle, as always, is to reconstruct from a new basis oppressive social organizations.

The summer after Goddard I wanted to do more experiments exploring the links among erotic fantasy, nakedness, acting out, and ceremony. TPG was in residence at the University of Rhode Island, and I was leading a student workshop. I took as my prototype for the U.R.I. experiments an "ecstasy dance" I helped stage in March, 1969, as part of a class I was teaching at N.Y.U. The 1969 dance was done at the Performing Garage. It was based on keeping a steady beat/rhythm for a number of hours, from 1 A.M. to dawn. The ten participants danced in a circle throughout the night. After a few hours of dancing I began to project my fantasies onto the "blank screen" of the monotonous dancing rhythm. Here are some of my notebook entries from that period, both before and after the ecstasy dance.

> 8 January. The outstanding feature of a ritual is that participation in the ritual is a transformation. A new order or new state of being is reached through participation in the ritual.
> 10 February. Ceremony = structured, elegant, meaningful activity. Repetition. Ritual = change in status + ceremony. In private life the echoes (sublimation) of older rituals are dimly recalled. Even in the way we sit around a supper table.
> 6 March. The more monotonous the dancing rhythm the more likely to have hallucinations.
> 13 April. All night dance discussion. Possible to get into trance if we give up ego and judging mind. Give ourselves to the group. Group consciousness.
> Ecstasy begins lower. OM sound. Abandon yourself. Drop into the world arising.
>> Abandon
>> Arise
>> Within
>> Without (self)
>> Outer same/inner movement
> Games during all night dance. Eyes closed. Sitting cross-legged in a circle. Who is next? Where? Peeking? Gathering peripheral information. What time is it? Who is copping out?

At about the same time as the ecstasy dance I began a series of exercises with the Group that I called the "Real Touch Exercise." Performing *Dionysus in 69* three times a week led to a numbing of sensual feeling. To the audience the caressing seemed genuine, even erotic; to the performers it was routine. The "Real Touch Exercise" was:

> Touch each other. Start without stylization—perfectly natural touching. Either *casual,* such as a handshake, backslap, smile, glance, gesture. Or *friendly* such as an embrace, cheek kiss, ass grab, armlock. Or *intimate* such as kiss, fondle, explore. The exercise is over when the limits of natural physical expression have been reached and recognized.

The exercise was done usually by three people, What happened, for examples:

1. Lila lightly kisses Bob. Bob embraces Harry. Harry laughs nervously. Harry rubs Lila's hair, nuzzles her ear. Lila shakes Bob's shoulders, massages him. Bob kisses Lila's forehead, embraces her, tries to go further—kisses her mouth. She pulls back. Harry shakes Bob's hand. Lila squeezes Harry's chest standing behind him. Bob lies in Lila's lap, plays with her hair, then stops. She looks down at him. Harry takes Lila's hand and walks with her. Puts his arm on her shoulder. Lila puts Bob's head in her lap, caresses him, kisses him, then pulls away. Bob takes Harry for a walk, arm on his shoulder. Harry puts his hands on Lila's shoulder, then gives her a comradelike slap on the shoulder. Lila kisses Harry full on the mouth. He responds. Bob stands behind Lila, nuzzles her neck, puts his hands across her breasts, swings her gently back and forth. Lila caresses the back of Bob's thighs. Harry gives Bob a back rub.

2. All smile at each other. John moves in closer. He blows his nose. Arlene rubs John's hair, he reciprocates. Gloria touches Arlene's face under her left eye. John plays with Arlene's hand. Arlene lets herself be played with. She plays with John's hand, explores it. John caresses Gloria's face. Gloria touches John's knee. Arlene lies in John's lap. He touches her thigh, caresses her face self-consciously. Gloria caresses John's hair. John lays Gloria down, plays with her upper arm. She reaches out and plays with him. He touches her face, she plays with his face. He approaches her breasts with his hands. Arlene watches. John lifts Gloria's shirt. She caresses his head with her thigh. Arlene appears left out. This has lasted about five minutes and is like a teen-age make-out without kissing. John peck-kisses Gloria good-bye. Arlene rubs Gloria's back. John caresses Arlene's right hand. She smiles. Gloria kisses Arlene on both cheeks. John kisses

Arlene's neck. She responds, but only with one hand. Then with two wrapped around his head. John slaps Gloria's foot and then slaps her ass. Arlene twists John's arm in tomboy act. John lies in Arlene's lap, his hand around her left leg. Then he caresses her leg from knee to foot. She rubs his stomach. He rubs her back. Then he rubs her face and plays with her hair.

What was extraordinary is that people were so tentative with each other. In the context of the play there was much nakedness and eroticism. In workshop all was shyness, distance, and avoidance.

The 1971 U.R.I. ecstasy dance involved about thirty persons. It was staged in the theater where we performed *Commune*—the large scene shop in the new U.R.I. theater building. The participants were workshop people and some Group members; also two friends of workshop people. The rules of the dance were simple. A dancing circle had to be kept going; people could vary the tempo of the dance; if a person left the building for any reason, he could not reenter; outside the circle—and the room was very large—any mutually agreed activity could happen; no smoking, eating, drinking, drugs, or talking. For the dance the workshop people had constructed a central altar of fresh fruit and flowers, spilling from a cornucopia that was a toilet bowl; and they had filled the tub from *Commune* with steaming water. The lights were dim. The dance would last either until it was interrupted or until 2 P.M. the following day, whichever came sooner. It began at midnight. It ended at 6 A.M. when it was interrupted.

During the six-hour dance the rules were, as best I know, strictly observed. Some people reached trance. The music accompanying the dance varied from slow rhythmic beating to singing and shouting, and the dance steps varied accordingly. While the water stayed hot, people bathed in it. About half the people were, at one time or another, naked during the night. When the dance ended, people literally threw themselves on the fruit and devoured it.

Later in the week the Group discussed the dance. The workshop people held a separate discussion. Group members were very angry at me because they felt I had "used" the dance sexually. I was one of several people who made love during the night. I defended myself by saying that I had not violated any of the rules. "Come off it," someone said, "you made the rules!" I got angry back. "The workshop made the rules! And I wasn't the only one to fuck! Why are you so pissed off at me?" However hard I defended myself, I felt guilty. The charges struck home. Was the ecstasy dance just an ornate structure sheltering simple erotic impulses? But at the same time I wondered what was wrong with that. I knew that orgies were times when people agreed to suspend customary rules of sexual behavior; that in licensing licentious behavior many societies controlled it.

A woman said that the dance made her "feel dirty" and betrayed by me. In retrospect it seems that we were all trying to work out something concerning my identity in the Group. As a parent I was not entitled to sexual liberties. As a director I ought not manipulate people. But as a peer . . . ? Someone suggested that we stage another ecstasy dance. "This time to *really* explore ecstasy. We'll keep the exact same rhythm for twelve hours, on the beach, during the day." This adventure in pure torture was rejected. Discussion soon shifted to a lobster bake. People felt that if "ecstasy dance" was just a fancy name for "party," then we should throw the party without benefit of title. But the lobster bake was not like the ecstasy dance. The rules of the dance made it into a game and a ritual. Internalized restraints were exteriorized and made visible in the strict rules of the dance. This in turn lowered anxieties. The ecstasy dance was not Saturnalia, but in structure it was parallel. And I wondered if theater was not a kind of "time out" from everyday behavior; a special situation where people are trained to act out in public their fantasies of power, violence, conflict, and eroticism.

Ambiguities revealed by the U.R.I. ecstasy dance are not limited to it. Environmental theater space is erotic. The erotic parts of the body are those places where the viscera is at the body surface or where the body is turned inside out: genitals, anus, lips, mouth, tongue. Only slightly less erotic are the eyes, ears, armpits, crotch, back of the neck, base of the spine, and fingertips—all areas of extreme sensitivity. Paul Schilder points out that sensations at body openings are not felt "at the actual point of the opening, but about one centimetre inside the body. . . . That the most sensitive zones of the body are near the openings, but one or two centimetres deeper in the body." [17] The essence of eating, breathing, and sexual intercourse is *penetration,* the entering into the body, and the going out from the body. In Chapter 1, I spoke of a sense of visceral space—or, perhaps more precisely,

[17] Schilder (1970), 88.

a visceral sense of space—and I cited Kaplan's view that the proscenium theater is an architectural version of a specific body state. I propose that the body state of environmental theater—the spatial mood—is erotic: the inside-outness of the body translated into theater architecture. Orthodox theater spaces emphasize the eyes and ears; environmental spaces emphasize the nose and mouth.

Experiments like the ecstasy dance—and the many "gropes" and smelling and tasting exercises that I have devised—are literally ways of "working in the dark" where people know each other by touch, taste, and smell; where talking is banished so that unsublimated pleasure and unrepressed disgust can be given full play. I want to know my colleagues not only by the sound of their voices and the look of their bodies but also by the smells of their skins and the tastes of their flesh.[18]

Eroticism and nakedness are not identical, though they converge in many particulars. Physical and psychic nakedness are not identical either, but they, too, converge. "Choices 1," developed by the Group and the Firehouse Theater in 1969, is very different from "Choices 2." But these differences are largely a matter of different settings and different participants. Goddard students had stakes different from those of the professional performers of TPG and the Firehouse. At the Firehouse:

> Three spaces clearly marked out and brightly lit. The rest of the theater room dark.
>
> Space 1. Positive interaction among clothed people.
>
> Space 2. Positive or negative interaction among naked people.
>
> Space 3. Negative interaction among clothed or naked people.
>
> A performer may not move from one lit space to another without first spending some time in the darkened portions of the room.
>
> No more than three people in any of the lit spaces. No speaking. Nonverbal sounds permitted.
>
> The exercise is over when there are fewer than two people in *each* of the three spaces. For example, if Space 1 is empty, Space 2 has one person, and Space 3 has one person, the exercise is over.

[18] I agree with Marcuse (1955), 36: "Smell and taste give, as it were, unsublimated pleasures *per se* (and unrepressed disgust). They relate (and separate) individuals immediately without generalized and conventionalized forms of consciousness, morality, aesthetics."

"Choices 1" took more than three hours. I did not participate. The exercise had many qualities of dance. The Firehouse space was made of many levels of different heights and contained many curved forms. It encouraged a variety of encounters. Things happened among people both in the lit spaces and elsewhere. Because of the focused, bright theater lighting, each of the three spaces became a stage. Some of the events on these stages were very powerful: confrontations that began in slow motion—like animals sniffing each other out—gradually accelerating, freezing, transforming, tangling, untangling. Some encounters were sexual. The naked space usually had three persons feeling each other out with curiosity and delicacy. There was a particularly intense encounter among three women none of whom, to my knowledge, was homosexual. The sense of strangers meeting in a special intimate way was founded on fact, because the Group and the Firehouse had just met two days before. The friendships started during the Group's three-day visit to Minneapolis endure even now. "Choices 1" transcended its origins as an exercise and became a dance-drama about initiating friendships, renewing acquaintances, and, occasionally, ritual combats.

"Choices 1" became drama accidentally—but what could be more natural among people all of whom were performers? *Clothes,* on the other hand, was intended as an improvisatory dance-drama—a public version of an improvisation first done in workshop. *Clothes* "premiered" at U.R.I. about three weeks after the ecstasy dance. I did it again—with another group of people—at the Vancouver Art Gallery in September, 1972. The scenario quoted below I wrote out after the U.R.I. performance; then I used this scenario for the Vancouver performance.

> After completing psychophysical exercises while the audience enters, the performers lie on the floor. Each performer listens to his own breathing rhythms and to whatever other noises he can hear. Slowly he develops these sounds into a precise rhythm; and he enunciates this rhythm.
>
> Each performer keeps his own basic rhythm throughout the piece.
>
> When the rhythms have been established, the director says: "Someone get up. Move in a slow dance of your own making. Listen to your own rhythms, and the rhythms of the others." This person is First Dancer. As he moves, First Dancer sings his own name.
>
> Always following the director's instructions, this is what happens: First Dancer picks any number of others to dance

with him, as mirrors and alter egos. The Dancers sing their own names. After a few minutes of dancing they go to a central place, maybe a platform or two. First Dancer positions the others, treating them like store mannequins. He puts arms in place, adjusts heads, arranges the Dancers each in a distinct pose. Then, by touching each Dancer on the lips, he silences them. Then he positions himself and is silent.

The only sounds in the room are the rhythms of the other performers still lying on the floor.

The others rise, and each moves in slow motion, making a move only while making a sound. Thus the moves are staccato and very slow. The overall effect is of movement as if under strobes. The performers approach spectators and without words solicit clothes, jewelry, personal effects. This phase of gathering stuff may take an hour or more. It continues until everyone has been approached at least once, and perhaps many times.

While gathering stuff the performers arrange the stuff on the frozen Dancers. The Dancers are slowly adorned, overdressed, in the accumulated properties of the audience.

At U.R.I. there were six Dancers positioned on an arrangement of three curved platforms each about two feet high. There were about seventy-five spectators. Four of the Dancers were standing; two were lying down. The fifteen performers gathering stuff moved through the theater very slowly and with such clear intentions that a spectator could see a performer approaching for several minutes prior to any direct solicitation. There was plenty of time to decide whether or not to contribute. Many took off clothing and dangled it as bait to attract performers. Others allowed performers to undress them. By the time the gathering was over six males were totally stripped, and two females were stripped to their underpants. The Dancers were grotesquely arrayed—literally buried under a staggering collection of stuff. The clothes were not just tossed on but carefully arranged. The Dancers looked like figures from a wax museum or like the dead adorned for their trip to the underworld. The clothes were so heavy that the two Dancers lying down told me later that they had trouble breathing.

In Vancouver the performers not only dressed the Dancers but also made patterns of clothes on the floor, finally outlining a cross that cut the room into four sections. Performers approached spectators many times insistently demanding clothes. By the time the gathering phase was over many spectators were naked or near naked. In Vancouver there were four Dancers, six performers, and about fifty spectators. I began the Vancouver performance by vaguely outlining the piece and telling people that anyone could participate. Only two of the performers/Dancers were from my Vancouver workshop. The rest were audience.

> When the director sees that most of the things have been gathered, he says "Freeze." This direction is given to everyone in the room. Then the director says: "You have three minutes to bring your things to the center, if you wish." As time passes, the director counts it down. When the three minutes are up, he says: "Anyone who has not had anything taken or has given nothing please leave."

At U.R.I. two people left. At Vancouver a man left and then came back five minutes later. "Yes, I've given something." Later it turned out he was referring to his attention, not to anything material. There is no way of checking up, nor any need to do so. The director's instructions throughout are guidelines. Sometimes the most interesting things happen when an instruction is ignored or changed. The director should never insist on his version of an event or exercise.

By asking everyone who has not contributed to leave, a community of sorts is established. Everyone in the room has participated as either a Dancer, a performer, or a giver of clothes. At U.R.I. about five persons came forward during the three-minute grace period. Two of these were women from the Group who gave all of their remaining clothes.

> Spectators are invited to walk around the room looking at the Dancers. A museum tour. Performers and Dancers remain frozen. After about five minutes the director helps form the spectators into a single line. He tells them to file past the Dancers as a crowd in mourning files past a bier. Also to begin singing a chant—either a known song or something the people invent.
>
> After the procession the spectators go anyplace in the theater, preferably high up. First Dancer is told he can move, and one by one, he "frees" the other Dancers. They take in everyone in the theater, preferably one at a time.
>
> Very slowly the Dancers divest themselves of their costumes and lay all the articles on the floor in neat piles. Shoes in one place, shirts in another, pants in another, sweaters in another; and so on. All the clothes are displayed as in a bazaar, or in a hangar or gym after a disaster. Or the way loot might be shown after a major heist. Spectators are in-

vited to walk around, look at the stuff. Items may be examined but not removed. No talking.

After about fifteen minutes of window-shopping the director asks everyone in the theater to climb to the highest places in the theater. From the high places, one at a time, people begin looking for their things and identifying them. "My red sweater. "My gold wristwatch." "My corduroy pants." "My yellow underwear." "My white sneakers." And so on. The naming continues until everything is named.

It is during this phase that I realized how many things people carry with them on a summer's evening. The naming took more than one-half hour both at U.R.I. and in Vancouver. The naming itself is a kind of music. Two people start to speak at once, one backs off, the other hesitates and then goes on. Between speakers there are pauses of varying durations. Sounds come from different parts of the room. During this phase the audience senses itself as a community—a group somehow "in this thing together."

> When the naming of things is over, people come down one at a time and gather their things; dress; say what they want to say; leave. The performance is over when everyone is gone.

During this phase spectators became performers. The whole room was a stage and those sitting in the scaffolding a captive audience. They can't leave—their clothes are on the floor! At U.R.I. I asked the workshop people to sit in a circle on the floor; but in Vancouver everyone but the speaker was in the scaffolding. People spoke as they gathered their things. Some made farewell speeches, some performed dances, some told jokes, some waxed philosophical. There was dialogue. The Vancouver audience was given to humor and the performing of routines while dressing. Spectators at U.R.I. gathered their clothes into bundles, said relatively few words, and dressed outside the theater. On both occasions I left when there were about ten persons remaining.

Clothes comes out of several earlier exercises: "Dressing and Undressing" (see Chapter 4), where people exchange clothes while telling stories; "Recapitulation" (see Chapter 8), where dancing rhythms are discovered by listening to the sounds coming from *within* one's body; "Arrangements" (see Chapter 4), which is the prototype for *Clothes*. *Clothes* develops slowly in harmony with an audience that is drawn deeper into the action as time goes on. When spectators exercise, lie down, and dance; when they give things or have them taken; when they examine their own things worn by the Dancers and then laid out on the floor; when they identify by name each of their things; when they claim their things, dress, and address their fellow spectators—at each point they participate in a drama that is made from them and their own attitudes toward their property. *Clothes* is as close as I have yet come to invoking a sense of genuine community in the theater.

But *Clothes* does not come out of my head, or even from the theater. It is part of a larger scheme of *social nakedness*. Of the thousands of examples of social nakedness in North American society I have participated in a few. Let us not consider just now spectators who freely stripped and joined the dances or "rituals" of *Dionysus in 69;* or my own well-publicized stripping at the New York premiere of *Paradise Now.* My first experience of social nakedness was at the mass protest against the invasion of Cambodia in May, 1970. More than 100,000 people assembled in Washington. The President was fenced off by a cordon of D.C. Transit Authority buses which surrounded the White House on every side. Shades of covered wagons! The speeches were routine, and it was a very hot day, with temperatures well into the nineties. About ten thousand people gathered around the reflecting pool in front of the Lincoln Memorial. Soon kids were wading and splashing; singing, dancing, shouting. Then a few stripped, and then more and more, and it was not long before hundreds of naked youths were celebrating in the Pool to the delight of thousands and the cooler gaze of Washington cops.

In the summer of 1970 TPG was in residence at SUNY New Paltz. In the afternoons we often went to Low Falls, an accessible wood, stream, and waterfall in the foothills of the Adirondacks. Always there were from thirty to several hundred naked kids. The next summer we were in residence at U.R.I. and lived on a farm in Narragansett. Often Group members would sunbathe in the backyard, and casual nudity was common in the house. In the summer of 1972 we were in residence at the University of British Columbia in Vancouver. Adjacent to U.B.C. is Wreck Beach, about one mile of unofficially authorized "nude" bay front. On any sunny day it was crowded with more than a thousand naked people, ranging in age from infants to the aged, but predominantly young people.

During the sixties many middle-class children rejected the life-styles of their parents. Behind these life-styles lay the American economic-political system. The Protestant ethic came in for

Photographs 21, 22, and 23. The Birth Ritual of *Dionysus* performed in costume—as it was until November 1968, four months after the play opened. (*Raeanne Rubenstein*)

Photographs 24, 25, and 26. The naked Birth Ritual followed by the ecstasy dance celebrating the birth of Dionysus. Sometimes the audience joined in the dancing. (*Frederick Eberstadt*)

Photograph 27. Pentheus dancing naked before he is brought by Dionysus to be dismembered by the Bacchantes (*Frederick Eberstadt*)

Photograph 28. Agave speaks to Dionysus. She is standing amid the corpses of the men she and her sisters have killed. (*Frederick Eberstadt*)

a particularly heavy shelling. First the beatniks and then the hippies rejected the ideals and practices of mainstream America. The rebels were known by their clothes which resembled nostalgic throwbacks to pioneer days of the nineteenth century: homespun, long-haired, moustaches and beards, denims, casual. The hippie movement, however, was no fad: It signaled a deep disaffection and alienation that we have not heard the end of. But also never underestimate the resiliency and cunning of the Yankee entrepreneur spirit. The wholesalers of style soon enough absorbed the hippie look and its revolutionary rhetoric: It suited fantasies of the American Dream. Bankers sported long hair, sideburns, boots, and denim; the Chrysler Corporation proclaimed "The Dodge Rebellion," and Ford came out with lines of cars named after exterminated breeds of horses.

Nakedness appeared to be one sure refuge from the purveyors of trade. Nakedness as a way of dressing is beyond the pale—it generates no need for clothing stores, mills, designers, or wholesalers. But even nakedness was soon appropriated for its erotic cash value by the "entertainment industry" that began turning out books, magazines, films, and stage shows whose only purpose was to convert the prurient interest into cash. Thus the double bind: To support the "sexploitation industry" is to strengthen those who treat human beings as objects; to oppose it is to strengthen those who want to clamp censorship on expression.

Why did the young create a new leisure class—why not a new working class? Simply because it is the entire *idea of productivity* that has been called into question. The American working class supports the idea of productivity and therefore offers no acceptable alternative to the rebels. Instead, the working class itself needs reformation. The only acceptable models were those people rejected by America, people "good Americans" think of as useless and worthless: Indians, blacks, Third World people, and the "primitive people" who live "close to nature." The serious, deep contradictions laid bare by the rebellion of middle-class youth have not been dealt with. But the style of "going naked" seems to have taken root.

If going naked is a rejection of the system, it is also an affirmation of the body. In public performances this affirmation is touched with exhibitionism. I don't use the term clinically. I mean a delight in showing off, in displaying the body. Coupled with exhibitionism is a certain amount of voyeurism. The one who wants to be looked at is complemented by the one who wants to look. There was understandably a lot of this in *Dionysus in 69,* a play largely based on the relationship between exhibitionists and voyeurs. That this relationship sometimes borders close on prostitution (intentional or unintentional) should not surprise us. As Eric Bentley has it, "we shouldn't need Jean Genet to tell us that the whorehouse is itself a theatre. It is the legitimate theatre's illegitimate-sister institution." Bentley goes on to say:

> What then, finally, to make of the naked American of the new theatre? For one thing, he or she is but old whore writ large. If stripping has many meanings, one of the first is undoubtedly the invitation to the sexual dance. To take off your clothes says: make love to me. In the theatre this is usually a little on the symbolic side, but the message is understood, even when the love is only made with the eyes. Above all, it is understood on the actor's side of the footlights. For the actor knows he is a whore and that violation by the eyes is humanly as thoroughgoing as any other. The wish to be naked on stage is the wish to offer oneself. I do not say "give oneself," as these are not amateurs, and admission is not free. The front rows at *Oh! Calcutta!* now go for twenty-five dollars a seat.[19]

Bentley goes too far—and not far enough. Surely there is a connection between the liberating ambitions of "going naked" and the whorelike qualities of some plays; but there is a difference between whoring sex shows and *Dionysus in 69*. But the differences among body liberation, serious art, and sex shows are of degree. They each center on the body: the first as celebration, the second as symbolic or metaphoric "objective correlative," and the third as merchandise. And in each there is more than a pinch of the other two.

When *Dionysus in 69* opened, there were *no naked scenes* in it. It was not until December, 1968, that we did the birth and death rituals naked; and some weeks later before we did the ecstasy dance naked. The first naked work I ever did in the theater was in February, 1968, with T.P.G. It was a phallic dance in which the women celebrated the maleness of the men. Nakedness was voluntary, but by the end of the exercise all but two people were naked. Then in May, 1968, we rehearsed the ecstasy dance of *Dionysus* naked. But during performances the most that ever happened before December, 1968, was that some of the women removed their shirts and danced bare-

[19] Bentley (1972), 377.

breasted. Writing of her experiences performing naked in the role of Dionysus, Joan MacIntosh says:

> The first speech as Dionysus is the hardest part of the play for me. To emerge vulnerable and naked and address the audience and say I am a god. Absurd and untrue. I didn't believe and therefore the audience didn't believe. Eyes glazed, body mobilized and defensive. Rehearsed with R.S. Told him I felt like a fraud, doing that. He said expose that, deal with that, don't cover it up. . . . The absurdity of telling 250 people that I am a god makes me laugh and the audience laughs with me and gradually the strength comes and the self-mockery fades away.[20]

Gleaning my own notes for that period reveals how difficult the move to nakedness was.

> November. You can be naked through clothes or through skin. Costumes are too easy. Either do show naked as sacred act or dressed and let nakedness come through street clothes.
> 4 December. No more costumes. Street clothes. Everyone naked for birth ritual. Ecstasy dance naked? All naked for death ritual. Naked until end. Bodies washed—people gather clothes, dress.
> 6 December. Naked = shock. Holy because so stark.
> 8 December. Nudity is a risk. Not a risk for the audience who will (and did) keep their distance. But a risk for each performer to do what is most difficult: be naked without being either abstract or strip-tease sexual. M.'s birth rhythm during the Agave scene was at once specific, exploratory, revealing, "unaesthetic" in the best sense, and committed. She actualized the physical rhythms of birthing. C.'s going into the audience was another inventive, dangerous, committed act.
> Audience encounters good. As we get more authentic, expect more encounters. The encounters will begin to shape some parts of the performance.
> 8 December (mimeo notes). I noticed a "blindness" in our nudity. We did not want to see ourselves so naked. The "numbness" that people said they felt was a severe form of this blindness. More moderate forms were people literally keeping their eyes closed; people not leaving the mats; people relating to the others through touch and sound but not through sight.
> The nudity clarified certain things: (1) The birth ritual is a birthing, not only of Dionysus, but sympathetically of each

[20] MacIntosh in The Performance Group (1971), no page.

of us through him. (2) Undressing before the birth ritual is a sacred and surgical preparation; at once full of portents and (clinically) sterile. It is a way of clearing the way. (3) we leave the fetal meditation to birth ourselves.

The ecstasy dance is an ordeal/celebration. To leave the mats is to negotiate with the profane world. Leaving takes courage and incorporates the knowledge that life must be lived and life is not pure. The audience may participate clothed outside the mats; but they must not come onto the mats unless they are as we are.

The second phase of the nudity—the death ritual and body pile—is more clearly defined. It is the second half of the birth ritual; it is the result of profanation and at the same time itself a sacred act. To die is natural. To kill is either obscene or sacred or both.

For birth the audience is invited or at least permitted to participate. For death the audience is challenged. "Are you people proud of this?" Agave asks.

Rarely did spectators participate in the birth ritual. They were more likely to join in the ecstasy dance celebrating Dionysus' birth that follows the ritual. And on some nights people intervened to prevent Pentheus from being sacrificed, or they joined in sacrificing him. In both cases spectators stripped and died/killed with the performers. But with very few exceptions none of the naked spectators ever engaged the performers erotically. *Dionysus in 69* was risky erotically only during the caress scene, or during some of the choruses delivered in the nearly dark theater. Whenever performers invited the audience to *touch,* or touched spectators erotically, there was a good chance that the touching would be reciprocated. Sometimes the touching got heavy. Male spectators especially would go as far as they could. Male homosexuals ditto. Less frequently female spectators would come on. I know of no lesbian come-ons.

TPG's inexperience with nakedness in *Dionysus* led us to more experiments in workshop, especially to exploring the relationship between physical and psychic nakedness—between nakedness and vulnerability. The most important of these are mirror exercises. Mirror exercises are well known in theater and dance. There are many children's games that involve mimicry and more subtle kinds of mirroring. In fact, mirroring can be traced to the earliest experiences of infancy. It is in these experiences that I locate the sources of psychic nakedness, vulnerability, and that *special kind of sharing* unique to theater. The late child psychologist D. W. Winnicott:

Whereas inner psychic reality has a kind of location in the mind or in the belly or in the head or somewhere within the bounds of the individual's personality, and whereas what is called external reality is located outside those bounds, playing and cultural experience can be given a location if one uses the concept of the potential space between the mother and the baby.[21]

Now at some point the baby takes a look round. Perhaps a baby at the breast does not look at the breast. Looking at the face is more likely to be a feature. What does the baby see there? . . . What does the baby see when he or she looks at the mother's face? I am suggesting that, ordinarily, what the baby sees is himself or herself. In other words the mother is looking at the baby and *what she looks like is related to what she sees there.*[22]

The theatrical event is fundamentally a mirroring; an ensemble company is a group of mirrors reflecting each other. Not fixed, dead mirrors that give back a reduced reflection of surfaces, but organic mirrors that interpret, transform, amplify, and relate both surfaces and depths, bringing people together in what can only be described as an intensive dance. Birdwhistell's film studies confirm this.[23] Experiencing me-in-you and you-in-me is characteristic of theater—and of other intimate relationships. Theater's specialty is in making public what usually are private affairs.

The raising to consciousness of mirroring can happen naturally over a long period of time, as among friends; it can be determined biologically, as between mother and infant; or it can be trained, as in mirror exercises. Almost every exercise described in this book can be handled as a mirror exercise. Of the many that could be discussed from this point of view I will select only two.

"Chinese Prop." *A* stands behind *B*, and *C* stands behind *D*. They position themselves so that *A-B* is face to face with *C-D*. *A* whispers to *B* who says what he hears out loud to *D*. Then *C* whispers to *D* who says what he hears out loud to *B*.

[21] Winnicott (1971), 53.
[22] Winnicott (1971), 112.
[23] See Birdwhistell (1970), 12–23, 47–50, 147–155.

A and *C* have complete freedom of what to say. *B* and *D* have complete freedom of how to say.

Anyone from among those watching may substitute for any of the participants at any time.

"Chinese Prop" takes a long time to get anywhere. People are initially shy and uncomfortable with a difficult, unnatural situation. People speak in clichés; they move stiffly and self-consciously. Only after a long while do individuals give over to their partners, and instead of having four people, we have two couples, *A-B* and *C-D*. Still more time passes before these couples fuse and two entities, *AB* and *CD,* confront each other. If this fusion occurs, the exercise reveals some startling shapes, sounds, and rhythms. Each entity moves with a dancelike intensity and conviction; language is heightened often turning to song; unpredictable things are said.

What's happening? Ego boundaries between individuals are breaking down. The progression:

$$A.\ B.\ C.\ D. \longrightarrow A\text{–}B{:}C\text{–}D \longrightarrow AB{:}CD \longrightarrow ABCD$$

is one of breakdown and reformation on the basis of mirroring until from four individuals one entity emerges. When the exercise works, no individual feels responsible for what is going on. Consequently inhibitions diminish. Communication that commences as from one individual to another becomes from one extended person to another (*AB* to *CD*) and ultimately to a dance-theater form in which only one extended organism is speaking/moving. Neither *A* nor *B* is speaking to either *C* or *D*. The communication is from one extended person to another. The couple *A-B* is in a mirror relationship with itself. What *A-B* says/does is not the expression of either *A* or *B*. Neither is it the sum of two individual expressions. It is the expression of the relationship *A-B*. Between the two extended people still another mirror develops, so that what goes on among the two entities is neither the expression of *AB* nor of *CD* but of the relationship *AB:CD*. As the exercise continues, the ego boundaries are lowered still further. The moving/speaking becomes more "surprising" to those doing it as well as to observers who know the participants well. What happens is not expected of *A, B, C,* or *D* or even of *AB* or *CD*. Ultimately, *ABCD* is expressing itself. Of course, substituting any of the four people starts the whole process over again from the beginning. The relationship *A-E:C-D* is altogether different from the relationship *A-*B:*C-D*. "Chinese Prop" plays easier than it reads. What is asked of participants is patience.

"Double Mirror" is even more closely linked to Winnicott's idea of mirroring than is "Chinese Prop." However, I developed "Double Mirror" before I read Winnicott. "Double Mirror" grows out of many theater mirror games and from childhood mimicry and games like "Patty Cake, Patty Cake." In all these the fun is both in seeing yourself reflected in the actions of others and in repeating the actions of others so that they are trapped in their own gestures and sounds. Also it becomes hard to locate where the *original* is—who is mirroring whom? Mirror exercises take two or more voices/gestures but only one action. Feedback involves more than one person but only one action; it is as if one person's head were exploded so that one person becomes several people.

> *"Double Mirror."* Performers sit in an ample, irregular circle. Someone comes to the center. Two others come to the center and take the same positions as *A. B* and *C* mirror *A.* Everything *A* says or does is repeated by both *B* and *C.* They do not wait for *A* to finish a sentence or a gesture. They mirror *A* word for word, move for move. There is no time for "reflection" or judgment. The mirrors must pay such close attention to *A* that they do not think about what they are doing or have any idea of what *A* is doing. A good set of mirrors is less than a full word behind *A.*
>
> Careful attention is given to the tiniest details. A curl to the lips, a slur, a stutter, a hand gesture, a jaunt in the walk, breathing, the "uhh" sounds people use to fill in with, averted glances, stifled laughter—all the things that people *cancel out* or *ignore* or *slip* by. These *forgotten bits of communication* are especially difficult and important.
>
> The mirrors position themselves in a triangular relationship to *A,* so that neither mirror is face to face with *A* or out of *A*'s field of vision.

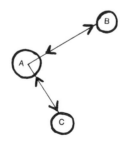

From time to time others replace *B* and *C.*

Despite attending to details, the mirrors do not ape *A*. What is happening is that the mirrors are giving *A* back to himself. The mirrors do what they perceive. They help *A* raise his consciousness of himself, particularly in regard to his own forgotten bits of communication. What the mirrors see in *A* is in fact *A*'s version of what he sees in his mirrors. The double mirror is truly a double mirror. Subject and reflections are versions of each other. *A*'s perception of himself-as-real is confirmed in his experience of the mirrors who are giving him back . . . himself. What is being exercised is not sight but insight; and that of all three people. The space between mirrors and *A* is an exteriorized version of an inner space, a space that is neither me nor not-me but the me-that-is-between-me-and-the-others. This space is a paradigm of performance space. It is organic, alive.

> When I look I am seen, so I exist.
> I can now afford to look and see.
> I now look creatively and what I apperceive I also perceive.
> In fact I take care not to see what is not there to be seen (unless I am tired).[24]

"Double Mirror" is not an exercise for beginners—it is for people who already know each other well. It is an exhausting exercise, literally emptying people out. It is a whole body exercise dealing with voice, movement, feelings, self, and others simultaneously.

"Double Mirror" is a deep exercise. It retrieves feelings, gestures, and body states from the past; it gets at *sources*. That which is deep is "long abiding, the cause or motive behind whole systems of fluctuating behavior, an enduring or prevailing urgency."[25] Sometimes the words come up the way Carlos Castaneda felt after chewing some peyote buttons:

> What followed next was not speech; it was the feeling of my unvoiced thoughts coming out of my mouth in a sort of liquid form. It was an effortless sensation of vomiting without the contractions of the diaphragm. It was a pleasant flow of liquid words.[26]

That's how I felt when I did the "Double Mirror" in Vancouver

[24] Winnicott (1971), 114.
[25] Kaplan's definition, in a letter to me.
[26] Castaneda (1968), 32.

in 1972. Other experiences with the exercise have not been so good for me.

What is marvelous about "Double Mirror" is that you see/hear yourself telling your own story at the moment that you are telling it. The feeling of support this gives is indescribable. I felt I needed no justification for doing what I was doing. My experiential world was all-inclusive, narcissistic to a degree I can't put into words; oceanic, endless, satisfying. I tested limits: I shouted, stamped, cried, insulted the mirrors. When something in me (*me?*) was convinced that I could not offend the mirrors, drive them to *stop mirroring me* and say instead: "Okay, we've had enough of *you,* now listen to us and we'll tell you what we *really* think of you!"—then I felt deeply relieved, and things came up (in Castaneda's sense) that I didn't know were there. I was fully accepted, present. I heard myself-in-things, and I began to work-things-out from inside myself.

There is no more succinct description of "Double Mirror" than Winnicott's "the face that reflects what is there to be seen."

Psychic nakedness and physical nakedness are sometimes identical. In this chapter I have tried to show what I mean by that assertion. It is not an easy subject. I cannot be conclusive about it. I end this chapter by referring to a scene from *Commune* where David Angel, performed by Stephen Borst, walks around the theater twice, naked, followed by Lizzie and Clementine, dressed. The nakedness actually begins a scene earlier. David is stripped, tied by the feet, held by the arms in a spread-eagle, and brutally interrogated by Fearless. The interrogation is an adaptation from Marlowe's *Edward II,* Act V, Scene 5, combined with elements of common police practice and Charles Manson's account at his trial of how he was treated. The interrogation is also a sexual abuse. Fearless accuses David of being a homosexual and threatens to urinate on him. Immediately after interrogating David, Fearless walks up to the women and asks them if they "know what a sex orgy is." Spalding and Bruce who have been holding David spread-eagle become his comforters. They lie down next to him, cover him with their bodies, caress him, tell him to "speak no more, rest, I won't leave you comfortless."

In their arms David begins to dream: "In the last days there will be a big earthquake that will open the world for all those who love. That's us. We shall be saved!" He jumps to his feet, exhilarated, and begins a slow, strutting dance not unlike the black funeral struts of New Orleans. It is a fantasy dance, a march around the room in his head. He is in jail, he is free. He is condemned, he is saved. He is alone, he is followed by two women. He is David Angel, he is Jesus Christ. He is on the way to the gas chamber, he is on the way to Calvary. He is Stephen Borst, he is a performer. He is dressed in glory, he is naked. As he dances, the women sing:

> I shall march through Death Valley with my angelic band
> I shall pass through your cities with my fan in my hand
> And around thee, O Los Angeles, my armies will encamp
> While I search my holy temple with my bright burning lamp.

This is a reprise of the opening of *Commune*. In that first dancing all the performers invite the spectators to join the dancing. Usually many do. Now there are only three dancers —naked David, followed by Lizzie and Clementine. No invitations to the audience. During the first dance everyone held hands; during the second Lizzie and Clementine hold hands, but David is out of reach. They gesture to him but never reach/touch him.

During the first circling of the room David looks at the spectators and says to some of them: "I don't care what I look like to you. I don't care what you think of me. I don't care what you do with me. I've always been yours anyway." Invariably portions of this speech evoke smiles, sometimes giggles. People respond to David: "Man, I think you are beautiful!" As if to reassure him, to get in touch. I hear in David's speech two voices. The first is of the character David Angel, a man condemned to die, like so many others, whose entire life has been a preparation for that condemnation; a man dreaming on the glory of ultimate surrender. The second voice is Stephen Borst's. He is speaking for all performers: "You are the audience and I am a performer. Here I am, this is me, I belong to you." Stephen Borst is vulnerable.

At the end of the first circling of the room Fearless resumes his questioning of the women. They stop dancing and enter onto the center of the Wave. They stand still. Everyone is quiet.

David continues to circle the room. He is no longer strutting. He is just walking. He fixes his attention on a spectator: "I've eaten out of your garbage cans." On another: "I've worn your secondhand clothes." Another: "I've taken things and given them away again the next second." Then he stops walking; he stands in front of a spectator. "I've given everything I have away. Everything." He drops his hands to his sides. "Take, this is my body." Sometimes the spectator touches David, or speaks to him, or makes a wisecrack. More often nothing is said. After about ten seconds David turns away, squats, awaits the next scene. He dresses after the Dune Buggy Race about three minutes later.

The scene has had another ending. The last bit of dialogue used to be: "Take, *eat,* this is my body." Then David takes hold of the flesh around his stomach and pulls it out, as if his flesh were his clothes. The gesture of pulling his flesh was grotesque. It looked as if David could unzip his skin and step out of his body. The word "eat" embarrassed people. Although the words were those of Christ at the Last Supper, the allusion was too ridiculously sexual. Spectators often tittered, As in the successive versions of the My Lai scene (see Chapter 2), David's naked walk was smoothed out, given "dignity."

David Angel's nakedness—or is it Stephen Borst's?—is more difficult than the mass nakedness of *Dionysus in 69.* The one-to-one contacts, the simplicity, the duration, and the aloneness of David are startling. Through David the audience sees Stephen Borst. It is more astonishing these days to see one man, naked, simply walking around a room than to see a group in the midst of a dramatic action "celebrating the flesh" by whipping it into a frenzy or dressing it in lights, music, or meaning. David Angel's dance becomes a walk that is not dramatic, nor is it a celebration. It is a showing.

The actor, at least in part, is creator, model, and creation rolled into one. He must not be shameless as that leads to exhibitionism.
He must have courage, but not merely the courage to exhibit himself—a passive courage, we might say: the courage of the defenseless, the courage to reveal himself. . . .
The actor must not illustrate but accomplish an "act of the soul" by means of his own organism.
Jerzy Grotowski

The Mother is not an ordinary human being like you and me. She has a tremendous force behind her. She can do whatever she likes. She is very highly concentrated.
Vinnie of Sri Aurobindo Ashram

4 Performer

Stanislavski brought to the word "actor" a dignity it never previously had. He made of the actor a humanist and psychologist, a person who understands and expresses the feelings, motives, actions, and strategies of human behavior. Stanislavski deplored actors who allowed themselves to be exploited by managers. He denounced lazy, indulgent, show-off, prostituted actors who lived for applause. The great Russian actor-director insisted that the actor live his life "in art"—a state of rigorous training, self-examination, high ethical standards, and refined good taste on and off stage. To achieve this the actor learned how to be "natural" in front of an audience; this was a complicated, demanding task.

Vsevolod Meyerhold—Stanislavski's pupil, rival, friend, and (virtual) successor—turned the master's teachings upside down even before Stanislavski wrote them out. Meyerhold wanted theater-in-the-theater—"style" and the "grotesque."

The grotesque aims to subordinate psychologism to a decorative task. That is why in every theatre which has been dominated by the grotesque the aspect of design in its widest sense has been so important (for example, the Japanese theatre). Not only the settings, the architecture of the stage, and the theatre itself are decorative, but also the mime, movements, gestures and poses of the actors. Through being decorative they become expressive. For this reason the technique of the grotesque contains elements of the dance; only with the help of the dance is it possible to subordinate conceptions to a decorative task.[1]

The dance is not "natural" in Stanislavski's sense. It is carefully composed, not to duplicate everyday rhythms, but to express feelings and situations. The great argument of modern theater between the naturalists and the theatricalists boils down to this: *Where does human truth lie? On the surface, in the behavior men show every day, or in the depths, behind social masks?* The naturalists strive for a replication of just those everyday details that represent the essential man. The theatricalists strive for means to penetrate or surpass the masks of daily life in order to reveal the essential man. Stanislavski and Brecht are naturalists. Artaud and Grotowski are theatricalists. As in all great arguments most people take a little bit of this side and a little bit of that side. But it is good to know the argument in its barest form.

Applying the principle of theatricalism to environmental theater means applying the principle of *whole design* to every aspect of the production from performer training, to arrangement and use of text, to shaping the space, and all technical elements. No part of the work is frozen or predetermined. Some very hard work is necessary if the performer is to develop the courage and technique to lay his mask aside and *show himself as he is in the extreme situation of the action he is playing.* This is not Stanislavski's famous "as if." This is the actual situation of the action, not its imaginary projection. This is the "what is." Environmental theater performing is both naturalistic (= "show himself as he is") and theatricalistic (= "in the extreme situation of the action").

This act of spiritual nakedness is all there is to performing. This act of dis/covery is not character work in the orthodox sense. But neither is it unlike character work. It takes place in the difficult area between character and work-on-oneself. The action of the play is arrived at through a cyclic process in which the performer's responses are the basis for the work; the performer's own self is exteriorized and transformed into the scenic givens of the production. These givens comprise the mise-en-scène and

[1] Meyerhold (1969 [1911–1912]), 141.

are, in a sense, character. But the response of the performer to each given may at any time evoke a new given and change the mise-en-scène. The process is ruthless, ceaseless.

The great argument is reflected in many lesser debates, none more fiercely waged than that between advocates of spontaneity and discipline. Again Meyerhold, who is uncanny in his up-to-dateness.

> Does the display of emotion really diminish the self-discipline of the actor? Real live men danced in living movements around the altar of Dionysus; their emotions seemed to burn uncontrollably inflamed to extreme ecstasy by the fire on the altar. Yet the ritual in honor of the god of wine was composed of predetermined rhythms, steps and gestures. That is one example of the actor's self-discipline unaffected by the display of emotion. In the dance the Greek was bound by a whole series of traditional rules, yet he was at liberty to introduce as much personal invention as he wished.[2]

One of the aims of this chapter is to show some techniques of achieving spontaneity and discipline simultaneously. "Spontaneity and discipline, far from weakening each other, mutually reinforce themselves; what is elementary feeds what is constructed, and vice-versa, to become the real sources of a kind of acting that glows." [3]

During their visit to New York in March, 1971, members of the Japanese National Theater came to the Garage and showed The Performance Group some examples of their work. Mansaku Nomura did a selection from a Kyogen play. I loved the simplicity and discipline of his performing, the clarity of the gestures, the sudden shifts in tempo and voice. I asked him if everything was scored.

"Yes," he said.

"But what about your feelings *inside* the score? Do· they change?"

"Of course," Nomura answered. "Each audience affects me differently—and what I feel completely changes the texture of my performing. I work from the moment."

This was identical to the answer I got from Ryczard Cieslak when I spoke to him about his work as the Fool in *Apocalypsis* and the Prince in *The Constant Prince*. Stephen Borst of The

---

[2] Meyerhold (1969), 129–130. Written in 1911–1912.
[3] Grotowski (1968), 121.

Performance Group defined character as "a set of physical and vocal actions constructed of relative movements and inflections." The circle is *never closed*. The score always allows the performer the freedom to express himself spontaneously. To provide such liberty, that is the function of a score.

"The actor is a human being who has dis/covered and un/covered himself so much that he re/veals [= unveils] something of man. He is the miracle." [4] I call actors in this sense—actors who are working toward dis/covery—"performers." The performer does not play a role (re/cover) so much as remove resistances and blocks that prevent him from acting through, wholly following, the impulses that come from within him in response to the actions of a role. In performing, the role remains itself, the performer remains himself. Also the performer is equally adept at singing, dancing, speaking, moving; he is in contact with his own centers; he is able to relate freely to others. Clearly this is an ideal picture. In plain fact, some of the most interesting performing occurs around areas of resistance, places of special turbulence, where the performer's life-in-the-theater is at stake.

Actor training in America is a crippled enterprise because it is an enterprise. Universities and schools as much as individuals guard what they have, market their own special approaches, jealously compete with each other. Instead of the exchange of techniques that characterizes a wholesome tradition, training is marked by secret approaches and special effects. So much of our critical machinery is geared for taking things apart, tearing them down, and so little dedicated to support. There are few places where students learn through apprenticeship and example, the best methods.

In the deepest sense no written account can substitute for *presence,* and presence is the fundamental aspect of training. I believe in apprenticeship: conscious observation and imitation, seasoned with critical questioning and experimentation. Presence is possible only in safe places, in moments of trust when ego-boundaries dissolve, or at least thin out. Training is the struggle to make places safe, to encourage trust in the middle of a social system that breeds danger and apprehension. The exercises described in this chapter are meant to suggest *a whole approach to performing*—one that encompasses staging, playwriting, and environmental design as well as performer training. I consider this whole approach traditional, though it is not the tradition of indus-

[4] Grotowski during an address at New York University, December 13, 1971.

trialized Western theater. Rather I draw from the traditions of communal peoples: the traditions of Asian theaters; the traditions of medieval and early Renaissance Western theater; the tradition of Greek theater before Aristotle. The roots of these traditions are joined.

The exercises presented here and the system that generates them are the barest beginnings toward refinding a traditional approach to performer training. The freedom of a tradition is identical to the freedom of a score. A score is tradition in miniature. I learned my work here and there, from different masters. And I have watched many people work and I have taken what I could from what I saw.

Most important by far has been the work of the performers of The Performance Group. No matter where an exercise comes from, or what associations it brings, once the performers begin working with it they make it their own. All training is one-to-one, extraordinarily intimate, the process of giving birth over and over again. Many exercises are found, worked on for a while, and then given up; perhaps they will return later, or be done again in a different way. A few exercises persist, especially those for the body core and the voice work. But no exercise is sacrosanct.

I don't write this chapter this chapter as a "how to" manual, a popular mechanics of environmental theater training. The exercises are offered as a concrete way of understanding some of what TPG does; and through the Group an insight into environmental theater as a whole. Also it is in the training that the problem of person vis-à-vis role is most poignantly put. To learn the exercises one must study with a teacher, not a book. And your teacher has had to have studied with his teacher; and so on. The avant-garde is the most radical (= to the roots) version of the traditional.

There are four steps to the performer's process. One doesn't go up these the way one goes up a staircase. They happen simultaneously, each feeding the others. The four steps are life-rhythms—like breathing, eating, sleeping; they sustain a performer without exhausting him. The four steps are:

1. Getting in touch with yourself.
2. Getting in touch with yourself face to face with others.
3. Relating to others without narrative or other highly formalized structures.
4. Relating to others within narrative or other highly formalized structures.

Performers skilled in these steps return to the beginnings about twice a year. They start with the most basic exercises (and what is most basic will vary from performer to performer) and play through them. In doing so they find new exercises for themselves and develop these on the spot. These new exercises are variations on themes—sometimes the variations are a long way from where the performer started. Doing the exercises means drawing on both their sources: disciplined patterns learned from a teacher and intimate impulses and associations evoked from deep within oneself. These impulses and associations express themselves within the discipline of the exercises, throughout the whole body and voice. The movements and sounds thus expressed become new disciplined patterns that are used to explore still more impulses and associations. In this way the work is self-generating.

One doesn't master the first phase before going on to the second. There is no such thing as absolute mastery. The work is like the horizon at sea—you always approach its finality without ever achieving it. Each step of the work depends on the others. For example, a performer gets in touch with himself only to the degree that he can relate to others. Each person finds his own way of doing the work. This personal search changes as people change, and the work changes as the group doing it changes. The work is intimate, but it cannot be done alone. Doing it alone converts it into meditation, which has great value but not for performance.

Just as there are cycles in every individual's approach to the work, so there are group cycles. The exercises are done in a space where individuals can see and hear each other. Even if a performer chooses to do the work absolutely alone, the energies of the others pass through him. Sometimes the work is done with partners or by the entire group practicing together. There are various techniques for this kind of group work. Periods of contact alternate with periods of solitude. Doing the exercises in a space where other people are also working—and where that work makes movements and sounds—subtly but deeply tunes people in to each other.

Each step of the work has exercises associated with it; these are:

1. Getting in touch with yourself: psychophysical-association exercises, basic verbophysical exercises in breathing, moving, resonating.
2. Getting in touch with yourself face to face with others:

taking in, giving over during partner work, name circles, exchanges, songs.

3. Relating to others without narrative or other highly formalized structures: witness games, confrontations, rolling, carrying, jumping, flying, trust exercises.

4. Relating to others within narrative or other highly formalized structures: improvisations, scenes, open workshops, rehearsals, open rehearsals, performances, scored roles.

The first two premises of the work are that the performer is a creator and that the performer is a worker who must not be exploited by directors, managers, producers, or audiences. The performer's responsibilities are that he cannot be self-indulgent or lazy, he must give over to the discipline of the work, and he must respect the work of others. Sooner or later the work affects his daily living—drugs are incompatible with this work, as is hysterical, depressive, or other pathological behavior. Even tobacco and alcohol interfere with the work by debilitating the body and siphoning energies. The performer learns to work for himself, to kick out his feelings even when he is scared or ashamed. Otherwise, if he keeps bottled up, he will be resentful of his colleagues and the work. All this adds up to performing as a life's work.

Process—a term used often in environmental theater—means "*getting* there" rather than "getting *there*," emphasis on the doing, not the done. But the differences between process and product are not absolute. For the spectator the play is a product. The task of environmental theater is to make process part of each performance. For the performer most of his daily work is process. If he knows where he's going and how he's going to get there, he cannot invent or discover in response to known and unknown obstacles. A performer deep in process is satisfied with *any point* in his work provided he is in touch with that point. The ultimate of the work is identical to its immediacy: to be alive to the here and now, to express oneself here and now. What an immense risk that is! Those who love products value things and make things of all living beings. Those who love process value living and make living beings of all things. Choose.

Many actors reject process; they think training is something that prepares them for performing. "Once I get through this," they say to themselves, "then I can perform, and perform." But training gains in importance as the person matures. Not only is

there new work to be learned, but there are habits to be un-
learned, long-hidden blocks suddenly revealed. The body offers
more resistance as a person gets older; each resistance must be
faced, understood, dealt with. Public success also threatens the
performer. The tendency is to freeze what the public applauds.
Without success the performer feels bitter; with it he cultivates
lies. Many young actors freeze themselves in a pathetic hope of
ambering their talents. They learn too late that creativity's cake
must always be eaten to be had.

Process = that state of being when the performer doesn't care
how he looks or sounds, is not even conscious of the effect of
his work. He gives over everything he is to the work at hand,
surrenders to the impulse, seeks only to make contact with his
partners. Process = participating concretely in the here and now.
Process = revealing associations, following wherever they lead,
to the very end.[5] Process is not improvisation or chaos. Both
improvisation and chaos are useful sometimes. But process is a
conversation between spontaneity and discipline. Discipline without process is mechanical; process without discipline is impossible.

All performing work begins and ends in the body. When I
talk of spirit or mind or feelings or psyche, I mean dimensions
of the body. The body is an organism of endless adaptability.
A knee can think, a finger laugh, a belly cry, a brain walk, and a
buttock listen. All the body's sensory, intellectual, and emotional
functions can be performed by many organs. Changes in mood
are reflected in changes in chemistry, blood pressure, breathing,
pulse, vascular dilation, sweating, and so on; and many so-called
involuntary activities can be trained and consciously controlled.
This is no news to yogis whose systems are based on the knowledge
that the body is one, interconnected whole. Furthermore, the body
doesn't end at the skin. The idea that people generate "auras"
of various kinds is true. Also group energies are greater than
and different from either individual energies or the sum of
individual energies.

For the purpose of training I isolated four body systems: gut,

---

[5] Except for physical violence, which I forbid not for aesthetic but for
ethical and practical reasons, there is nothing that *a priori* should not be
done on stage. As for physical violence I think there is an aesthetic advantage to *ritual combats*. In this matter I am deeply influenced by ethology.
I think man's performance behavior can be traced to roots in animal ceremony—especially mating dances and the displacement of aggression into
gestures of submission and triumph. See Konrad Lorenz's *On Aggression*.

spine, extremities, and face.[6] I arrived at this division after watching many performers for hundreds of hours. Time and again I saw people using only their hands and faces, illustrating play texts by reducing the art of acting to a kind of public speaking. I felt the most efficient way to help actors make contact with their bodies was initially to ignore the arms, hands, legs, and feet—forcing the actors to use their body cores.

The gut system is the source, the first house of performance. The gut begins in the mouth, nose, ears, eyes, and sinuses, focuses into the throat, then leads to the lungs and stomach; it includes all the organs of digestion; the heart; the liver, spleen, and bladder; the anal and urinary sphincters; the genitals. For all its many parts the gut is remarkably harmonic. Five rhythms interplay. For women there are seven: the swift, lifelong heartbeat; the powerful in-out of breathing; the slow but deep contractions of the digestive system; the contractions and release of excretion; the climaxes of sexual orgasm; the menstrual cycle; the gestation, birth, and nursing of infants. All these rhythms comprise the gut's primitive dialogue with the outside world. Food is separated into nourishment and waste; breath is separated into usable oxygen and exhaled carbon dioxide; seminal fluids and menstrual blood are discharged; occasionally a baby is started and brought into the world precocious and neotonous. Each gut system rhythm has its own clock, from the more than once a second of the heart to the once in nine months of birthing. Even in sleep the body is not shut off, just internalized; plainly there is a relationship between the gut system and dreaming.

But for all this activity many people I've worked with are dead in their guts. The first exercises help the performer get in touch with himself—let him know he has a gut: a complicated, willful, sometimes whimsical, powerful, and responsive lifeline in, through, and out from his center.[7]

> *Sphincters.* Stand with eyes closed, lower jaw relaxed, knees flexed just enough to maintain an erect posture. Con-

[6] Of course the body can be "divided" in many different ways, depending upon one's purposes and needs. Practitioners of hatha-yoga, for example, divide the body into Upper (head and neck), Middle (trunk, arms, hands, and genitals), and Lower (buttocks, rectum, legs, and feet).

[7] Both the Greek and the Hindu sense of center is of the navel, or of the area of the body between navel and genitals. Ditto for Buddhist opinion. The prenatal infant is connected to the mother directly from the gut; this fact of biology is carried over into mythology.

tract the lips into a tight circle, relax. Repeat. Then contract the anal and urinary sphincters, relax. Repeat. Then all sphincters in unison; sequentially in different rhythms; in different combinations. Repeat lying on back, on stomach.

Touching sound. Lie on back, eyes closed, relaxed. Inhale until lungs are full. Hands over the bottom of the belly so one can feel the diaphragm working. Let the breath out with no attempt either to make or to inhibit sound. Usually there is a slight touching of sound, an "ahhhhhhhhh."

Panting. Position as in touching sound. Breathe in and out first slowly and then more rapidly through the mouth. Don't cheat—don't take a lungful of air and let it out in bursts. True panting is a way of breathing; it can be maintained indefinitely. After panting soundlessly pant with sound, each pant having its own sound. Pant up and down the scales. Pant a song.

Swallowing. Stand relaxed, jaws loose but mouth closed. Gather spit and then swallow it slowly, feeling it go down the throat and into the stomach. Take a mouthful of banana, chew it for a full minute, swallow it slowly. Trace the route of the banana on the outside of the chest with your hand.

Touching sound and ﹅panting are basic vocal exercises; the voice is part of the gut system. Through these exercises the performer learns to acknowledge the workings of his gut—breathing, salivating, swallowing, gurgling, burping, rumbling, farting, excreting. The first lesson is to become aware that *something is always going on in the body.* Then the performer learns that the guts begin in and around his face and end in and around his anus and genitals. Slowly the work makes connections between these terminals, moving from both ends into the middle. The performer senses that his breathing is a way of getting the outside into the center of his body, and that vocal production—of sounds or words or songs—is a way of letting the outside know what is going on inside the body. The first vocalizations are versions of gut-sounds: gurgles, sobs, heaves, gags, vomits, spits; then laughs, cries, shrieks; finally tones, scales, songs.

At the start many performers are unaware of their *body cores,* unable to locate their centers. These people must learn to stand still, to listen to themselves from the inside, not to resist impulses originating in the gut. I tell beginners to relax the face, forget about the hands, and express what they feel by varying the depth and rhythm of their breathing.

In each person's search for his center the director must be careful not to intrude. Some people have high centers, others low;

some have off-center centers. The director must not impose his own sense of center on the performer. People with weak senses of their center are very open to suggestion; an eager director can badly mislead a struggling performer. At most the director approaches the performer with his hands, touching the performer, helping him feel the outer shape of the body.

Wherever an individual's deep center is, there are surface spots at the base of the neck, the base of the spine, the navel, the anus, and the genitals that are terminals—places where body energy comes to and flows from. These points are contact areas on the body surface for energy centers deep in the body core. Body core exercises start with an awareness of these surface contact areas. Slowly the performer begins to follow the lines of energy from these contact areas to deep sources within the body core. The exercises include reacting to the environment through breathing rhythm, speaking words without intonation—expression coming entirely from variations in breathing rhythm and contractions and flexings of the body core, especially the stomach muscles.

Such exercises are part of the second step of the work. Before learning them in detail the performer learns several basic psychophysical association exercises: the head, hip, and body rolls—all gut exercises.

Head roll.[8] Standing relaxed. Locate the joint at the base of the neck. This is usually prominent when the head is bent slightly forward. Begin rotating the head, in either direction, pivoting from the joint at the base of the neck. Do not push the head but let it fall in every direction in turn. The head falls forward, a slight energy moves it to one side until it falls in that direction, then a slight energy moves it back until it falls backward, then a slight energy to the other side, then forward again, etc. The head rolls with no predetermined rhythm. The rhythm will naturally adapt itself to the associations; and the rhythm will change, perhaps frequently. Breathing is deep and adapts itself to what's happening. Usually the eyes are closed.

Hip roll. Standing relaxed. Slowly bend over until the head is hanging between the legs. Shake out vigorously. Instructor forcefully taps the flat bone at the base of the spine. Slowly rise and stand relaxed. Then gently begin a

[8] The head roll is a gut exercise because it does not deal with the surface of the face or scalp but with the insides of the face. The movement of the head, pivoting from the base of the neck, stimulates the digestive system and causes reactions throughout the rest of the guts.

circular motion of the pelvis originating from the flat bone at the base of the spine—not unlike the grind of a stripper's bump-and-grind. The pelvis is rotated as if there were something in front that it is moving toward and something behind it is moving toward. Do not rotate the upper thighs and knees, or the whole trunk. Isolate the pelvis. Often people will rotate the pelvis too vigorously, shutting out many rhythms and associations.

Body roll. Standing relaxed. Slowly bend over as at the start of the hip roll. From this position rotate the body first to the side, then back, then to the other side, and then forward. The entire torso rolls on the joint at the base of the spine.

Hands and shoulders relaxed. Make sure the head goes all the way back and hangs loose. Tension causes great difficulties and can result in serious muscle strains.

This exercise often causes dizziness and nausea at first. Invariably people lose balance and fall. Sometimes there is vomiting—especially if a person has eaten less than two hours before work. Also there is severe anxiety because of the sudden and continuous shifts in body attitudes. When a person is all the way back, he is open, vulnerable to attack on the face, neck, throat, chest, stomach, and genitals. This defenseless position is followed at once by the very protected position of the head tucked between the legs and the gut and genitals shielded by the back and buttocks.

If the body roll is done regularly, and correct breathing maintained, the dizziness, nausea, and loss of footing will, in most cases, pass. Breathe in while the head is falling back, and breathe out when the head is falling forward. Do not try to control the depth of the breathing or the overall rhythm of the exercise.

These difficult exercises are not gymnastics. There is no perfect way of doing them, no ideal model that the beginner emulates. The prescribed movements are an armature, a framework that can be discarded once the performer finds his own way. At first, however, the instructor must help beginners sense their blocks. The instructor insists that the basic movements are accomplished; that the body is relaxed; that the breathing is free and deep. Points of tension are the neck, shoulders, thighs, anal and genital sphincters, throat. The head roll depends on letting the head go all the way back, all the way to the side, all the way front. The body roll depends on letting the head go all the way back, on keeping the shoulders and arms relaxed, on pivoting the whole upper body on the joint at the base of the spine. Beginners like to hold on, to keep their heads looking forward; their breathing is shallow and forced; they are grim and silent. A common fantasy accompanying the dizziness, falling, and vomiting is that the body will break open and all kinds of horrid things will spill out: shit, vomit, urine, half-digested food, foul gases, the guts themselves—all the dark secrets of the inside. These fears are physicalizations of psychic facts. In truth, the association exercises will help the performer spill his guts.

I keep talking about "associations" without once explaining what I mean. Associations ought not to be defined before a performer has experienced them. Silence and teaching the mechanics are the best rules for the first weeks of work. If a performer insists, saying, "I won't go on unless you explain!" keep quiet. Let him make up his own mind. It is his choice to stay or go. From the start he learns that *this is his work, he does it for himself, he takes responsibility for it.*

An association is something private. It is presumptuous for one person to define it for another. All I can do is say what associations have been for me. When I let my head go, give over to my body, do the exercise without judging myself, without measuring against an ideal; and if I am working in a *safe place,* a space where I do not fear intrusion, spying, or the judgment of others, then I begin to "think my own thoughts." For myself these have sometimes been like daydreams—fantasies of things I wanted or feared; or talking to myself; or hypnagogic hallucinations; [9] or even realities identical to night dreams. Sometimes my associations have been states of exaltation, raised body-consciousness; sometimes a feeling of ecstasy or separation from the body—like floating, astral projection, or levitation; sometimes a heightened awareness of part of my body as when I felt I was laughing with the small of my back while doing a back bend. Often I think of the exercise itself, of when it will be over, of what people think of me doing it, of how it may help me, and so on. I consider these kinds of thoughts to be blocks.

Association exercises are a way of surrendering to the body. They give experiences counter to the view that the mind and body are separate entities in relentless combat. There is no "mind over body" or "body over mind" in the association exercises. The exercises lead to "whole body thinking" in which feelings flow

[9] According to Freud (1961, written 1900), hypnagogic hallucinations "are images, often very vivid and rapidly changing, which are apt to appear —quite habitually in some people—during the period of falling asleep; and they may also persist for a time after the eyes have been opened."

to and from all parts of the body with no distinction between "body" and "mind." Associations last anywhere from a few seconds to an hour or more. One can't force associations any more than one can force night dreams. But there are ways to follow associations through to the end. During an association there are choices—an image or feeling (or whatever the association is) "presents" itself, then another, and another. Usually, at some moment, two associations will occur simultaneously, or a dull weariness will appear to drown out an association. The performer has the chance to choose which association to focus on, or whether or not to let the level of drowsiness rise so that all associations are washed out. The important thing is that the performer make his choice instantly about which association to follow. Because there is a choice, one has the option of ending the associations by considering the alternatives. But if one chooses randomly and immediately, the associations will usually continue, often in an unexpected direction. I used to think the performer should pick the more "difficult" association—the one he feared most—but such choosing would reflect judgment, a removal from the immediacy of the situation. An instant, random choice allows the performer to stay with the flow. As for a rising level of drowsiness there is no way to fight it and maintain a free flow. Instead, if one allows the drowsiness full play, perhaps even falling asleep, new associations may occur.

An association ends when it ends. For me there is a sudden blankness at the end, or a sharp return to the place where I'm working. Sometimes I realize that the ending is false, that I've cut off prematurely. There's no way to know for sure, and one shouldn't worry about it. Going to the very end means going as far as one can at this time.[10]

[10] The technique of random expression of inner states is the chief technique of psychoanalysis. The difference being that in analysis the body is kept generally still, and the expression is verbalized. The technique is also like "stream of consciousness" and "automatic writing" techniques popular earlier in the century. All of these techniques are related to the belief that underneath surface phenomena resides a more primitive, more true (that is, less conditioned by social circumstances) human consciousness. This is a modern, Western version of old worldwide beliefs in the multiplicity of consciousness and the existence of many parallel, simultaneous realities. Arieti (1948a, 1948b) connects the way schizophrenics think with dreams and free association. He says this way has a special logic which he calls "paleologic"—old logic. This paleologic is not causal, not Aristotelian. It works by linking predicates rather than subjects, and is entirely concrete. Paleologic creates *private languages* that must be interpreted to be comprehended. Poetry is a form of semiprivate language, an art form with

At first doing the exercises will result in muscle pain, physical exhaustion, loss of breath, and dizziness. One should push through these obstacles. But sharp pains—cramps, stabs, straining tendons and ligaments—are signals to ease off. Otherwise damage may be done. Injuries caused by overexertion are symptoms of fears of getting in too close a touch with oneself. Overzealousness leading to injury is pseudo-heroism. Properly done, the exercises help each person strike a balance between the disciplined demands of the work and the limits of the body. The exercises are themselves paradigms of environmental theater where performing is a combination of the scored mise-en-scène and the free-flowing feelings and personal associations of each performer.

I've described only three gut exercises out of dozens. The head, hip, and body rolls are step one exercises. There are gut exercises for step two. The step one exercises can become step two if they are done with partners. For example, the body roll can be done with one person rolling and another kneeling behind keeping a hand on the flat bone at the base of the spine. The kneeling performer harmonizes his breathing with the person rolling. The contact between the two performers will expand until it includes a constellation of body signals—breathing, touch, sweat, smell, vocalizations. Each person will have his own associations, but these will occur in a context of expanded consciousness, in the space shared by the two performers.

Stephen Borst, who has been doing the exercises for several years, says of them:

> It's important for me to experience the mortality of my body. Every day I begin the association exercises again and have to overcome gravity again. There is no final solution to these problems. I laugh and cry at the same time so much because of the incredible irony of the desire to be infinite—and fly—and the absolute mortality of the body. It is finally a great laugh-cry to experience these simultaneously.

Other gut system exercises include "taking in," an exercise that relates swallowing-vomiting to what a person sees and ties

---

just enough public language to make it accessible. The associations a performer has are not shown as such to the audience. These associations underly the *public languages* of performance. Workshops and rehearsals are necessary so that the performer can become aware of his associations and in order to find objective correlatives linking these private associations to the public languages of performance. I am indebted to Ralph Ortiz for bringing Arieti's work to my attention.

Photograph 29. Makbeth's *first* banquet—invented by TPG. Duncan is arriving at Inverness: He is the meal's main course. Awaiting him, the Makbeths and their friends devour each other. The three Dark Powers stand to one side, intervening only to serve one person to another. Throughout the meal they sing Shakespeare's lines to the tune of "Happy Days Are Here Again." (*Frederick Eberstadt*)

breathing rhythms to digestive rhythms; snout and tasting exercises such as the one with the basket of fruit described in Chapter 1; listening exercises in which performers translate what they hear inside their own bodies into movements of the gut and/or into vocalizations.

Many gut exercises are about eating—taking something into the body and transforming it. In July, 1971, I ran an exercise with the workshop students at the University of Rhode Island that carried some of these themes through to a conclusion. (Improvisations like this are part of step four work.)

A circle with a clearly defined center. Everyone around the circle, no one in it.

Someone goes into the center and offers himself as the Meal. He closes his eyes and keeps them closed until the end of his participation in the center. If the Meal opens his eyes and sees the Eater(s), he cannot participate further but must leave the exercise. This provision is necessary because the Meal must give himself over entirely to his fantasies concerning the Eaters, and the Eaters must enjoy absolutely the liberties of anonymity.

The Meal awaits the Eaters who come in any number. They make no noise except what is necessary for eating. They may eat anywhere and anything on the Meal's body, but without causing sharp pain or injury. They may nibble, suck, lick, and bite—but not bruise, draw blood, or in any way treat the Meal violently. If Eaters feel violence, they should express it in the fierceness with which they chew, swallow, and breathe. The Eaters may undress the Meal and position him. The Meal remains passive—he belongs to the Eaters.

While being eaten the Meal utters whatever sounds are there; he lets his breathing rhythms go free.

Witnesses around the periphery of the circle keep silent, contacting the action with their eyes and breathing rhythms. They can move to observe, or to get away from seeing. They may enter the circle and become Eaters whenever they wish.

Eaters may leave the Meal whenever they wish. When the Meal is alone, or when the Meal says "stop" (which he may do at *any time*), the director makes sure that everyone has returned to the periphery of the circle before allowing the Meal to open his eyes. The Meal then takes in *everyone* around the circle before returning to the periphery himself.

A new Meal offers himself. The exercise continues until there are no more Meals and/or no more Eaters.

This exercise is one of many about cannibalism. Some of this work has found its way into performance—for example, the cannibalistic banquets of *Makbeth*. Eating exercises that come from listening to the sounds within the body and the vocalizing these and using the vocalizations as the basis of a dance took on for the Group in 1970 a definite and repeatable pattern: that of identifying, fattening, murdering, cannibalizing, and resurrecting a group leader, or scapegoat. Philip Slater has detected the same pattern in Training Groups: "What is particularly compelling about the attack [on the leader] is the variety of fantasy themes associated with it: themes of group murder, of cannibalism, of orgy." [11] I am especially interested in these themes because they are basic dramatic stories, found in innumerable variations in many cultures. Tragedy can be viewed as a cannibalistic sharing of a leader's special power, the distribution of his *mana*. No wonder Aristotle found the effects of tragedy cathartic—working directly on the guts. I feel that the essential theatrical themes do not find their only, or even chief, sources in literature but in the experiences of the body.

For each of the body systems—gut, spine, extremities, face— there are association exercises, partner work, trust exercises, confrontations, and improvisations. But the work is not dry, as such cataloging may make it seem. The majority of exercises happen only once. When the director understands the work, he learns how to create exercises on the spot, letting go into his own impulses and associations, in this way strengthening his ability to contribute. The director risks failure along with the performers; he trains his skills slowly. It is not necessary to finish every exercise or complete a round so that everyone has a chance to do an exercise. Work will begin, some performers will participate, and then the work may be put aside. I have returned to some exercises after more than a year of letting them stand incomplete. Occasionally an exercise is so appropriate that it is used over and over. The work is systematic but not linear.

I could describe much of what happens at every workshop over a year's time. That would fill many thick volumes but wouldn't bring the reader closer to the essence of the work. The work congeals around those performers whose problems and bursts of growth show themselves suddenly and must be dealt with immediately; it grows when the director is in a fertile,

[11] Slater (1966), 24.

imaginative period; it grows when the group senses itself and peer relationships replace parent-child relationships. I am not giving here a chronological account of the work.

I start work on the spine system simultaneously with work on the gut. These two systems are so basic to performer development, and so closely linked to each other, that neither can be given primacy. (Work on the extremities and face is deferred.) The spine system runs from the joint at the base of the neck used as the pivot for the head roll to the flat bone at the base of the backbone used as the pivot for the hip and body rolls. At these joints the spine and gut systems meet.

The spine supports the body core and contains it as in a large basket. The spine is not rigid; it is flexible, supple, like a strong tree that gives in wind. Chronic back trouble plagues more performers than any other complaint. Backs are stiff, locked, tight; there are pulled muscles, spasms, wrenches, and vague, persistent pains at the base of the spine. Sometime the cause of back troubles is a weak set of stomach muscles. But often back complaints are psychogenic. The base of the spine and its surrounding musculature is a magnet for every kind of anxiety and archaic fear. The spine exercises contact these fears, helping the performer to grow aware of them and confront them, working through them. Sometimes it's as easy as bringing an association out to be recognized, and the the back muscles relax and the body is liberated. Usually it's not so easy.

There are three kinds of association exercises for the spine: bends, balances, and separations.

Bends. Mechanically these are simple—the difficulty is in doing them slowly and not blanking out on the associations. Breathing should be free; the performer should make whatever sounds he wants.

Note: few people can do these exercises completely at the start. Don't strain. Do as much as possible. As time passes, there will be improvement. The exercises develop self-trust if done easily and persistently. Letting yourself do it is as important as being able to do it.

Kneeling back bend. Kneel with the thighs, buttocks, and back all in one line. Then slowly, vertebra by vertebra, starting from the base of the neck, go over until the head touches the ground in front of you. Keep the head relaxed, the shoulders and arms relaxed. Breathe through a slightly open mouth. Then slowly, vertebra by vertebra, lift with the energy coming from the joint at the base of the spine. Continue upward past the upright starting position, let the head fall back, and slowly bend backward until the head touches the ground behind you. Keep the back arched, and the shoulders and arms relaxed. Once the head is touching the ground, slowly rotate it as far as possible to one side and then to the other. Then lift, maintaining the arch in the back. The energy center is the small of the back, as if you're being gently pushed up. Use the muscles in the back and stomach, not in the thighs and shoulders. Do not swim up—flow up.

Repeat several times.

Standing back bend. This is the same as the kneeling back bend except that the performer is standing. Drop the body core forward until the head is between the legs. Then lift yourself, vertebra by vertebra, beginning at the base of the spine, until upright. Let the head fall back, and slowly bend backward, keeping shoulders and arms relaxed, until the hands touch the floor. Then support yourself with the hands, maintaining an arch in the back, making a full, round bridge. Then lift, maintaining the arch in the back. The energy center is the small of the back.

Repeat several times.

Note: These bends usually cannot be done completely at the start. Go back as far as is comfortable, and as far as one can recover using the muscles of the back and stomach. Steadily, over the weeks, the performer will be able to go back farther until the entire movement is possible.

The kneeling and standing back bends make excellent partner exercises. Give over to the partner who does most of the muscle work. In the kneeling back bend especially the partner straddles the one bending and carefully lets him down. Then, after the head has touched the ground and been rotated, the performer's head is lifted a few inches off the ground, and the whole torso is vigorously bounced up and down. The partner is careful not to let the other's head hit the floor. Both people let out sounds. A variation of the standing back bend is for the partner to help the other come from the first position to the upright position by gently rotating the head and making certain that the neck muscles are relaxed. Then, when the performer is upright, the partner literally drops the performer's head back, cradling it so that there is no muscle pull. These exercises—somewhere between step two and step three work—build trust; they ought not to be done by people who do not trust each other. There are other exercises to initiate trust and confront mistrust.

Balance exercises are all well known. From yoga there are

various headstands, shoulder stands, and tree poses. Always the temptation is to rush through the balance exercises, showing off how well one does them. In fact, the balance exercises are excellent meditations. Also, when one is upside down, it is comparatively easy to sense the separations between the vertebrae, tensions in the shoulders, chest, pelvis, spine, and legs. Each tension can be relaxed while maintaining balance. Upside down, the body is like a set of children's blocks, each standing on the other rather precariously. The job is to build the blocks higher, in different arrangements, and then to move them around without toppling.

Each exercise evokes different associations in each performer —but there is one associational pattern I have observed repeatedly during the headstand. When a group all stand on their heads together and begin talking to each other, they seem to become children between the ages of five and eight. Voices rise in pitch, giggling begins, tensions subside, and a special euphoria takes over.

Separations help performers experience different parts of the body as individual units. Particularly helpful are lifting the torso from the bottom of the rib cage and rotating it first to the left and then to the right; lifting the shoulder from a relaxed, or bottom, position, to a middle position, to a high position; turning the neck sharply from center to either hard left or hard right; rotating the whole torso as far as possible to the left and to the right while keeping the arms at shoulder level and moving the head either in the direction of the rotation or in the opposite direction.

Let me emphasize that these are association exercises, not gymnastics. Nothing is worse for the performer than "movement exercises" or abstract "body work." Don't treat the body as a thing. *Your body is not your "instrument"; your body is you.*

The third system is the extremities—shoulders, arms, elbows, wrists, hands, fingers; thighs and buttocks, legs, knees, ankles, feet, toes. There are exercises for each of these. Some can be done simultaneously with exercises for other body systems. For example, one may do the hip roll and a hand roll at the same time. In fact, the exercises for the extremities are, in part, variations of exercises for the gut and spine systems. The extremity exercises are rolls, shakes, wiggles, throws, grasps, and separations. It is important that the performer understand the amount and complexity of the creative work a hand, a foot, or a finger can do. Because people are so naturally expressive with their hands—hands and speech are intimately linked—they forget that the hands can be developed as independent, primary means of communication, as indeed they are for the deaf or in the mudra system of Indian theater. In some cultures the feet are almost as well developed communicators as the hands.

Exercises for the face start with total relaxation of the facial mask. And a mask is exactly what the face is. Early in life people learn to "put on a face," and the repertory of faces grows until it is nearly endless. Each person has an extensive repertory with limitless variations adapting automatically to the situation at hand. Among the apparently well behaved American middle class, politeness often means controlling the face so that little or no expression shows. A model of American heroism is the "poker face," a blank expression concealing all feeling. Anyone who, as an adult, has reexamined the way he uses his face is bound to have discovered his own clichés, as unmistakable as his handwriting. To relax the face one lets the lower jaw go slack, mouth slightly open, with no attempt to control drooling. Breathing is deep, eyes droopy, cheeks patted loose. Many exercises retain a relaxed face as a way of encouraging body core expression. But other exercises work on the face mask itself.

> *Pulling in, stretching out.* Two performers sit opposite each other. *A* begins to work his face into a doglike snout. He closes his eyes, tenses and points his lips, sucks his chin in, collapes his cheeks, etc. *B* helps him by telling him what parts of his face need working. Both performers use their hands to help *A* mold his face. As soon as *A* has pulled in as much as he can, he slowly, step by step, relaxes his face, letting it pass through a normal mask and then into a stretching out—making everything as wide as possible: gaping mouth, stretched cheeks, bugged eyes, raised eyebrows, extended neck. Again *B* helps. Then *B* does the exercise with the help of *A*.

The face exercises can be extended to the whole body, which takes on the qualities of the facial masks. Sound and movement are produced naturally as a consequence of the total physicalization. Making these extreme masks by the entire group at once can lead to extraordinary improvisations and confrontations.

Only rarely are associations or gestures uncovered by the exercises kept for performances. The main purpose of the exercises is to help people get in touch with themselves, find relationships with others, develop group consciousness, relate inner states to outer states. The exercises are a way of limbering up the association process so that the performer will be able to contact his feelings during performances. The exercises help the performer feel more comfortable with sudden, sometimes unpredictable, changes in mood and expression; swift flashes of anger and joy; and the majestically capricious manner in which body states evoke feeling states and vice versa. I say capricious because changes occur suddenly, unexpectedly, making connections that are as refreshing as they are far-fetched. Links that couldn't possibly be thought up, images that couldn't be invented, happen and stick. In a real way the performer is broadened and deepened; his self-awareness grows. Ultimately, the score of a performance works the way the exercises do: as evocative circumstances within which dangerous and astonishing connections are made not by effort, cunning, or preplanning, but in the natural flow of events, as if by accident. The greater the distance between cause and effect, the better. In doing the work the performer concentrates entirely on causes, on following the process through. What it looks like, what it sounds like, is of no matter to him. These things are considered later, during discussions of the work; they are the primary province of the director who keeps a trained outside eye on the effects of the work and the possible use of these effects in a mise-en-scène.

Thus far I've described exercises that pertain mostly to the first step of performer development. The second step—getting in touch with yourself face to face with others—means expressing what's in you even though there's another person facing you, watching you. That's a very hard thing to do—it means keeping the in-touchness of the first step, with open channels throughout the body, while being conscious of another person. This other person is also keeping his in-touchness in front of you. The relationship between the two people is *not dialogue*. The performers are not trying to say something *to* each other. Each is expressing himself. Dialogue is give-and-take. Being face to face is all give: training the performer to express himself without fear of judgment, his own or another's. Trusting himself to be himself here and now in front of another.

In the theater, at least, a performer has to trust his partners. Once there is trust, almost anything can happen. Before you can trust others you have to learn to trust yourself. The first step of performer development takes the most time because it is so difficult for a person to learn to trust his own impulses. The second step expands the circle of trust to include at least one other person. It is important that while working on this second step the performer not "act" or "pursue objectives" or in any way mask his personal commitment, or ease over the difficulty of what he is doing. A simple starting exercise of step two work—an exercise I often use at the first workshop—is the "Name Circle."

> Everyone sit in a circle. One person names the others, one at a time, taking enough time to look at each person carefully, readjusting breathing rhythms and body behavior. If there is a mistake, a lapse, or a change in name, these are corrected by the person whose name has been forgotten, mispronounced, distorted, or mistaken. After one person finishes naming everyone, another begins.

Sometimes people take new names, or are given new names, that stick. The names of the characters in *Commune* were found in the "Name Circle," and the exercise itself was part of the performance for nearly a year. The "Name Circle" is an exercise that can be done repeatedly, especially to relax tensions and bring people back to a basic corroboration of each other. Sometimes a person going around the circle forgets to name himself. He should be told, "You have forgotten someone."

A somewhat more complicated step two exercise is "Dressing and Undressing."

> Everyone puts an article of his clothing in the center of a circle and then sits around the circle. A person goes to the center and begins telling a story about himself. As he talks, he takes off some or all of his clothes and puts on as much or as little of the clothing in the circle as he wants. He wears the new clothing either conventionally or in new ways—a T-shirt as pants, for example.
>
> The performer concentrates on changing clothes, not on the story he is telling, which therefore may become halting, rambling, incoherent.
>
> When there are no more clothes in the circle, or when no one enters to tell a story, this phase of the exercise is over.
>
> Then people go to those whose clothes they are wearing and return the clothes by slowly undressing and handing the articles back to their owners. Everyone dresses in his own clothes.

Most people have trouble telling their story while sorting through the clothes, dressing, and undressing. However, when they give themselves to the action of the clothes, their story gets freer, more self-expressive, less set-up; it takes on the rhythm of the story-teller. The costume assembled by the performer also reflects his mood, and frequently fishes things from far inside.

In "Dressing and Undressing" the director reminds the performer to keep exchanging clothes as long as he is in the center, and to keep talking. Even if the performer is "talking nonsense," the director persists in urging him to continue; it is frequently in nonsense that the most powerful associations occur. Also, while the performer's conscious attention is occupied by a simple task, deeper things come through.

Neither the "Name Circle" nor "Dressing and Undressing" stretches language toward song or brings into play the parts of the body where breath, guts, and speaking converge. The confrontation hip roll does.

> Two people face each other, about three feet apart. Each begins the hip roll. After a few seconds each person begins to *speak words*. These words are not spoken to the other, they are not dialogue. They are spoken in front of the other person, with the eyes open and looking at the other person. Energies flow back and forth but not as dialogue.

Confrontation hip roll is the fundamental verbophysical exercise. The presence of the other stimulates a response; a feedback situation develops. The responses are in words because the process of the exercise is to give verbal life to physical impulses, to allow the performer to distort the sound of words while not losing the ability to say words.

Glassy eyes, looking away, shut eyes, stopping the roll, dialogue or anger at the director, dialogue with the other performer, all indicate blocks. Patience and persistence is the best course for the director to take. Sometimes a bitter confrontation between one or both of the participants and the director is unavoidable. Then the director must not hold back his feelings, whatever they are. When carried through, the confrontation hip roll releases tensions from a deep level, often a sexual level, and the performer reveals things—to himself as well as to others—that he maybe was unaware of. The confrontation hip roll is the first exercise using words where the performer discovers what he feels while he is doing the exercise. It is in the realm of dis/covery rather than expression.

Another verbophysical exercise is the "Open Sound."

A performer goes to the center of the circle, lies on his back, eyes closed. Others go to him, touch him at places of tension, talk to him, helping him relax and getting his breathing in touch with his feelings. Then the performer touches sound; the sound should come through unobstructed. If there is a catch in the throat, or anywhere, a tightness in the chest, a failure to breathe deeply, the others tell the performer about it.

The performer's head is tilted back so that the air passage from throat to lungs is absolutely straight. Often, as he continues to make sounds, he is lifted onto the back of one or two others and bent over so that the spine is relaxed and the body lies in an arch. Sometimes he is lifted and carried, jogged slightly. Someone is always near his neck and head supporting them so that the performer can relax completely. Others are near his stomach and genitals. There is a great deal of touching, pressing, stroking, and whispering.

The sounds that come out of the performer are often very deep and perhaps frightening if one has not heard them before. A backlog of sounds is run: tears, sobs, laughter, shrieks. Sometimes it is not possible to tell if the person is belly-laughing or belly-crying.

The exercise frequently goes through two or more complete cycles of rising and subsiding sounds. The director must be careful not to cut the exercise off short. The rhythms of the completed exercise are: lying back and breathing—soft sound —tilting head back and louder sounds—lifting—carrying— very loud sounds—putting down—sobbing/laughing—relaxed, quiet breathing.

When the performer is exhausted, literally empty of sounds, and is put down for the last time, he is asked to open his eyes and take in the others one at a time. Someone kneels at the performer's head so that he does not have to use any muscles other than his eyes to go around the circle. Contact is maintained until everyone has been taken in.

No rush. A single performer may take as long as a half hour with this exercise.

Other verbophysical exercises are "Song and Dance" and "Foot Song."

"Song and Dance." Everyone lies on his back. Then one person rises and sings a verse of a well-known song. Those who know the song sing along, but only one verse. Then another person, another verse, and so on, with less and less time between verses until there is a spontaneous flow of song on song, a kind quick-changing game of follow-the-leader.

Accompanying each song are movements, with the originator of the song being the leader and the singers the followers.

Ultimately there develops a flow of songs and dances that is spontaneous yet familiar.

"Foot Song." Everyone lies on his back. One person up at a time. This person touches ones lying using only his feet. He talks-sings while touching people with his feet. Words are not thought out. People on the ground make sounds without words. The person standing has his eyes open; others have their eyes shut.

After everyone has been the person using feet, everyone gets up together, eyes closed, sensing each other only by using bodies and feet, no hands or faces.

Each of these verbophysical exercises is part of a comprehensive verbophysical wheel. Every kind of sound on the wheel is connected to all the other sounds; and each is a function of breathing/moving, the wheel's hub.

Have each performer go around the wheel in either direction without missing any stop.

An interesting step two exercise that combines speaking and doing is "Locating a Relationship in the Body." This exercise is from March, 1970, when the Group was first dealing with the problem of "body thinking."

After the association exercises everyone squat. One at a time people go to others and say something. The director helps people find the places in their bodies that the words show in or relate to.

This exercise works out differently every time it is done. In April, 1970:

> M. to W.: I have trouble dealing with my mortality.
> Director to M.: What do you mean?
> M.: I can't explain it. [*Pause.*] It's about death, about time.
> Director: Where do you feel it in your body?
> M.: I don't know exactly. I feel high. Like I'm floating.
> [*He breathes deeply.*]
> Director: Where else?
> M.: In my knees.
> Director: Let it gather there, let the feeling come together
> there. Deal with your mortality and death from your knees.
> [*M. slowly collapses from his knees and falls over hard
> on the floor, ending spread-eagle, legs very stiff.*]

.   .   .   .   .

> S. to I.: I blocked you out and I don't want to. [*This
> spoken very quietly, almost as if taking it back or talking
> to himself.*]
> Director: Shout. [*S. does.*] Louder. [*Director helps S. into
> a back bend to open his voice.*] Now, again [*S. shouts from
> this position and makes contact.*]
> L.: [*Shouting back, but his words are slurred.*] I don't
> want to either!

These confrontations are banal; they are not the great poetry of
drama. But feelings acknowledged, no matter how banal, are the
sources of genuine performing, no matter how poetic. The greatest
block is fear—fear of seeming banal and trivial, fear of appearing
foolish, fear of shame. Once the performer is able to give up
his mask of being special and great, and his mask of being
polite and in good taste, and his mask of "I won't let myself be
found out," he is ready to start experiencing the feelings of sublime
poetry. W. B. Yeats:

> I must lie down where all the ladders start,
> In the foul rag-and-bone shop of the heart.

Step three of the performer's process is relating to others without narrative or other highly formalized structures. Step three
is about trust, relating, witnessing, and sharing.

> *"Making Friends."* Go to someone in the room, take him
> to another place in the room that is safe for you, play a
> game with him that is fun for both of you.

Not so easy, most of the time "Making Friends" ends amid a ruin
of small talk and awkwardness or pretended fun. Lives are spent
pretending we're enjoying a situation in which we share space

with people we don't know. Step three goes back to the beginnings of relatedness.

Simple movement exercises help people tune in to their partners.

"At His Pace" (from Catherine Farinon-Smith). A person begins to walk or move around the space. Someone joins and tries to move at the same pace. This is not slavish imitation but a try at getting inside the movement of the other, giving yourself over to the other.

"Looking Back." A person crosses from one side of the space to another. A second person does the same. Their paths cross. After passing each other both stop, turn, look back, take each other in, and continue on their ways.

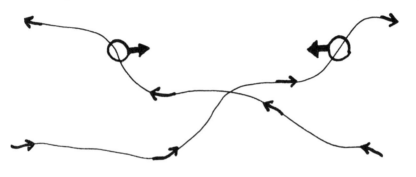

"Blind Leader." Someone is blindfolded and put in the center of the group. The others protect him from danger. The blind person leads the others. They surround and follow the blind leader. The leader doesn't know where he's going because he's blind. The others follow a blind leader for whose safety they are responsible.

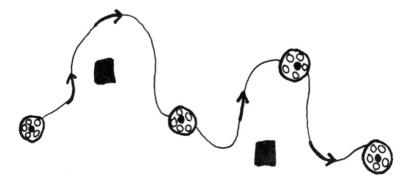

"Surge." Everyone stand against a wall. One person on impulse moves to another wall, or large object in the room. Everyone follows, moving in the same way as the first person (walking, running, crawling, etc.). Everyone bunches up, breathes deeply, relaxes, spreads out. Someone else moves on impulse, and so on.

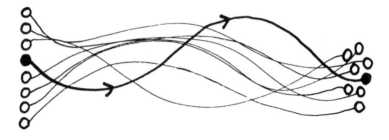

"Swarm." A leaderless group moving together at the same speed in the same manner.

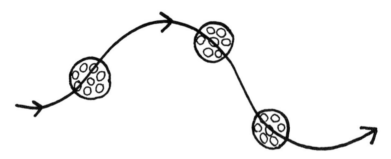

These simple exercises put people in touch with each other, with the group. Other exercises such as "Trust" or "Flying" help performers learn the physical basis of trust.

"Trust." Group forms a tight circle no more than five feet in diameter. Someone goes to the center, closes his eyes, and begins to fall in one direction or another, maintaining enough rigidity in his body so that he topples over like a tree. He is caught by the others, returned to an upright position, passed around the circle, lifted overhead, etc.

"Flying." Group lines up in two columns facing each other, arms outstretched forming a landing cradle. Someone goes to a high place, five to eight feet, and jumps off into the arms of those waiting.

The Living Theater used "Flying" in *Mysteries,* and The Performance Group uses it in *Commune.* Many exercises can be invented from the principle that the individual needs the group and that each member of the group needs every other member. If this is not true, it is good to find out early and take the necessary steps.

A more complicated situation is one in which the feelings and fantasies regarding group trust are given play. Hostility, aggression, resentment, betrayal, and anger are all possible outcomes of doubts regarding trust. Hidden affection is also the result of doubts regarding trust. Self-pity, which is usually a compound feeling, needs to be broken down into its components of affection, betrayal, fear, and anger.

> *"Rolling."* A rectangle of mats about thirty by fifteen feet. A person presents himself by lying down on one of the ends of the rectangle. He closes his eyes and relaxes. He puts his hands over his head so as not to roll on them. Three or four others come to him and begin rolling him. They roll him up the rectangle to the other end, stop, and then roll him back. They are careful not to roll him off the mats, twist his body, pull his hair, etc. The person being rolled makes whatever sounds are there. The rollers are silent. The exercise continues until there are less than three rollers or until the one being rolled says "Stop." Then another person presents himself, and so on.

I first did "Rolling" at Goddard College in September, 1970. Resentments had been building, and tempers were short. There were some direct confrontations among members of the Group, but bad feelings persisted. One performer in particular felt she couldn't trust the others. I asked her to pick three people she trusted least and three she trusted most. Then she was the one rolled with the three people she trusted most rolling her. As the exercise went on, I substituted the three she trusted least. The substitutions were done in such a way so as not to disrupt the rhythms of rolling. When she opened her eyes at the end of the exercise and saw that she had been handled by the "unsafe" people, she cried. "I didn't know you from the others," she said. Often feelings of mistrust are projections of one's own doubts and fears.

Part of step three is to bring others into your world, not just to do something in front of them but to do things in relation to them or with them.

"Witness." After finishing the association exercises everyone goes into a squat. No one can see more than a small
circle around his feet, as heads are kept down. No peeking.

A person gets up, chooses any number of others—from
no one to everyone—arranges them in any way, and then
does something in front of them, or with them. The act may
relate directly to the witnesses, like embracing, or it may
simply be something the person wants the witnesses to see.
The person doing the action is free to use sound. The witnesses remain silent unless told by the person to make
sound.

When the person is finished, and all witnesses have resumed squatting, he squats and says, "Done." Someone else
rises and begins.

Note: The director must participate in this exercise. No
one can be outside it. The *only* witnesses are those chosen by
each person.

Because of the nature of "Witness," I will not report anything
I have seen except to say that the actions are sometimes extreme
and revealing. Things come out that otherwise would remain
concealed for months, if not permanently.

"Witness" raises three points not directly tied to any particular
step of performer development, but important to them all: (1) no
reprisals or blackmail, (2) no judgments, (3) nonparticipation
of the director in the exercises. Only in regard to the first point
may I be absolute. The work will not advance if people gossip
about it outside of workshop, using workshop as a way of getting
information to be used at other times in other places. Workshop
must be treated by all as a relationship like that between lawyer
and client or priest and confessor. A few words of gossip can
ruin a month's work.

On the other hand whatever reactions occur during the workshop—no matter how personal these reactions are—ought to be
expressed in the here and now of the workshop. It is a very
delicate matter how. In outward appearance there may be very
little difference between support and judgment; but in effect there
is all the difference in the world. Generally, those watching an
exercise do not express their reactions visibly or in sound. Most
reactions can be translated into breathing rhythms. These will
usually not disturb those doing an exercise. Sometimes, however,
audible and visible reactions are good—these can support persons
going through difficult passages. What is to be avoided are claques
and other forms of self-indulgence, or sneers and other forms
of put-down judgments. Occasionally, even in the midst of an

exercise, someone feels he must interrupt. He should do so clearly and plainly. Then either his interruption will be accepted —made part of the exercise—or rejected. Most often it is preferable to set aside the natural rhythm of give-and-take and put things in sequence. This way each person has a chance to have his say-and-do to the utmost. Once a person, or team, is done, then another can enter the exercise, feeding feelings directly into the work. These matters are subtle, and nothing of what I've said ought to be considered absolute.

As for the participation of the director in the work, I strongly believe he should enter only when the exercise cannot be done without him, as in "witness," or when it does not need his attention, as when an experienced group is doing the initial psychophysical exercises. When there is more than one director in a group, then, of course, the directors not directing participate. However, I don't think directors should drop in on the work to find out what it's like or to learn more about the performer's process. These admirable intentions should be worked out by the director in someone else's workshop where he can genuinely be one of the performers. The director's wish to *temporarily* divest himself of his authority and become "just one of the performers" is arrogant. The performers work daily developing their skills. The director serves them best by functioning as an outside eye or an intervening helper. He is not entitled to the role of king-in-disguise.

All this changes if the director is not king. In TPG a change in Group structure means I am no longer the sole leader. There is collective leadership and collaboration on artistic matters. I will discuss this development in Chapter 8. As the Group changed from an autocratic parental kind to a collaborative colleague kind, I found it both easier and more necessary to participate in the work. Still, I usually do not participate in the same way as the others. While the performers do association exercises, I do yoga; I participate in those workshop exercises that do not need me to be outside; when others direct workshop exercises, I participate. In other words, instead of staying outside except when it is necessary to be in, I am now inside except when it is necessary to stay out.

If "Witness" is a public showing, "Boatrock" is a secret sharing.

> Two persons sit on the floor facing each other, their legs over each other's thighs and their hands grasping each other at the wrists so that as one goes down on his back, the other

is pulled into a sitting position. They begin rocking each other, not helping but falling into dead weight, so that both partners tire quickly. When both are exhausted, they fall into each other's arms. One person tells a story to the other; a story that is true, secret, and a kind of confession: a story the teller doesn't want to tell out loud. When *A* is finished, the partners rock again to exhaustion. Then *B* tells his story.

"Boatrock" is an exercise in fundamental stage communication, dialogue stripped to its beginnings: one person telling another something, one person contacting another. It is also an exercise in presence, trust, and giving over. Like all step three exercises, "Boatrock" is collaborative.

Sharing has its aggressive side, too. Relating to others includes getting angry at them, confronting them, facing off against them. There are many ways to confronting. A person can "call a circle" and invite everyone else to witness/participate in the confrontation. He can arrange to be alone with another, or have a private meeting in a "safe place" where two or more people can deal with each other. He can transform his feelings into sound and movement or in other ways inject his feelings directly into the work. The only thing a performer ought not do is stuff his feelings: Blocked feelings consume a great deal of energy. A person has to concentrate on holding himself in, shutting off. This blocking cuts off responsiveness not only in the area of suppression but in many other areas as well.

Exercises that stimulate aggressive actions—like those that stimulate affectionate actions—need not start with some incident in mind. The formal structure of the exercise is itself a stimulus evoking concrete images, associations, memories, and impulses. (Aggressive exercises are as much grounded in presence and trust as are affectionate exercises; in both cases actual feelings flow through formal structures. These structures are, in turn, given shape by the feelings that flow through them. It is like the banks of a river that are constantly being re-formed by the water that flows through them.) One of the richest aggressive confrontation exercises is "Ritual Combat," developed from ideas of Konrad Lorenz—specifically his discussion of display and submission dances and the triumph ceremony of geese.[12]

A combat zone is marked out, usually a circle of about twenty feet in diameter. *A* comes to the center and issues a challenge by means of a dance. If the challenge is not

[12] Lorenz (1967), 125–132, 174–179.

taken up, *A* retires. If it is taken up, *A* and *B* perform a display dance face to face, an overt provocation. People on the sidelines choose sides and show their support.

Combat starts when both *A* and *B* are finished dancing. No rush, nor surprise attacks. Combat involves sound, movement, and total body commitment—but no physical contact. Each time a combatant strikes, the other receives the "blow" in his body, from a distance. The wounded one then responds. There are no misses; every blow wounds. There are no recoveries; once a person is wounded, he carries that wound throughout the entire combat. Every combat ends in the death of one or both of the combatants.

For example, *A* thrusts with his left arm in a pistonlike motion. *A* must continue this motion for the entire fight. *B* is wounded in the stomach and doubles over. *B* must remain doubled over for the entire fight. From his doubled-over position *B* delivers a brutal kick which breaks *A*'s shoulder. *A*'s shoulder is slumped; his other arm continues to thrust in the pistonlike motion. *A* delivers a kick that downs *B,* breaking one leg. From this disabled position *B* bites through *A*'s ankle, and *A* falls. And so on until death.

Because of the totality and intensity of the commitment, the combat is brief. Usually a minute or less is enough to score a death.

If one of the adversaries survives, he is the winner, and he is entitled to dance a triumph dance over the corpse of the loser. The winner's supporters join in this dance. The supporters of the loser claim his body, grieve over it, and then resurrect him. Then the two dances merge into one celebration.

The pattern of "Ritual Combat" is classic: presentation and display; preparatory war dance; combat; triumph dance and lament; resurrection; celebration. "Ritual Combat" combines intensity, formality, personal commitment to an action, storyshowing, dance, and group celebration in a way that verges on true drama. Several times I've used this exercise as the core of long improvisations. Things can get complicated, almost epic, involving wars between cities, the coronation of rival kings, combat between culture heroes, trance dancing, slavery, and ornate triumph ceremonies.

"Ritual Combat" is either step three or step four work depending on how fully the combat is embroidered with dramatic elements. Most step four work—relating to others within narrative or other highly formalized structures—are improvisations, scenes, rehearsals, open rehearsals, performances, scored roles: the familiar stuff of theater. In step four work the performer combines spontaneity, personalization, and interaction with objective meanings, ikonography, and mise-en-scène.

In July, 1971, I improvised "Arrangements" with the U.R.I. workshop. Later I reinvented a version of "Arrangements" as *Clothes* (see Chapter 3). All the director's words written below were noted by me after the exercise that was improvised.

> *"Arrangements."* Everyone lies on the floor in silence. Then people rise one at a time and move in slow motion to the highest places in the space. As they move, they say names very quietly. Their own names, names of others in the workshop, names of people they know, mythical or legendary names, names of the dead—names. They speak in slow motion so that the names are turned into sounds, slurred, like speaking under water.
>
> As each person gets to the highest place he chooses for himself, he freezes. When everyone is frozen, the director says, "Take off your cothes and throw them down in slow motion." The clothes are taken off slowly, they are held out slowly, but of course they drop according to Newton's laws. When all the clothes are dropped, the director says, "Those who are dressed go and pick up the clothes that have been thrown down and bring them to the center of the space."

Note: Undressing is "offered" rather than "required." When I saw that some people did not undress, I used that in the improvisation. In a genuinely collaborative situation the director is free to ask for anything, and the performer is free to reject anything. Thus the work between them keeps its qualities of living tissue.

> When the clothes are collected in the center, the people bringing them stop saying the names as soon as they put the clothes down. They freeze in whatever positions they are when the clothes they are carrying touch the floor. When all the clothes have been brought to the center, the people in high places stop calling names.
>
> Then, silently, in slow motion, the people in high places come down, claim their clothes, dress, and find a safe place to lie down and close their eyes.
>
> The people in the center unfreeze, look at the ones who are lying down. The director says, "If you want to join someone lying down, take off your clothes, go to the person you want to join, put your clothes next to that person, arranging your clothes in the position you want to be in, and return to where you came from, saying your own name all

the while. Then look back at yourself lying next to the one
you wanted to join."

When the clothes have been placed and everyone has gone
back to where he came from, the director says, "Those lying
down get up and see if there are clothes next to you. If
there are, take them to the person they belong to, moving
in slow motion, saying his or her name as you move. If
there are no clothes next to you, simply sit still and watch."

When all the clothes are returned and the people are all
dressed, allow silence to last a long time.

This is typical of improvisations incorporating recurrent themes
in my work: undressing, exchange of clothes, clothes as an image
of the person, freezing, slow motion, a person's being-in-clothes
and a person's being-separate-from-his-clothes. I don't know
exactly what I am working out for myself in exercises like
"Arrangements," but I am deeply implicated in the improvisation.

In all the steps of the work, but especially in step four, the
director's fantasies, associations, and body idioms are reflected in
the work. It is in this work that the risks of manipulation and
acting out are greatest. The director is not a performer—he doesn't
follow his impulses in the same way as the performers do. Instead,
he directs and follows his impulses to use others to make his
own fantasies concrete. In step four often the director is not
helping the performer but collaborating with him in building an
imaginary, concrete world. In the tender, extreme give-and-take
between director and performer both find out a great deal about
each other. The work is dangerous. Sometimes performers will
feel used, even embarrassed, by what the director suggests. Sometimes the director will feel bottled up, angry, and resentful if
he must censor his impulses. The work is a struggle to find the
terms through which the director's impulses and the performer's
impulses may converge and play freely with each other. Necessarily this will be a small proportion of the work tried. This
kind of work takes mutual trust. Most of the time the performers
work from their own impulses and the director watches. But
in an improvisation like "Arrangements" the director is working
deep from his own barely-conscious. This kind of work is most
rewarding when the director's suggestions are suitable armatures
for the performer's own explorations: when director and performers are truly tuned in to each other.

It isn't enough for the performer to be himself in a performance
or to be the director's surrogate. Creativity starts from the self
but feeds into a larger, collective structure. In the theater this

larger structure is called *action*. During the last part of his life Stanislavski turned to the problem of identifying action. His "logic of physical actions" has two parts—the details of the score and the connections among all these details. Each detail is a fulfillment of its own needs—for example, a halfback stretching his body so that he is horizontal to the football field while making an effort to catch the ball. Performers in theater strive for the same purity of detailed action, an absolute identity between act and objective. But it is harder to get this kind of purity in theater because the physical task is complicated by psychological and mise-en-scènic considerations.

The ultimate problem of step four is to construct a score for each performer that makes sense to the audience (the *connections* of the logic of physical action) while freeing each performer to pursue each action for its own sake (the *details* of physical action). When this ideal state is achieved—it never is—then each performer is wholly committed to each moment of the performance, and the performance-as-a-unit will make sense to the audience. The equivalent in football is a perfectly played game before a stadium full of *aficionados*. Thus the theory may be correct, but its application is impossible. Either the play makes sense but lacks conviction in performance, or the performers are really into it but the audience can't make heads or tails out of what's happening.

The best technique I know of to achieve a score made from the logic of physical actions is to relocate questions ordinarily asked intellectually so that they are asked of other parts of the body. For example, in *Commune,* when Clementine thrusts downward with her arm, hand, and fingers, pushing her fingers into Lizzie's belly at the climax of the Sharon Tate murder scene, the question for the performer is not *"Why* do I stab Lizzie?" but *"How* do I stab Lizzie?" The question of "how" is put to Clementine's arm, hand, and fingers; to her belly and shoulders; her face, teeth, and tongue. If each detail of the action is in place, if the connections between the details are strong and logical, then the whole action will be so together that *any answer to the question of "why" is correct.* (Or, to put it another way, knowing "how" makes knowing "why" unnecessary.) In fact, the answer to "why" will change from performance to performance, depending upon the immediate circumstances of the night. This changing response to "why" within a fixed set of actions is what is meant by "the performer is free within his score." It is exactly as Grotowski says:

> The actor's score consists of the elements of human contact: "give and take." Take other people, confront them with oneself, one's own experiences and thoughts, and give a reply. In these somewhat intimate human encounters there is always this element of "give and take." The process is repeated, but always *hic et nunc* [here and now], that is to say, it is never quite the same.[13]

Here and now. A tension, confrontation, contact, exchange—between the performer and the text; between the performer and his actions; between the performer and his partners; between the performer and the spectators; between the spectator and other spectators.

While working on *Makbeth* we couldn't find the actions of the play. We tried many different exercises, but nothing worked. We *knew* what the actions were, but we couldn't connect them to the body, or link them to each other. The poetry of the great soliloquies sounded extraneous. Peter Brook saw a performance and suggested an exercise. "Have the actors say the lines as fast as possible; have them recite the whole play in a half hour. In this way the action underneath the psychology and poetry of the lines will be flushed out into the open." We tried the exercise. It was not a cure-all, but it helped. Forced to give up tricks and superficial personalizations, without time to reflect on how beautiful the language was, the performers *felt through* the words to the action. (Feeling through is the body's equivalent to seeing through; it means to perceive an action through what was previously an opaque or deadening barrier. In many Shakespearean productions the master's poetry is just such a barrier.) Faced with a merciless task—saying the lines so fast they could not possibly think about what they were saying—things began to happen: shouts, laughter in unexpected places, fierce whispers; the actions became visible the way a landscape emerges from a lifting fog. The rehearsal began with people sitting in a large circle, but soon performers were up and moving. New relationships erupted as if from beneath a sea of words. Strong logical actions that defined the flow of whole scenes swept away the previous, too-highly-individualized treatments of text.

Unfortunately, the Group was unable to follow through on the exercise. Terrible problems were shaking the Group to its foundations. *Makbeth* never achieved the rush, force, clarity, and beauty it had that rehearsal. But I use Brook's exercise now when faced with a problem of not seeing the forest for the trees; or when

[13] Grotowski (1968), 212.

things are bogged down in muddy detail; or when a text is encrusted with meaning.

Steadily in 1969 and 1970 the Group worked on the idea that *feelings must flow freely through a set score of physical actions*. This idea was put to a severe test during the spring of 1971 when the Group developed a new version of *Commune.* Originally *Commune* was composed of nine performers, an assistant director, and myself; we did the daily work. We were assisted by Paul Epstein and Jerry Rojo, who worked with us occasionally. In the spring of 1971 we were looking for ways to free ourselves from relationships based on characters who were no longer in the play and performers who were no longer in the Group. *Commune* had to be remade for six performers. One afternoon I asked the performers to run through the play silently, playing every action but carefully avoiding dialogue substitutes such as nodding the head to signal Yes. I wanted to test the actions for clarity, coherence, and wholeness. Whenever an action was unclear or unfulfilled, the run-through was stopped, and we worked on the detail.

Many actions were revealed as superfluous, others as unclear. Over the next few weeks much fat was cut from *Commune,* a very painful operation. For the first time a clear story was discovered at the core of *Commune,* and that story was embodied in a scenic rhythm. The work confirmed an opinion of Meyerhold's:

> Any dramatic work which is imbued with the quality of true theatricality is amenable to total schematization, even to the extent of temporarily removing the dialog with which the skeleton of the scenario is embellished. In this form, schematically and mimetically performed, a genuinely theatrical play can still stir the spectator, simply because the scenario is constructed from traditional, truly theatrical elements.[14]

The work of finding the actions of a play fails when the director or performers are impatient. Finding the action-score of a play takes hundreds, maybe thousands, of hours; most of this time is spent on solutions that will ultimately be rejected. Discovering the logic of actions—and ruthlessly revising the mise-en-scène in terms of this logic—doesn't come automatically, easily, or naturally. Tempers are short, the work grueling and repetitive. Many rehearsals go on for hours and end with no measurable gains. The goodwill of the company is tested.

[14] Meyerhold (1969, written in 1914), 150–151.

Ultimately, I am not even certain that all changes in the direction of clarity are for the best. I believe things can become too clear, too easy and simpleminded. That art is best that incorporates irrelevancies, lapses of logic, unresolvable tensions. Incorporating mistakes does not mean eliminating them. Franz Kafka: "Leopards break into the temple and drink to the dregs what is in the sacrificial pitchers; this is repeated over and over again; finally it can be calculated in advance and it becomes part of the ceremony."

From all this work each performer begins to find his role. A role is a theatrical entity, not a psychological being. Great errors are made because performers and directors think of characters as people rather than as *dramatis personae:* masks of dramatic action. A role conforms to the logic of theater, not the logic of any other life system. To think of a role as a person is like picnicking on a landscape painting.

Theatrical logic is about *doing, showing, impersonating, singing, dancing, and playing.* These are the resources a performer calls on when preparing a role. Whatever "psychology" there is in a role is the psychology of the performer, his own personal being. The performer's contingent experiences confront the transcendent elements of the scored role. But it is not a simple confrontation of two self-contained entities. The score is made by the performer, out of the performer. He is his own material; he does not have the buffer of a medium. Theater is not an art that detaches itself from its creators at the point of completion; there is no way of exhibiting a performance without at the same time exhibiting the performers. And the experience of the performance for the audience are the innumerable and deep points of contact and interpenetration of performer and performance. These can be listed in only the most generalized way.

Performer	*Performance*
Person	Role
Self	Story, text, action
Immediate	Timeless
Continuous	Intermittent
Contingent	Transcendent
Here, now	Without time or place
Actual	Reactualization [15]
Unexpected	Already known
Experience	Metaphor or analogy
For the last time	Again and again

[15] For a discussion of the concepts of "actual" and "reactualization" see Eliade (1965) and Schechner (1970a).

This way of working is different from that of the orthodox theater. In orthodox theater the actor wants to "get inside" the character; rehearsals concentrate on techniques that help the actor "lose himself in" the role. Devices such as emotional recall help the actor find in his own past analogue to the experiences of the character he is "portraying" so that *he can feel what the character is supposed to have felt.* In short, the character is assumed to be a person, and the actor's job is to become that person. Environmental theater does away with the "there are two people" assumption. Rather, there is the role and the person of the performer; both role and performer are plainly perceivable by the spectator. *The feelings are those of the performer as stimulated by the actions of the role at the moment of performance.*

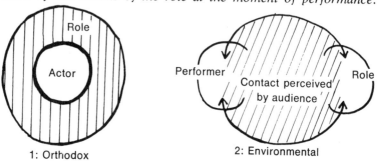

1: Orthodox   2: Environmental

The orthodox actor vanishes inside his role. The environmental theater performer is in a perceivable relationship with the role. What the audience experiences is neither the performer nor the role but the relationship between the two. This relationship is immediate; it exists only in the here and now of performance. The performer doesn't try to mask his difficulties; his way of dealing with the role is a major part of the interest in the performance. The performer and the role are open to each other; the performer uses "his role as if it were a surgeon's scalpel, to dissect himself." [16] The reverse is also true: The performer's way of dealing with the role illuminates it.

Most performances in environmental theater do not achieve the purity of model 2. There remain degrees of orthodox acting. But I believe the model is attainable. It is a question of training performers, directors, and audiences to look at theater not as a reflection or duplication of reality—as secondary realities—but as itself a primary kind of reality, and then to interest people in the process of this performance reality.

[16] Grotowski (1968), 37.

Earlier in the chapter I discussed verbophysical exercises. I want now to return to the subject of voice training. Voice work is intrinsic to every step of the training. While doing the association exercises performers are encouraged to make whatever sounds they wish. These sounds are not forced; they are a function of the physical work and of the associations. If a person unaccustomed to the way The Performance Group does the opening exercises were to listen to the first hour of a workshop, he would possibly think people were mad, in great pain, hysterical, in the throes of trance or orgasm. Every conceivable sound is made, from laughing to screaming, sobbing, heavy breathing, moaning, gurgling, singing, shouting, reciting tongue-twisters, doing scales, etc.

The body shapes the voice; controls its intensity, volume, pitch, rhythm, duration, variety, and timbre. In the verbophysical exercises the performer does not think about what to say. He doesn't use the voice as the means of saying what he knows; he uses the voice as a *means of finding out what he is saying.* Using the voice need not be an expression of something more basic; using the voice is in itself an essential act. In this way new sounds, new songs, new languages, are possible. Dialogue is not limited to verbal language or to the usual ways of using verbal languages. Sometimes by simply singing a song while doing a massive exercise like the body roll uncovers new feelings, new ways of singing. Sometimes performers "speak" with each other by breathing-and-dancing, a form of unverbal, soundless language. The unverbal is the sonic counterpart of the unconscious—a system of linguistic relationships not yet formed into ordinary speech or song. Just as unconsciousness is continuously communicating with consciousness through daydreams and nightdreams, fantasies, and associations, so the unverbal is always communicating with the verbal through the "uhhs" and "ohhs" that accompany speech, breathing sounds, body sounds like digestion, ringing in the ears, swallowing, and the noises polite people learn to ignore and suppress such as sudden gasps, sobs, laughs, moans, shrieks. The association work helps the performer engage these sounds.

Once the voice is on its way to becoming free, once it no longer is the servant of grammar, decorum, or literary poetry, it can *make as well as use language.* Jerome Rothenberg in his dense, extremely rich preface to the extraordinary book *Technicians of the Sacred* puts it this way:

Poems are carried by the voice & are sung or chanted in specific situations. Under such circumstances, runs the easy answer, the "poem" would simply be the words-of-the-song. But a little later the question arises: what *are* the words & where do they begin & end? The translation, as printed, may show the "meaningful" element only, often no more than a single, isolated "line"; thus

> *A splinter of stone which is white* (Bushman)
> *Semen white like the mist* (Australian)
> *My-shining-hours* (Chippewa: single word)
> etc.

but in practice the one "line" will likely be repeated until its burden has been exhausted. (Is it "single" then?) It may be altered phonetically & the words distorted from their "normal" forms. Vocables with no fixed meanings may be intercalated. All of these devices will be creating a greater & greater gap between the "meaningful" residue in the translation & what-was-actually-there. We will have a different "poem" depending where we catch the movement, & we may start to ask: Is something within this work the "poem," or is everything?

Rothenberg answers his own question.

> The animal-body-rootedness of "primitive" poetry: recognition of a "physical" basis for the poem within a man's body —or as an act of the body & mind together, breath &/or spirit; in many cases too the direct & open handling of sexual imagery & (in the "events") of sexual activities as key factors in creating of the sacred; the poet as shaman, or primitive shaman as poet & seer thru control of the means just stated: an open "visionary" situation prior to all system-making ("priesthood") in which the man creates thru dream (image) & word (song), "that Reason may have ideas to build on" (W. Blake).[17]

It is not as difficult as it may seem to employ these concepts. Paul Epstein in working out the music for *Makbeth* approached sound *topographically,* as shapes rather than noises. For example, here is Epstein's text for Lady Makbeth's reading of Makbeth's famous letter.

[17] Rothenberg, ed. (1968), xxi–xxiv.

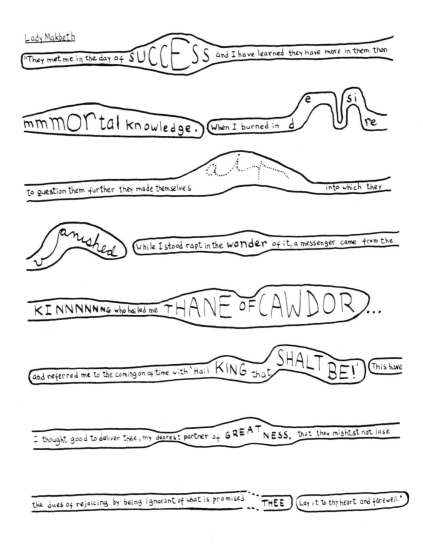

Lady Makbeth

"They met me in the day of SUCCESS and I have learned they have more in them than mmmORtal knowledge. When I burned in desire To question them further they made themselves into which they vanished While I stood rapt in the wonder of it, a messenger came from the KINNNNNNG who hailed me THANE OF CAWDOR... and referred me to the coming on of time with 'Hail KING that SHALT BE!' This have I thought good to deliver thee, my dearest partner of GREATNESS, that thou mightst not lose the dues of rejoicing by being ignorant of what is promised THEE Lay it to thy heart and farewell.'

Epstein instructs the performers: "The graphic notation suggesting a heightened treatment of key words. The notation is both an approximate transcription/interpretation of things done in rehearsal and a score to be reinterpreted by the performer." The music of *Makbeth* was worked out collaboratively by Epstein and the performers within the environment at the Garage. (Unlike the rest of the production, Epstein composed the music after the Group's return from Yugoslavia.) Epstein's piece *Concert for TPG* is similarly a collaboration.[18]

Epstein writes of *Makbeth:*

> In much of the music of *Makbeth* the selection of text, on the basis of phonetic content as well as meaning, was a major part of the compositional task. "Text setting" came to mean literally that, placing pieces of text in relation to one another and to a context of scenic action. Duncan's funeral procession reverses itself to become Makbeth's coronation march. The transition is made musically as the funeral chants are replaced by miniature fanfares, the themes of the text fragments changing from purification and sleep to duty, honor, and the crown. . . .
>
> While Makbeth murders Duncan, the Dark Powers play out a scene of carousal that is parallel in its overall rhythmic shape. As Makbeth addresses the dagger and gradually moves towards action, the sounds of carousal are languorously seductive. Fragments of text resonate from one part of the scene to the other, and the sinuous phrases of inflected speech relate the carousal to Makbeth's lust for the crown. Both scenes climax at the same time, and the sound of the Dark Powers subsides into whispered phrases, the words chosen as much from their high sibilant content as for their sense.[19]

Makbeth is not an opera but an attempt to bring back into Western theater the sonic complexities, possibilities, ranges, and gut meanings of Asian and "primitive" theaters where there is no hard division between music, dance, and drama.

In some ways voice work transcends all of the four steps

---

[18] The second part of *Concert*, "Intersections 7," is printed in *Scripts 2*, Vol. 1, No. 2 (December, 1971), 62–70. There Epstein lays out the uses of space, the special notation for *Concert*, and rehearsal procedures.

[19] Epstein's two-part essay "Music and Theatre" lays out his aesthetics and procedures. See *Performance* (Vol. 1, Nos. 2 and 4 [1972]). Epstein and I have worked together since the founding of the New Orleans Group in 1965.

of performer development. Voice work is at the same time the most sophisticated and the most primitive element in training and performance. The voice is identical to the breath—to the ancient notion of *spirit,* of life coming from outside and possessing the body, or of man's essential inner life.[20] Sound is to breath what gesture is to movement. People are always breathing and therefore always making some ground noise; but sounding the breath is signaling, and the range of signals and languages is incalculable. Claude Lévi-Strauss understands, as few people do, that questions of vocalities touch the basic issues of human culture.

> . . . innumerable societies, both past and present, have conceived of the relation between the spoken language and singing or chanting as analogous to that between the continuous and the intermittent. This is tantamount to saying that, within culture, singing or chanting differs from the spoken language as culture differs from nature; whether sung or not, the sacred discourse of myth stands in the same contrast to profane discourse. Again, singing and musical instruments are often compared to masks; they are the acoustic equivalents of what actual masks represent on the plastic level (and, for this reason, in South America especially, they are associated, mentally and physically, with masks).[21]

Lévi-Strauss sets up several transformational pairs of opposites:

continuous	intermittent
spoken	sung/chanted
profane	sacred
everyday	mythic
unadorned	masked
nature	culture

The first terms are the more inclusive, the matrices of the second. But the second terms decay (in the musical sense) into the first. For example, the face is usually unadorned, unmasked; but it is by painting the face, dressing it, imitating it, distorting it that masks are made and worn; and when the ceremony/celebration is over and the mask taken off and/or destroyed, the face remains as before.

[20] The etymology of *spirit* is enlightening in this regard. Its Latin root is *spirare* = to breathe, an onomatopoetic word. The Latin *spiritus* = breath of life, life itself, soul—as well as a simple breath. Derivatives include actions as diverse as conspire, inspire, perspire, transpire, and aspire.

[21] Lévi-Strauss (1969b), 28.

This same transformational exaltation characterizes performing. Out of the daily tasks of training and rehearsing, a performance arises, step by step. It is performed for as many times as it is. Then it is dismantled. A similar rhythm affects every performer. He arrives at the theater before show time; prepares himself in some way for the peculiar excitement of performing; performs; when the show is over, he goes through some procedures of coming down, restoring himself to a level state again. The sequence warmup–perform–cool-down is one action unit. Performance itself is a heightened activity, an exalted state that is intermittent, sacred, mythic, and masked. It is a special way man has of singing.

The performer has qualities of the healer and the ecstatic. "The shaman becomes the exemplar and model for all those who seek to acquire power. The shaman is the man who *knows* and *remembers,* that is, who understands the mysteries of life and death." [22] Few performers in the West achieve this understanding, but the echoes and the aspirations remain. The work of environmental theater is to stir those coals, to raise the temperature of theater.

> The medicine man is a professional dealer in all kinds of anxieties connected with body destruction and primal scenes. He has been initiated by having his own corruptible intestines removed, i.e., by having undergone the punishment for his body destruction fantasies, but also by over-compensating this anxiety position. . . . The reparation fantasies which always follow body destruction trends, are introverted towards his own body, and then reextroverted towards his patients, whom he heals by stimulating their own reparation fantasies. In healing them he heals himself, by a permanent series of reparations. [23]

A performance is always about at least two things: the performer's body and the story. The performance stimulates the audience to react *in their bodies* to what's happening to the performer. The stories are variations on a few basic themes, all of them involving dismemberment and reparation. The performer says to the audience: "Watch my insides being removed, watch as I spill my guts in front of you, to you, for you; watch how I am healed." In watching, the audience participates in a cycle

[22] Eliade (1965), 102.
[23] Roheim (1969, written in 1945), 191.

of conflict, agony, death, dismemberment, and repair. True, the story being told may have great consequences and meanings on the social level. But at the same time a profound visceral experience is taking place, touching off deep reverberations in the audience. During each performance the performer tries to find for himself—and undergo in front of the audience—the process of birthing, growing, opening up, spilling out, dying, and rebirthing. This is the life-rhythm mystery of theater, "live theater." This is the kernel of theater's most personal experience, located at that place where art, medicine, and religion intersect.

Lone Bear or Empty Wagon of the Kiowa
was so clumsy a shaman that the ethnographer
could see him fumble red clay from his
pouch and chew it in his mouth, later to be
spit out as his own "blood." Such events
explain why shamanism sometimes has to be
taught. Shamanistic "tricks" point to another
role of the shaman, that of self-impresario and
entertainer. The stage magician is still another
scion of the magician-shaman-showman.
Weston La Barre

One becomes what one displays. The wearers
of masks *are* really the mythical ancestors
portrayed by their masks. But the same results
—that is, total transformation of the
individual into something *other*—are to be
expected from the various signs and symbols
that are sometimes merely indicated on the
costume or directly on the body: one assumes
the power of magical flight by wearing an
eagle feather, or even a highly stylized
drawing of such a feather; and so on.
Mircea Eliade

5 Shaman

What is the difference between rehearsal and preparation? A play
on Broadway gathers its cast together about six weeks before
opening. They rehearse five or six days a week, six or seven
hours a day. What are these 240 hours spent on doing? The actors
read the play, memorize its lines; they move on the stage,
memorize those movements; they learn how to behave in each
others' company so that the audience will be able to enjoy the
performance by sharing one illusion or another with the actors.
In a very good performance the reality created by rehearsing
is extremely convincing, moving, and meaningful. Rehearsal, in
essence, is not much different in high-school plays, off Broadway,
in the regional theater, or on Broadway. Rehearsal is a way of
making unknown material (the play to be performed) so familiar
to the actors that the audience can successfully believe that what
they see is a way of living. The professional actor is a person

who is skilled in this kind of magic deception; or invocation of belief.

Workshop with Grotowski, Chaikin, Brook, André Gregory, or TPG is not very like rehearsal in the orthodox theater. Much of the time in workshop is not spent memorizing lines or gestures or in any other way repeating what will later be done in performance. I have described some of the Group's workshop procedures, and although the other groups will have different exercises and different ways of getting at the work, the underlying structure will be the same: Workshop advances the development of the company, not necessarily the development of a particular performance. The fundamental difference between a rehearsal and a workshop is that a rehearsal is aimed at *one set of gestures relevant to one production.* The deepest way rehearsal is make-believe is that its purpose is to help everyone support the illusion that a one-time event is for all times. Thus when we see a finished, professional production of, say, *Mourning Becomes Electra,* the audience is helped to believe that these actors are part of the same family or at least that they know each other very well.

Workshop works toward the same goal, but authentically. The idea of a workshop is to help the performers get to know each other well enough so that the relationships ultimately presented on stage are founded on actual knowing among the group members. Group work is a hothouse way of developing small communities, families, in-groups, cells; the exercises stimulate not only self-knowledge but knowledge concerning the others and knowledge of the self-and-others. Not any others, or a generalized Other, but *these others here with me now.* If that sense of being-with-the-others is highly developed, audience and performers alike get a sense of ensemble.

Among the Australian aborigines there is no need to rehearse or run workshops. Any performances the widely scattered, small aborigine bands do are done for themselves; properly speaking there is no audience. And there is no need to do anything special about teaching the dance steps or songs. These the children see and hear from birth. Or they have dreams that reveal the shape and words of new dances and songs. Or, when the ceremonies are near, the men take the boys to a secluded spot and show them the dances, teach them the songs, educate them in the lore of the tribe. The boys are initiated, not rehearsed: They join the men in what the men for a long time have known and done. (This way of preparation, apprenticeship, used to be popular in the arts. It is a method I respect.) Also, of course, there is no need among the aborigines for workshop. The members of the group already know each other very well, having lived together all their lives. In fact, the people stage rough equivalents to encounter sessions to help relieve the pressures of anger, resentment, and hurt feelings that build up among familylike groups. At these times individuals are encouraged to express in word-duels all that has offended them. These word-duels serve not only to let off steam but also as entertainment.[1]

Communal peoples—a term I prefer to the pejorative "primitive"—do not rehearse or run workshops. But they spend many hours *preparing* their performances. What are these preparations, and why have them? Among the aborigines:

> Although short in themselves, these dances usually require several hours of preparation, mainly for decorating the dancers' bodies and the sacred paraphernalia carried or used in the dances. Members of each cult-lodge carry out these preparations with extreme care, with the older members supervising each detail and instructing younger members on the correct designs. . . . The preparations are thought by the Aborigines to be at least as important as the actual dances. This is not so much a matter of craftsmanship or artistry as propriety; that is, each design or piece of paraphernalia is judged by the older men in terms of whether or not it includes all the traditionally correct elements for the particular ceremony being performed. . . . A neat, carefully painted body design is enjoyed by the lodge members but is not required for the ceremony. In short, craftsmanship and artistry are permitted and even, in an informal way, encouraged, but only if they do not in any way violate the themes set down by tradition.[2]

Thus, one function of preparation is to keep the contact with tradition, the past, the Ancestors, the Dream Time: The Eternal Present. This historical function—or is it the opposite, a means of obliterating history?—is especially important in nonliterate cultures where the past cannot be deposited in books. Preparation = tradition-in-action.

E. T. Kirby in his important article, "The Mask: Abstract

[1] The practice of word-duels is widespread enough to be called general. It is a highly specialized art among the Eskimos and some Siberian peoples, but it is also practiced in Oceania, Melanesia, Africa, the Americas. The idea is to express one's feelings regarding wrongs publicly; then to somehow make up formally, usually through exchange of gifts.

[2] Gould (1969), 109–110.

Theatre, Primitive and Modern," discusses several aborigine performances in which the performers are

> totally transformed into an "ancestor" with tufts of down applied with blood in red, white and black geometrical patterns over the whole body and face, the form of which is also altered by a headdress (simple or fairly elaborate) that extends this same decoration. Parts of the design are said to refer to objects in nature, plants, or animals, or to places associated with the particular myth performed, but the forms have no similarity with those referenced, and their relation to those forms or to the body on which they are shown is unclear and occult, at best. Abstraction thus supports an "enforced connection" between earth, plant, animal, and man in the re-creation of an ancestor who was associated, in essence, with them, and the abstraction, as such, retains the mystery of that association. Such costumes, creating of the performer an *Ubermarionette,* take several hours to prepare and apply, while the performance in which they appear lasts about five minutes. . . .
>
> As enactments the performances are very simple. Consequently, their form, the nature of the beginning and end of each, takes on even greater significance. Characteristically, each enactment begins with the costumed performer or performers hidden at some distance from the audience, behind a bush or in a gully, and then appearing to advance toward the audience with the peculiar high-knee action. The effect is that of the supernatural appearing out of the natural world. At the end of each short enactment, the performers are "released" by the audience, a member of which will knock off the performer's headpiece, lay a hand on his head or strike a staff on the ground (depending upon the particular tribe). The audience thus retains or regains control over the supernatural.[3]

I prefer *transformation* to Kirby's *abstraction.* Abstraction implies a distillation of events and patterns, whereas transformation implies a change in the level, intensity, and actual shape of the reality being performed. In the dances Kirby describes, the preparation is a way of *changing the order of things* so that the performers may make the metaphysical leap. They are then brought back to a mundane level of experience by the spectators. The preparation is quite literally a "send-off," and the final audience gesture is a "bring-down."

[3] E. T. Kirby (1972), 10, 12.

Once transformed, the performer exists in a trance. He is not separate from that which possesses him, or that with which he is identified. Unlike orthodox theater where the *willing* suspension of disbelief means that always there is a second reality—"the real world"—shadowing the performance reality, there is in the aborigine performance a change in realities so that during the performance there is *only one reality:* the one being performed. Rehearsal is a way of emphasizing the performance structure so that "the real world" can be successfully relegated to a shadow, a disbelief that can be suspended; preparation is a way of getting out of "the real world" or—more accurately—of invoking another world of reality that wholly occupies space/time until the performance is ended by some kind of de-preparation, or bring-down. It is this sense of getting ready, going up, and coming down that we call ecstasy; and although orthodox theater has some of it, there it is sensed as "magic," a kind of trick that pleases. Ecstasy does not stimulate free pleasure but a kind of reverential fear.

Even in extended performances among communal peoples—performances that may take months or years to complete—there is a lingering sense of ecstasy: of invoking a new order of things that exist only for the time being. The masters of ecstasy are called shamans. Before I can examine shamanism and its relation to performance, more has to be said about theater in communal societies; about preparation.

In eastern Australia there is an initiation ceremony called a *bora.* It is worth examining because its structure is a paradigm of initiation ceremonies everywhere, even of such watered-down rites as bar mitzvah. The boys to be initiated are "kidnapped" from their homes and taken to a secluded spot in the bush where they are instructed in the lore, songs, and dances of their people. This schooling lasts for months. Meanwhile, in the main camp the women mourn the death of their boy-children and prepare for a feast at the same time. They know that the death of the boys will inevitably lead to the birth of new, young men. Eliade outlines the structure of the ceremony:

> First, the preparation of the "sacred ground" where the men will remain in isolation during the festival; second, the separation of the novices from their mothers and, in general, from all women; third, their segregation in the bush, or in a special isolated cam, where they will be instructed in the religious traditions of the tribe; fourth, certain operations performed on the novices, usually circumcision, the extrac-

tion of a tooth, or subincision, but sometimes scarring or pulling out the hair. Throughout the period of the initiation, the novices must behave in a special way; they undergo a number of ordeals, and are subjected to various dietary taboos and prohibitions.[4]

The function of all this is to

> reactualize the mythical period in which the bora was held for the first time. Not only does the sacred ground imitate the exemplary model, Baiamai's first camp, but the ritual performed reiterates Baiamai's gestures and acts. In short, what is involved is a reactualization of Baiamai's creative work, and hence a regeneration of the world. . . . For what is involved here is a fundamental conception in archaic religions—the repetition of a ritual founded by Divine Beings implies the reactualization of the original Time when the rite was first performed. This is why a rite has efficacy—it participates in the completeness of the sacred primordial Time. The rite makes the myth present. Everything that the myth tells of the time of beginning, the *bugari* times, the rite reactualizes, shows it is happening *here and now*.[5]

The details of the preparations are extremely important. The grounds must be laid out in a certain pattern; the dances danced in a certain way. It is not a question of beauty, or feel, but of *correctness*. "Sometimes there are gestures whose meaning seems to have been forgotten, but they are still repeated because they were made by the mythical beings when the ceremony was inaugurated." [6] Exact preparations and exact performance assure that the link between past and present will not be broken.

Transformation is not limited to making one person into another. and one place into another. Transformation identifies person-time-place. The successful transformation of any one element involves the transformation of the other two. One cannot rehearse a transformation. One gets ready, makes preparations. If these preparations are correct, the transformation will take place.

Let us not think only of transformation but also of transformer: the means by which one thing is changed into another, or the link between two separate realms. In communities with utter

4 Eliade (1965), 4–5.
5 Eliade (1965), 6.
6 Eliade (1965), 6–7.

solidarity such as those I have referred to in Australia there is no need for a special person to serve as a transformer. Anyone, given the proper circumstances, can serve as the transformer. On some occasions everyone, or a large proportion of the community, is a transformer. But in other societies it is necessary, for very complicated reasons, for specially trained people to act as transformers on behalf of the entire community. These people are shamans. A shaman is the transformer = the one who is transformed = the surrogate = the link = the one who connects different realms of reality = the one who facilitates change by embodying change = the one who by changing himself helps others change. The shaman is a professional transformer, and very much like the theater performer.

Shamanism is "a method, a psychic technique" of which the "fundamental characteristic . . . is ecstasy, interpreted as the soul forsaking the body. No one has yet shown that the ecstatic experience is the creation of a particular historical civilization or a particular culture cycle. In all probability the ecstatic experience, in its many aspects, is coexistent with the human condition." [7] Shamanism is a performance full of costumes, special languages and poetries, songs, dances, and magic routines. It originates very early in man's history—at least as far back as the Alpine Paleolithic some 30,000 to 50,000 years ago. Apparently shamanism originated in central Asia and from there spread all across the northern hemisphere, so that shamanism is evidenced in America, Asia, Europe, and the Middle East. Historical and structural evidence connects shamanism with Greek, Chinese, Japanese, Indian, and Korean theater; and also with many proto-theatrical ceremonies in Europe, the Middle East, and both North and South America. I am not going to examine these historical connections, though I believe such a study is urgently needed. I will concentrate on structural affinities.

Studies of shamans agree on several points. (1) The shaman is not psychotic, though he may display psychotic symptoms.

[7] Eliade (1965), 100–101. There is a growing literature on shamanism as it relates to performance. I recommend Shirokogoroff (1935), Roheim (1950, 1969), Lévi-Strauss (1963), Eliade (1964, 1965), Lommel (1967), Rothenberg (1968), and La Barre (1972). It is becoming clearer that in shamanism we may have a proto-performance of immense importance to theater, psychiatry, religion, and medicine. It is no accident that these seemingly different occupations share so much. Apparently the connections are more than structural: There are actual, historical links, and most probably a common source.

"He is, above all, a sick man who has been cured, who has succeeded in curing himself." [8] (2) The shaman works by performing—that is, by singing, dancing, going into or invoking trance, transforming himself into animals or other nonhuman beings. (3) The shaman deals with the body. His is not an art that can be practiced at a distance, such as writing. The shaman stands close to his patient, ministers directly to him, touches him, and extracts from him the *substance* of the disease: a rock, feather, bone, what have you. (4) The audience is "a sort of gravitational field within which the relationship between sorcerer and bewitched is located and defined." [9] If the shaman fails to cure a patient, this is not the failure of the system but an indication of a particular shaman's feebleness, or the resistance of the patient, or the power of the disease.

A shaman becomes a shaman because he is "called," and then trained. His training is done either by other shamans or through dreams and visions. Often there is a combination of human and visionary instruction.[10] An Eskimo shaman, Isaac Tens, tells of his call:

> Then my heart started to beat fast, and I began to tremble, just as had happened before. . . . My flesh seemed to be boiling. . . . My body was quivering. While I remained in this state, I began to sing. A chant was coming out of me without my being able to do anything to stop it. Many things appeared to me presently: huge birds and other animals. . . . These were visible only to me, not to the others in my house. Such visions happen when a man is about to become a shaman; they occur of their own accord. The songs force themselves out complete without any attempt to compose them. But I learned and memorized those songs by repeating them.[11]

Similarly for the instruction of an Australian shaman:

> At sunset the shaman's soul meets somewhere the shadow of a dead ancestor. The shadow asks the soul whether it shall go with it. The shaman's soul answers yes. . . . Then

[8] Eliade (1964), 27. Compare Laing's ideas about psychosis.

[9] Lévi-Strauss (1963), 168.

[10] A contemporary but already classic account of an old shaman instructing a young student is contained in the work of Castaneda (1968, 1971, 1972).

[11] Rothenberg (1968), 424.

they go on together, either at once into the kingdom of the dead or to a place in this world at which the spirits of the dead have gathered. . . . The spirits begin to sing and dance. . . . When the dance is over the spirits release the shaman's soul and his helping spirit brings it back to his body. When the shaman wakes, his experiences with the spirits seem to him like a dream. From now on he thinks of nothing but the dances which he has seen and his soul keeps on going back to the spirits to learn more and more about the dances. . . . Then he will first explain the dances to his wife and sing them to her, and after that he will teach them to everyone else.[12]

The shaman does not learn information. He learns what and how to perform. He learns a technique. He is not a transmitter of ideas but a transformer of doings.

The shaman is feared and prized by his people. He is a little crazy. He is "the exemplar and model for all those who seek to acquire power; [he] is the man who *knows* and remembers." [13] He is also an entertainer, a magician, a trickster.

What is this performance? Risking a rash generalization on the basis of a few observations, we shall say that it always involves the shaman's enactment of the "call," of the initial crisis which brought him the revelation of his condition. But we must not be deceived by the word *performance*. The shaman does not limit himself to reproducing or miming certain events. He actually relives them in all their vividness, originality, and violence. And since he returns to his normal state at the end of the seance, we may say, borrowing a key term from psychoanalysis, that he *abreacts*. In psychoanalysis, abreaction refers to the decisive moment in the treatment when the patient intensively relives the initial situation from which his disturbance stems, before he ultimately overcomes it. In this sense, the shaman is a professional abreactor.[14]

What Dream Time is for the aborigines the enactment of the crisis of the call is for the shaman: both reactualize past events, show them as happening here and now. Although the shaman's call seems to be a private event (especially in Lévi-Strauss's rather limiting analogy), it is, in truth, a public performance whose importance comes from the acceptance it finds with its audience.

[12] Lommel (1967), 138–139.
[13] Eliade (1965), 102.
[14] Lévi-Strauss (1963), 180–181.

Lest the reader think that shamanistic performances are always heavy, Castagné describes a Kirgiz-Tatar who

> runs around the tent, springing, roaring, leaping; he barks like a dog, sniffs at the audience, lows like an ox, bellows, cries, bleats like a lamb, grunts like a pig, whinnies, coos, imitating with remarkable accuracy the cries of animals, the songs of birds, the sounds of their flight, and so on, all of which greatly impresses the audience.[15]

This is not an isolated or unusual example. Shamans are audience-oriented; their performances are designed to involve, please, scare, and affect audiences. Traditional shaman's costume includes drum, tambourine, headdress of horns, skins, and feathers, skin coat, rags, tatters, emblems. Often a performance is supported by many props and by assistants who provide visual and sound effects. Among shamans there is much competition. And even those skeptics who want to expose shamanism as a hoax find themselves ineluctably drawn into the system.[16] This is because the system allows no objective reference point against which the shaman's effectiveness can be measured. At most, individual shamans can be judged ineffective; this in no way disturbs belief in the system that extends throughout the society. Shamanism exists within the field of audience belief.

> The rhythmic music and singing, and later the dancing of the shaman, gradually involve every participant more and more in a collective action. When the audience begins to repeat the refrains together with the assistants, only those who are defective fail to join the chorus. . . . When the shaman feels that the audience is with him and follows him he becomes still more active and this effort is transmitted to his audience. After shamanizing, the audience recollects various moments of the performance, their great psychological emotion and the hallucinations of sight and hearing which they have experienced. They then have a deep satisfaction—much greater than that from emotions produced by theatri-

---

[15] Quoted by Eliade (1964), 97.

[16] Lévi-Strauss discusses the question of the intrasubjectivity of the belief in shamans. Castaneda's experiences with Don Juan are convincing examples of the assertion that doing is believing. The difference between shamanistic belief and an audience's belief in a theater performance is that we limit our believing to the time/place of the performance. Shamanistic belief extends to include the whole society all the time. The performance does not create belief in the shaman, it merely concretizes that belief.

cal and musical performances, literature and general artistic phenomena of the European complex, because in shamanizing the audience at the same time acts and participates.[17]

Except for certain experiences of religious ecstasy there is nothing in the West to match shamanism.[18]

The shamanistic performance is not mere spectacle. It is also high drama. The shaman struggles with-for-through the patient's body in order to find the disease and exorcise it. *The drama is to go into the patient's body and take from it the disease.* This is a personalized version of an ancient and worldwide story: the descent into the underworld, the perilous journey, the struggle against nonhuman beings waged by a person and his non-human allies, ultimate confrontation with the Great Beast, victory, triumphant return carrying a trophy. Often the shaman will show a bloody feather, or pebble, or other concrete manifestation of the disease he has vanquished. Only on the surface is there a one-to-one relationship between shaman and patient. The sick man summons the shaman. The main problem is diagnostic: Of what is the sick man sick? The cure is not a remedy but a diagnosis. Once the disease can be identified, located, and publicly exposed, it will go away, the patient will be cured. Or it will not go away, and the patient will die. The disease is something concrete and "bad" that has *gone into* the patient, and the shaman is asked *to get the bad out.* To do this the shaman does not work alone. He is a shaman because he can call on "allies" or "helpers" or "familiars" who are more powerful than he but responsive to his call. They assist him or, more exactly, *take him over and use his body as the field for their work.* The patient's body and the shaman's body are a battlefield where a war is waged between shaman-possessed-by-his-allies and disease-who-possesses-the-patient; a war that is also a game of hide-go-seek. Thus the shaman is as transparent as the sick man; and the essential relationship is between shaman transformed and sick man transformed.

[17] Shirokogoroff (1936), quoted in Lewis (1971), 53.

[18] Undeniably, the experience of believers at a revival meeting or faith healing or snake handling Protestant service is a species of religious ecstasy with the preacher performing as shaman. Also the several varieties of black churches in North and South America and the Caribbean combine elements of African shamanism (voodoo and other practices) with fundamentalist Protestantism. Of course, early Christianity is imbued with shamanistic elements. The claim of the fundamentalist churches that they carry the germ of the authentic early church is valid.

Surrounding and determining this complex is the community who are present not as neutral or even interested bystanders, but as a kind of Greek chorus. They assist, comment, criticize, participate, evaluate; they move in and out of the action; sometimes they occupy the foreground and sometimes the background. They are deeply implicated in the struggle, and they hang on the outcome. For their lives are at stake as well as the lives of shaman and patient. The entire field of the shamanistic drama can be drawn like this:

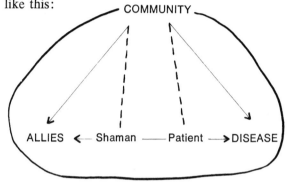

The community infiltrates and determines the entire performance. This is seen as true if we ask what the disease is and what the allies are. Insofar as the disease is more than a biological fact, it is an embodiment of the community's curses, aggressive feelings, death wishes, hostility, etc. This value system must be understood relativistically. The disease is whatever the community dislikes, fears, holds to be taboo, resists, resents, cannot face. In order to objectify, exteriorize, and come to terms with these feelings, they are projected onto the sick man who may or may not also suffer from a biological illness. Of course the sick man is part of the community, and he unconsciously collaborates in becoming sick. The allies are not so easy to identify. They are not simply the opposite of the disease. The allies—like the shaman—are not at the center of the community, but on its extreme edge. The allies, like the shaman, are necessary but feared; an agent of good but a possessor of very menacing powers. The medicine of the shaman is homeopathic: It fights the disease on the disease's terms with the disease's weapons and cannot structurally be distinguished from the disease. That is, the shaman-transformed is just as much a function of the community's unconscious collective emotional life as is the disease. Thus at any moment the shaman may find himself not a celebrated hero but an outcast. Oedipus the King becomes the untouchable exile at Colonus. But while he is in the community's favor, no trick, magic, sleight of hand, cunning, faking, or even out-and-out lying will displease the people. For the shaman exists as shaman only within the field of the audience's wishes. In this dreamlike world anything wished for is possible.

The disease is an idea: the incarnation of a communal antiwish (= the curse, the demon, black magic). The power of the disease is equal to and opposite to the power of the shaman. But the shaman is also an idea (= the magic incantation, the allies, white magic). Both shaman and disease are creatures of the community. The shaman = the good forces = the positive side of the community = solidarity, unity, oneness, wholeness. The disease = the bad forces = the negative side of the community = disruption, fragmentation, disunity, separation. For traditional communities the great evil is fragmentation, the ultimate punishment, ostracism.

Thus I think I am justified in saying that the true confrontation in a shamanistic performance is between two contradictory sides of the community's psychosocial life. And that this psychosocial life is extremely manichaean, a perpetual struggle between good and bad, light and dark, us and them, here and there, in-the-village and outside, life and death, human beings and nonhuman beings. Anyone who bridges these terrible gaps, who in some way eliminates, modifies, or transforms these absolute polarities, is to be sought after, implored, used, and feared.

Shamanism develops in societies where daily existence is, or has been, precarious. It is more usual to find shamanism among hunting cultures than in agricultures. In farming there is a regularity to life, and rituals tend toward seasonal celebrations of bounty. In hunting, however, there is always doubt that food will be found; and the lives of the hunters are in jeopardy. In other words, the manichaean vision develops out of reality.

There is no reason to believe that our society, for all its technological sophistication, is not open to shamanistic revival. Certainly the knowledge that nuclear weapons exist makes life among us precarious. Even more directly, the great cities of the world are indeed jungles, full of immediate dangers. And the dangers are the sudden kills associated with hunting societies, not the slow kills of drought or even flood and famine associated with agriculture.

I think I am also correct in saying that shamanistic performances work through the contradictions and gaps in a community's psychosocial life. The contradictions are not resolved with finality but simply appeased for the time being. A patient recovers, or dies. But somewhere else the struggle goes on. The drama is not temporary; the disease cannot be allayed once and for all. The shamanistic performance is a testing of the community's responsiveness to its own psychosocial needs. This responsiveness is always being projected, localized somewhere within the community. The shaman is used to seek out exactly where the struggle is at the moment; he is a human divining rod.

Is the performer a shaman? If so, how? If not, why not? If he is not a shaman, ought he to be one? If so, how? These questions can be boiled down to: Is the theater the place where we localize and act through our own or our community's psychosocial life? If not, why not? If so, how?

Philip Slater writes:

> Another example of the way in which formal structures help disconnect the individual from his or her organic milieu is the drama. Drama as we know it has many roots, but in part it serves as both a substitute for, and a vehicle for the erosion of, community life. Drama, as opposed to ritual enactment, begins when street life ends—when one cannot assume that he will "run into" the people he wants to see in the normal course of a day.
>
> The most powerful source of drama is the family—the great tragedies are almost all family affairs. In a simple community when a family crisis occurs people run into the street and the community gathers around to mediate, nourish, and absorb. As a community becomes larger, less integrated, more impersonal, the capacity of the family to generate drama does not change, but it can no longer be shared. The community becomes privatized, the family isolated, the streets empty. It is at this point that drama in the form familiar to us begins to emerge—as if people had to have some place to go with their collective responsivity. Into the hole left by the retirement of the family inside the dwelling is poured a dramatic scene, enacted by performers.
>
> We can see this transition most clearly in Greek drama, which generally takes place in the street outside the family home. Indeed, the killings and mutilations usually take place *inside* the home, offstage, and then are reported to the chorus just as if they, and the audience, were villagers gathered in the street. Athens in the period when Greek drama was at its peak had witnessed a rapid urbanization, with shrinking and isolation of the family unit, not unlike what we have experienced during the past century.
>
> Occasionally performers have tried to ply their trade in

communities that have not lost their social responsivity, with unfortunate results. The simple people forget the artificiality of the setting and are prone to enter the action. A villain risks his life in such a setting. We smile condescendingly at this behavior, but it is this responsivity and sense of interconnectedness that make such communities secure and nourishing social environments—environments that "work." It is not that they are childish or stupid, only that their social impulses are still working in an intense and automatic way, whereas ours have atrophied. Supposedly we have substituted "rational," "reasoned," or "judicious" behavior for this responsivity, but how poorly it works can be seen at a glance. Referral agencies, mental hospitals, prisons, and nursing homes are a few of the tardy, impersonal, inhumane, and generally rather dilapidated mechanisms we have evolved to replace this naive responsivity.

The drama, meanwhile, is one of the principal devices we have for deadening this response. We are conditioned very early to look on passively while people are being beaten, killed, or suffering in every conceivable way. The ultimate success of the drama in anesthetizing our social responses is apparent in phenomena such as My Lai and the Kitty Genovese murder. The theatre helps train us in non-responsiveness so that the formal institutions that depend for their existence on our social narcosis can survive.

It is the theatre itself that has begun to develop an antidote to this condition, not without considerable resistance from its case-hardened audiences. Environmental theatre seems almost to pinpoint this issue—not only in its efforts to engage the audience in action, but in its impulse to return to the street.[19]

Even more absolutely than stage drama, television is the great deadener. At suppertime, and again before sleep, millions of citizens are shown the horrors of war, sandwiched between the most orally gratifying (or stimulating) commercials so that people dying and people buying are connected at the deepest level, and pleasantly. One watches the misery that is "news" with detachment, or relish; and one's supper and dreams are full of the uneasiness of induced detachment. Or, worse, of induced gratification. Like Romans at their gladiatorial games we see "reality" acted out in front of us, but are powerless to do more than raise or lower our thumbs. The gesture is meaningless because the performers who are saved from death at this show will die at some future show. We watch not staged fights among individuals, or even vast spectacles in the mountain lakes of north Italy, as

[19] Philip Slater, "Earthwalk" [to be published].

the Romans did. We watch whole "worlds"—arranged in great teams of First, Second, and Third. And more domestic excitements of "street violence" and "hijackings." All real enough but de-realized by the distance, detachment, separation, and narcosis of TV. The interludes are made of "human interest" stories and the perpetuals: sports and weather.

Need we ask why what is happening to us is happening? Yes.

What are the "deep structures" of shamanism? And how do these relate to theater in industrialized societies? First I do not say that shamanism is the only source of theater, though I do think it is one of two sources. The other is puberty initiation rituals of boys. I think that it can be demonstrated that the phenomenon called drama—whether it occurs in ancient Greece, medieval or modern Europe, China, Japan, India, or Africa—can be shown to derive from either shamanism or initiation rituals, or combinations of the two. I am asserting this in the strictest historical sense. I will not try to prove it here because it is only tangent to my purposes in writing this book. What is of concern here are the *structural* affinities between shamanism and performance, between the shaman and the performer.

The deep structure of shamanistic performance is a protagonist-antagonist conflict by means of which the secret wishes of the community are exposed and redistributed. Shamanism's function is social homeostasis. Shamanism cannot exist in isolation; it is inconceivable in individual terms. This may at first appear strange because the shaman is a person who is often treated as an outcast, a person so feared and so weird in his look and behavior that people keep their distance from him. But, as we have seen, the shaman functions as a repository for the community's wishes and antiwishes; he is an incarnation of projections, fantasies, legends, and "powers" that originate outside him, possess him, use him, transform him, energize him, and enable him to do what he does. However, the shaman need not be "pure." He is himself just as he is the community's repository and screen. Therefore it is not damaging to find shamans who are self-serving, cunning, tricky, egocentric, and anything else their personalities make of them. The shaman's slyness, in fact, may be a display of qualities the community secretly admires. A shaman, unlike a priest, is encouraged to show his faults. A priest displays only the "better" half of a man; he is expected to repress all that does not serve the institution he represents. The shaman expresses what everyone else represses. He is not a keeper of the holy, as the priest is.

Quite the opposite, the holy keeps—and plays with—the shaman. The shaman is the vessel through which all that is powerful chooses to express itself. And these powers are inherent in the community itself, are the community. The shaman is preinstitutional; his social work is privatized, localized. Priests are created when the homeostatic process is institutionalized, regularized, arranged into entirely known values. Frozen.

The shaman is a kind of jokester, fraud, showman; the performer is a kind of holy man, curer, vessel, expresser of taboo subjects. I don't think the performer is a run-down shaman, but I do think that when a society develops institutions to replace the shaman, then the performer as we know him arises: Every church needs its juggler, and no matter how priest-oriented a society, the perplexing mixture of holy man and trickster who is the shaman is resurgent in the performer. The performer is the shaman to societies with an organized priesthood.

There attaches to the actor through the centuries a taint of the prostitute, the trickster, the sham, the phony. And also a touch of sacredness and awe. There is also more than a little rivalry between the church and the theater. This is because the actor, like the priest, contacts the powers-that-be and is able to enact a eucharist all his own, a transmigration of spirits no less miraculous than anything the Catholic church, or any other, is able to cook up. Only the church keeps its miracles for itself, and uses them to educate, manipulate, extort, and rule the people. The actor more openly sells what he does, and he liberates the people by making them laugh at what the church demands everyone bow their heads before. Or if the actor puts his public in awe, it is in awe of his performance, not of the ideology that supposedly supports the performance. In short, the actor acting exposes as a lie the bag of miracles every church attributes to a so-called Divine.

But the shaman is again something special. He is a church-without-a-church. What the shaman is unable not to do the actor trains himself to simulate. The shaman is the one who cannot prevent the spirits from possessing him and who, ultimately, gives in to the "call." The shaman makes a career out of what he is powerless to stop. If later he becomes a flimflam man, so what? The community has already possessed him, is using him. The actor trains himself to induce the spirits to enter him, or to simulate the effect of the spirits entering him. The actor makes a career out of pretending to be a shaman.

I make a distinction between "actor" and "performer." The

actor leans in the direction of simulation and pretend, the performer in the direction of achieving by rigorous, disciplined means what the shaman is powerless to prevent. The actor can exist anywhere, even in the most alienated, priest-ridden society. The performer can exist only within a community. That is why in our days the performer exists only as part of the ensemble, the group, the commune: a community within the alienated society at large.

There is more to the problem. The actor makes a career out of pretending to be shaman—this is the beginnings of the identification between the prostitute and the actor. The prostitute is a woman who *stands for* another woman in the eyes of men. Prostitute = substitute. This standing for is a show, an entertainment based on the fantasy projections of the client who asks of the prostitute little else than that she be a blank screen. An encounter with a prostitute is a micro-theatrical performance. The actor is a man who stands for other people in the eyes of the audience. I know that there are male prostitutes and female actors. But, for whatever reasons, over the centuries most prostitutes have been women and most actors have been men. I think this is not inbred into the human species but a historical circumstance and changeable. It is in fact changing. And I do not think I am too bold in saying that as one career opens up to recruits from the opposite sex, the other does also. In a fundamental way theater and prostitution are public and private versions of each other. I also think that if either profession were absolutely perfected, the other would vanish. So those who wish to end prostitution need only perfect theater—and vice versa.

The shaman is in his way a public prostitute—a man who stands for someone, or something, else. He introjects the fantasies projected onto him. This introjection is so complete that the shaman often believes he is the god, demon, person, animal, or thing he is possessed by. Similarly for the performer who trains himself to *accept trance and possession; and to find the ways into and out of unusual states of consciousness and doingness*. The performer acts through circumstances on behalf of the audience who witnesses his behavior. The performer also originates that behavior because in modern societies self-consciousness is a privileged value, something sought after and trained for.

And it is self-consciousness that sets the performer off from the shaman. Something happens to the shaman; he is "called." He does what he does and at most assists his "calling." But the performer tries very hard to exist sequentially in two different states of being. During training, preparation, and rehearsal the performer wants to be aware of what is happening to him—he wants *to choose to let it happen*. He wants to compose it himself, make the performance himself: be entirely conscious of his participation in an event that, beyond its emotional components, has political, personal, and social "statements" to make. The performer wants to have effects and to know the effects he has. And then, at the decisive hours of performance, he wants to be able to let everything go, to perform "without anticipation," to fall entirely into the spell of the performance, to "give up" his consciousness to the "action."

This set of tasks is incredibly difficult to achieve and has many self-contradictions built into it. But it is what Brecht sought, and what so many people who persist in doing theater in modern societies feel to be the only way. I turn over the contradictions. I try to work them out in rehearsals and performances. Up to today I have found no rock-bottom answers.

Words and magic were in the beginning one
and the same thing, and even today words
retain much of their magical power. By words
one of us can give to another the greatest
happiness or bring about utter despair; by
words the teacher imparts his knowledge
to the student; by words the orator sweeps his
audience with him and determines its
judgements and decisions. Words call forth
emotions and are universally the means by
which we influence our fellow-creatures.
Therefore let us not despise the use of words
in psycho-therapy and let us be content if we
may overhear the words which pass between
the analyst and the patient.
Sigmund Freud

The heat was so intense that from time to time
boys were told to place fresh cattle dung
on the ground so that those delivering
addresses could stand in it now and again
to cool their feet. . . . In these invocations
grievances, both real and imagined, are made
public, not with the purpose of complicating
the issue or inflaming passions, but because
it is the rule of such gatherings that everything
a man has in his heart against others must
be revealed and no bitterness kept secret.
E. E. Evans-Pritchard

6 Therapy

The impact of various psychotherapies on contemporary performing styles cannot be overestimated. In workshops since the days of
Stanislavski the emphasis has been on the "work on oneself."
This no longer stops with mastery of theatrical techniques such
as speaking, moving, singing, and dancing. Working on oneself
includes knowing about one's past and how that past shapes
the present; it includes removing "blocks," or impasses of a
neurotic or otherwise psychopathologic kind. Techniques of working on oneself include various exercises adapted from group
therapy, Gestalt therapy, psychoanalysis, and other therapies.
Rehearsals are no longer repetitions of material designed to

provide an "interpretation" of the play being produced. Rehearsals include "confrontation" with the material; using the material as a way of evoking associations in the performers. These associations become the subjects of the drama, and the audience sees not merely the production of a play but the use of "the role as a trampoline, an instrument with which to study what is hidden behind our everyday mask—the innermost core of our personality—in order to sacrifice it, expose it." [1]

At least since Freud the inner life of individuals has become the subject of much study and art. And this inner life displays as much fundamental sameness among individuals as does the outer social life. We are each ourselves, unique; but each of us is much like the others in terms of life crises, psychic careers, and frailties. Traditionally drama took the outer life in crisis as its mode of action. The introduction of psychology as a major field of human knowledge meant that drama would somehow have to make the inside outside—into a mode of action—or cease being important. Dramatists were quick to answer the challenge and the plays of Chekhov, Toller, Pirandello, Ionesco, Genet, and Becket do exteriorize the inner life transforming it into a mode of action. But practitioners of stagecraft have been slower to answer the challenge. Meyerhold did to a degree; Artaud saw what had to be done but could not do it. Only with the development of environmental theater over the past fifteen years has stagecraft caught up with playwriting. The inside is the outside now in the work of Grotowski, Chaikin, Brook, and others. Surprisingly, this transformation has brought contemporary theater close to the theater of many "primitive" peoples whose performances have always been an exteriorization of inner states.

Therapy is based on psychology which is based on a single, unverifiable, undeniable premise: that people have an inner life —some of it conscious and much of it unconscious. This inner life is related to displayed behavior in a very complicated manner. A special mode of circuitry relates inner life to behavior. In fact, behavior is the visible aspect of inner life just as inner life is the invisible aspect of behavior. The unconscious is that part of the inner life of which the individual is only indirectly aware, mostly through free associations, slips of the tongue, fantasies, and dreams. It is this realm of associations, slips, fantasies, and dreams that the environmental theater is especially concerned with. It is genuinely a new theater.

[1] Grotowski (1968), 37.

Am I saying that less than one hundred years ago people didn't know they had an inner life? No, but I'm saying something almost as radical. There was no way of talking about that inner life or incarnating it in art. Although the inner life was always present, it was not comprehensible until psychology and psychoanalysis developed a vocabulary and methodology to handle it. This work is still rough. And although the field is specialized, the consequences of the discoveries are universal; as are, for example, the consequences of the postulates of modern physics.

Often enough the work of TPG has been a groping—blind steps into an unknown prompted by the need for survival, or by curiosity, or by themes uncovered in the plays we were working on. Or from the intimate needs of individuals in the Group. At each step these intimate needs have been acknowledged. I believe it necessary that these needs not be nurtured privately but brought into the open—"dealt with." Thus, there is a very strong therapeutic dimension to the work. Furthermore, I believe that healthy persons (= whole persons = self-aware persons) are more able to create full, rich, and suggestive art than are wounded, fragmented persons. We may never be able to heal ourselves, but at least we do not cherish our wounds.

TPG's experience with therapy has taken three forms. First, we spent more than seven months in a weekly program of group encounter sessions directed by Larry Sacharow, Judy Altenhaus, and, occasionally, Fred Altenhaus. From this work—and other techniques in the air in the late sixties—we adopted/adapted a number of exercises. Secondly, our very basic workshop work is strongly therapeutic. This derives from the commitment to "lifework," to a theater that transcends what theater usually is in our society; it is closely related to concepts articulated by Grotowski in *Towards a Poor Theatre*. Also it comes from a convergence of ideas in Western psychotherapy, Zen, and yoga: an opening to the East with large consequences not only in theater but across a wide range of American experiences. (America particularly seems prone to these Asian influences. After all, the original Americans came to these continents via Siberia-Alaska; and the Americas face the Pacific as well as the Atlantic. This Pacific-facing may ultimately prove more important than our Atlantic past. We are learning again that the world is truly round.) Thirdly, the style of TPG's public performances has correctly been *accused* of being therapeutic. This is not the only thing these performances are. Like many other events performances are *overdetermined:* more goes on in them than is necessary for their existence; this richness of many converging sources results in an equivalent richness of radiating divergent energies. Or is this just my fancy way to justify confusion?

Each of these kinds of therapeutic experiences needs to be examined. The question for me has never been: "Theater *or* therapy?" but *"What are the ways in which theater can be/ought to be/is therapeutic?* Or, posing the question in a large scope, what is the health-giving function of theater on both the individual and the social levels? Is there a homeostatic function of theater? In what way is an art that is *acting* also an *acting out* and/or an *acting through?* How do these terms relate to each other? What is the role of the perfomer? Is he shaman, doctor, artist; or sick person, neurotic, everyman? In exploring the medical functions of performance I suggest the addition of therapy to the list of theater's functions that already includes entertainment, education, initiation, worship, economics, and aesthetics. In function, too, theater is overdetermined. Not that all performances show all the possible theatrical functions.

It is not experiments like Moreno's psychodrama that uncover theater's therapeutic function. Psychodrama strips theater of its nontherapeutic functions and leaves it impoverished and localized; bereft of the cultural and historical reverberations that make a performance of *Oedipus* something different from just an oedipus complex. The therapeutic function is elicited by—or at least indicated by—generalized *yearnings* felt by many individuals in industrialized societies. These yearnings can be categorized:

> 1. *Wholeness.* Participatory democracy. Self-determination on the individual, local, community, national, and international levels. Therapies which aim for Oneness, Unity, the First or Last Cause. "Getting It Together." Total Theater. Intermedia. Integrated Electric Circuitry. An end to the dichotomies:
>
> | | |
> |---|---|
> | a whole person | not mind/body/spirit |
> | families | not individuals |
> | communities | not government vs. governed |
> | jobs like play | not alienated "work" |
> | art where we are | not far away, in museums |
> | one world in peace | not nations at war |
> | man one with nature | not ecological destruction |
>
> 2. *"Process" and organic growth.* An end to the assembly line where a person does not do a "whole thing" but is fragmented and turned into a machine. Therefore, "process

not product." Also: organic foods, "turn people into artists not onto art," idealistic Marxism where the means of production are in the hands of the people, and "do your own thing."

3. *Concreteness.* Down with theories, abstractions, generalizations: the "biggies" of thought, art, industry, education, government. Instant history: "Tomorrow Now!" "Power to the People!" Make your demands known by acting them out. Street and guerrilla theater. Marches, demonstrations, take-overs. Urban warfare. Revolutionary rhetoric. Digging the immediate. Sensory awareness, concrete poetry, earth art, Happenings, pornography, turbulence, and discontinuity instead of an artificial smoothness and conformity. "Blow your image."

4. *Religious, transcendental experience.* Eastern philosophies and disciplines, especially those that are compatible with "electric circuitry." Alpha-wave meditation: biofeedback; TM, Zen, yoga, and so on. Messianism, Charles Manson and the Family, epiphanies, psychedelics. Ways to truth through surrender of the self, or breaking down ego boundaries. Searches for answer to eschatological questions: What is the meaning/purpose of life? Sacralization of everyday life; making all gestures meaningful. Encounter groups, marathons, theater made in, by, and for communes. Tribalism, rock festivals like Woodstock, trips, freak-outs, ecstasies.

This collection of hopes, slogans, pop history, charlatanism, rip-off, energy, enthusiasm, and idealism reads a touch quaint even now. In some ways the sixties were full of "nativistic movements" and "crisis cults"—attempts to go forward and backward at the same time, to plug new and shocking information into systems not equipped to handle the load. But it is wrong to dismiss the period, or too easily reject its impulses. Wholeness, process/organic growth, concreteness, religious, transcendental experience are each ways of saying the same thing: Links must be discovered or forged between industrial societies and nonindustrial ones, between individualistic and communal cultures. And a vast reform in the direction of communality—or at least a revision of individualism—is necessary. This reform and revision will leave no aspect of modern society untouched; not economics, government, social life, personal life, aesthetics, or anything else.

Theater takes a pivotal position in these movements because the movements are histrionic: a way of focusing attention and demanding change. The marches, demonstrations, street and guerrilla theaters, arrests of well-known and unknown people were for show: symbolic gestures. (One of the great differences between the white liberal-radical movements and the black revolutionary movements is that underneath the black talk is actuality, not symbolism. In such groups as the Weathermen, white radicals tried to adapt black stances but not very successfully. The fact is that the plight of blacks in America is many times more desperate than the plight of whites. In the black experience there is a basis for genuine revolution; in the white experience there is a basis for symbolic or hoped-for revolution. This is nowhere made clearer than in comparing the trials of the Black Panthers to the trials of white radicals, especially the Chicago Seven. Mr. Eight—Bobby Seale, a black—was "separated" from the trial of the others, all white.) I call the great actions of the late sixties symbolic—even with all their violence and qualities of ultimate confrontation—because the proclaimed stakes were way out of line with the actual stakes. Ultimately, each demonstration was exactly that: a way of showing, not a way of doing; to "seize" a building did not mean to actually engage in the kind of insurrection practiced by Mao or Castro; rather the American actions were gestures, rehearsals, theater pieces designed to show what could happen, or what the protestors somewhere felt deeply ambivalent about. Each symbolic act was a kind of kidnapping of conscience to be held in jeopardy until a ransom of action was paid: ending the War in Vietnam, sharing the governance of the universities with students, and so on. The goal was not to overthrow the system, or even the government, but to make the system respond.

The peculiar quality of the late sixties was one of "rehearsal," or "When I make demands, treat me as an adult; when the conflict is for real and I can get hurt, treat me as a child." It was a world in which everything changed and remained the same. A world of messiahs and Utopian proclamations: Paradise *Now!* Behind each promise lurked a betrayal. Around 1971 the curtain came down. The struggle resumes, but with different strategies.

Theater, as always, was both a part of the period and a reflection of it. Many felt that the theater should no longer deal with illusions of any kind. The theater was "real"; as real as anything else in life. A confusion was promoted that made it hard to tell which theatrical action was "real" and which was "acted." The confusions that Pirandello and Genet treat from the distance of prescheming and writing out the sequence of whirligigs and dizzying effects were introjected directly into the heart of the performing process: into rehearsals, improvisations, performances. Not even the actors knew what/who was what. Theater went into the streets; the streets surged into the theaters. Theater became a testing ground and initiator of social changes, a laboratory; a place not merely to watch things but to *do* things. I shared in these actions.

Insofar as theater is an active agent and laboratory of change and transformation—for the theater workers and/or audiences—insofar as theater is a place where change occurs, theater becomes its own subject. An inversion of orthodox arrangements happens. The classical subjects of theater—the great dramas, for example—are no longer "presented." They are used as a means to look at other subjects, or as lenses to focus attention on changes taking place in the performers themselves. Instead of seeing Hamlet through the experience of Laurence Olivier, we witness Judith Malina through the actions of Antigone. Instead of the audience remaining rather comfortable in the dark anonymity and passivity of the auditorium, spectators are put on the stage, in the light, and told to act. The performer is trained not to pretend but to be himself. The mechanics of the theater—lights, stage machinery, scenery—which had for so long served to create an illusion, are exposed, shown as they are, opened to public viewing. Rehearsals themselves, once the most cherished secret operation, are made public; and the fundamental *strategies* of theater are put at the disposal of spectators who participate in determining how the play should go, what it means and whether or not the performers should finish it. In short, *letting the secrets out and demystifying theater* becomes a prime theatrical purpose.

These phenomena can be examined from all kinds of perspectives. For example: The people have been tricked for years by "magic" ideologies and the duplicity of politicians; the workings of government and business have been hidden; vast populations live their lives according to illusions and false dreams. The theater, in its very substance, must act against these lies. Or: The work of Freud and many other psychologists has revealed the workings of the unconscious; once these workings are "revealed," they are, by definition, conscious: the "backstage" areas of individual thought and feelings are now public. The theater ought to do likewise. Or: The historical experience of World War II, Nazism, the Cold War, the Pax Americana, and neo-imperialism has shown everyone that the myths and ideologies of the Western cultural complex are lies. Theater must show these myths for what they are. Or: Everywhere people are taking power into their own hands; a great social revolution is occurring hand in hand with a revolution of consciousness. The "Third World" of people, of ideas, of feelings, is rising up against the oppressors and building a new world. Theater participates in this revolution. Or: The Western nations that have dominated the world are disintegrating; the English, French, and German empires are gone; America is discredited. As usual, decadence and chaos mark the death throes of a culture. Theater suffers with the rest. There are as many more "ors" as there are perspectives to current events. We live in a relativistic age where events are comprehensible only when measured against other events.

In this book I am measuring theater against many non-theatrical events. I maintain that there is a give-and take among technical, personal, cultural, and historical matters. I say that theater is structurally and functionally related to rituals, cere-monies, and social gatherings of many kinds; to myth, folklore, and ways of story-telling; to playing, games, and athletics; to shamanism, therapy, and religion. This is nothing new. What may be new is that I insist that the most technical aspects of theater —training, rehearsal, staging—are understandable only when one grasps the larger dimensions of theatrical sources and processes. And that questions of who the performer is when he performs, what a character is, what the relationships are between performers and spectators, and all other matters of a seemingly "just theatrical" nature are genuinely consequential to society at large. In short, that theater is a model of the innumerable ways men have of *actively* integrating their feelings, wishes, fantasies, and dreams with the facts of the natural world. I am not aiming for a single view of theater, a key to fit all locks. Rather I want to follow to their roots the impulses that make theater inevitable whenever human beings congregate. I believe theater is coexistent with the human condition, and a basic element of this condition.

Theater as therapy, therapy as theater, therapy in theater, therapy for theater, therapy and theater—add them up and they are but aspects of an aspect. But in defining what theatrical purposes therapy serves we may discover what therapeutic functions theater has. This, in turn, will illuminate the relation-ships among performers and between performers and spectators. At one level, of course, performers are not shamans; they play the shamanic role only when it is projected on them by spectators. But on another level performers invite the fantastic, empowering identifications spectators insist on awarding them. Actors, like gods, are nourished by those who worship them. And inevitably the performer introjects what has been projected on him; he becomes what is expected of him. For example, here is Jason Bosseau who, for several months, played the role of Dionysus in *Dionysus in 69*.

> I am not interested in acting. I am involved in the life process of becoming whole. I do many technical exercises which organically suit that process. They act as a catalyst for my ability to let essence flow, to let my soul speak through my mind and body. The impulse becomes the action. The body is free to fly. The mind is liberated from tensions of the body, and flows with sounds, feelings, vibrations, everything. Everything becomes/is the flow. Mind/body are one. Thoughts/feelings/sounds/movements/vibrations are one. The flow pounds in my being, pulsates, jerks, explodes, retreats, bounces, settles, redefines itself, reintegrates itself and feeds everything from the depths of my gut to the outermost limitlessness of the universe.[2]

That's the way it feels to be a god among men, even for a night.

But the shaman's role is dangerous, precarious. The Performance Group's experiences with encounter group therapy began when Patrick McDermott stopped rehearsal one afternoon in November, 1968, and demanded that we "stop sweeping shit under the rug and start dealing with each other." The Group had been in existence exactly one year; we were performing *Dionysus* three nights a week and rehearsing *Makbeth* days. From the beginning many TPG exercises were "confrontations" (a term taken from therapy and Grotowski). Two or more people face each other and say/do what they feel about each other. The performances themselves were used as confrontations, but it was impossible to be direct and honest in front of two hundred people some of whom wanted blood. And as director I was excused from the public confrontations. This was wrong because much of the tension centered on me. So intrigues developed, tensions built, the work snagged.

We needed to know more about each other. We had to find

[2] Jason Bosseau in The Performance Group (1970), no page.

ways of unblocking communication. Our work was unusual, and we didn't know how it was affecting us. We didn't know when we were "acting" and when we were "being." Or how to act and be simultaneously. Entries from my notebook that fall:

In standard acting the performer "takes on" the "life" of the "character." In Brechtian acting the performer "stands outside" the character and "comments." Here the performer "confronts" not only the character (in fact, less the character) but the *action:* the ritual-like movement of events. In simple terms, the physical presence of the performer = the physical presence of the action.

The audience is not merely a witness to the interpenetration but a participant. Concretely, four elements interact: space, reactualized event, performer, and audience.

The consequences for the performer are that he is inside the action but present through it. Either he is transparent and the action is visible through him; or the action is transparent and the performer is visible through it. Thus the performer's problems are not only technical and professional but personal and private.

The performer's life is "on the line"—visible and threatened. This results in confusions and interpenetrations between the performer's "daily life" and his "working life." It also leads to deep audience involvement because what they are seeing is someone *actually going through* something; or going through *to* something.

Performers are no longer evaluatable on the basis of orthodox criteria but on their ability to incarnate:
duration/length . . . intensity/temperature . . . conviction/sincerity
To be authentic = to spend irrevocably. Like the Eastern mystics. Rites of passage. Irrevocable giving or exchange. To be inauthentic = to use the "tricks of the trade."
authentic = to exhaust
inauthentic = to conserve
When the system is perfected, the performer will be able to choose which situations demand authentic and which inauthentic treatment. Confrontations like Ritual Combat are examples of authentic performing. They are usually short, of high intensity, and performed with high conviction. Cage's random concerts are examples of inauthentic performing. They are of open duration—that is, theoretically endless, of low intensity, and performed without high conviction.

There is a danger to our way of working. A special insanity, both in the performers and in the audience—the re-creation of a nonliterate, intensely committed, sacral experience.

To conceive of a medievalism armed with modern technology is to glimpse the darker and more tyrannical side of a new art I am in the process of exploring. To say the least —like Frankenstein—I am ambivalent. But I cannot turn back.

The advantage of a secular life is that events are neutral; the disadvantage is in increased reification and alienation. The advantage of a sacred life is that events are meaningful; the disadvantage is that persons are punished cruelly for trespasses against meaning. Our work, and our times, are tending toward the sacred.

Two weeks after writing out these thoughts I devised the following exercise:

Death move. Shephard climbs a tower—during *Dionysus* —takes a push-up position over Jason, suddenly drops on Jason, forcing Jason's air (guts) out. *Murder with the central body.*

What else usually associated with the extremities can we do with the central body? And vice versa?

Usually Extremity: eating, caressing, smiling, crying, holding, killing, pointing, walking, talking, scratching, tickling, seeing, hearing, carrying.

Usually Central Body: breathing, heartbeating, digesting, fucking, hiding, dying, hunting, feeling "deep inside," stomach rumbling.

Exercise: Articulate each of these as they usually are; transform them into actions for other parts of the body. For example, have your hand breathe, your stomach cry, your arm hide, your back point.

Still two weeks later:

The rage in me against the Group as a whole (strange how it does not focus in on the "guilty" individuals) for a continuing—though somewhat improving—pattern of lateness/absence. The feeling that they do not work as hard as I do, do not commit as much, are not as determined; do not really care, in fact. Knowledge that I depend on them for my work and therefore consider their absences/latenesses as personal betrayals of me.

It is this quality of betrayal that is the most difficult to really understand, tying in, as it does, to my other patterns of neurotic (or what have you) behavior:

One nexus:
    Porn—love—children—"other" women—Joan

Connectives: ↓

        humiliation—work (writing, directing)

2nd Nexus: ↓
   Betrayal—rage—paranoia

Connectives: ↓

      "they don't work as hard"
      "they don't want as much"
      "they are not as good as I"

3rd Nexus: ↓

Omniscience—omnipotence—invulnerability.

These five systems all seem tightly related; they all feed into each other; they do not function independently.

Somehow I believe archaically that I can do work, live, love, gratify alone. But also I know—perhaps also archaically—that I can do nothing alone. This is what G. was trying to tell me this morning about acknowledging his existence, his contribution to my life process.

And J.'s and the Group's. And to acknowledge it in fact is also to permit disruptions—to turn over to others—more or less, but in increasing amounts—the possibility of influencing my life; my life "course." . . . To realize that I am not what I put myself out as being. I am not self-contained, invincible, and untouchable.

I do not like to be touched. For those hands on my surface, those unsolicited hands, can suddenly plunge into me and bring up guts.

At the time the Group got involved in group therapy I was still in psychoanalysis seeing an analyst three times weekly. Several other Group members were seeing therapists or analysts also. Sacharow, who led most of the sessions at the Garage, worked at Daytop Village, an addict treatment center, and directed Daytop's theatrical hit, *The Concept*. We had our sessions every Thursday afternoon, usually for about four hours. Attendance was not mandatory, but considerable group pressure meant that nearly everyone always attended. The sessions were modeled on the Daytop techniques and on the methods of Gestalt therapy. The confrontations were direct, often brutal, and much anger was expressed. People made contact with past experiences, especially those relating to their parents. The most intimate relationships were opened for all of us to witness and sometimes participate in. I found the sessions hard because so much anger was directed at me. I began to understand how much I functioned as the Group's parent, and how destructive this was. But changing was not easy because I liked being the Group's parent.

The sessions formalized the ways in which our private lives were involved in the work. Things that had been done blindly were brought into the light of awareness. But full integration of private psychic life and performing life did not take place. Much blurring was eliminated: the "confrontations" were dropped from *Dionysus in 69*, and we developed *Makbeth* along lines that were more orthodox. Some rituals of the Sacharow sessions still characterize TPG work. Sitting in a circle to discuss things; expressing feelings as directly as possible; full expression of anger and other "negative" feelings through any means except physical violence. If someone is troubled, he may "call a circle" and present his trouble to the whole Group; or he may take another person aside and speak with him privately. If someone feels that another is "coming out sideways"—indirectly and vaguely expressing feelings—the "sideways" person will be asked to say clearly what's on his mind. We've developed exercises—like the mirror work discussed in Chapter 3—designed to "blow your image": show a person in a new and maybe uncomfortable light. We resist "dumping": projecting your problems on another or blaming everyone for your own misfortunes. And we try to make the working space "safe," a place where people can follow their impulses, express their feelings, discover themselves and others without fear of being put down.

Therapy is not magic. The Performance Group with whom Sacharow worked broke up less than eight months after the encounter sessions ended. In some ways the sessions brought about the breakup. Among the things we learned was that we were not able to work together.

The breakup of the Group was a terrible period to live through. It came to a head during the fall-winter of 1969–1970. Notebook entries:

> *25 September 1969.* What is it in human nature that makes outwardly enforced discipline necessary—continually necessary? . . . B.—is he lazy? Too simple a diagnosis—but also accurate. Somehow he chooses self-pity, narcissistic and ineffectual anger, sarcasm instead of facing his own qualities

and problems forthrightly. Needing both voice work and the confidence that voice work would bring—he avoids voice work. Needing almost continual probing and experimenting with his role, he settles for clichés.

What should my reaction be? Simple anger seems too primitive. Detailed analysis wasteful. Perhaps simply to demand a discipline. "At least once a day go over your scenes." Have him explore through actions new ways of doing his scenes.

27 September. Lateness—what to do? Fines are simple, hateful—but simple. And it is objective and across the board. Always had difficulties with fines—to make someone pay $5 for 5 minutes. In psychoanalysis being late = cheating yourself—but that is a one-to-one activity and the patient pays. Here the person being paid is late—and the lateness is (1) disruptive of the whole group and (2) contagious and cumulative, if unpunished. Fines are the only way—strictly enforced, not with any apologies. And across the board.

25 November. Must surpass "acting"—only the truth of the individual experience—the direct confrontation between action and self—can surpass acting. No one (except possibly L. and W.) has surpassed acting and really confronted the actions of *Makbeth*.

27 November. Thanksgiving at the theater. Almost empty. Lucky if we have 60 people. Worried about a commercial failure. Death of the theater. Efforts to maintain full-scale full-time company blown to bits. . . . Other, more difficult realization is that the performers here, (excepting L., W., and V.) are not very good; and many of them—in their mid-20's—have stopped growing. That is why workshops are so important now. To sift out the whole and the growable from the mean, the stunted, the resentful, and the impossible.

There is still in this Group after all this time a fear of revealing each other to each other. We close up physically— we cover our faces with our hands—we hide our voices and feelings.

14 December. Snowy Sunday. Extremely depressed about the theater. It's like running a grocery store. Always something to do—very often this something is not creative. I have not created an organization—that is, there is no associate director to direct and I want a leave of absence very badly—a long leave for writing and traveling. There is no general manager to keep the business going. There is not even a loyal group of actors. Some (I think B. chief among them) bad-mouth the performance, distrust me. I am, as Makbeth says, "sick at heart." . . . I am drained emotionally, physically, financially. I do not see a way out except resignation—except saying, "I will not work here anymore."

When I left TDR, I wanted to devote myself to theater and writing. I have not done so. I am devoting myself to caretaking and some patchwork thinking. I have failed.

I do not want another two years of furious anger leading to people-ruined concepts, torn-up hearts, hatreds, distrust. . . . The end of things is as unbearable as the beginning of things.

16 December. Problems in TPG started with sucking and breast feeding: mothering. Now weaning. Some (B., Q., K.) yearn toward narcissism; they seek Grot or their own way. Or K. refuses to be weaned. B. goes toward narcissism. Others also closed off—like F. A few—L., and the new people, and possibly W.—seek relationships. Only in relationships is a creative collaboration that invokes and utilizes celebration and sharing possible.

3 January 1970. Quite frankly, the problems with the play are overshadowed by and are functions of the problems within the Group.

5 January 1970. Waiting for B. at O'John's. The end of the working relationship (formally) which ended sometime ago. Difficult for me to organize my thoughts or feelings—afraid. The stored-up anger—but now it is beyond anger: what would anger help? The fear—wishing to avoid the meeting/confrontation—knowing it is inevitable. Wanting to sidestep the pain of his hatred and contempt; of my own feelings. . . . I think firing someone from the Group is tantamount to killing them and I suffer the anxiety and guilt of a murderer.

Firing B. precipitated the blow-up. The question was whether or not I had the right to fire someone. The debate was not about legalities—as TPG was then structured I had the legal right. It was a question of good faith. I acted in bad faith: By using my legal powers I made it impossible for the Group to survive. My alternative was to quit the Group, abandoning its "properties"—the name, the Garage, the material copyrighted by the Group, the reputation of the work. As things happened, those who sided with me did not use the Garage again for some months. But we kept the legal entity, "The Performance Group." Or rather I kept it. It was not until the spring of 1972 that the Group was restructured so that all members were part of the corporation and five Group members elected to the board of directors. If the Group is to schism again, I cannot run off with it.

When the Group was reconstituted in March, 1970, I knew that the work would have to change. That I would have to be less of a parent and more of a colleague. Also I knew that I had deep resistances to changing the work, and accepting a new role. Those who chose to continue working with me knew of these problems. So we went on together, eyes open. There was no question of returning again to some kind of formalized group therapy. In fact, as time went on, people began to recognize that some of the Daytop techniques—developed as they were to cope with addiction to hard drugs, heroin mostly—promoted a family relationship in which the therapist became a father figure. In using these techniques in the Group I replaced the therapist. So instead of therapy easing our problems, it fed them. Also we learned that anger is not the only feeling that people repress; and that too much of a concentration on releasing anger can lead to blocking other feelings.

For a time we concentrated on the immediate tasks at hand. We researched *Commune,* developing its script along with its actions; we concentrated on our own exercises and in much intense vocal work; we ran workshops for students first at New Paltz and then at Goddard. But the interest in therapy did not vanish. It shifted from a Daytop orientation to a more general interest in Gestalt therapy. The work of Perls, Goodman, Naranjo, and others [3] was of interest because the "general principles" of Gestalt therapy coincided with our theater work. According to Naranjo, these principles are:

> 1. Valuation of actuality: temporal (present versus past or future), spatial (present versus absent), and substantial (act versus symbol).
> 2. Valuation of awareness and the acceptance of experience.
> 3. Valuation of wholeness, or responsibility.

In turn these principles are actuated by techniques of "present-centeredness," which Naranjo describes as "the outspoken request to the patient to attend to and express what enters his present field of awareness. This will most often be coupled with the instruction to suspend reasoning in favor of pure self-observation. This second is the *presentification* of the past or future (or fantasy

[3] There is a wide body of work by and about Gestalt therapists. I can suggest the following: Perls, Hefferline, and Goodman, *Gestalt Therapy* (New York: Dell, 1965); Perls, *Gestalt Therapy Verbatim* (Lafayette, California: Real People Press, 1969); Fagan and Shepherd, eds., *Gestalt Therapy Now* (New York: Harper Colophon, 1971).

in general)." [4] Ideas like this did not so much bring us new exercises as confirm a direction we were already strong in. A similar ratification came from studies individual members made of Zen and yoga.

In practical terms the work on present-centeredness begins with the association exercises. Here the performer learns how to be aware of his associations and to "follow them" (i.e., maintain his awareness) even while performing rigorous physical work. More, the quality of the physical work influences and is influenced by the associations. This is not left to chance. After performers have learned the shapes of the basic exercises I sometimes ask them to sing a song while doing an exercise. The melody and words of the song are conditioned by the shape of the physical work and the quality of the association. Or, sometimes, I may ask a performer to *actualize* an association—make it into breathing, movement, sound. In other words, instead of having the association exist *in relation to the physical work,* the performer *translates the association into the physical work*. This actualizing may lead to discoveries of unique ways of moving, breathing, speaking, or singing—unique in terms of what this particular performer is accustomed to doing.

Group support comes in three ways. Sometimes everyone watches what's happening, intervening only to ask a question or report what's happening. For example, "What's happening to your left arm?" or "Your eyes are squinting and your fists are clenched." These interventions are ways to help the performer be aware in the present of what he is doing. The second means of support is to ignore the performer doing something special. By not paying attention the rest of the group is saying that the performer can use the space as he feels fit; that his associations do not frighten, disgust, embarrass, or shock his colleagues. This kind of formal ignoring is very supportive, and many people are able to go much further than they could working alone in a empty room. It is of course possible for more than one person to be off on a deep trip at the same time.

The third kind of support is interaction among those having associations. This interaction is not psychodrama. People do not take identifiable parts in someone else's memories or fantasies. Quite the contrary, the interaction and contact is on the basis of mutual associations, one thing sparking another, the spontaneous construction of a performance world arising from the simultaneous

[4] Naranjo (1970), 50, 53.

triggering of several chains of associations. Out of the most personal and interiorized impulses comes an increasingly scenic and harmonious total effect. I have seen many exercise periods culminate in singing, dancing, exploring sounds, a kind of group dance-music theater.

From the outside, workshops like these appear at first to be madhouses, but from within they are both liberating and disciplined. They provide each performer with a range of possibilities that he can later call on in rehearsals. Once something is externalized, it is demystified and workable; grist for the mill. To act a secret out in front of one's colleagues is to shatter its terrifying grip. One might not even know the nature of the secret. The secret is its actualization. Not only is a block removed, but many things tied to the block, dammed up behind it, are liberated, too. Each liberated impulse is raw material for further work. Rehearsals are reductions and refinements of workshops, and performances are reductions and refinements of rehearsals. The workshop is the first circle of creativity, and this circle must be as wide as possible—for every succeeding circle will be more limited.

Many blocks not only occur in the body but are *about the body*. The performer is especially prone to *body destruction fantasies*. He fears that harm will come to his own body, often from within. Hours of training are spent in helping the performer develop confidence in his own body. But with growing confidence there sometimes occurs a splitting off so that the performer thinks of his body as an "instrument"—something outside himself which he plays as a violinist plays a violin. Fears of injury do not diminish with increasing mastery of such skills as acrobatics, tumbling, fencing, wrestling; or with less strenuous body skills such as speaking, singing, dance-movement. The tensions are often extreme and hard to control. When working with people who are not actors, and who have few ambitions to become actors, I find them relaxed about their bodies, if unskilled. But performers are very cautious, protective. Furthermore, they are prone to minor injuries that occur suddenly, reach an immediate crisis, and subside. Things like "pulling a muscle," "twisting an ankle," or "hurting my hand," or even more chronic complaints like headache, backache, stomach pains, "stiffness." I do not look lightly on any of these conditions; but I do separate them from the few serious injuries or illnesses that I have encountered among performers. I think that the chronic and minor complaints are psychogenic and are related to body destruction fantasies.

Roheim points out what many psychoanalysts confirm: that "the dreamer's environment is built up out of his or her own body." [5] The landscape of a dream is not external, but representations and elaborations of the dreamer's body. "Every image in the dream, whether human, animal, vegetable, or mineral, is taken to represent an alienated portion of the self." [6] Gestalt therapists will ask patients to play out their dreams, becoming in turn each object they have dreamed. "By re-experiencing and retelling the dream over and over again in the present tense, from the standpoint of each image, the patient can begin to reclaim these alienated fragments." [7] This process of reclamation is similar to rehearsal where, in the Balinese description, "the dance goes into the body." During rehearsal performers learn things that are external to their bodies (i.e., to themselves) so completely and deeply that ultimately these "alienated fragments" appear to originate from inside the performer.

But rehearsal is still more complicated than this; and there are many different kinds of rehearsals. In an example like the Balinese—or our own ballet—where the movements are traditional, having originated back in history, the performer indeed is learning something external to himself and integrating this new material into his body. But the integration is so complete, if successful, that the performer becomes possessed by the new material, becomes an incarnation of some preexistent form. The performer's own body is absorbed by the body of the dance he is dancing. Watching a Balinese master like Kakul of Batuan teach children to dance is to see an old man literally sculpt, pound, smooth, pull, push, guide, and control a young human being. Kakul stands behind his pupil and moves the child's body, making instant corrections not verbally but by actually putting the body right. Sooner or later, if the pupil surrenders to the dance (gives over to Kakul), the "dance goes into the body." Kakul can step back, make fewer and fewer corrections. And then a third phase begins—that in which the dancer *interprets* the dance: makes changes in the traditional gestures. These changes are tiny variations, but these variations are what gives each dancer his or her personal quality. If the variations are too great, Kakul makes corrections; if there are no variations, the dance is mechanical, dead.

In Western theater the performer invents his own gestures.

[5] Roheim (1952), 18.
[6] Enright (1970), 121.
[7] Enright (1970), 121.

Most of the time this is done casually, and little can be said of such work. But when performers work consciously on the structure of their gestures, on the ikonography, their work is very close to what Enright describes as the therapeutic process. Gestures are found that are revealing of the performer and suited to the material being performed. If there is a killing by knife—as in the TPG *Makbeth* or *Commune*—then one must search for ways to make the body into a knife—after having decided that the knife would come from inside the body, rather than use a prop. The problem is one of how to hold the fingers and hand, how to adjust the arm, how to relate the arm to the shoulder, the shoulder to the neck and head; how to organize the entire body. This problem is not mechanical. The action of becoming-a-knife is one in which material is found *inside the performer*—a kind of waking dream—brought outside, examined, worked on, and slowly, step by step reintegrated into the performer's behavior. The gesture of the knife is not found all at once. If it were, the process would be easy and brief. Nor do we know beforehand what we are looking for. We know an approach: that the gesture is *important to the people doing it* and that the *gesture must communicate to others*. What makes the work so painstaking is that many gestures suit one or the other of the necessary conditions, but very few gestures suit both. Or, once a gesture is found that is suitable, it may not effectively relate to other actions in the performance. But if the right gesture is found, the work then shifts to helping the performer accept this gesture as his own.

Contrary to what one might expect, this is not easy. Even though the gesture originates within the performer, he treats it as something alien, difficult, and even threatening. He performs it "from a distance," without conviction, as if it were someone else's. The same problem Kakul faces with his pupil is now faced by the director. The gesture must "go into the body"—the same body from whence it came. The means of getting it there are not much different from those Kakul uses. The gesture is repeated again and again; it is learned. But why is this so?

I think many gestures that performers invent are like their own dreams. These dreams are frequently variations of body destruction fantasies. I consider it decisive that theater is so often about violence and violent sexuality. This recurrent subject matter characterizes "the world of theater" and sets it off from, say, "the world of painting," which includes landscapes, still life, and portraits as well as violent themes. Many theater gestures are hard to accept, painful to reintegrate into the performer's psychic life. The task of reintegration is complicated by the fact that stage environments are not neutral. They are literally dream worlds, extensions of the performer's body; a stage setting or an environment is fundamentally animistic: alive as a dream-object is alive. The performer works in a place where all the things he sees and touches are extensions of his body. He uses his actual body in spaces that are extensions of his fantasy body. Archaic myths of separation and reunion, dismemberment and reparation, are the basic actions of all drama. Fears of bodily harm are always being stirred by the very act of performing. I do not know whether people who are prone to such anxieties are drawn to careers on the stage or whether engaging in such careers stimulates these anxieties. Probably some of both.

Part of the director's job is to help performers see themselves, to become *aware* of what they are experiencing. This awareness is not an intellectualizing but an understanding with the whole mind/body. A block is not usually an inactivity; it is usually an action repeated blindly, with seeming purpose but without the performer's awareness: a compulsion. A block is a barrier that obscures all that is behind it. One doesn't dynamite a block. It needs to be examined, understood, integrated into the performer's field of self-awareness.

> At the end of the association exercises F. begins pounding the floor with her fists. She hits the floor hard but not nearly hard enough to express her rage, grief, frustration: whatever it is that is causing the gesture. To strike with the force that she shows in her belly and shoulders would be to shatter her hands. Her voice, which is naturally strong but often choked into whispering or gasping, is barely audible. She sounds as if someone has a hand at her throat.
>
> As I watch her, I see a bottleneck. There is terrific energy below in her belly and genitals. This energy is squeezed off at her throat. Her head hangs limp, blank except for tears which stream mutely down her cheeks like blood. She is not sobbing; she is making no sound at all. The surges of energy originating in her belly and genitals sweep upward, are blocked at the top of the chest and throat, and sweep outward into her shoulders, arms, and hands. There is a secondary block in her shoulders, a restraint so that when she pounds her hands on the floor she doesn't hurt herself.
>
> After a long while I go over to her, explain what I see, how her body looks to me. I draw her a picture of her body as I see it with the energy below, the blocks, and the energy

flow. I give her some cushions to pound on so that she can
hit as hard as she wants to without breaking her bones.

As the energy is allowed to flow through her shoulders to
her arms and hands—as she begins to pound the cushions—
her throat opens up and she begins to scream.

F.'s problem did not just go away. Giving her the cushions
—and the permission to get angry and scream—did not remove
her block. During performances she still spoke as if there were
a hand at her throat. At other times she would begin a sentence
and then lose the end of it, as if speaking out loud frightened
her back into silence. But the morning I drew her a picture of her
body marked a turning point.

The solution is not a direct confrontation such as "Open your
throat and let it all come through." This kind of instruction
confuses the performer because it simply asks her to do precisely
what she cannot do. It is like shouting to a drowning man: "Just
swim and you'll be all right!" Wallen emphasizes the correct
response which is as applicable to workshop as it is to therapy:

> The therapist works to unblock the impulse so that it can
> organize the field. He may do this by taking the resistance,
> the muscular resistance to crying [for example], as the figure
> of the patient's attention. In other words, instead of em-
> phasizing "You want to cry," he emphasizes "*How* are you
> preventing yourself from crying?" He goes back over and
> over again the problem of "what are you doing that pre-
> vents you from getting what you want at this moment, in
> this immediate situation?" [8]

Thus in showing F. a picture of herself I encouraged her to see
how she was preventing herself from shouting and pounding
her fists. Then by allowing her body to take on the shape of its
resistance she began to learn the means of overcoming it. She
began to find out *for herself* what her own means of resistance
were at that moment.

In the terms of Gestalt therapy F.'s problem is technically
described as "retroflection . . . negating, holding back, or balancing
the impulse tension by additional opposing sensorimotor tension." [9]
This is a good definition of a block. Instead of overcoming blocks

[8] Wallen (1970), 12–13.

[9] Enright (1970, 112. Enright identifies retroflection with Reich's "character armor." The performer wants to hold onto what he's got rather than
risk himself. Often the performer doesn't even know he's wearing his armor
—it has become a genuine "second nature."

by forcing one's way through them, it is better to have the performer act out the block itself. But sometimes a block will not present itself so dramatically as in F.'s case. It will simply be an inability to make contact with oneself, and therefore an inability to contact others. An exercise I like as a means of becoming aware of these subtle blocks is "Circle Walk":

> The performer walks in a circle whose perimeter is patrolled by other performers so that the one walking is absolutely free to let go without fear of injury by collision. As he walks, the director describes to him how his body looks. "Your chin is jutting out, your left arm is swinging behind you, your feet are hitting the floor hard on the heels." The descriptions are given with enough time between so that the performer is able to exaggerate whatever behavior is being described. He juts his chin out as far as he can; he swings his left arm as far behind as he can; he stomps his heels into the ground. Descriptions and exaggerations continue until the performer can do no more. He relaxes, continues walking. Perhaps a few cycles are repeated.

In "Circle Walk" the performer becomes a caricature of himself; or, if he repeats several cycles, he becomes successive caricatures. These exaggerated images are often revealing and ultimately relaxing. They help the performer experience in large terms what perhaps he only barely perceived; and it allows him to be in a direct and surrendered relationship not only to the person telling him what he is doing but to all the others who maintain the circle.

Once a performer acknowledges a block not as an idea or a theory about his past, but as a condition of his body, he is more able to be flexible in regard to it. Of course, people are frightened of blocks: A block is the incarnation of a fear. And often this fear is of discovering what the block blocks. A double bind. Paradoxically, what the body shows is precisely what the performer wants to hide. In an exercise like "Circle Walk" the character armor is exaggerated to such a degree that it can be examined-in-action, brought to the surface as an immediate condition of the body. Once the block is brought out into the open this way, it is no longer so likely to dominate and inhibit the performer. Sometimes a "breakthrough" happens, and the block is entirely overcome. More frequently, after many exercises, a small advance is made, a touch of suppleness is introduced into places where all was stiffness.

This kind of "therapeutic" work is located in the body and is communicated from body to body. In cultures where a tradition clearly delineates what the moves of a performance are—as in Bali—the teacher can give the moves to the student, manipulating the body until the moves are entirely integrated. Not far from this kind of training is the work that I saw at the kathakali training school in Kerala, India. At the Kalamandalam, as it is called, there is a mixture of Western and Indian methods. (Or, perhaps because of the ultimately Indo-European source of these methods, I only thought I saw a mixture of old and new.) Much of the instruction consists in having accomplished performer-teachers watch, coach, correct, and intervene in the work of the students—much as acting is taught at hundreds of schools in America. But there is a special period of the year toward the end of the rainy season when students are "given the massage." This is called Chavitti Uzhicchil.

> The body is rubbed with a mixture of sesame oil, coconut oil, and melted butter. Then the student lies down, his face and chest touching the ground. His thighs are spread outward and the knees rest on pieces of wood about seven inches high. The lower part of the legs is folded inward, the feet touching each other. In this position the upper and lower part of the body touch the ground while the lumbar region is pushed up by the pieces of wood. The guru, supporting himself on a horizontal beam running at the height of his shoulders, begins to "massage" the body of the student gently with his right foot and toes. But, while "massaging," he pushes downward on the lumbar region. Gradually, he brings the lower part of the abdomen to ground level. By now, the knees are the only part of the body which do not touch the ground. The purpose of the massage is to change the position of the kneecaps so that the basic position and stage gait can be performed easily. The "massage" lasts about half an hour. It is very painful.[10]

I do not think that the only purpose of exercises like Chavitti Uzhicchil is to strengthen or change the body. An underlying purpose is the relationship between student and teacher: *a way of bringing the two together in a physical way within the terms of a given tradition.* The tradition transmitted in and through the body is an objective correlative, a medium for the love that the two people feel for each other. I think that all such teaching

[10] Barba (1967), 48.

body-to-body is erotic, life-giving, and is the most fundamental quality of teaching. Lovemaking without a tradition to be transmitted is a personal, intimate act and little more. Transmitting a tradition without lovemaking is a mechanical act and can never achieve the fullness or depth of the kathakali or Balinese way.

The transmission of knowledge body-to-body is not a random or improvised activity. Centuries of study have developed many traditions, particularly throughout Asia. The kathakali dancer knows of the energy centers in his body and is trained to use them. These are in his face-mask, lower back of the neck, lower middle back, hands, thighs, knees, and the "palm" of the feet. The main energy center is the lower middle back. But the location of energy centers does not seem to be uniform in all cultures or even in all groups within a culture. For example, Hatha-yoga is organized around different *asanas* (poses) and breathing rhythms. The breath is absolutely central, and so the main energy centers are in the solar plexus and the lower belly (diaphragm). Aikido, a rather recent discipline that synthesizes a number of systems, emphasizes *ki,* a difficult-to-translate concept of mind/body unity. The *ki* can be sent anywhere but its home is the "single spot in the lower abdomen."

> Zen and Yoga, seated meditation and mizogi breathing all consist in training this part of the body. Why is the lower abdomen so vital both to spiritual unification and to that of the body and the spirit? The spirit inhabits the body. Vaguely attempting to unify the spirit alone, therefore, is impossible. . . . To concentrate our spirit in one place, we use the single spot in the lower abdomen. We speak of the "single spot": because to talk of the diaphragm or the lower abdomen invites the danger that the student will tense that part of his anatomy. This is not our aim; we are striving to concentrate the spirit.[11]

In karate "the center of power and concentration is the *tanden* (area behind the navel) which is the center of the body's gravity."[12] For t'ai-chi "only in the flexibility of the waist is there true strength, for the waist is the foundation of all bodily movement."[13] Burmese bando stresses the thrusting power of the head,

[11] Tohei (1968), 16.
[12] Nakayama (1970), 8.
[13] Draeger and Smith (1969), 158.

shoulders, elbows, hips, knees, and feet.[14] Many Asian dances and body/spirit disciplines derive from the double source of observing animals and military training. These sources are not, after all, so different. The movements of stalking and animal combat have a ritual and dancelike quality. Military combat before the advent of modern, long-range weapons also had qualities of the hunt, close combat, and dance. Military training emphasized endurance, speed, grace, and balance. Men were taught to seek out the weak spots of adversaries and to fight from their own base of strength. Ritualized combat is the source not only of sports like sumo, judo, or bando but also of dance theater like kathakali, chow, and no.

All Asian dance masters agree on the unity of mind/body and the concentration of this power in a single place, usually the lower abdomen. The mind/body is concrete, locatable, and trainable. In Asian traditions there is nothing obscure or mystical about this training. Usually it begins early in life, reaching an intensity of concentration during adolescence. The mature artist continues training, but in a less concentrated way; also he is expected to serve as a teacher. The greatest artists teach young children. There are some forms in which children are the major performers. The Balinese legong, for example, can be danced only by girls under the age of twelve. The premise of training is that *the whole human being can be trained*. This training occurs in cycles. First the teacher works body-to-body with the student, doing the moves of the work with the student. Then, at a certain point, the "dance goes into the body" and concentrates at the "single spot." This concentrated knowledge/energy is sent to different parts of the body. From this time on the training occurs both inside the student and from the outside. A dialogue between teacher and that part of the student that *knows* adds to the student's knowledge. More and more is sent into the body; and the body grows deeper in its actual knowledge.

This way of training is possible because Asians make no separation between spirit and body. This dichotomy is part of the Western tradition of "soul." Perhaps ultimately the idea of a soul separate from the body derives from shamanism and the belief in the flight of the soul from the body—astral-projection or ecstasy. The idea of soul separate from body has many consequences including belief in personal immortality (one soul can inhabit

[14] Draeger and Smith (1969), 158.

many bodies, each in sequence). Whatever its other consequences, the idea of a spirit separate from the body creates grave difficulties for performer training. The performer thinks of "his body" as a vessel, an instrument, a possession; he trains "his body" and not "himself." Training deteriorates into gymnastics, routine, a deadening repetition without growth of knowledge or insight. As soon as the performer is "finished" with his training, he abandons it. Like education in general, it is regarded as a tool, a skill, something to be "acquired" and used as a means to greater ends. For the Asian performer training is part of a lifelong cycle of give-and-take; the primary means of personal growth. To the Western performer training is an alienated means to a desired end. This *instrumental* view of training is opposite to the Asian *holistic* view.

Changing viewpoints means changing life-styles. Obviously this kind of change is not easy. I have not yet done enough work concerning the direct transmission of knowledge body-to-body. Also Americans have no authentic tradition in the Asian sense of tradition. But in the association exercises and the varieties of exercises that derive from them there is a kind of tradition that can be transmitted body-to-body. (It is not enough to learn about how to transmit body-to-body by studying things like yoga or aikido. We must be able to communicate *our own work* body-to-body.) The task is not as idealistic or hairbrained as it might first appear. Alongside the currently dominant Western tradition of mind-body dichotomy is another tradition of mind/body unity. This second tradition is visible in contemporary psychotherapeutic techniques. It can be traced back to the Renaissance ideal of a "whole man," to Greek ideals of the balance between the physical and the mental. The Greeks were also influenced by Near Eastern and Egyptian ideas concerning metempsychosis—the passage of the soul from one body to another; the mind-body dichotomy. So there is a fault in the Western approach to these matters.

Exercises like "Chinese Prop," "Double Mirror," "Circle Walk," "Locating a Relationship in the Body," "Confrontation Hip Roll," and "Giving Over the Head"—all described in this book—are examples of body-to-body communication. Any number of exercises can be generated from the simple principle: People communicate not only with words but with their whole bodies; if words are disallowed, other means of communication will be found. For example:

"Totem Animal." Find "your animal" in yourself. Do not worry if it is not a "natural" animal; it may be your own kind of unicorn or griffin. Don't worry if it's not an animal you know beforehand.

Find your animal's place in the space, its home. Find its language, its way of expressing itself and being. No words. Find its characteristic gestures. Find its friends and enemies. Explore spaces away from home.

Make contact with other animals. Both friends and enemies.

"Yourself in Your Environment" (from Janie Rhyne). Pick from various sizes and shapes of paper one "you can imagine as representing you as you feel in your personal environment at this moment. Choose one drawing tool: pencil, crayon, chalk, paint, or even an ink-soaked rag that you can hold in your hand."

Sit where you won't be distracted. Concentrate a few moments on the blank sheet. Begin to make a drawing on the paper and consider its placement as representing where you are in your environment right now. "In a corner? In the middle? At the bottom or top? Off to one side?" Then actually put yourself in the space as you have drawn yourself.

Then begin to extend the size and directions of your drawing. Do this "in any way that feels like you living from your center and in relationship to the boundaries of your chosen environment." [15] Then actually move about the space using your drawing as a map.

These simple exercises are ways of *doing with the body* what one usually is only barely aware of with the mind. They are not exercises that cut off or shut off the mind. They treat the mind and body as a single unit and admit of the possibility that the center of this single unit may be anywhere within the whole organism. The Rhyne exercise encourages the performer to move from an abstract or reified expression of self in the drawing to actually putting himself into the situation of the drawing, as if the drawing were a map of the theater space, thus integrating the performer into that space. The whole space becomes, for the moment, the performer's body, and his body becomes the center, for him, of the space. He is his own center in a space that is himself.

This work doesn't come easily. Nor does it yield the kind of instant success sometimes claimed by followers of the "Growth

[15] Rhyne (1970), 279–280.

Movement." [16] The process of integrating mind and body by concentrating on physicalizing experience—acting through crisis, learning body languages—is part of old, worthy systems that reach near perfection in the arts-skills-therapies-philosophies of yoga and Zen. This kind of body knowledge is good for performers of whom it can truly be said: *I am what I do, and I do with who I am.*

The aim of body-to-body work is to increase flexibility, to free performers from the bonds of single-bodiedness—for people are single-bodied in the same way that they are single-minded. But the more secure a person is in his sense of center—the *ki*—the more able he is to move from that center, to send energy from the center to different parts of the body, to realign himself in response to the situation, to respond to others fully, unclouded by fantasy, projections, and introjections.

Problems surrounding fantasy, projection, and introjection are extremely complicated because these very blocks are often also a performer's stock-in-trade. One of the chief tools of the Stanislavski system is "emotional recall"—a way to focus one's past on the present situation of a performance. Performers construct fantasy-projected situations using their colleagues as screens on which to project a situation parallel to that of the scene being performed. For example, Joan MacIntosh associates her own mother with the Lady in Blue of *Commune*. "I used to look at my mother's huge belly—she was eight months' pregnant with my brother, and I was only nine years old at the time—and want to break it open with my fingers and take the baby away." That association is actualized at the moment Clementine jabs her fingers—the knife—into the belly of the performer playing the Lady in Blue. And again when Clementine says, of the murdered Lady, "And I knew that if I cut open her belly I could have her baby!" I don't object to using associations this way. A role is enriched, doubled or tripled. But I do think ultimately we must seek present-centered techniques, ways to perform an action in which the performer is entirely present in the action. Often,

---

[16] Characteristic of California's many therapies is the idea of instant and permanent wholeness, eradication of suffering, an end to anxiety. Also characteristic is how swiftly one therapy follows another, each proclaimed by adherents to be *the* method. Such a wild profusion of truth! Much of the "Growth Movement" is a distortion of Asian disciplines of acceptance and knowing through disciplined doing. Present-centeredness in yoga and Zen is not a rejection of the past, a cure for suffering, or a version of hedonism. It is not utopian. It does not end suffering but the sense of suffering in suffering. In other words, it ends self-pity.

in fact, this is the case: Associations are not planned in advance; they happen spontaneously, evoked by the immediate circumstances of the physical actions.

No matter how helpful projections and introjections are in actual performing, they can be very destructive of group life. Technically, a projection is believing that someone else is behaving/feeling a certain way when, in fact, you are behaving/feeling that way. The other person is a screen on which you project your own behavior/feelings. Introjection occurs when you take behavior from another "without assimilation or integration with the self." [17] Introjection goes deeper than parroting line readings. On one level a relationship based on introjection appears to be a genuine friendship, like the relationship between a younger and older brother or sister. But on another level there is resentment. The introjector feels possessed, deprived of the ability to act on his own; he feels he is becoming another person, but not successfully. The introjected feels consumed, the object of hungry attention; he wants nothing more than to be left alone. I remember a performer coming up to me, embracing me, and saying: "Richard, I want to get inside you, to get into your guts, to be one with you." I stiffened, cut off, fortified my defenses. Introjector-introjected relationships develop subtly. Frequently they occur between the director and one or more performers, especially if the group has not reached peer-group status but is still modeled on the parent-child relationship. Whenever there is an introjector-introjected relationship, there is a good chance that "I love you" means "I resent you." The introjector is ashamed to admit to feelings of inadequacy; or he overadmits them and blackmails. The introjected is fearful of losing an adoring friend. There isn't an easy solution to these problems. As I said, the performer's stock-in-trade includes using the very psychic situations that, when they intrude on one's personal life, block healthy relationships. My only advice is an analogy taken from pharmacy: A little dose is medicine, a heavy dose is poison.

At the start of this chapter I noted that TPG used therapy in three interrelated ways. These were: (1) the weekly encounter group sessions held during 1968–1969, (2) in workshop, (3) in performances. The ways that therapy enters our performances is both obvious and subtle. For a time during *Dionysus in 69* we actually employed encounter group techniques during the per-

[17] Enright (1970), 112.

formances. These "confrontations" were dropped when they became avoidances rather than public confessions. Performers were playing at or pretending to reveal themselves. *Makbeth* had very few directly therapeutic techniques. The Group was at the breaking point when we made *Makbeth.* The performance revealed those tensions. In *Commune,* however, a new try was made at bringing therapeutic techniques into the performance. We did this in a subtle way: by building each role out of material that was important to the performer playing the role.

Commune is a composed piece rather than a version of an already existing text, as *Dionysus* and *Makbeth* were. *Commune* was composed over a year by gathering together material from American history, American literature, scenes from Shakespeare and Marlowe, and events from our own lives. These events were not acted out during the performance, but they were worked on during workshop and rehearsal. What survived in the performance was a series of events that joined together documentary and well-known happenings to more obscure and personal happenings. Thus, for example, the relevance of MacIntosh's pregnant mother to the Lady in Blue. A good deal of other material was also used. None of it is visible as story. This intimate stuff determines the basic rhythms of the play, the ordering of events, the tone of scenes, the underlying structure.

The inner lives of the performers give coloring, tone, rhythm, and attitude to all the behavior displayed in the performance. This inner life varies greatly from night to night. Therefore, although the physical score remains the same, the feel of the play changes for each performance. The inner lives also color the surrounding psychic and physical geography. It is not an exaggeration to say that the environment becomes a kind of dream-scape —extensions of the performers' bodies as they are projected into space by the actions of the play. The play is a collective dream, and the dream includes the audience. What TPG does with a high degree of consciousness other groups do automatically. Our times are imbued with a "therapeutic consciousness." People are concerned with inner states and blocks caused by neurotic disturbances and distortions. In my opinion the best performances occur at the intersection of choice, fantasy, and dream.

The orthodox view of characterization is that the actor finds in his own life or in observations of others ("studies") parallels to the life of the character. The audience sees the character focused through the prism of the actor.

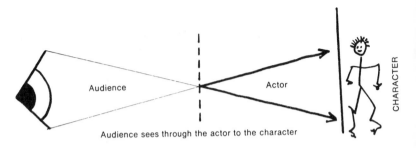

Audience sees through the actor to the character

When Olivier plays Othello, he finds in his own life aspects that are relevant to Othello's life. Olivier may use emotional recall so that at a given moment—say when Othello discovers that Desdemona is innocent—the "proper emotion" is displayed. Olivier recalls the precise circumstances of some deep loss in his own life. Recollecting these brings tears to Olivier's eyes. The audience sees Othello weeping.

In environmental theater the situation is reversed. Using the actions of the character as his focus, the performer illuminates his own life. The audience sees the performer through the prism of the character.

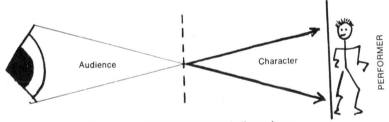

Audience sees through the character to the performer.

For example, when Borst plays David Angel in *Commune,* he uses certain actions of Charles Manson in prison to awaken in himself personal responses. Borst doesn't know before beginning rehearsals what these responses will be, or even which of Manson's actions will be used in the actual performance. It takes a long time to go through the material finding actions that are both personally suitable and objectively usable in a public performance. A scene like the one in which David is strapped on the floor, interrogated, and tortured is made from material drawn from Marlowe's *Edward II,* Ralph Ortiz's *The Sky Is Falling,* TPG's *Government Anarchy,* and the Manson trial. What unifies the scene is Borst's performing. And what makes this performing possible are the intimate associations stirred by the actions of the scene. A feedback is set up in which Borst and his colleagues search for elements that are personally evocative; and the more elements that are found, the more that is evoked. From all the material—both objective (in the play) and subjective (Borst's associations)—some is selected and organized into the scene. The scene is built as a whole, not with the words coming first or the actions coming first. Both are invented/selected together, over many hours of rehearsal. Ultimately, what the audience sees when David Angel is interrogated and tortured is the response of Borst to these actions. This is what Grotowski calls "psychic penetration," the performer using "his role as if it were a surgeon's scalpel to dissect himself." [18] The main organizing force in orthodox theater characterization is the role; in environmental theater it is the performer.

Instead of seeing the character through the prism of the actor's work, audiences at environmental theater see the performer through the prism of the actions invented/discovered to probe/illustrate/reveal the character. It is a complicated business. Instead of "interpreting the role" the performer uses the role as a means of finding out things about himself; in the process of self-discovery he also finds out things about the situation of the character. The differences between the orthodox and the environmental approaches are not as absolute as it would seem. It is a question of emphasis and working methods, rehearsal techniques. In orthodox theater the role exists outside the performer—like a suit of clothes, a blueprint, a project to be fulfilled, and objective to be realized. In environmental theater the role is as unknown as the performer playing it; the two are in a dialectical relationship, and each illuminates the other. The process is a spiralling series of tension-release cycles. Finding out what the role is and what it is becoming, experiencing it in its changes, are what rehearsals are for. Rehearsals are not to practice the finished thing, but to prepare for something to happen.

Audiences at environmental theater watch performers wrestling with roles. The struggle is not resolved in rehearsals; the performance is not a settled sequence. That watching a performer struggle with his role is an engrossing experience to many spectators is itself an indication of the widespread impact of psychotherapies. Therapy's most general effect has been to awaken a *sensitivity to process*. People are no longer satisfied with sitting

[18] Grotowski (1968), 37.

back and seeing something. They move around the action, they examine it with curiosity, skepticism, and involvement. They want to know how and why something came about. They demand to be let in on *what's behind what happens*. The subjects of drama are exploded and imploded beyond and behind "action" to include the closest scrutiny of processes and causes.

The demand that theater open its process of creativity to public viewing doesn't stop with the performers and their characterizations. It is also seen in staging, the workings of the environment, and in the other aspects of production. Spectators are brought onto the stage, put in the very place where the performance is happening. Visible is the stage machinery; eliminated are separations between onstage and offstage. Even the distinction between rehearsal and finished performance is blurred. Rehearsals are open to the public; performances include stops and repetitions of scenes. Mistakes are not covered up. All of these changes open the performance up, revealing the inner life of performing. Performing itself becomes a kind of therapeutic activity. The inner life of theater becomes theater's subject. Perhaps even a little narcissistically the theater concentrates on its own processes. But even as this special kind of performing gains acceptance, new possibilities challenge its existence. Playwrights are writing scripts that I for one want to direct. But how can one do "finished scripts" in an environmental theater?

We too shall become solemn, fat, and
Ubu-like and shall publish extremely classical
books which will probably lead to our
becoming mayors of small towns where, when
we become academicians, the blockheads
constituting the local intelligentsia will present
us with Sèvres vases, while they present their
mustaches on velvet cushions to our children.
And another lot of young people will appear,
and consider us completely out of date,
and they will write ballads to express their
loathing of us, and that is just the way
things should always be.
Alfred Jarry

I'm not sure if an ensemble company like
The Performance Group would give the play
the right feel. I'm not being specific about
your group because I've never seen them but
every ensemble group that I've seen always
works best from a piece which they originate
along with a director and writer. If they
attempt plays it always seems that the play
takes a back seat to the ensemble and director.
Sam Shepard

7 Playwright

In April, 1972, after seven months in Asia, Joan MacIntosh and
I came back to America. Things had changed in America, and
in our perception of ourselves, our friends, and our work. When
we got back, we did not want to resume work on *Don Juan*
immediately. Instead we wanted to work on a finished script.
The rest of the Group had come to the same conclusion on their
own. Everyone believed that working on a script would give us
all the chance to get back together again. Some of the energy
needed to compose a text could be spent on learning about each
other, reintegrating Joan and me back into the company. Also
the skills of the company were advanced enough to be tested
against the restrictive disciplines of working from a text.

I had not directed a "regular play" since the 1967 New Orleans
Group production of Ionesco's *Victims of Duty. Dionysus in 69,*

Makbeth, and *Commune* all ended with settled scripts, but each started from various points other than a settled script. What I like about working from a script is that the ground rules are already laid out. By reading the play one knows pretty well what the general flow of the action will be, what the themes are, and what the production will look like. What is unknown are the exact points of contact between performers and text, the interaction among the performers, and the effect of the audience on the production. At least I thought I knew the ground rules as we began working on Sam Shepard's *The Tooth of Crime.*

At this writing, we are very much in the middle of the work, and some of my expectations have been ambushed by situations I could not have predicted. I know my work in environmental theater has changed the way I work on a script and the way the performers work. And because several of the environmental theaters have indicated that they plan to work from scripts, I think TPG's experiences with Shepard's play are worth noting.

TPG uses words in its productions. Often these words have been pushed, pulled, punched out of shape: transformed into sounds without regard for denotation; made into guts, extruded from guts. Words have been treated *operatically,* except that our criterion for distortion is not music but the feelings of the performers as revealed through highly disciplined exercises. But the effect is similar to opera: a musical treatment of words.

Listening to the poetries and dramas of African peoples, Oceanic peoples, the Japanese, and others, one can't escape the fact that everywhere words are used as sounds. The voice is a marvelously flexible instrument, a specialized way of breathing; almost every part of the body can be used as a resonator. Furthermore, since human beings are all one species, *anyone can learn to make the sounds anyone else can make.* So-called impossible vocalizations such as Japanese gutturals are available to anyone wishing to train. This discovery concerning the universality of vocalization is leading to a great revolution in voice training and to a revaluation of text in the theater.

After reading Shepard's *The Tooth of Crime* I wrote him:

> I want to look at the play nakedly, approach its language not as a dialect but as a way into the heart of the play and a way to uncover things in the performers playing the roles. I can't say what the results will be because our way of working is truly to let the rehearsal process take its own course, uncover what is to be uncovered. We find the style

of a production by rehearsing it. . . . Most directors and actors start with a "guiding idea," an "image to be realized," a "preexistent action." I don't, the Group doesn't. We start with only what is there, the barest facts: seven performers and a collection of words organized under role headings.

The Tooth of Crime builds from an identity between the languages of rock music, crime, and big business. A "hit" in one world is the same as or different from a "hit" in another; a "big killing" is/isn't murder; a "contract" is a contract is a contract. In the world of *Tooth* rock stars move up in the ratings according to how much turf they control—they earn turf by killing their rivals. In a society controlled by Keepers and informed by image-makers, there is more than a touch of the Roman gladiatorial games—all observed from home, on TV. The streets are controlled by the packs, the gangs, the cross-syndicates.

Shepard is a master of the language of the world he has created. In addition to the languages of rock music, street gangs, the Mafia, and the image-makers, Shepard invents a language spoken by Crow, the "gypsy killer," the young punk moving in on the turf of established stars. Crow's language is somewhat like that of Burgess-Kubrick's *Clockwork Orange*. The meeting between Crow and the old man, Hoss, is a conflict of idioms. At one point Hoss pleads, "Hey, can't you back the language up, man, I'm too old to follow the flash." The big scene of the play is a song duel between Hoss and Crow. This duel, in fact, has many prototypes—from the once popular "Battle of the Bands" to the ritual combats of certain Eskimo peoples:

In Alaska and in Greenland all disputes except murder are settled by a song duel. In these areas an Eskimo male is often as acclaimed for his ability to sing insults as for his hunting prowess. The song duel consists of lampoons, insults, and obscenities and the disputants sing to each other and, of course, to their delighted audience. . . . The verses are earthy and very much to the point; they are intended to humiliate, and no physical deformity, personal shame, or family trouble is sacred. As verse after verse is sung in turn by the opponents the audience begins to take sides; it applauds one singer a bit longer and laughs a bit louder at his lampoons. Finally, he is the only one to get applause, and he thereby becomes the winner of a bloodless contest. The loser suffers a great punishment, for disapproval of the

Photograph 30. First round of the fight between Hoss and Crow in *The Tooth of Crime*. Hoss, played by Spalding Gray, faces Crow (in leg brace), played by Timothy Shelton. (*Frederick Eberstadt*)

Photograph 31. Second round of the fight: The action moves in a circle around the theater. The audience either follows or turns to watch. (*Frederick Eberstadt*)

Photograph 32. During the second round, the keepers (officials) are alone in the fight ring as audience and other performers have moved to the far side of the theater. Standing, Elizabeth LeCompte; seated, Stephen Borst. (*Frederick Eberstadt*)

Photograph 33. After the fight: Crow teaches Hoss how to be a Gypsy. Cheyenne, played by James Griffiths, accompanies the lesson on the drums. (*Frederick Eberstadt*)

Photograph 34. As the audience crowds around, Becky, played by Joan MacIntosh, lives through a "make-out" session in the backseat of a car while Hoss, now an old man, looks on. (*Frederick Eberstadt*)

community is very difficult to bear in a group as small as that of the Eskimo.[1]

This is exactly the structure of the Hoss-Crow duel. Hoss loses; he is stripped of his authority, his machismo. What is most interesting to me about the duel is "the belief that language (i.e., poetry) can make-things-present by naming them." [2] Many times in *Tooth* Shepard uses language in the way that Emenau says Hindus do:

> It is noteworthy and perhaps to be interpreted as a general tendency in Hindu culture to *raise certain aspects of the subliminal to consciousness,* that Hinduism in general and the Tantric sects in particular make extensive use in ritual and religious practice generally, not only of the intrinsically meaningless gestures (of the dance and iconography), but also of *intrinsically meaningless vocables.* For example, the famous *om* and *hum* and the not so famous *hrim, hram, phat,* and many others, are meaningless, religious noises in origin, whatever symbolic meanings are given to them by the developed dogma.[3]

Or in the terms of Birdwhistell:

> Since regularities appear in the stream of movement and in the stream of audible behavior around certain syntactic forms, it is possible to state that body motion and spoken "languages" do not constitute independent systems at the level of communication. By a logic, not yet known, they are interinfluencing and probably interdependent.[4]

All this confirms what dancers and theater performers have known for hundreds of years. But this knowledge is just at this moment being raised to a kind of scientific consciousness characteristic of Western thought. As such it is available as a tool, just like other technologies. Shepard's play uses this tool and scrutinizes it. In this way *The Tooth of Crime* is about performing and about techniques that TPG has helped develop.

But I must not speak of our work on *Tooth* as if it were finished. Working on the play raises the issues of language—of the concrete essence of the word, of how words are emptied of

[1] Farb (1969), 68–69.
[2] Rothenberg (1968), 385.
[3] Emenau (1942), 149.
[4] Birdwhistell (1970), 130.

meaning and filled with new significances. The more we work, the more we find that Shepard's words are bound to music, specifically rock music. Shepard is a musician as well as writer. He composed a score for *Tooth*, but we did not want to use his score for several reasons. In my first letter to Shepard I said:

> We start with the belief that music is essential to the play—but without knowing what shape that music will take. We do not play electrified instruments and do not import outsiders into our productions so I would say, probably, we will not use electric music done electrically. We will have to find out how to do electric music with our bodies. . . . The problem becomes for us: How do we make the kind of music necessary for your play without microphones, electric guitars, and so on? I think we can make the necessary music because I don't think rock is a function of mechanics but of some movement within the human spirit. One of the things we have to find out is precisely what that movement is, *what does it sound like?* In other words, the problem isn't how to play rock, but how to find the cause from which rock springs. Then to play that cause.

Shepard's own music—we heard it on tape—is based on rock chord progressions. Using it would have been acceptable but not as suitable to the complexities of *Tooth* as the project TPG embarked on. I have nothing against electrically amplified music—but Group members don't play it. We are committed to making the sounds in our plays with our own bodies. This commitment has not attained the status of dogma—in fact, as we worked on *Tooth*, we used what musical instruments Group members knew or could learn: violin, saxophone, melodica, harmonica, fife, and drums. For a few months there was a clarinet—but the woman who played it left the Group.

I rejected amplified music for *Tooth* because the sound of it is so overstimulating that everything else goes dim—it's like having a bright light flash in your eyes and trying to see clearly after it's been turned off. Also there is the basic issue of theater as a handcraft. Electronic equipment puts the actors and their story at a disadvantage. The audience gets its kicks—but without ever having spent the body power and attention of getting there. Electric energy is a kind of narcotic.

Anyway, we're far enough on the other side of the rock era to do a play that gets at the heart of some of rock's ideas without having to rely on the actual music. The fact that Group performers are not musicians in the usual sense is an advantage. We've had to probe to what the music is about. And rather than rely heavily on pure references or parody we've been able to use a good deal of irony. A style is held up in a certain light, and it refracts many different colors. For example, when we play "When the Saints Go Marching In"—one of the few quotation songs we use—it's a victory march for Hoss, and a dirge for his whole era.

But this is getting ahead of the process. While waiting for Shepard's reply to my letter, we went ahead and began working on his play. The first problem was to approach the language concretely. I did not want us to work "around a table" figuring out what the play meant; or even discussing its story. I wanted to start with some actual experience of its very rich, troubling, and difficult language: a poetry as dense as any in the modern theater. First we sang the play as if it were an opera. Every line was sung, sometimes as recitative, sometimes as aria, sometimes solo, and sometimes in chorus. Then we sang the play as a kind of Jagger-like talking jazz. (Later we saw Jagger's film, *Performance;* I think that the style of the film has influenced our work on *Tooth.*) Then we read the play "naturalistically," as if every scene were taken directly from life. In none of these explorations were we trying to figure out the dialogue from the point of view of characterization. The performers were feeling the language out, weighing it, discovering how it moved, what its possibilities were. The text was treated concretely—not simply as sound nor simply as denotation, but as meaning conditioned by sound. The performers used a "verbophysical" approach: taking sentences and distorting their usual intonation according to the physical impulses in and among the performers. Once we went through the play speaking the lines as fast as possible. New ways of saying the words were found. Later, while working on the fight scene, I massaged the performer playing Crow while other performers accompanied him on musical instruments as he worked through his lines. As I pushed and pounded his flesh, he began to discover new relationships to the language. Some of these soundings —instead of the orthodox "readings"—were retained for the fight scene.

At the same time performers began making up melodies and trying out rhythms for the songs. A great deal of Shepard's play deals with the different images people wear like masks; and also the contrast between the styles of one era versus the styles of another. The conflict between Hoss and Crow is aptly described as "a styles match." Performers tried to find well-known styles:

the vocal mannerisms of a movie star, the beat of a rock musician, the walk of a superstar athlete. These styles were then taken to the extreme, extended, put under a scenic microscope. Barry Klein, our technical director, went through Shepard's text and made a list of every song, every musician, and even phrases and words that alluded to music. Then Barry made a three-hour tape of all the music. We read the play to the music. The tape recorder was so loud the performers could not hear each other. Gestures were exaggerated. From where I sat it looked like a silent movie. Next we did an improvisation containing all the main actions of the script as the performers understood them while listening to the Klein tape.

Each of these efforts was an attempt to get into Shepard's play without intellectualizing about it. There would be time enough later to evaluate, discuss and rationalize what the work was about. But the initial thrust of the work was entirely concrete. And it was a meeting between the performers and Shepard's language.

As we were doing this work, Shepard wrote me:

> I got a lot of conflicting feelings and thoughts about the whole thing. First off, it's nice to know that you begin work without any preconceptions. But you gotta understand that this play for *me* is very preconceived. I got exact diagrams and pictures in my head about how it should be done. . . . This play is built like *High Noon,* like a machine Western. It's gotta work with all its insides hanging out. You know what I mean. I'm really not trying to pull artistic priority bullshit because to me the play stands outside me on its own. It's like a kid brother that I wanna protect. . . .
>
> The other doubt I have is about the music. Most of it is very simple Rock progressions from Velvet Underground to The Who. It's gotta be electric! No other way for it to work. The songs were all built for electric guitar, keyboard, bass and drums. All the music is written down and fits each section of the play according to the emotional line that's going down. It's gotta be played by Rock musicians who've got their chops. Actors who aren't musicians just couldn't handle it.

On every point Shepard was correct. But I didn't want to give up on doing *The Tooth of Crime.* And it was Shepard's very objections that fired my enthusiasm even more than before I got his letter.

His preconceptions are built into the text. There is no way around them. They are the sinews of the play. And even if we were to reject Shepard's composed score, the music has to follow the progression he outlined because that progression is embedded in the rhythm of the language. A finished script like *The Tooth of Crime* enters rehearsal steps ahead of the performers and director. The script has a claim on completeness. The writer is infected with the disease that made him write, and this disease takes on a more profound form once the play is completed by the writer: The actions are embedded in the script; they *are* the script. But the first task of the performers is to try the play in every way possible except as the writer has indicated; to lay the words as bare as possible by avoiding doing what the words insist be done. It doesn't matter that later the performers come back to the very actions called for in the script. If Lady Macbeth is to walk in her sleep as Shakespeare describes, it is because no other way is possible, other ways having been tried and rejected.

We kept working on *Tooth* while waiting for Shepard's reply to my second letter, which said in part:

> We accept your words as written, and the parts that they are organized into, and the basic flow of the action. But the rest of the scenic activity is our responsibility; we must work long and hard *to find our own places within the world of your script*. Or, to put it another way, we accept your script as *part of an artwork yet to be completed*. . . . Our five years of work entitles us to the claim of creativity, just as your work as a playwright entitles you to the identical claim. We don't want to dismember your work, or to do it against its own grain; but we want to accept it as a living term of an artwork of which we are the other living term; and together to bring the performance into existence.

I appreciated Shepard's preconceptions, but could not accept them as the basis of my work.

The issue is the relationship of the playwright to the production. Is the play the fountainhead and goal of production? In the old days the actor was used to express the essential theater that was presumed to be the ideas of the playwright. Then a revolution occurred, and the script was used to express the essential theater that was presumed to be the feelings of the performers. The locus of the essential theater shifted from the page to somewhere between the navel and genitals of each performer. Historically speaking both extremes were necessary. In my opinion the vaunted "authority of the playwright" was largely a convenient fiction developed by directors of the late nineteenth century in order to bring actors and managers under the control of the directors. Remember, the theater was in a bad way. Star actors and greedy managers controlled the stage. There were hardly any rehearsals, no coherence to productions, and not many worthy new plays. The riddle of chicken-and-egg is insoluble; but as the theater became more unified under the guiding hands of directors like Saxe-Meiningen, André Antoine, and, sublimely, Stanislavski, writers of profound talents turned to the theater, and the end of the nineteenth century saw a flowering unmatched since the Renaissance: Henrik Ibsen, August Strindberg, Anton Chekhov, Frank Wedekind, Alfred Jarry, to name just a few. The directors claimed that they were "serving" the playwright, "realizing" his ideas. In this way the directors could not be accused of the same egocentrism they detested in the stars.

Perhaps unconsciously but nevertheless powerfully the directors drew on the tradition of exegesis. Exegesis is originally the "official" interpretation of Scripture; and in Judeo-Christian tradition exegesis carries with it the authority of (canon) law. Exegesis is a way of interpreting the Bible so that the congregation of the faithful can be guided in their actions; a way of resolving the ambiguities of the Word into the clarity of law. In his original form an exegete is a guide, a director, an interpreter. Of course, the Word is intrinsically ambiguous, and so the ages reveal many exegetic variations. The tradition of exegesis is firmly enough rooted in European culture that it was relatively easy to make the transformation: The playwright became God (often absent but always all-powerful), his play the Bible, the director the exegete, the actors the celebrants, and the audience the congregation of the faithful. This pattern was reinforced by the parallel development of modern, mass education. Modern education was also based on the exegetic tradition; and literary texts of all kinds have been interpreted as if they were the Bible. Explication of the text, in fact, has been the major tendency of modern literary criticism. There is no better confession of faith than a term paper written to satisfy the exegetic insights of the professor. Finally, exegesis in the theater was confirmed by the emergence of the brilliant playwrights of a period that extended from Ibsen to Genet.

Until the antiliterary revolution in the theater—first unsuccessfully fought by the surrealists in the twenties and Artaud in the thirties and then triumphant in the fifties and sixties—the playwright held sway. Then the writer was out, and only now is he being invited back in. But on what basis? Some, of course, want to forgive and forget. Others, following Cocteau's dream, want poets *of* the theater not poets *in* the theater. I propose that the playwright develop his own particular skills to the highest degree. These skills are literary, poetic, the mastery of language as distinct from the mastery of action.

If one examines the *texts* of the nonliterary theater, one discovers an abundance of literature, *pure* literature, stuff never intended for the theater. For example, Grotowski's use of T. S. Eliot, Dostoevski, Simone Weil, and the Bible in *Apocalypsis Cum Figuris;* the Open Theater's use of the Bible in *The Serpent;* the Manhattan Project's use of Lewis Carroll's *Alice* books in *Alice in Wonderland;* TPG's use of American Colonial writings, Henry David Thoreau, Herman Melville, and the Bible in *Commune;* Peter Brook's work with Ted Hughes in *Orghast*. What is one to make of this spate of purely literary text in a theater most noteworthy for its proclaimed antiliterary intentions? What I see is a sharp division made between the *craftsmen of words* and the *craftsmen of actions*. Because the texts do not inherently carry with them intractable associations of actions, the directors and performers were able to confront these texts with actions that arose from the associations of the performers rather than from the dictates of the authors. In other words, the performers were free to develop *to the end* their own actions.

For example, as the Polish Theater Laboratory program accurately describes a scene from *Apocalypsis:*

> In the scene of drunken gibberings cut by dancing and the singing of *Quantanamera* everyone stands bunched together in the middle of the room shouting each other down with quotations from the Bible, while the Simpleton scampers around them trying to attract their attention. But the words of the Bible assume lewd and sickening overtones in the context of their behavior. Simon Peter drools through his sleep about something to do with incest. Lazarus gleefully recalls his gruesome misfortune. Judas harps provocatively away at his garbled parables. Mary Magdalene flaunts her physical attractions. John recites chilling passages from Revelations which become gross sexual allusions.

Or in the Manhattan Project's *Alice in Wonderland* Alice's meeting with the caterpillar is staged as an encounter between a girl from the Bronx and a stoned-out psychedelic freak. Or in *Commune* where the quotation from the Bible concerning "and all those who believed were together and had all things in common as every man had need" is used as the basis for the scene where the performers actually steal things from the audience.

Using well-known literary texts not only lets the performers invent their own actions, but it encourages a kind of blasphemy and irony. The Bible with its profound associations and long history is especially useful in this way. But these very opportunities are also a severe limitation. The classic texts are perhaps too well known; irony and blasphemy are too easy a response. But the opposite responses of high seriousness and faith are insupportable. Once again theaters are turning to playwrights because the writers can provide a personal and to some degree original vision. But I believe that if playwriting is again to become important to the theater, it will not be because writers master dramatic and theatrical action but because they provide to the masters of that craft a mastery of their own: writing. The writer is a master of words, and the performer is a master of scenes. The director is a master of, as Antoine said long ago, "a view of the whole." [5] Without playwrights the theater is impoverished in the direction of irony, fragmentation, and—ironically enough!—exegesis, for the actions of performers taking off from the "great texts" is nothing so much as a further elaboration of what those texts might mean. Now that performers have begun to learn to use words not only as dialogue but as song; now that scenes can be exploded to fill whole spaces; now that audiences can watch, collaborate, participate, influence, and even dominate performances—the time is ready to include again in the theater masters of the literary arts.

Shepard responded to my second letter:

> I've decided to be adventurous and let you go ahead with
> *Tooth*. Your enthusiasm is hard to deny. I think your group
> will probably come up with a powerful production although
> it may be far from what I had in mind. The main reluctance
> I have is that the play will become over-physicalized and
> the language will fall into the background. But time will tell.

This is a danger. The task for the Group is to integrate language, music, and gesture. I know this much: Some of *Tooth* is acted in a much more quiet, concise way than TPG's other works. But some of it is in familiar Performance Group style. I am very aware that the production will open after I finish this book. That

[5] Antoine, in Cole and Chinoy, eds. (1953, 1963 [1903]), 93.

makes me reluctant to say too much, because there is a great deal of rehearsing still to be done.

But a few more thoughts. When we began working knowing that we would do the play publicly, we searched through the text for whatever personal associations each performer could find. I also contributed some of my associations. The director is not absent from this phase of the work. We began assembling musical instruments, including car parts from junkyards. Much of the play's imagery concerns automobiles. Slowly some scenic shapes emerged from hours of working in small rooms both in Berkeley, California, and Vancouver, Canada. Jerry Rojo came to Vancouver for three weeks, and together we designed the environment. It is a modular environment—capable of endless variations like a giant tinker-toy. As we worked on *Tooth,* it took on the shape of a contemporary opera. More than half the play consisted of music or musical accompaniment to heightened speech. The music took on a variety of tones. We did fourteen work-in-progress performances of *Tooth* in Vancouver during September, 1972. Ron Verzuh thought this:

> The play involves virtually everything that you and I have experienced in the past one and a half decades pinching in a bit of American history just as if it were the quintessential MSG in some special aliment. *The Tooth of Crime* is not a play that is easily described. It creates a fantasy world that leans toward being exclusively the individual's perceptions. I thought of the films *Zacharia*, Farina's *Been Down So Long Etc.* and Kerouac's book *On the Road.* Then into music, I heard blends of everything from Haley, to blues, Dylan, Beatles, and Miles Davis. A modern rock-jazz nuance in the variety of sounds. It seemed to me to evolve as a cross between *Rebel Without a Cause* and *A Clockwork Orange.* Pictures of Brando with cycle, Hendrix, and James Dean adorned the labyrinthian, plywood setting. Where does that take your mind? *Tooth* was a combination of sights, sounds, experiences from the past and mysteriously from the future puddinged together and stirred—constantly stirred.[6]

Of course reviews like this please me; and perhaps I am being immodest in quoting Verzuh. But what I want to point out is that *Tooth* seems to be stirring *associations in the audience* rather than simply presenting incarnations of associations in the performers. It is outer-directed. Meyerhold said it with clarity and finality in his 1936 lecture on Chaplin.

[6] Verzuh in *The Peak* (Vancouver: Wednesday, September 20, 1972), 17.

I have come to regard the *mise-en-scène* not as something which works directly on the spectator but rather as a series of "passes," each intended to evoke some association or other in the spectator (some premeditated, others outside my control). Your imagination is activated, your fantasy stimulated, and a whole chorus of associations is set off. A multitude of accumulated associations gives birth to new worlds—whole films which have never got beyond the cutting-room. You can no longer distinguish between what the director is responsible for and what is inspired by the associations which have invaded your imagination.[7]

It is interesting that Meyerhold is talking about film, because the techniques of film—especially montage, quick-cutting, musical back-up, and ikonographic gesturing—have heavily influenced my work in *Commune* and *The Tooth of Crime*. In fact, when Rojo and I worked out the environment for *Tooth,* we thought it would offer the audience a filmlike experience. The environment is a large, centrally situated structure more than thirty feet in diameter, with several towers rising twelve and sixteen feet. No spectator can see everywhere because the environment fills the space. To improve sight-lines somewhat Rojo had the idea of cutting windows in the environment. This had the effect of framing and focusing scenes and scene fragments. Sitting in one part of the environment, a spectator could see a hand, a face, or a whole scene through one or more frames. As we worked through August, a few people came to watch rehearsals and commented how much the performance felt like a film.

Then on September 11 the first full audience saw the play. More than 225 people filled the stage of the Frederic Wood Theater. The audience was on stage, the house empty. But instead of staying seated and peering through the complicated environment, the audience got up and followed the scenes from place to place. *The Tooth of Crime*—which is often a contrast between the people-crowded public life of a star and the lonely cut-off life in a mansion: "insulated from what's really happening by our own fame"—became both a street play and a public tour of a Hollywood mansion. The performance didn't lose its filmlike quality; added was the feel of a street scene and guided tour. So you never know until the audience is there what the play will be like. If the performers are masters of action on one level, the audience is the master on another.

[7] Meyerhold (1969 [1936]), 318–319.

From then on the performances had a medieval or Elizabethan feel. Performers played many speeches directly out to spectators who were crowding in on the action. Asides made sense. A deep identification was possible between spectators and performers. A special kind of rhetorical speaking filled a place between the music and the intimate, private, quiet scenes.

Several years ago I argued forcibly that play texts were mere pretexts out of which the performance is made; material to be used, distorted, dismembered, reassembled. I wanted to do a thorough job of debunking the classics. It was necessary to redress an indecent imbalance in which living artists bowed down to dead gods. I still believe in the collages of *Dionysus, Makbeth,* and *Commune.* But, generally speaking, I want to turn to other work—work that includes the playwright. We have moved beyond the point when actors acted with their faces, hands, and voices. The rebirth of the whole performer demands the reintegration of the writer into the theater.

People will work with scripts; people will work without scripts; people will use scripts as material; people will work with the playwright present as part of the theater group; people will work with a script sent from afar by a living writer, as Shepard sent *The Tooth of Crime.* Each of these ways of working is supportable, and in the same group. A repertory of different kinds of work —classic, contemporary, collage, improvised—is more than possible: It is necessary. The shaman who dances in animal skins is sometimes called Master of Animals, though it is not clear who is the master and who the servant. So, too, the performer, the director, the playwright.

Men can and do destroy the humanity of other men, and the condition of this possibility is that we are interdependent. We are not self-contained monads producing no effects on each other except our reflections. We are both acted upon, changed for good or ill, by other men; and we are agents who act upon others to affect them in different ways. Each of us is the other to the others.
R. D. Laing

All murders are family murders, either within a literal family or in family-replica situations.
David Cooper

8 Groups

There is no audience participation in primeval or contemporary shamanistic performances because there is no audience. Rather there are circles of increasing intensity approaching ecstasy. Those in the most heated-up center—say the shaman, the dancers, the patient (if it is a curing ceremony)—are doing what we would call performing; the others in the audience are not disinterested spectators or even people there just to be entertained or educated. The audience has such a high stake in what's going on that we cannot call these spectators an audience: They are a community of participants. Their support is decisive to the outcome of the ceremony, to its efficacy; their corroborative singing and dancing, the *heat of their attention,* must in a real way match the heat of the ceremonial center.

Nowhere is this clearer than in initiation ceremonies where an actual transformation of boys into men takes place under the guidance of the whole adult male population of a village. Not every adult is at the center of the ceremony. Indeed some men just watch. But this watching, as well as the fuller kind of participation through dancing or drama, is a *condition of the ceremony.* There is no way of conceiving an initiation proceeding without the attention of the already initiated. And usually such ceremonies are structured so that over a period of hours, days, weeks, or months *each* of the adults has a part to play in the center as well as spending much time on the outer rim. So that during the whole course of the initiation everyone has had the chance —indeed has been required—to be both player and spectator. This is as true of the initiates as of the others. Much of the ceremony is staged for them; they are a special audience. But at moments of crisis the boys are brought into the drama; the drama is acted *through* and *on* them: They are circumcised or put through some other ordeal; their bodies are scarred or written on in the physical language of the ceremony; they sing and dance. Ultimately the separation between the initiates and the initiated is eliminated; this is the function of the ceremony. A drama has taken place, and its social function has been to eradicate distinctions between outsider and insider, spectator and performer, boy and adult, novice and initiate.

Kenneth Read describes what it feels like to be drawn into a performance of this kind. Read witnessed the prenuptial celebration of a Highlands New Guinea people.

> The house was packed to its capacity, but in the blackness I was unable to discover so much as a single feature of the man who sat beside me. Almost immediately, enveloped in disembodied voices, I felt the first stirrings of a curious panic, a fear that if I relaxed my objectivity for so much as a moment I would lose my identity. At the same time the possibility that this could happen seemed immensely attractive. The air was thick with pungent odors, with the smell of unwashed bodies and stranger aromatic overtones that pricked my nostrils and my eyes. But it was the singing, reverberating in the confined space and pounding incessantly against my ears, that rose to cloud my mind with the fumes of a collective emotion almost too powerful for my independent will. Momentarily the night vanished, and my purpose, even the circumstances of my presence in the village were no longer important. I stood poised at a threshold promising a release from the doubts and anxieties that separate us from one another, offering, if one took the step demanded, a surety, a comforting acceptance such as those who share an ultimate commitment may experience..Even though the words were unintelligible, the massed voices were like a hand held toward me, a proffered embrace.
>
> . . . The songs followed one another without a perceptible break, a single shrill and keening voice lifting now and then to point the way to a new set. As the others joined in strongly, I felt close to the very things that eluded me in my

day-to-day investigations, brought into physical confrontation with the intangible realm of hopes and shared ideas for which words and actions, though they are all we have, are quite inadequate expressions. In analytic language, the situation could be accommodated under the rubric of a rite of separation—an event by which a young girl in her father's house, surrounded by her kinsmen, was brought to the morning of the day on which she must assume a new status and be transferred to her husband's people, but its quality could not be conveyed in any professional terms. While the voices swelled inside the house, mounting to a climax, the barriers of my alien life dissolved. The sound engulfed me, bearing me with it beyond the house and into the empty spaces of the revolving universe. Thus sustained, I was one of the innumerable companies of men who, back to the shrouded entrance of the human race, have sat at night by fires and filled the forest clearings and the wilderness with recitals of their own uniqueness.[1]

I, too, have sat among these same New Guinea highlanders at song and known the synesthesia Read describes where one smells with the fingers and hears with the feet. During experiences like that the "collective" is not only the people but the place they are in, the music, the heat, and time itself, which no longer moves but collects in a heap like fallen snow. Wholeness is so total it is bizarre to speak of distinctions like "spectator" and "performer."

The theater Read describes can be called tribal, or ritual, or collective; it can be represented by a simple model.

There is no distance, aesthetic or other, between performer and community. Spectators and performers exchange roles. Many rites are structured around a contrapuntal dynamic in which a person is at one time a spectator and at another a performer. The efficacy of rites is their ability to transform people and things into "new" or "different" people or things. This ability-to-transform is part of the essential structure of rites, a core of wholeness, oneness,

[1] Read (1965), 251–252.

indissolubility guaranteed not by freezing roles but by demonstrating that each is potentially the other. With the advent of Greek drama—and forms of African, Indian, Chinese, and Japanese drama, too [2]—fixed role separations are introduced. In the Greek theater one can still discern the development of drama from shamanistic rituals.[3]

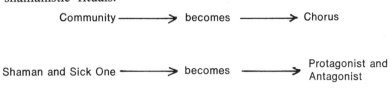

In their part of the world the Athenians invented the audience as an assembly whose *only* role in the drama is to watch. The audience is literally situated outside the circle of action, and a physical distance separates spectators from chorus and performers. The chorus, in fact, serves as an intermediary linking audience and performers. So perfectly is the Greek amphitheater an architectural version of the Greek conception of drama that a scale

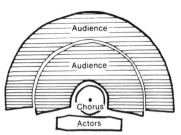

Altar of Dionysus at center of dancing-circle

[2] Evidence is mounting that many, if not most, dramatic forms of the northern hemisphere derived from prehistoric, circumpolar shamanistic ceremonies. These ceremonies of Eurasian origins concerned hunting and fertility; also, frequently, curing and initiation. Each place where this Paleolithic shamanism encountered local cultures a certain kind of drama developed which used costumes, story-telling, dancing, song, and specialized (professional) people: performers. Definite connections link Far Eastern, Indian, Middle Eastern, European, and American drama. The African case appears special, but ultimately I think African drama will also be linked to the worldwide system.

[3] See La Barre (1972), 441 and 470–471.

drawing of the theater at Epidaurus (fourth century B.C.) is a fine model of the Greek idea of drama.

The audience outnumbers the performers by about fifteen thousand to three actors and either fifty, twelve, or fifteen members of the chorus.[4] In any case, the intimacy of tribal performances that involve a few dozen or at most some hundreds of people is gone. The Greeks made a very strict separation between the actors and the chorus. "The actors were hired by the state, and their proper place was upon the stage. The term 'hypokrites,' or 'actor,' was never applied to the members of the chorus."[5] The actors remained on the stage—a raised platform behind the orchestra or dancing-circle. The chorus remained in the circle. The chorus physically stands between the actors and the audience and is a double agent functioning on behalf of both the audience and the characters of the drama. The whole circle of tribal theater is broken. The audience does not surround the performance but is in a compromised relationship both face to face with it and more than halfway wrapped around it.

The progression—historical and conceptual—can be presented this way: [6]

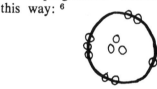 

Top   Side

Shamanistic circle. Performance space is continuous with the terrain. No audience as such.

Top   Side

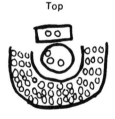 

Greek theatre, hewn out of the terrain. Audience

[4] The number of actors increased from one to three as the numbers in the chorus fluctuated, first coming down from fifty to twelve and then increasing to fifteen.

[5] Haigh (1907), 221.

[6] Thanks to Brooks McNamara for helping me think through these ideas.

Top   Side

Roman Stadium, free standing—can be built anywhere.

Accompanying the separation of the theater from the natural landscape is the development of the audience, professional actors, and stories and/or events that "take place" not in the place of the theater but in some imaginary place, or distant place, that the theater space represents—either symbolically or mimetically. The whole process of identification with the landscape and subsequent separations and transformations occur in Europe during the Middle Ages. The development of the Elizabethan playhouse is not a replication at a later date of the Greek theater, but a more or less independent development from such shamanistic theater spaces as the Cornish Round or the arena in which the Castle of Perseverance was staged. These, in turn, came from even earlier celebrations that joined Christian and pagan European rites. What is convincing is how the modern European theater originated at least twice, following a similar pattern independently both times. Thus the pattern that shows a close identification between the uses of terrain-as-theater and the introduction of the audience along with the theater-as-a-separate-place indicates that we are dealing with a structural phenomenon, and not just a single, unique historical occurrence. To generalize: As long as there is no audience, there will be no theater space separable from the terrain—whether this terrain be a field, a mountaintop, a temple step, or the village square. Once there is an audience as such, a theater space will develop. Or perhaps the process moves in the other direction: Once there is a separate space, the audience will develop.

The contemporary situation of the television audience discloses a unique structure. The stage is in one place, and the audience is scattered in many places. The possibilities for mimetic performances and a complete mix-up between "real" and "performed" are incalculable. Whatever "happens" *on* TV is a performance.

The "audience" at Shea Stadium watching the Jets play football are "performers" for me in my living room watching "the game." At the stadium maybe I am watching mostly the game, but at home I am part of a much more extensive performance. I listen to the commentators, see many commercials, watch some plays two or three times, observe the fans in the stadium, and maybe am involved in something lively and domestic in my own apartment. But because I am removed from the stadium in time/space, I cannot participate in *that* event in any way. My cheers fall on players who cannot hear me. I am watching a "live" event—something that is happening and in doubt—and I cannot feed in my energy to somehow affect, or at least express, how I view the events. Some participatory appetite is stimulated without any chance of being consummated. More appetites are stimulated by the commercials, and the wish-to-buy completes the cycle, or at least one becomes aware of it. One result is the food-and-drink gorging that goes on in response to TV viewing.

"Live" broadcasting must be understood in a special way. It is "morning" on the forbidding moon surface, but evening in my comfortable bedroom; it is a crowd of important world leaders that I seen in Peking, but just my wife and I at home; it is chilly, windy, and noisy at Shea Stadium, but warm and quiet in my living room. TV connects wildly different environments —but "media" is a funny word for TV because no mediation whatever occurs between these environments. The TV situation induces "audiences" within audiences, "spaces" within spaces. A model of the Jets' game on TV:

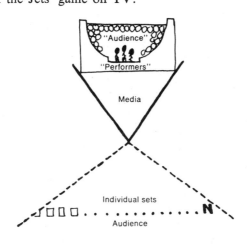

Attempts at "participatory broadcasting" are naïve. These experiments sidestep the essential problem: The audience is scattered, individualized, impotent. An actual community situation is impossible because community depends on *presence,* the convergence of many sense and space fields. The scattered audience is in many different fields, reacting in diverse ways. All feedback passes through media point M, and spectators cannot get in direct, unmediated contact with each other. At most feedback can be indicative of feeling; it cannot be spontaneously expressive of feeling. The need for M is more than a convenience: It puts control of the situation into the hands of whoever controls M. All feedback goes through M, just as the performance goes through M. Feedback becomes another element in the performance, grist for the performance mill operated by those who control M. Only in an illusory way do those "out there" control the performance, or interrupt it, or change its direction—all of which is possible in participatory theater. What really happens in TV is that the participators are fed into the system and become part of the performance for all other viewers; the participator is maximally manipulatable.

The existence of the audience introduces *aesthetics* into the theater. For the audience are those people who are interested in what's going on not from the point of view of having something directly at stake—as, for example, the families of a couple getting married do. The audience watches the event for event's own sake and can appreciate the way in which the performance takes place. This interest in "the way in which" replaces a more immediate concern with "what is happening." Participation is not just a naïve doing something, but a deeper having something at stake in the performance. Of course the families watching the wedding are concerned with the way the ceremony appears. But to the degree that the marriage is economically, personally, and socially important to the families—say a fortune is at stake—the more the focus will be on that it takes place, and the less it will be on how it takes place. But audiences are detached, interested in how, in spectacle, and get involved mainly in secondary, empathetic or sympathetic ways. Problems of how to make this kind of aestheticized audience participate—want to have a stake in the performance—are not easily settled. Many environmental theater designs try to restore the unbroken circle of shamanistic ceremonies. This is seen most clearly in performances staged in "found space"—the streets, mountainsides, meadows—where the performance space is continuous with the terrain.

In other words, aesthetics is a kind of self-consciousness about performing. When the audience is separated from the performance, the performance becomes autonomous. It is no longer tied to the here-and-now of ceremony. It has available to it the past, an ability to re-present events from other times and places. Ceremony makes the past and distant actually present by means of hierophany or "reactualization." The aesthetic mode is to *re-present* the past and distant. A contemporary wish is to somehow combine the aesthetic and the ceremonial. However, the differences between the aesthetic and the ceremonial are very basic and cannot be easily reconciled. The aesthetic mode encourages analysis and self- and other criticism through the observation of action from a distance. Contradictions that ritual theater resolves in an overwhelming celebration of group solidarity are, in Greek drama, laid bare for all to see, and left raw. The "resolutions" that conclude many Greek dramas are often mere formalities, survivals of shamanistic communion. Once there is an audience, there is distance, fragmentation, analysis, criticism, and objectivity. Read's experience in New Guinea is unthinkable at Epidaurus.

It is my thesis in this chapter that the need to form groups —think of how many groups have been formed in the past ten years!—is an attempt to restore wholeness and community to theater. But the group-makers also need to retain abilities of analysis, criticism, and objectivity introduced into Western drama by the Greeks. Group theaters identify with *both* tribal and Greek theaters; they want to live in both New Guinea and Athens. Thus are we involved in a deep, painful, and irresolvable contradiction. For it is not possible for the audience to exist and not exist at the same time. Nor can spectators simply be asked to participate. Nor is it possible to create a community in the span of a few hours. Nor can I give up my need for wholeness and community. Living through these difficulties has caused some theaters to turn inward, making of themselves examples of group life and collective creativity.

This truly agonizing situation can be put in the terms of a logical problem: If there were primeval circumpolar shamanistic performance cultures characterized by costuming, dancing, and story-telling by means of symbolic action and based on community-wholeness and the inseparability of performers and spectators; and if, into this scheme, as a result of contact with this circumpolar culture, peoples as diverse as East Asians, Asian and American Indians, Iranians, and Greeks introduced the idea of the audience as a separate assembly of people whose role in the theater is to watch; and if contemporary groups want to achieve the wholeness of the tribal experience of the primeval shamanist performance cultures without sacrificing the objectivity, analysis, and self-critical abilities of audience theaters, then: Are there means of achieving both kinds of theater simultaneously; of resolving the contradictions setting tribal and audience theaters off from each other? Are there ways of going on other than turning inward to form self-contained communes, in-groups, elites, or congregations making each theater group into a community-in-itself?

We have not yet solved this problem. All I can do is describe the TPG experiences that inevitably led me to formulate the problem as I have just done.

How much has changed from the earliest theaters to the present day. The dancing shamans of the European caves danced deep in the earth. The ceremonial places are "reached only after hazardous crevasses, low seams, and slippery tunnels have been traversed, with feeble lights battling the unknown eternal darkness. . . . The adytum of the cave at Clotilde in Spain must be crawled to, reverently or ridiculously, on hands and knees. And only after slithering through a culvert-like tunnel and inching up a rock chimney, a foot on each side above the abyss, can one make the hour's walk through devious corridors to view, finally, the famous 'Dancing Sorcerer' at Trois Frères." [7] Jean Genet, writing in 1954 a preface to *The Maids,* made much the same point regarding his hopes for modern theater:

> I have spoken of communion. The modern theatre is a di-version. It is sometimes, rarely, an estimable diversion. The word somewhat suggests the idea of dispersion. I know of no plays that link the spectators, be it only for an hour. Quite the contrary, they isolate them further. Sartre once told me, however, of having experienced this religious fervor during a theatrical performance: in a prison camp, at Christmas time, a group of soldiers, mediocre actors, had staged a French play evoking some theme I no longer recall —revolt or captivity or courage—and the far-away home-land was suddenly present, not on the stage, but in the hall. A clandestine theatre, to which one would go in secret, at night, and masked, a theatre in the catacombs, may still be possible.[8]

[7] La Barre (1972), 397.
[8] Genet (1963), 40.

Some modern theaters have attempted a kind of inaccessibility, an ordeal of entry, a rite of passage in order to stimulate, if not communion, at least reverberations of a communal spirit. The commercial theater charges money, and that is all. But we have lost touch with the work that earns the money. Dollars are no longer an accurate translation of a certain quantity of sweat, a sacrifice made to attend the theater. So our modern group theaters invent new entrance procedures. I myself am very fond of these: some way of greeting the spectators as they enter, of making a demand of some immediate, bodily kind.

In *Dionysus in 69* spectators were admitted to the Garage one at a time. This caused consternation among some. People resisted being separated from their dates, friends, spouses. But I wanted spectators to be confronted by the space, to enter it with surprise or anxiety or delight not blanked out by the presence of a known other. We did not let friends follow friends into the theater but separated people by four or five other people. Each person met the space alone, and found a place in it. For several months after November, 1968, performers met spectators inside the entrance door and carried them to places in the theater. Spectators were literally kidnapped. I got the idea from Van Gennep:

> Carrying and being carried is one of the practices which is found more or less universally in the various ceremonies through which a person passes in the course of a lifetime. The subject must not touch the ground for a specific length of time. He is carried in someone's arms or in a litter, placed on a horse, an ox, or in a carriage; he is placed on a mat which is movable or fastened, on a scaffold or an elevated seat, or on a throne. This rite is basically different from that of straddling something or being transported over something, although the two are sometimes combined. The idea is that the person should be raised above or lifted onto something.[9]

I quoted Van Gennep to the Group and added in my notes:

> As Dionysus says: "I shall bring you there. Someone else will bring you home. Carried high. A sight for all eyes." Later we shall establish the carrying home of Pentheus. For now, let us score the opening ceremonies of carrying each other and members of the audience. Carrying over or across. Carrying fast and slow. Carried by one or by many.

[9] Van Gennep (1960 [1908]), 185.

To enter the environment for *Makbeth* spectators had to enter a door on Wooster Street, go upstairs over the theater, pass through a complicated maze one at a time, and descend down a narrow, steep stairway into the theater. Brooks McNamara, designer of the maze, says this about it:

> The maze was originally conceived as a series of corridors beneath a high platform in a corner of the first floor of the Performing Garage. The audience was to pass through the corridors before entering the main environment. Like the performance itself, the maze was seen as an attempt to create a new organization of the Macbeth legend, previous performances of *Macbeth,* and the performance which was to take place. . . . As the concept for the maze became more complex, it outgrew the space available under the twelve-foot platform. We decided to move the maze upstairs to a large room on the second floor of the Garage. . . . At this point I left for England. A new idea came to me after spending a few minutes in the hall of mirrors at the Battersea Fun Fair in London. In the hall of mirrors the walls of each chamber were made up of four by eight foot frames, some of which contained mirrors and others heavy sheets of plate glass. Still others were completely open, allowing movement from one chamber to another. Once inside the hall it became difficult to distinguish the door to an adjoining chamber from a glass wall or mirror. It seemed to me that something of the confusion of the hall of mirrors would give the maze a vitality and complexity not present in the early models. A second experience—a visit to the Chamber of Horrors at Madame Tussaud's Wax Museum—suggested a further possibility. The light in the Chamber of Horrors is intentionally bad. The level of light in the room constantly changes and the light sources are placed so that it is often very difficult to see an exhibit; most often the tableaux are half hidden by shadows. The result is that spectators and exhibits often seem to merge, with tableaux apparently coming to life. I decided that I wanted a similar effect in the maze.[10]

Of course the original maze at Minos' palace in Crete serves the same purpose: to contain the horror locked within and to frustrate the heroes who attempt to penetrate to the heart of darkness.

A theater that demands of its audiences even a touch of this

[10] McNamara's written account accompanying drawings and models of the maze; unpublished.

kind of adventure is going beyond the blandness of buying a ticket. In *Commune* the entrance procedure was simplest of all, and intimate. We would not admit anyone who did not take his shoes off and leave them near the door. I have discussed this in Chapter 2. I enjoy "working the door" for TPG plays not only because I like seeing the audience enter filling up the theater invitingly the way water fills a bathtub, but also because of the many changes people go through when they realize that a ticket is not all they need to gain entrance. In fact, many people come to TPG plays free; but no one enters except through ceremony.

Whatever the opening ceremonies, they do not convert an audience into a community. Sometimes the ceremonies make people think, or stir feelings; mostly people think the ceremonies are cute, or another annoyance one must put up with off off-Broadway: avant-garde affectation. Certainly the ceremonies are pale versions of the ridiculous-sacred climbs through the primeval caves of the dancing shamans. Furthermore, whatever effect the ceremonies may have on spectators, they do little to the performers. The group experience begins somewhere else; and it is more than a mere ritualistic embellishment of an aesthetic event.

I think that fundamentally the formation of a group is an attempt to create a family, but a family structured from the assumption that the dominance of the parents can be eliminated and that repression can be reduced if not eradicated. A nonparental, unrepressive family is surely not the kind of family I was brought up in. To develop such a family means to fly in the face of many traditions. And to assert that the function of the new family is to make plays—to show performances—is to heap difficulty upon difficulty. TPG has never come close to what David Cooper describes as a commune. But our struggles are in the direction Cooper outlines, and over the issues he identifies.

> A commune is a microsocial structure that achieves a viable dialectic between solitude and being-with-others; it implies either a common residence for the members, or at least a common work and experience area, around which residential situations may spread out peripherally; it means that love relationships become diffused between members of the commune network far more than is the case with the family system, and this means, of course, that sexual relationships are not restricted to some socially approved two-person, man-woman arrangement; above all, because this strikes most centrally at repression, it means that children should have

totally free access to adults beyond their biological parental couple.[11]

Now: On the surface Cooper does not apply to TPG. We have no children; we have not been a sexually free group; we live together only a few months of the year. But Cooper has described a subtext that operates strongly in the themes and processes of our work. And because performing is a special kind of work in which symbolic representation, acting out, and actuality interpenetrate, much of the history of TPG could be summarized as a development from a father-dominated family into a more flexible sibling family and from here toward some kind of non-family collective.

From my point of view the basic struggle from the beginning of TPG in November, 1967, until Joan MacIntosh and I left for Asia in October, 1971, was around what my role in the group should be. This struggle—and sometimes it also seemed like a quest—took many forms. During the time Joan and I were away—about seven months—the Group changed, and when we were reintegrated into TPG during the spring and summer of 1972, it was on a different basis from before.

I began the Group as a workshop after announcing to my classes at N.Y.U. and to some friends that I wanted to continue work I started while with the New Orleans Group (1965–1967).[12] Also during the first three weeks of November I was in Grotowski's N.Y.U. workshop, and I wanted to apply some of what I was learning. During October I coordinated the planning for a street theater piece, *Guerrilla Warfare,* which was staged simultaneously in many areas of Manhattan on October 28.[13] Some of the people I met while planning *Guerrilla Warfare* wanted to continue working with me. The workshop met at first once a week. Soon, however, meetings were increased until by mid-December we were meeting three and then four times a week in the evenings.

I never directly selected who was to form the nucleus of TPG.

[11] Cooper (1970), 44–45.

[12] The NOG was founded and directed by Franklin Adams, Paul Epstein, and me in 1965. We wanted to work in intermedia, Happenings, and environmental theater. We collaborated on several pieces including the May, 1967, production of Eugene Ionesco's *Victims of Duty.* After I left New Orleans Adams and Epstein kept the NOG going until Epstein left in 1969.

[13] *Guerrilla Warfare* was based on a scenario I wrote called "Public Events for the Radical Theatre" (see *Public Domain,* 201–207). Accounts of *Guerrilla Warfare* appear in *The New York Times,* October 29, 1967, and the *Village Voice,* November 1, 1967.

I simply announced very strict standards of attendance for the workshop. A person had to be on time; if he missed more than one workshop, he would not be let back in. The work itself was physically difficult, combining exercises I learned from Grotowski with NOG work, tumbling, and some encounter group techniques. Although I was not entirely conscious of it at the time, the fact that many of the people in the workshop were also in my classes reinforced my authority greatly. Also in no small way I encouraged my own elevation as a father-leader. I was about ten years older than most of the people. By mid-January there were about ten people left from an original twenty-five. We decided to form a group and do our own version of Euripides' *The Bacchae*.[14] But "we" is a tricky word. A corporation was formed by me in which I held all the powers. I took out a personal loan from a commercial bank in order to have enough money to look for a permanent theater space. Luckily Patrick McDermott and William Shephard found the Garage, and I rented it.

Soon a very complicated situation had grown up. Even at this distance I am not able to untangle it completely. Legally, The Performance Group was a nonprofit, tax-exempt corporation, with me as its executive officer. Theatrically, TPG was a theater of amateurs, myself included, training ourselves. We were fortunate in finding a theater space ideally suited to the new style of work we were doing. Group-wise I became a guru, loved and hated by the people I worked with. The nature of some of the exercises —the gropes, the hours-long improvisations evoking both mythic and intimate material, encounter and confrontation work—corroborated my position. Also I had difficulty speaking to people personally, one to one, in simple conversation. I was most relaxed in a highly structured situation—such as teaching exercises, arranging the rules for a theater game, outlining the shape of an improvisation. When I was confronted, I remained silent, justifying my lack of reaction by saying to myself that the performer needed me as a screen on which to project his/her feelings. Often I would communicate to the whole Group by writing out my notes and distributing them. I discouraged any kind of discussion during workshops. In fact, we followed strict procedures of silence. Every feeling that came up was focused into the work, made part of the work. I saw little of group members outside of the work. In fact, I was very uncomfortable when a few of them wanted to become my friends.

[14] See *Dionysus in 69,* The Performance Group (1970).

But this situation was not stable. The commercial success of *Dionysus in 69* put off the inevitable reckoning—after all, maybe I did have some "magic" (went the legend), because the play was a hit. But even as the Garage resounded to full houses, things within the Group were deteriorating. Rehearsals for *Makbeth* during the 1968–1969 season went very slowly. Our own experience with a formal therapy group (see Chapter 6) demystified my position in the Group. I began to have deep doubts about my leadership abilities and about the structure of the Group. At the time I didn't know what was going on, and I fought desperately to keep my powers. Later I read Slater's excellent summary of the dynamic.

> . . . the initial view of him [the leader] is highly suffused with an exaggerated and idealized parental image. But this fantasy of the group leader's omniscience is obviously doomed to decay. In the first place, it is based in considerable part on the feelings of abject dependence which are aroused by the initial lack of structure in the situation. The feeling calls for the desire and also activates the world-view appropriate to the feeling when it was first experienced. Relative to the helpless child the parent *is* omnipotent, and whenever such helplessness is felt again, authority figures will tend to be viewed in the same way. But as the group members gain inner strength this perception will correspondingly wither.
>
> In the second place, transference reactions bloom most richly in the absence of stimuli, . . . and it is easiest to attach an idealized parental image to the group leader when he is unknown. . . . Insofar as he does nothing and says nothing, the fantasy of his omniscience can be maintained. . . . His nonretaliatory detachment bolsters and colors this fantasy, enabling the members to see him as "invulnerable" and a "superman." But gradually he, too, reveals more and more, and when he speaks he becomes mortal and fallible again and seems quite unsatisfactory by contrast with the idealized paternal image against which he has been silhouetted. Hence the members fluctuate in their attitudes toward him, seeing him now as omniscient, now as incompetent, and circulating bizarre rumors which serve to support both views.
>
> In time, the group leader is stripped of his magical image altogether—his secrets fathomed, his bag of tricks up-ended —and appears in all his naked mortality, a mere human, although apparently clever and well-intentioned. A revolt occurring this late in the game carries no thrill and yields

no sense of triumph. If it is not a god but only a mere human who has been conquered and eaten, then what has the group achieved, and what has it added to itself? [15]

The revolt came very late in the game. All during the spring of 1969 I felt my authority slipping away, and I did not want to let it go. In rereading letters written to me by a Group member I realize how stupid I was. The arguments for sharing power, gracefully abdicating my omnipotence, were clear and well taken. But something in me made me want to hold on with a desperation that I can only describe in retrospect as life-saving. Somewhere I felt that if I let go, I would go down.

Instead of letting go I tightened up. On July 27, 1969, I read and posted the following notice:

> RS has following powers:
>   1. To admit and dismiss members of the Group.
>   2. To determine what plays should be produced, the casting, and directing assignments.
>   3. To set workshop work and rehearsals both in terms of the nature of the work and their scheduling.
>   4. To supervise the planning of the environment and other artistic but non-performance matters.
>   5. To set fines for failure to do work, or disruption of work.
>   This does not signal an end to open discussion. I wish people to feel free to express their opinions. But discussion will not occur during exploratory work where it is necessary to get into the work and not evaluate it too soon.
> Performers have following responsibilities:
>   1. To perform.
>   2. To be in workshops.
>   3. To run workshops where assigned by RS.
>   4. To direct plays or projects where assigned by RS.

Behind this incredible document was another, drawn by the TPG lawyer at my request, and dated July 1, 1969:

> This will confirm the understanding reached between you and the Board of Directors of The Wooster Group, Inc., whereby we have employed you as Executive Director and Artistic Director of the corporation and of The Performance Group. . . .
>   We confirm that, in this capacity, you are to have sole

---

[15] Slater (1966), 79–81.

charge of all artistic matters and overall administrative control of all operations, including, without limitation, the right to hire and fire members of The Performance Group and other employees, to select the works to be presented, to fix hours and places of employment, determine use of the theatre and to establish rules and procedures for the group members and employees, subject only to the powers granted to this Board by statute, our certificate of incorporation and by-laws.

We understand that in the past you have referred certain matters affecting The Performance Group and the theatre to the members of the group to decide. To the extent that you wish to do so, this is to confirm your authority to continue this practice and to extend or restrict the areas or subject matter to be treated this way, but in case of any dispute between the members of the group and you, it is our intention, and we hereby agree, that your decision shall prevail.

In the notice of July 27 I gave as my reasons for "clarifying" TPG structure:

1. Confusion of legislation for participation. The two are far from identical.

2. Confusion of argument for collaboration. Ditto.

3. Necessary to put most of Group's energies into the immense and interesting problems of *Makbeth,* professional improvement, exploration of self.

4. Experience over the past year has shown:

A. Not growing fast or largely enough as performers.
B. Increasing number of enervating and mind-wasting disputes.
C. Decreasing concentration on work.
D. Preoccupation with "interpersonal communication" which in many instances does not communicate but rather develops a private (to individuals, to the Group) code.
E. Group has not emerged either as functioning community or functioning theatre.
F. People who needed special work did not get it.
G. People who had developed capabilities not sufficiently challenged.
H. Increasing self-indulgence on the part of the Group as a whole. Individually people want to work. Together, the work is sometimes avoided.

5. Therefore I am returning to some old disciplines which I feel most strongly will help us become finer performers and more whole persons.

It is hard for me to assess now (November, 1972) my feelings then (July, 1969). I was scared, disappointed, threatened; I had no faith in the way the work was going. I did not enjoy *Dionysus in 69* because images I had in my head were not being played out in the theater. Every time a performer would make a suggestion either about the mise-en-scène or about Group structure I read it as an attack on me. My experience in the Sacharow group sessions did not facilitate my dealings with the others. The groups gave us a frame of reference, but this frame was of anger, resentment, and perpetuation of the parent-child relationship.

The capper was the work on *Makbeth*. I had no confidence that the Group could do the play. Some of the best performers I could no longer speak to, no less work with; two others were leaving the Group, one permanently and one on a "leave of absence." I was afraid of failure. What if the critics hated *Makbeth;* what if there were no audiences?

The critics hated *Makbeth;* there were no audiences. The Group was plunged into its deepest crisis. Exactly a year before the *Makbeth* crisis that exploded the Group, I wrote another note to the Group dated December 10, 1968:

On Rules & The Withering Away of the Director

In all perfectable societies the perfect state is one in which there are neither rulers nor ruled, but rather a harmonious unity in which all live with all. Not in peace, for that would be tedium, but in overt agreement over goals and procedures; active differences coming only over means and only to determine the "better way." These differences are worked out through discussion and action, a new "chairman" emerging for each encounter. The whole society is one rooted in trust and flowering in productivity.

Such a society does not yet exist; probably has not yet existed.

Rules measure the distance between where we are and that perfect state that is the end goal of perfectable societies. Rules are a confession of inadequacy; an admission of imperfectibility. Where rules exist, something is wrong.

I am a a relativist. I do not believe I will live in a perfect state; I do not think I am living the worst of all possible states. I do not believe either in artistic anarchy or artistic totalitarianism. Artistic totalitarianism is a situation in which a man's whimsy = law. It is a situation which has traditionally been dominated by tyrants, but one in which the "people" (of a small group) could also be dominant. By that I mean, if a person decided not to do the work and by that decision he interrupted the work of all the others, his act would be (for him valid) for the others totalitarian.

The rules we have are essentially of two kinds: (1) societal and (2) artistic. The first kind—be on time, attend —keep us in existence and prepare the time/space for our work. The second kind—surpass yourself, express yourself within the terms of the work—are the root of our art. Insofar as we believe in the second kind, the first kind of rule will wither away. No one would miss work he found absolutely necessary and productive.

However, the human psychophysical mechanism (from toe to soul) is extraordinarily complicated, deceptive, and cunning. We too often ask someone to be "human" when human beings can be nothing else but human. No desire for perfectibility will eliminate the beautiful complications of the non-perfect human being. Rules are established as boundaries, touchstones, guideposts. Within the brackets of the rules

the performer and the director are free. Our rules are to us what the circular arena and the limit of three actors was to the Greeks. Sometimes our rules are viewed as tyrannical episodes—the "acting out" of RS. In some views they are that; RS is no more perfect or perfectible than any other person.

The only specialty he can claim is that he is more knowledgable about the process we are embarked on; and that he recognizes the restraints of rules and their necessity: the fact that they free more than they inhibit.

The time may come in The Performance Group when disciplinary societal rules are not necessary and artistic rules are simply implicit in our work. That would mean that TPG was fairly close to being a model of the perfect society. I would welcome, though I do not expect, that time.

Until then I would like you to think of the proposition that the rule of law is a circumscription that draws the area of our creativity and freedom; and not be swayed by the all too simple belief that any limitation is tyrannical.

Endnote on infallibility:
  I am very aware that I am most fallible; that as a human being I am not complete. Not "through" as the existentialists would say. I hope not to be "through" until I am dead. Completion is not a state but a process and by definition an impossible project for the human being—but one which must occupy all who wish to be wise.
  The nature of our work is innovative and experimental. That means a high proportion of failure. To do our own work is to fail much of the time. Your failure will be not to be able to answer specifically the questions of situation and specificity; not to be able to express effectively the answers when you have found them; and more tasks as well that we will come to later. My failure will be in concepts relating to the mise-en-scène; in allowing myself to be "subjective" but not "personal" in dealing with each of you; and more that I will come to later.
  I believe that we need presently, and for some time to come, rules. Perfection is not my game; process is. A word, I might say, that few of us understand though many of us choose to use it either as a cloak or a dagger.

But instead of moving in the direction vaguely outlined in the above, a movement toward communality and collective decision-making, we moved to crisis, confusion, disruption, and explosion. As I tightened my authoritarian grip, the group members increased their pressures against me. It was a classic situation. It also interiorized and then projected the situation from *Makbeth*. In some way I was playing old Duncan, and I was doomed. As Slater points out, the patterning of group life on a mythic model is common:

> We seem to be dealing here with something akin to the magical force or *mana* of many nonliterate peoples. This force resides in the idealized parental image, and is present in the group leader only so long as he is identified with that image. . . . What the group wants most when it revolts is to believe in its own strength and dependability. It will be successful as a group insofar as the members are willing to depend on each other rather than on the leader, and this will occur when the group as a whole is perceived as strong and able.[16]

[16] Slater (1966), 81.

Thus the attack on me, and my bitter defense and counter-attack, was not pure, but dripping with old themes some of which we had rehearsed for more than a year and were performing nightly. And the conflict left no one the richer because it finally was a kind of stalemate. I fired people; people fired me. We argued, fought, made public pronouncements. Box office receipts were seized, legal notices sent. When January was over, *Makbeth* closed, and the Group split irreparably. I cannot speak for the others, but I did not feel triumphant, just exhausted. It was like the crisis of a sickness, a horrible but necessary vomiting of hatred and personal failure. And, just maybe, the chance for another beginning.

Before discussing the new beginning I want to reflect a moment on TPG in terms of the thesis in this chapter: the contradictory need for communal and analytic experience. TPG began as a workshop, but I knew from the start that I wanted to direct a theater. I think everyone in the workshop wanted a theater. We shared a hope that this theater could be made on a different basis from the commercial theaters. We did not want the part-time, amateurish off off-Broadway kind of theater in which people held second jobs and were unable to give enough time to training or rehearsal. We did not want a stepping-stone theater in which people stayed just long enough to get known. However, I reacted negatively to suggestions that we form a community. I identified community with self-indulgence, freak-outs, undisguised pursuit of pleasures, especially sexual pleasures, at the expense of discipline, productivity, and what I called "professionalism." I was trained as a critic and editor; my N.Y.U. job was as a professor. Expectedly I leaned toward ·the classical end of the scale. For all the reputation about being "dionysian," I *taught about* dionysian patterns—I did not live those patterns. At the same time I felt an overwhelming excitement during some performances of *Dionysus* and during some workshops.[17] Something *more than* theatre was happening. This "more than" was the making of personal bonds among TPG members; suggesting ways of communal experience to audiences: in other words, the shamanistic kind of performance. But even as I was fascinated by this, drawn to it, I could not give myself over to it. I was afraid of what would happen to me, to my reputation, to the work I wanted to do. I did not trust the Group, which means I did

---

[17] For a discussion of this excitement see my "Politics of Ecstasy" and "Negotiations with Environments" in *Public Domain* (1968); and my notes in *Dionysus in 69* (1970).

not trust the people I was working with. Finally, they did not trust me either. As I lost my magic hold over them—as I became less and less a father—I substituted raw authority: I became a boss.

Subsequently I discerned different models of group structure. TPG began with the *leader outside the group*.

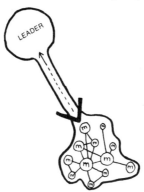

The ego boundaries of people in the group are weak while the leader's boundaries are strong and fiercely defended. He is outside, above, beyond, more powerful; the sense of identity of individual group members depends on the leader's attention, praise or punishment, assistance, and personal presence. He is the father to the group. There are frequent *emotional epidemics* in the group to which the leader is immune. Cliques, struggles, ganging up, and dumping on a scapegoat characterize group life. The leader is envied and hated for his immunity, unassailability, and invulnerability. In this kind of group, rebellion against the leader is inevitable; and if the rebellion is thwarted, members feel depressed. A group with the leader outside can be transformed into its opposite, *a group in the leader*. This did not happen to TPG, but it is the kind of structure the Manson family has.

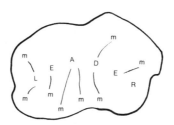

The leader is a messiah, a god, a supermind, the one to whom all is revealed. The members' ego boundaries are completely dissolved; they live in and through the leader whose fantasy life becomes the actual life of the group. In fact, the leader is the only *person* in the group. The others are absorbed into him, they are parts of him, extensions of his body. Without his "love" they are nothing. Members spend hours interpreting the leader's actions, telling stories about him, embroidering his legends, adoring him, and keeping their experience of him in a perpetual mysterious elation. Like Mel Lyman of Boston's Fort Hill Commune, or The Mother of the Aurobindo Ashram of Pondicherry, members may think of their leader as the Avatar, the literal incarnation of god. The leader does not communicate in only a direct, discursive manner but through parables, mysterious gestures, and allegories of action. The leader *manifests* himself. Heinlein's *Stranger in a Strange Land* is about the cult of such a leader, as is the New Testament.

TPG moved not toward this extreme, but often unshakably stable, structure, but toward other, more moderate, models. First we became a group with the leader in the group as a special member.

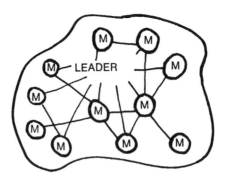

In this kind of group the leader has specific and well-known powers. He gives to the other members of the group but does not reveal as much to them as they do to each other and to him. There is still a large degree of mystification; the leader retains his function as a screen. He is not stripped of his parental role. This kind of group is unstable. The leader's unveiling of himself is deeply manipulative: It is a surface off which the others confront each other. The leader guides his behavior according to how he perceives the needs of the performers. The leader suffers delusions of omniscience: He *knows* what the others need. The others resent the fact that the leader's participation is somehow arranged, that he has jump on them. Let me be clear: It is not that the leader sits at home planning how he will behave at workshop; it is that he does not release his own feelings to the degree he expects others to do so. Thereby an irreversible imbalance is set up that gives the leader a manipulating upper hand.

TPG was this way from March, 1970, until after my departure for Asia in October, 1971. This very defensive and unstable group structure was my reaction to the terrors of the breakup of January, 1970. It was from this stance that we made the first versions of *Commune*. But with Joan and me gone the Group changed—if TPG were to survive, it had to change. I knew that when I went away: another subtle manipulation perhaps. But I didn't recognize the dimensions of the changes until after our return in April, 1972. A few weeks after Joan and I got back the Group had a party. After supper people launched into me. They said things they had been feeling for two years; everyone wanted to make sure that I understood that things would not pick up in April where they left off in October. Person after person said angrily that they felt I had used them in making *Commune;* that they were not entirely conscious during rehearsals; that they didn't feel that the play meant what they wanted it to mean.

This second revolution was different from the explosion of 1969–1970. During the first period of TPG I was secretive, autocratic, and distant. During the second period—the making of *Commune*—I was more like a broken-field runner, shifting my position in order to keep from being downed. In 1972 everyone wanted to keep working together—but in ways that were conscious and collaborative. We sought a form of structure that would be *conscious, stable, and creative:* a difficult combination. As best I can perceive it, this kind of structure could take two shapes, with one leading to the other.

In A. there is a single leader who leads with the consent and collaboration of the members. Many powers are shared and leadership diffuses. The leader interacts genuinely with members, taking the same risks they do. He serves at their pleasure and may be replaced if they wish. A. is a democratic model. In B. we have the mythical leaderless group—perhaps as rare as the unicorn. Every member is the leader depending upon circumstances. Decisions are collective, or a particular situation calls for someone who leads and gives up leadership when the situation

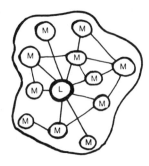 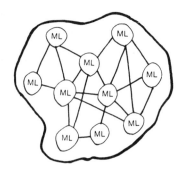

changes. In both A. and B. leadership is demystified, nonparental, and flexible. The democratic and collective (or participatory) models allow for effective interaction among members. In the parental model the interaction is almost all in terms of rivalry, either among siblings or between the members and the leader. In the messianic model there is total communion, merging, and adoration but little nonfantasized interaction. And there is no power—literally no *mana* or *anima*—outside the leader and what he bestows.

In point of legal fact TPG adopted a new structure in May, 1972. The corporation was restructured to include all members of the Group as members of the corporation; and no one who was not a Group member was included. The corporation members elect the board of directors who in turn elect the officers of the Group. Elizabeth Le Compte, Joan MacIntosh, Stephen Borst, Spalding Gray, Jerry Rojo, and I all wanted to be on the board and were elected. Also elected to the board was Jeremy Nussbaum, the Group's lawyer. Borst and I were confirmed as coexecutive directors of the Group. The "power document" of July 1, 1969, was redrafted to include both Borst and me; and we serve only at the pleasure of the board; and the board only at the pleasure of the members. This legal restructuring was one face of a more complicated and still developing restructuring. Presently the Group is not yet a collective. But leadership is spread around with several of us making decisions. Also the Group as a whole is not only consulted (as always) but *empowered* to make decisions. It is in the area of workshops and rehearsals—the daily artistic work—that a good deal still needs to be done. I don't know what needs to be done, but the process of collaboration, participation, and collectivization is started, and not finished.

All kinds of groups can produce "good theater"—if by that one means performances that are moving and meaningful to audiences. But definitely different kinds of groups tend to produce different kinds of theater. The first kind of group is secretive in its actual distribution of power, and if it works, *the director seems to be absent,* as the skillful marionette manipulator stands above the performance he controls. The second kind of group produces hierophanies, extremely powerful but often mysterious and private images and acting out. This kind of messianic group blurs distinctions between out-of-the-theater reality and in-the-theater reality: The killings of Sharon Tate and her friends were, to members of the Manson family, a show, a performance, a real-life drama. The third kind of group shows the strong hand of the director. The fourth kind of group—especially the leaderless version—is the most flexible, capable of adapting its structure to meet different needs. Therefore the kind of performance such a group can make varies widely.

During the summer of 1972 a lot of the strictness of TPG work went out of style. For the first time we let people drop in on our rehearsals which were open unless we needed to work alone. This was a full reversal of previous policy where all rehearsals were closed except formal "open rehearsals." Previously we let a few special people in to see our work—a professional courtesy. But we kept a "holy space, holy time" attitude. That attitude pretty well went down the drain. Students, faculty, visitors, dropped in to our U.B.C. rehearsals and stayed for a few minutes or a few hours. Some people came back again and again. Unless we got into very personal stuff we did all our work with people there. When we had to be alone, there was no hesitation in asking people to leave. Usually we kicked them out for a comparatively brief time—an hour or so—and then, after we worked through what was troubling the work, we invited our guests back in.

This loosening affected the work on *The Tooth of Crime* by making it inevitable that soliloquies and audience asides would enter into the production. Also, for the first time, the audience was truly part of the creative process at the very first stages of the work. There was one truly extraordinary workshop-rehearsal in which Timothy Shelton, playing Crow, was "given the room" by me. I told him that the rehearsal room and everyone in it were his. We were investigating what it takes to kill someone without using physical violence. Tim absorbed the power in the room, and some amazing interactions took place between him and audience who just dropped in to see a rehearsal. The exercise took more than two hours. During that time Tim and two spectators played several scenes that not only found their way into *Tooth* but affected the lives of those involved, including Tim and me. Lasting relationships were started, insights achieved. It was not psychodrama, but working through a theatrical problem at the level of personal encounter. Tim was able to turn the *whole room* into the place of his exercise. For a few hours in that small rehearsal room there was no distinction between the space of the performers and the space of spectators. Scenes took place wherever Tim/Crow initiated them. It took him nearly two hours to "kill" one person. The struggle between them was incredible—ranging across the whole room, dancing, singing, arguing, wrestling, talking, whispering, touching. In the midst of this other people came and went, as their afternoon schedule dictated. A few people stayed, left, and came back an hour later. (The other performers were not there, though a few dropped in toward the end. I think this helped Tim feel freer.) As we work on the play even now, Tim and I refer back to that afternoon as a deep well.

If our rehearsals are more open, our workshop work is not. We do our daily exercises alone with each other. And the "work on ourselves" is done privately. But there's a loosening of secrecy, and to the extent that secrecy is a mystification—a way of stimulating the curiosity of outsiders—it must be abolished.

All this is connected to the changes in basic group structure. As leadership is decentralized, the mysterious *mana* connected with the leader and infused in "the work" is redistributed and reduced. The mystery is not simply shared; it is eliminated. Reconstruction on the level of legalism has consequences on the level of art. The most illuminating consequence is that the two levels are shown to be inseparable.

I want to say that no matter how bitter TPG history may appear in this summary of it, our experience is not atypical. And it beats the even more brutal and surely more reified crushings of the commercial theater. Many groups simply do not survive. Others undergo periodic revision and reformation under the most difficult auspices. Joseph Chaikin, usually reticent about such matters, writes of the Open Theater:

> Then *The Serpent:* starting from the beginning, we had a utopian community. It couldn't have been better: there was

not one wrong current. Everyone was deferential to everyone else, and we maintained a strict, though unspoken, rule of friendliness among one another. Then with the start of the preparation for the production there grew a kind of dismay, and that dismay was carried through in every step of the actual mounting of the *The Serpent*. The dismay that began at the beginning of the process continued throughout; it really got bad. Each performance was like a confirmation of our disappointment, in spite of, or in part because of, the public success. Then we went to Europe with it, and everything was difficult: people with each other, the actors in relation to the work, in relation to me, in relation to Van Itallie. Everything was off. Nothing was working. There was a sense of betrayal, that each of us had somehow betrayed the other. When we came back from the tour, it was a matter of whether or not to pick up the pieces.[18]

Chaikin's observations are interesting for another reason, too. Often audiences and critics judge the quality of life in a group by the quality and tone of that group's public works. A group that performs as an ensemble—authentically giving to and taking from each other on stage—is assumed to be a "together group." More so if the work is not an orthodox play, not a "pretend," but something the group itself made from scratch, showing the here-and-now feelings of the performers through a set of verbal and physical gestures that these very performers have worked out with each other over months or even years. Audiences believe that such group work is a showing of group life on a one-for-one basis. Thus the reactions to *The Serpent* and *Dionysus in 69*.

How easy things would be if this fantasy were true! Just as it would be nice if democratic societies produced the best art. But the life on stage may be the only time/place where a group is together, the only opportunity for group members to communicate with each other in an open, direct, structured, non-hostile way; or where the hostility is translated into acceptable gestures. There is, unfortunately, no easy relationship between the quality of life in a group and the quality of the group's work. By "quality" I mean not only excellence but *tone,* the modalities of a performance. Thus *Dionysus in 69* was misinterpreted and misunderstood. Some spectators who had been "wiped out" by the performance—wiped out by the way the Group *played together*—were wiped out a second time when they came upstairs

---

[18] Chaikin (1972), 106–107.

after a performance and saw us at each other's throats. These same spectators were dismayed when they asked to join TPG —thinking we were some kind of dionysian tribe—and were cruelly rebuffed.

At some level the life of the group determines the life of the work. But it is necessary to be delicate and discriminating before announcing what the relationship is between group life and work life. Most of the things I've described already—meetings, notes, letters, arguments, pronouncements—are visible aspects of an immensely complicated and mostly submerged set of *family* relations. One example of this is in the permissive touching that goes on in many groups. Cooper is correct when he notes:

> The very recently evolved tradition of touching and holding between people, the new tradition of hugging and kissing anyone on every encounter, not just on socially prescribed meetings, seems to me to be good, but essentially a desexualizing, anti-erotic maneuver. It introduces a warmth, but the freezing plates are turned on underneath to melt the warmth and to limit its extent. If one is going to get on to the transexual reality of orgasm that dialectically retains sexuality in the present new level of synthesis, one has to be open to further moves all the time.[19]

People close off as they introduce into the group certain of the taboos of family life. These are not only the restrictions couples put on other couples; but the kind of don't-touch-sexually that brothers and sisters get into: a sibling incest taboo. Laing notes that the "family" is imprinted early in life—a set of relations adopted from one's own actual family and then projected onto many subsequent situations. Often enough in workshop one runs up against these "families." They are not easy to identify with clarity or to deal with.

> The "family" is not an introjected object, but an introjected set of relations. . . . "Family" space and time is akin to mythic space and time, in that it tends to be ordered round a center and runs on repeating cycles. . . . The reprojection of the "family" is not simply a matter of projecting an "internal" object onto an external person. It is superimposition of one set of relations onto another: the two sets may match more or less. . . . It is never enough to think of spatial struc-

19 Cooper (1970), 111.

ture alone, much less of one inner object out of context. One should always look for a sequence of events in which more elements than one have their parts to play.[20]

In other words, the reprojection of the family is a drama; and it is usually a murder drama.

The "family" mapped onto the family, or carried over to other situations, is no simple set of introjected objects, but more a matrix for *dramas,* patterns of space-time sequences to be enacted. As in a *reel* of film, all elements are copresent, pre-set to unfold in sequence in time as a *film* on the screen. *The reel is the internal family.*[21]

As groups develop from parent-dominated or messianic to democratic or collective models, the inevitability of the patterning Laing describes diminishes; there is less acting out and more acting through. But the element of acting out never vanishes altogether—not from group life any more than from any other part of human life. In fact, groups tend to stimulate and evoke a high level of acting out especially if the work or task of the group is to act: to replicate in some way the creative energies and dynamic of childhood and/or adolescence. In such situations it would be unnatural not to expect memories, associations, and living patterns from these early times not to be present. And for almost everyone the experience of childhood and adolescence is the experience of being introduced to, living within, and breaking free from the family.

After the breakup of TPG in 1970 I was extremely confused. When Joan MacIntosh, Stephen Borst, and I decided to go on, I didn't know how to go on. I felt like the end of Samuel Beckett's *The Unnamable:* "I'll never know, in the silence you dont know, you must go on, I can't go on, I'll go on." We invited Spalding Gray to go on with us. Spalding had come into the Group at the very end of the *Makbeth* experience. And there were the "associate members"—people we worked with but who were not part of the daily work: Jerry Rojo, Paul Epstein; and Catherine Farinon-Smith of New Arts Management. Joan, Steve, Spalding, and I ran workshops, talked about "new people," started to get the Group together. At the same time we began work on *Commune.* New people came into the Group: James

---

[20] Laing (1969, 1971), 4–9.
[21] Laing (1969, 1971), 17.

Griffiths, Patric Epstein, Bruce White, Patricia Bower, Mik Cribben, Jayme Daniel; a little later Elizabeth LeCompte. The next year Patric, Bruce, Patricia, Mik, and Jayme left—but without an explosion, as a matter of course; and Maxine Herman, Timothy Shelton, and Converse Gurian came in. Then in 1972 Converse left, and later so did Maxine. That's where we are now as I write this: Joan, Steve, Spalding, Liz, Jim, Tim, and me. During the first months of 1970 we found, and then used often, an exercise I called "Recapitulation." I named it that because at the time I felt it summarized the action of *Commune*. From the perspective of now I think "Recapitulation" condensed fantasies of family life of the first Group, and maybe some of the life of the second Group before my departure for Asia.

The themes of "Recapitulation" came from my reading of Slater's *Microcosm:*

> A king is weak or powerful only in relation to his people, and he is made great by increasing the social distance between him and his subjects. Thus the way to exalt the king is to crouch down before him, a technique which was exhibited in one group when a member happily remarked, apropos of the leader, "not many fathers have thirteen children!" But in part this process of building up the king and freeing his narcissism is like fattening the lambs for the slaughter—the more magnified his image, the more the "subjects" get to "eat." His symbolic enrichment will ultimately lead to enriching themselves, for the greater the king the more noble the revolutionaries. This is pure magic, and occasionally backfires. . . .[22]

The mechanics of "Recapitulation" are simple. The performers lie on the floor and listen to the sounds inside themselves and in the room. Sounds come from passing traffic, from heartbeats, breathing, stomach rumbling, house noises. Each performer selects from what he hears a basic rhythm. He gets his breathing together with this rhythm. Slowly each performer discovers a beat, a song, a pattern-of-being-in-harmony-with-the-spaces-inside-him-and-outside-him. Performers rise, dance to these patterns, dance *in* the patterns. The dance is augmented by chanting and singing and builds to a paroxysm. Then everyone collapses on the floor. Soon they rise again, but this time they dance with each other, as a group.

After doing this exercise several times a week for a few weeks

[22] Slater (1966), 83–84.

I noticed a pattern emerging. Rhythms, configurations, and inter-actions occurred in an organized way. This shaping happened at a time when I was in crisis about *Commune*. I wrote in my notebook on May 21, 1970:

> The difficulties of constructing a text—to get it into narra-tive shape—not as an operatic conglomerate, or a pitiable anthology of scenes—but as something organic to us. . . . We don't have the nuts and bolts of scenic structure yet.

And also on May 21 I noted:

> An attempt to set and repeat elements of recapitulation dance. Joan, Jayme, Steve, Spalding in set configuration with Steve as leader. Steve should keep his gruesome smile.

Some other entries from around that time:

> Group is original community. Selection of leader parallels establishment of parliamentary democracy. Fattening of leader = materialism/industrialization = success. Group kills leader then finds new leader—killed—again, very fast, ritual combats. Only one is left. He sings "song of myself." Name game. Recapitulation.
>
> Totem feast. Cannibalism. Mana.

On May 21 and 22 we set the shape of "Recapitulation" and made it into a kind of performance adding and clarifying elements. I drew two models of fattening and then devouring the leader. In the first everyone brings things to the leader—good things for his ego to eat. Then when he is satisfied, stuffed, everyone jumps him, murders him, eats him. In the second model the same action is achieved indirectly, through a hierarchy. Some people feed others who, in turn, feed the leader. The attack is begun by those closest to the leader. Then everyone joins in the killing and feast-ing. Finally people rush off to hiding places to enjoy the cannibalistic communion meal. But eating the leader's flesh poisons everyone. They die and lie on the floor in grotesque configurations. Then someone comes back to life. The others slowly begin to call their own names. The living person begins a dance over the bodies of the callers. Another joins the living, and then another, until everyone is singing first one name and then another. This name-singing changes into a chant: "One of us, one of us, we accept you, one of us!" (Weirdly enough I took this chant from Todd Browning's film, *The Freaks.*) The con-figuration for "Recapitulation" was:

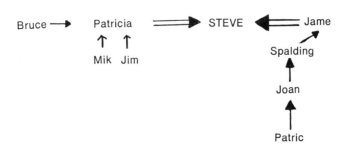

And the order of getting up was Jim, Jayme, Patricia, Steve, Joan, Spalding, Mik, Patric, and Bruce. I told the Group, "If someone doesn't respond, let him stay out/dead."

"Recapitulation" developed into a drama in its own right. It had seven movements: (1) birth, (2) finding sound and self, (3) coronation dance, (4) fattening the leader, (5) attack, kill, feast, (6) death of the victors, death of individuals, (7) resurrection and transformation into the group. Watching "Recapitulation," I felt I was observing a compressed history of TPG. Steve was playing me, I was murdered and consumed by those who performed in *Dionysus* and *Makbeth;* but they died, too. Out of all this ego, carnage, cannibalism, and destruction arose a new Group; a continuation of the old, but changed.

We did "Recapitulation" each Friday afternoon during the summer at the end of our week's work before Friday night's open rehearsal. It got a little longer as we added parts of *Commune* to it. It was a way of experiencing *Commune* with the body. It pressed all the work into fifteen or twenty incredibly intense minutes. It transformed rehearsals, unfinished improvisations, mise-en-scène meetings, and intellectualizations into a dance that by its nature had a beginning, middle, and end. It took *Commune* more than two years to catch up to "Recapitulation."

"Recapitulation" settled deep into our work. The exercise had roots in the first Group. We did work about eating, especially cannibalism, and totemistic cannibal feasting is the major image of *Makbeth.* The idea of making music from body and room sounds is used in *Clothes* and as the basis for Epstein's work in composing *Concert,* especially the jam session that ends "Intersections 7." "Recapitulation" is one example among many of gestures, associations, themes, and actions that carry over from one part of the work to another, from workshop to performance, from one group of people to other groups. If there is a tradition outside the Group in which we participate, there is another tradition in the Group that feeds and enriches the work. This internal tradition is what makes a group a group, what gives a group its own style almost regardless of who is monitoring that style at the moment. The style is something steady. It changes but more slowly than the personnel, because the style is a time-spore capable of blooming years after it has originated. As in families, group patterns persist for generations; the generations of a family are biological; the generations of a group are short.

The thoughts I have about groups—TPG and others; even the impulse to form communes—are mixed: at an impasse. Chaikin said to the Open Theater: "We have more or less said we are a task group: we work through problems in order to perform a work as a group." [23] I agree but add: Most of the life of the group is unknown, it is unconscious; it comes up in the style of the work, the ways people have of relating to each other. If we could take a twenty-four-hour year's long movie and then run it either fast or slow, we could see dance patterns, formal avoidances, homages, aggressive displays, flirtations, and untold other ways in which we human animal beings play with each other. Accelerating or retarding the action is a Brechtian device that gives us the proper distance from it to recognize it, to make it seem not our own, or surprising, and most important: revelatory of patterns. It is not possible for me to speak precisely about these patterns any more than I've done. Although TPG has no rules concerning group life (the punitive rules of the first Group went the way of that group), there are some principles that I think we try to follow.

1. The needs of all individuals in the Group ought to be expressed as clearly as possible. If someone broadcasts resentment—or any strong unarticulated feeling—others will ask what's the matter. This may lead to confrontations, discussions, a new direction in the work, changes.

2. Prior scheduling of rehearsals, or anything else, bends to take in whatever is happening among individuals. Even, if necessary, performances are postponed; I don't recall a performance ever being canceled because of a confrontation. There is a continuous interplay between "work life" and "personal life."

3. Each member finds for himself the work that suits him

[23] Chaikin (1972), 87.

Photograph 35. Makbeth is given his murder knife by his Lady. (*Frederick Eberstadt*)

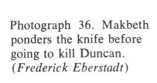

Photograph 36. Makbeth ponders the knife before going to kill Duncan. (*Frederick Eberstadt*)

Photograph 37. Makbeth returns bloody to Lady Makbeth. (*Frederick Eberstadt*)

Photographs 38 and 39. The *Makbeth* knife is used for the murders in *Commune.* (*Frederick Eberstadt*)

best. If this work isn't necessary for the Group, then the person will sooner or later leave the Group. In any case, the needs of the individual ought to be expressed, and the needs of the Group ought to be met.

4. Confrontations may be explosive and with everyone participating and witnessing; or they may be among just a few people, or just two, and quiet. There is no ritual to follow: only the need to keep the space between people open for communication.

5. Group life determines aesthetic life. That is, what a production is—or becomes—derives from what/who the Group is, and not the other way around. Roles are cast in accordance to what individuals in the Group need to do at a particular stage of their development. If a role is written for a man but a woman in the Group is ready to play that kind of role, then the role is made into a woman's role. If there are only six people in the Group and we want to do a play written for eight characters, a way is found in which we can combine roles—as was done in *Makbeth* and *The Tooth of Crime*. Or, if people leave the Group and it isn't the right time to bring new people in, a production is re-structured around those who are in the Group—as was done with *Commune*.

Confronting someone is hard. Resistances are like resistance to vomiting. You know you're sick and have to throw up what's offending your stomach. But you do everything you can to keep calm. Sooner or later the need is too great, the resistance is overcome. After the confrontation, if it has gone to the finish, there is relief and genuine calm. But no confrontation is once and for all. Each day's experiences bring up material that is either dealt with, forgotten, or repressed. (To repress something means that one has forgotten that he has forgotten: The repressed stuff is buried under at least two defensive operations.) Confrontations come from the gut; that is why they are like vomiting. Not every confrontation is public or loud; often it's just a matter of taking someone aside and talking.

I used to believe that confrontations could work with nonverbal expression just as easily as with words. I thought that every channel of communications was a translation of the verbal channel. My view of communicating was limited and word-oriented. I realize now that many different channels operate each in their own way; with distinct means of expression. So that the work of opening up new channels—bringing them to the attention of the performer—is not just a way of translating verbal language into nonverbal language; the new channel, whether it be unvoiced breathing, sounds, movements with the body core, finger gestures, or whatever, is a unique way of communicating what cannot be communicated in other ways. There is some redundancy among channels, but not as much as I thought. Although confrontations sometimes begin with excited shouting, maybe not even words, as an impasse is broken through, the participants ultimately must work things out more quietly, in conversation, working back into their relationship and dealing with each other with a minimum amount of projection-introjection.

What makes a theater group special is that its work is to perform. No matter what techniques are used to facilitate groupness, to bring all participants together, even to form a community: living together, talking out problems, sharing problems, making decisions collectively . . . finally if the community is a theater, the theater performs: for an audience. Without audiences the movement toward community could be completed without hindrance; or if a community failed, it would be due to inadequacies in the group or an outside social situation so hostile that no community could survive. But for theater communes there is the unique problem of the audience; a contradiction eating at the heart of the project.

The analytic function that the audience inevitably introduces into performance blocks every attempt at perfect union, communion. Some of the fine moments of workshop and performance are moments of communion. I cannot specify the scenes because these did not depend on a theatrical structure; they were genuinely communal despite theatrical structure: when that structure was overcome, transcended. The difference between such moments in workshop and in performance is that in workshop there is a chance to extend the communion, to wish that performance will never come, to joyfully abstain with going on, to savor a oneness-in-the-space-with-all-the-others. Or, as Stephen Borst once said after such an experience at New Paltz: "There's a little bit of you in each of me." Sometimes doing the association exercises is like that. Always the moment is evanescent.

But what of the same feeling when it occurs with an audience? Isn't that proof that it can happen, can be extended? Lots of theaters have tried to build a style from the belief that the audience and the performers together could form a community, no matter how temporary. Much of the work of the Living Theater was based on this belief. As the Living wrote of *Paradise Now:*

> The Revolution seeks to establish a State of Being of Interdependence between the Individual and the Collective, in which the individual is not sacrificed to the Collective nor the Collective to the individual. It is the premise of The Revolution that exterior changes or interior changes independent of each other are not sufficient. . . .
>
> The play is a voyage from the many to the one and from the one to the many. It is a spiritual voyage and a political voyage. It is an interior voyage and an exterior voyage. It is a voyage for the actors and the spectators. It begins in the present and moves into the future and returns to the present. The plot is The Revolution.
>
> The voyage is a vertical ascent toward Permanent Revolution.
>
> The Revolution of which the play speaks is The Beautiful Non-Violent Anarchist Revolution.[24]

But this is not what happened. What I've laid out in this chapter extends beyond The Performance Group. Wherever we are, we are *not* in a communal culture with shared goals and techniques. In theatrical terms this means: *No matter what reasons people have for coming to the theater, they are not there for the same reasons as the performers.* This divergence, in small matters as well as large, applies to the Living and its audience as well as every other theater in our culture. To every other theater that appeals for and gets an audience; even an audience of one.

The performers know something the audience does not. If nothing else, the performers know each other, and the audience does not. And if one starts with a theater full of people who do not know each other—as some have proposed—this is a guarantee of equality, not community. For community is based on mutual knowing not mutual ignorance. That is why so many attempts at improvisatory or game-theater end as painful displays of awkwardness and cliché.

If we are to get anywhere with the problem, we must admit the impasse; and know that the impasse is founded on rock. The best contemporary theaters acknowledge the impasse. Grotowski puts spectators in the midst of the performances—but the "witnesses" *(The Constant Prince),* the "living" (Akropolis), the "attenders" *(Apocalypsis)* are shut out of the performers' world. Grotowski brings two realms face-to-face; he denies any interaction. Robert Wilson invites spectators to join his company either as audience or as performers. In either case an ordeal

[24] The Living Theater (1971), 5–7.

awaits the enthusiasts. Those who climb a mountain to see the eight-day *Ka Mountain* or stick through the full twenty-four hours of *Overture* may be transported into a new realm of experience. But these hardy observers/participants are transformed into performers in the eyes of the less willing, less enduring spectators who come and go. Peter Schumann is always bringing people into his shows as singers, puppeteers, musicians, and craftsmen. The temporaries of the Bread and Puppet are similar to the chorus of Greek drama: intermediaries between the permanent puppets and the transient audience. None of these experiences resolves the impasse; each honestly admits it.

There is more to it—a special aspect of the impasse that comes from the fact that those group theaters that achieve an internal balance and some rapport with a public survive. The performers and directors get to know each other very well. The first, and second, blush of novelty wears off *within* the group. The demystification process eliminates many exercises, which are most useful when people are still getting to know each other. I know that each human being is bottomless and endlessly variable and new discoveries can be made throughout a long lifetime. But it is also true that people are consistent. The more you know about a person the harder it is to make big new discoveries; the longer people work together the less sweeping are changes within individuals. And as individuals grow toward or into middle age, the rate of change slows down. It all boils down to the truism that an intimate relationship of five years' standing is different from one of five months' standing. And, like it or not, people grow old in one direction only.

Most exercises cannot be repeated. Even the basic psychophysical exercises become routines if done with no relief or variations for years on end. And as leadership within the group decentralizes a new set of problems relating to keeping the creative juices flowing arises. The director is no longer the parent to be sounded off of; the performers are no longer children willingly screening the director's and each other's fantasies. Too much is known to keep the blush on the rose. The analogy between a stable group in its "middle years" and a marriage after four or five years is inescapable. The group moves toward institutionalizing its own methods, which were once radical; or it seeks ever more extreme and bizarre methods.

Is the solution permanent revolution? Should groups break up every few years so that routinization does not encase them in their own discoveries?

The problems of "middle-aged" groups are often overlooked. Most groups never reach this stage. They disintegrate early, or they explode when first coming up against the subtle, difficult problems of the "middle years" in the life of a group. Other groups try to work through these problems. This is what is happening (I think) in the Open Theater, the Polish Laboratory Theater, and TPG.

Stanislavski solved the problem by starting the studios—offshoot theaters designed to experiment using younger actors. This led to the great discoveries and methods of the Moscow Art Theater. But it did not prevent the MAT from ultimately fossilizing its methods, becoming a living museum-homage to its long-dead founder.

Only by de-mystifying group leadership can groups escape fossilization, which is nothing else than transforming the methods of the leader into a dogma. This transformation can occur in the leader's absence, after his death for example, just as easily as with his collaboration. In any case, dogma is the surest antidote to creativity.

I don't know what to do. I do know what not to do. Don't run away and start another group. Don't dig in and do the same old exercises one more time. Don't pretend nothing is wrong. Don't pretend people I know very well are strangers.

The pervasive crisis is a crisis in working methods and work goals. This kind of crisis is different from the wholly people-oriented crisis of younger groups. The group that survives intact demonstrates to itself that the people in it are not incompatible. Sometimes after this is known, the work crisis emerges. "So we can work together. What kind of work shall we do? How shall we do it?"

It seems that group theaters are being driven in two opposite directions. In order to work creatively theaters become collectives. This is a satisfying, dignified, personal-political arrangement for small groups. But insofar as groups succeed in getting themselves together, they find they are cut off from the society outside the group. It is possible to do as Schumann and Wilson have done, to make permanent theaters with temporary people—people on loan, as it were, from the audience. Or one can form an encapsulated work group such as the Polish Theater Laboratory.

I don't know about other theaters. But TPG structure appears temporary, a compromise: a tent in a windstorm. I turn the problem over and over. So do the others in the Group.

The task of the director in the stylized
theatre is to direct the actor rather than
control him (unlike the Meiningen director).
He serves purely as a bridge, linking the
soul of the author with the soul of the actor.
Having assimilated the author's creation,
the actor is left *alone,* face to face with the
spectator, and from the friction between
these two unadulterated elements, the actor's
creativity and the spectator's imagination,
a clear flame is kindled.
Vsevolod Meyerhold

Everything hangs on the 'story'; it is the heart
of the theatrical performance. For it is what
happens *between* people that provides them
with all the material that they can discuss,
criticize, alter. Even if the particular person
represented by the actor has ultimately
to fit into more than just the one episode,
it is mainly because the episode will be all the
more striking if it reaches fulfillment in a
particular person. The 'story' is the
theatre's great operation, the complete fitting
together of all the gestic incidents, embracing
the communications and impulses that must
now go to make up the audience's
entertainment.
Bertolt Brecht

9 Director

At one level, especially during the first phases of training, the
director acts as the neophyte performer's parent. Through the
director's guidance, and by submitting to the exercises the director
offers, the performer begins to find himself. The performer also
finds an enemy: the director. And, ultimately, a crisis is faced
for both director and performer. A small family is created by
workshop, and the struggles and rebellions characteristic of family
life are not foreign to life in a group theater. If the workshop is
temporary—say a specialized course offered by a director to
some fifteen actors over a period of two months—this crisis of
children vs. parent may never come. The course will end amid

thanks, even devotion; the process has no time to work itself out to a conclusion that liberates the actors from the director; or he/she from them. But in enterprises that achieve longer life this first, deep, definitive crisis is unavoidable.

If the parental crisis is faced and surpassed, the group enters a new phase. The parental function of the director is not discarded entirely; it is used selectively and with more and more consciousness. Each production, in fact, recapitulates the whole relationship; and there are cycles and phases within cycles and phases. The new phase, which succeeds the children-vs.-parent model, is that of All Are Brothers Together. This is a heady, delicious, brief moment in a group's life cycle. It is utopian in its ambitions, revolutionary in its spirit, celebratory in its mood, and comradely in its work. It assumes an equality among all members, divides work and responsibility and income equally. It is the famous "leaderless group." In my experience this Group of Comrades is short-lived because the wish to do something does not equal the ability to do something. And in the contradictions between what a person wants to do and what a person does arises new bitterness and, ultimately, a new hierarchy.

What kind of hierarchy? is the decisive question. The group can become reactionary and restore the parent-children phase. Or it can move toward a version of Communism: from each according to his abilities, to each according to his needs. However impossible this model may appear on the large stage of world political life, it is attainable within small groups. At least temporarily.

What happens now is extraordinary. Different people emerge into new roles. Different projects spring up, both within the group and outside it. Not only the director but others run exercises. The entire operation is heated up, without becoming hysterical. The group that had been self-isolating, focused almost entirely inward, built like a castle with walls and moat, all the energies directed toward the center, suddenly reverses its flow: The energy streams from the center into diverse places and projects; workshops and rehearsals that were "sacred" (closed) are now open, people just drop in to watch the work, sometimes to participate in it. Group members collaborate with outsiders on projects. The director's role is reduced, focused, and more flexible. He is no longer parent, enemy, outcast, savior, lover, friend, demigod. He is the one who is in charge of seeing that the story of the play gets played. And he doesn't do his job by himself.

For me personally the most important part of this development is that I am free of my own stereotypes. I no longer feel frozen in one mold or another. I play a number of roles consecutively and simultaneously, as do the others. The emergence is not into the clear light of rationality, but into a busy street of changing moods, roles, and activities. The focus is on work-being-done not on me-in-the-work.

I know that when I direct a play, I get totally absorbed in its web of themes, moods, actions, and people. And that writing about directing is the hardest thing for me to do because I know that everything I say is subjective. My theories bend like light around a strong gravitational source—the play I am currently directing. As I write, I am directing *The Tooth of Crime.* In my mind also are some projects for the future. Were this chapter to have been written while I was working on *Victims of Duty, Dionysus in 69, Makbeth,* or *Commune,* my ideas would be different in tone, if not in substance. As a director I do not stand off from the play I am working on or from the performers. I do not measure my responses beforehand. I don't come into rehearsals with a prompt-book under my arm, literally or figuratively. I get inside the play I am directing at a level that determines the rest of my life. I don't do this willfully. It happens because I love every play I direct, grow to know it intimately, and experience its faults as well as its beauties and pleasures. And each time I direct a play, I proclaim a method only to find out when I am finished that what I've found is not something general but the particular ways of directing the play I've directed.

Looking back over five years of working in environmental theater, I don't despair acknowledging that my own way of directing remains a mystery to me. Self-awareness is the hardest thing to achieve, and I have not achieved it. What I can write about are some specific techniques.

Early Work on a Project That Maybe Won't Be

The first thinking I do on a project is in pictures—drawings I make in my notebook—visual flashes of spaces-in-action. These *actograms* occur at the level where environment, physical action, knowledge of the performers, concept of the play, and my own drives are identical. TPG worked on *Don Juan* in collaboration with Megan Terry during the spring of 1971. Terry watched about five workshops, and during the summer she wrote a number of scenes some of which we rehearsed. The project was shelved

when Joan and I went to Asia. On June 21, 1971, I made the
first actograms of *Don Juan*.

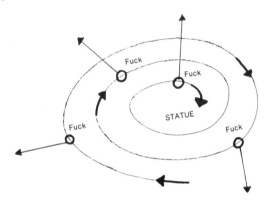

Notes accompanying the drawing say: "Running, DJ doesn't ever
want to get caught. To fuck = to get out of time. But at the end
stands the STONE STATUE: stasis. At the end of DJ's quest
—'keep moving on'—*pure quest*—at the end of his/her quest
is silence, stasis, immobility. Action: to (not) get caught." The
spiral shape of the first actogram gave way to another later
in the day.

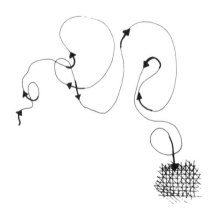

I titled this actogram "Don Juan's Moves."
During the summer everyone in the Group read the classic
Don Juan stories of Molière and Tirso de Molina. In workshop
we did an exercise about D.J. trying to get close to his love

—whatever his love might be. There were three characters: D.J., the Husband/Cuckold who is concerned only about his "property" (his Wife), and the Wife. D.J. could be a man or a woman. The Wife could either accept or reject the role of Sex Object. The exercise was designed to explore the relationships between eroticism, religion, and property. I asked myself: Should D.J. be one person or many, male or female? The work was stopped when the Group began to restructure *Commune*. I didn't think about *Don Juan* again until I was in Pondicherry, India, at the Aurobindo Ashram. On December 24, 1971, Joan and I saw The Mother, the incredibly ancient woman who heads the Ashram. Here is part of what I wrote in my notebook as I identified The Mother with Joan with D.J.:

> Core conflict: DJ in hell vs Lady DJ. He wants her to follow him. He wants NO FUNDAMENTAL CHANGE IN CONSCIOUSNESS AND EXPERIENCE. But she is GOING THROUGH A FUNDAMENTAL CHANGE.
>
> They start CLOSE, then their struggle begins—his to keep her, hers to get free. They END DISTANT & GETTING FURTHER AWAY.
>
> HIS TRAGEDY = LOSS OF HER = HER TRIUMPH = HER TRANSFORMATION.

Seeing The Mother, putting my head on her knee, left me with no easy feelings. I did drawing after drawing of her trying to isolate and understand my reactions to her.

> I remember very little of The Mother's room. Her profile, the line of people, a doll swan or a stuffed swan, French provincial furniture, the swan looking like The Mother, The Mother looking like the swan. . . . What an incredibly old woman and how concentrated in her neck, her cheeks, her right eye. Then when she smiles, her lower face, her mouth and chin, dissolves, disappears, is wholly fluid. I left trembling. I am confused, unknowing. CONFUSED, TREMBLING, WITHOUT KNOWLEDGE. Her look penetrated. She did NOT KNOW, she SAW.

At lunch I read one of The Mother's writings posted on the wall of the Ashram dining room:

> The future of the earth depends on a change of consciousness. The only hope for the future is in a change in man's

consciousness, and the change is bound to come. But it is left to men to decide if they will collaborate for this change or it will have to be enforced on them by the power of crashing circumstances.

Joan felt that changes were taking place in her, and the experience of the Ashram underlined that feeling. I identified *Don Juan* with powerful transformations in consciousness and with the emergence of woman power.

Early work is not making a prompt book. At the start of a project I think about my own life and of the people in the Group. To lay a foundation, one must dig deep, clear out spaces, rip up old things, turn over set ideas. At this level there is no separation between the personal, the given, and the found—between my fantasies, associations, experiences, workshops, texts, and the physical place I am when this kind of thinking occurs. Everything that happens later is in some way a transformation of the early work.

Seven Steps To Creating a Mise-en-scène

A mise-en-scène is *everything that comprises what the audience experiences.* To create a mise is to create something whole. Developing the mise is the director's main job. The most pragmatic, and succinct, definition of a mise-en-scène is Brecht's: "What comes before the spectator is the most frequently repeated of what has not been rejected." [1]

Work on a mise takes a long time. But it isn't gradual, like the blending of colors in a rainbow. It develops in breakthroughs, periods of apparent stalemate shattered by a burst of discoveries. I've seen lasting changes come from a few hours' work; and weeks of work where seemingly nothing happens. The quiet periods prepare for the (excuse me) dramatic changes. A performance goes through many transformations on its way to completion. And when it's complete, it is no longer worth performing.

As a matter of convenience I divide the process of creating a mise into seven steps. This arbitrary division is useful mainly as a teaching device. I ignore it while working.

    1. *Free workshop:* No attempt is made to work on a project. Exercises are reviewed and invented. Work on the

[1] Brecht (1964 [1948]), 204.

self, and on the group. Free workshop is the original void/ chaos out of which the definite order of a project may emerge. Free workshop continues through all phases of creating a mise-en-scène. Even in the last steps of rehearsal I recommend at least two hours of free workshop a day.

2. *Introduction of an action or text:* In *Dionysus in 69, Makbeth,* and *The Tooth of Crime* texts were used. *Commune* began with an awareness of certain themes, several scenes from Shakespeare and Marlowe, and exercises from free workshop, especially slow-motion running and the sound and movement exercise that became "Recapitulation."

These first two steps are like a vortex, drawing into the center of the work everything that is around it. The determining factor is not thematic but temporal; associations occur not according to categories but according to coexistence in time. Later thematic links are forged. For example, while starting to define the themes that would ultimately condense into *Commune,* the Group was also working on three scenes from Shakespeare and one from Marlowe. I selected these as acting exercises, assigning roles according to particular needs of particular performers. I didn't have *Commune* in mind (consciously). I think that *any scenes* we happened to be working with at that time would have been attracted to the center of the *Commune* vortex.

The Tempest, Act II, Scene 2: Trinculo and Stephano discover Caliban became the Temptations of Clementine— the transformation of Clementine from a stay-at-home to a member of the commune. *Commune* retains fragments of dialogue, and the whole songs, "I'll show thee the best springs . . ." and "No more dams I'll make for fish. . . ." In *The Tempest* scene is the root of the transformation from being an enslaved drudge to becoming a person capable of flying.

Edward II of Marlowe, Act V, Scene 5: Lightborn's murder of Edward becomes the Interrogation and Torture of David Angel. The Marlowe scene was combined with the arrest, trial, and Passion of Christ and Manson's account of his imprisonment, including dialogue from the transcript of his trial. These connections were easy because both Manson and Marlowe's Edward identify themselves with Christ.

King Lear, Act IV, Scene 6: Gloucester's attempt at suicide became the Blind Lizzie scene where she blindfolds herself and gropes through the space seeking the El Dorado signs that lead her to the edge of the Wave. Then she jumps off backward—into the arms of the others. Fragments of the *Lear* dialogue are combined with an account of the Sharon Tate murders. Simultaneously with Lizzie's groping around the space is the My Lai scene.

Richard II, Act I, Scene 2: Richard Courts Lady Anne became America Courts the World. Changing only a few words, this scene pitted all the men against all the women in an allegory of America's foreign policy. In February, 1971, the scene was dropped from *Commune,* with only one line—"Behold, this pattern of thy butcheries"—retained.

Except for America Courts the World, where satire and parody were intended, the actions/texts of Shakespeare and Marlowe were amalgamated and transmuted at a level where (I hope) they are fundamental to *Commune* and not intrusive literary allusions/quotations. Material from earlier theater can be brought into a production in the same way as personal material is brought in. Just as the performer refines, distorts, condenses, and selects from his life experiences, so fragments from earlier dramas can be worked into the play at hand. Only since the intrusion of stupid laws and notions regarding originality has this rich vein of creativity been stopped. Shakespeare and Molière without their plagiarisms would be much poorer playwrights. An art that is in essence transformational and transmutational should not surrender any of its sources, its deep springs. The modern idea of originality is a lawyer-capitalist construction geared to protecting private property and promoting money-making. It is anti-creative, and inhibits the reworking of old themes in the light of new experience. It is the constant reworking and elaboration of old material—call it plagiarism if you like—that is the strongest sinew of tradition.

3. *The project:* The time comes when an agreement—not always spoken—gives definition to the work: a *project* is launched. Discussions flow about themes, actions, meanings, structures. A condensation of interest leads to a basis for bringing things in and keeping things out. Themes, movement, environment, music, and characterization converge. The end is in sight. Formulations reached at this step are the basis for all subsequent transformations. At this step *The Bacchae* became *Dionysus in 69* and *Makbeth* got its "k."

4. *Performance space, roles:* The environmentalist gets to work—maybe even building part of the environment. Roles are defined and permanently assigned. This is a time of crisis and uncertainty because everyone is aware of the horrible gap between what the project sounds like and what it is. There seems to be no way to bridge this gap.

5. *Organization:* A text takes shape, scenes make sense, a sequence of events—scenic and/or textual—is agreed on, the environment built. Even business affairs like publicity, price of admission, posters, and so on are worked on. The mise appears finished—if this were an orthodox production, step 5 would be equivalent to rehearsals and at the end of it the play would open.

Steps three, four, and five draw limits, close avenues—pull the project together, get it in shape. A very hard decision comes at the end of step 5: The play could go on, but it must be taken apart again, thrown into deeper doubt than ever, and reconstructed. *The Tooth of Crime* was worked on from May to September 1972 before our work got through step 5. Then came a series of open rehearsals and work-in-progress performances in Vancouver, upstate New York, and Paris. These seventeen performances were difficult because in the Group's mind the play wasn't finished; but the audience came to see finished work. Even when the play was interrupted, when a scene was repeated, and when we did not complete the play—never having rehearsed the last scene—spectators acted as though they had seen a finished production. The difficulty was compounded by the fact that many spetactors liked the play very much. All the promptings were toward wrapping it up: rehearsing the last scene, polishing what we had, opening in New York. The Group did not want to do this, and we were helped by an accident. Spalding Gray, who plays Hoss in *Tooth,* developed a hernia and had to be operated on. He went into the hospital as soon as the Group returned from France. Physical work could not be resumed on *Tooth* until after a six-week pause. During that time we reread the play carefully—taking more than fifty hours of rehearsals to get through it. This work-around-a-table came after the play had been done seventeen times, and so our reference points were not academic or imaginary. The reworkings were very deep and rich.

6. *Open rehearsals and reconstructions:* Mise meetings, role exchanges, free workshops: working through the whole play again, from the start. The audience is invited into the

work—to view it, talk about it, and criticize it. The play is examined in hard-nosed theatrical terms: Does a scene work, does it hold the audience, is it clear?

For me this step is the hardest. The presence of an audience makes everyone want to set the piece. Failures are humiliating. There is a credibility gap between what the Group knows and what the audience knows. Insist as we may, spectators come to the theater to see a "finished piece." Only recently have we found a way of allaying this expectation. For *The Tooth of Crime* the announcements of open rehearsals are made to individuals. These people are invited to the rehearsals knowing that things may come up that require the Group to work alone; then the audience will be asked to leave. Only a few people show up for each rehearsal, usually less than ten. The performance develops vis-à-vis an interested audience that has come to see rehearsals, not finished shows. This kind of open rehearsal later gives way to more formal, publicly announced rehearsals. This second kind of open rehearsal is more like a performance. It is during these public open rehearsals that I grow stubborn. I fight to keep what I have and resist criticism. My stubbornness has at times been cataclysmic. If the director can keep himself open—really be able to take the play apart in front of strangers—the work can progress. If not, mistakes freeze into the mise-en-scène. *Makbeth* never got beyond step 6, and mistakes were frozen in. *Commune* opened in December, 1970, in the midst of step 6, and it took many months of arduous work to liberate the work from its early clichés.

Taking the play apart and reconstructing it makes everyone grasp the work in concrete theatrical terms. Open rehearsals leave no room for anyone to hide in abstractions or proclamations. The audience is there; either they get it or they don't. In step 6 the production emerges as something outside the performers and the director. It achieves an objective reality.

> 7. *Building scores:* The need is to locate the exact physical actions, musical tones, and rhythms that embody the themes and moods of the production. Rehearsals are often technical. A through-line is developed for each role. And the entire production is *tuned* the way a sailboat is tuned for racing: taut, sparse, efficient, active.

I used to believe that the score was exactly like a musical score, set in every detail. I don't think so now. The performer's score gives him anchor points—moments of contact, an underlying rhythm, secure details: places to go from and get to. As Ryczard Cieslak told me:

> The score is like a glass inside which a candle is burning. The glass is solid; it is there you can depend on it. It contains and guides the flame. But it is not the flame. The flame is my inner process each night. The flame is what illuminates the score, what the spectators see through the score. The flame is alive. Just as the flame in the glass moves, flutters, rises, falls, almost goes out, suddenly glows brightly, responds to each breath of wind—so my inner life varies from night to night, from moment to moment. The way I feel an association, the interior sense of my voice or a movement of my finger. I begin each night without anticipations. This is the hardest thing to learn. I do not prepare myself to feel anything. I do not say, "Last night, this scene was extraordinary, I will try to do that again." I want only to be receptive to what will happen.

> And I am ready to take what happens if I am secure in my score, knowing that, even if I feel a minimum, the glass will not break, the objective structure worked out over the months will help me through. But when a night comes that I can glow, shine, live, reveal—I am ready for it by not anticipating it. The score remains the same, but everything is different because I am different.[2]

Cieslak's metaphor of the glass and the flame is only an approximation; it is misleading insofar as it supposes that the score and the performer's inner life are separate: the container and the contained. The score is the most visible part of the performer's life as lived during the performance. The score is not hard like glass. It is a membrane, a skin of an extended life-system that only an ensemble/group can create. The score is alive, sensitive, and responsive. What each individual's inner life is to him the score is to the whole-group-in-performanc.

For the director the score is somewhat different than for the performer. The director is in the performance only by extension and identification. I go to each performance of a play I am directing not out of duty; and I am not bored. I experience the changes in the score, the variations and modulations, with an excitement. I reflect on the overall pattern of the performance:

[2] Personal conversation, 1970.

the development of the story, the leitmotifs. I concern myself with the arrangements and relationships among all theatrical languages: verbal, body, contact, and musical.

Open Rehearsals

Open rehearsals don't mean running a play in previews in order to make money before the critics murder the production. A genuine open rehearsal is showing the play, or parts of it, in an unfinished state. The audience is present so that the production can be revised in reference to how the audience reacts. Open rehearsals are a way of following through on Meyerhold's declaration of 1929: "We produce every play on the assumption that it will be still unfinished when it appears on the stage. We do this consciously because we realize that the crucial revision of a production is that which is made by the spectator." [3]

I want open rehearsals to accomplish the following:

1. Work on parts of the play that involve the audience such as the Tag Chorus of *Dionysus in 69,* the March to Death Valley of *Commune,* the soliloquies of *The Tooth of Crime.*

2. Locate difficult passages in the sense that a ship makes a difficult passage through shoal water. These passages may be problems for either the performers or the audience or both. For example, the first banquet scene of *Makbeth,* where the performers bite into each other, worked out okay in closed rehearsal but fell apart in front of an audience. The performers were rigid, inhibited, and terrified. The open rehearsals pointed to the kind of help needed in closed rehearsals.

3. Test the environment. No matter how carefully the construction is planned, many problems come to view once an audience uses the space. Only spectators can make these discoveries because over a period of a few days hundreds of different personalities explore thousands of possibilities.

4. Repeat scenes in different variations, different stagings. Not only can audience reactions be tested, but so can

[3] Meyerhold (1969 [1929]), 256.

performer reactions. Many scenes in TPG productions have developed this way. Sometimes there are discussions with spectators about variations. Always people stay after the rehearsals to talk to the director and individual performers. Playing variations has several advantages. First, one can experience the immediate changes in reaction; secondly, spectators learn the process from which plays are made—the cold task of selecting from alternatives.

5. Eliminate illusion-breeding "magic." By letting audiences participate in unfinished work—by insisting that the work be shown "in progress"—in the midst of the struggle to advance it—by washing dirty linen in public—a barrier is clearly confronted, and maybe lowered. The important thing is to distinguish between the dirty linen that is purely personal and must be dealt with behind closed doors (or trust is lost) and those problems that center on the production. Audiences have a great deal invested in the illusion that performers are special people (as distinct from people with special skills) who live magic lives vicariously for the audience. Performers are both terrified and immensely pleased by the roles projected onto them by the audience. The director too. Nothing shames a performer or director more than making a mistake and knowing that everyone knows that he has made a mistake. Open rehearsals help reduce the pressure for instant success; or for success that comes from living life vicariously. Often performers can feel the genuine warmth spectators have for them, and vice-versa. New, more relaxed and genuine audience-performer relationships can begin.

6. Spread word concerning a production. I don't believe in theatrical surprise. The only worthwhile surprise is watching an artist surpass himself/herself while doing the work. From this viewpoint each performance can be astonishing. Also, the monopoly reviewers have over the "reception" of new work must be broken—and the only weapon against the Reviewers' Trust is word-of-mouth. Open rehearsals give audiences a chance to make up their own minds, to tell their friends, to watch a play develop over a long period of time.

7. Abolish, or at least reduce, the distinction between rehearsal and performance. This is tied to the anti-illusionism of open rehearsals. I want people to become more aware of the crafts of theater-making and to confront the themes and rhythms of the work rather than either the personalities of the performers as such or a "character" into which the performer has vanished. I believe in a highly

conscious, critical, ironic middle ground. Too sharp a distinction between rehearsal and performance makes for evermore "safe" productions or more flashy techniques. Too much rides on the outcome of a single, opening night performance toward which all energies are directed. Performances are stuck in preparatory phases or frozen at a "successful" moment, losing vitality through routine repitition.

A few more words on points 5 and 7: The formidable task is to raise the consciousness of both audience and performers regarding not only each other but themselves. People become performers sometimes in order to live fantasy lives, magic lives. A performer with such illusions resists rehearsing in front of the people he wants to fool. Such a performer *performs rehearsing.* I have often found myself *performing directing* at open rehearsals. Becoming conscious of the game is the first step to ending it or changing it into something more wholesome. What is needed is a demystification of the entire process so that theater-workers can work on making theater just as construction workers work on a building while the sidewalk superintendents watch. With one great difference: The watchers at an open rehearsal may effect changes in the play.

Open rehearsals go along well until there is a stop. Up to the stop the rehearsal is like a performance. The stop introduces a strong tension. If the director speaks privately to the performers, the audience gets uneasy: They're being cheated from witnessing precisely what they came to witness. If the director speaks out loud to the performers, they get uneasy: They are being treated like children by a parental figure in front of guests. Only if the performers themselves stop the rehearsal and ask to repeat a scene or discuss something, is the situation relatively easy. The contradiction is simply stated, difficult to deal with: Performers don't want the parental aspects of the director-performer relationship exposed in public; the public wants either to see a finished performance or to be privy to intimacies concerning the rehearsal.

The director breaking in exposes the apparent diadic relationship between performers and spectators as an illusion. The actual relationship is triadic—with the director standing back because of convention. (In a symphony orchestra the director/conductor is present even though his role during an actual performance may be perfunctory. In music the illusion is the opposite to that of theater: The conductor appears to be more necessary during the performance than he actually is.) Not only is the apparent diad of theater an illusion, but the hidden third figure, the director, emerges in some kind of control. He interrupts, makes suggestions, requests different solutions to the problems at hand. Granted that the director's power is on loan from the performers—still, when the director interrupts, it is hard to not appear to be the *deus ex machina,* the Big Daddy.

These problems of director-performer communication in front of an audience must be worked on more deeply. I know that my own personality contributes to some of the difficulties TPG has had in open rehearsals. I tend to be more authoritarian in open rehearsals than I am in closed rehearsals. My Daddy role is puffed up, and I feel on the line. But I think the problems run deeper than my own inabilities. The performer's training is designed to support and enhance the diadic relationship. The director is supposed to prepare the performer for the diadic relationship. His work is out of sight by the time the performance is ready. At the moment the public is let into the theater the director is by convention supposed to retire. For, in fact, the director's chief role in orthodox theater is to serve as a surrogate public. If the director remains visible and active, then there are two publics, and perhaps a conflict between them. Which is the performer to pay attention to? During open rehearsal the performer plays with the spectators and then, suddenly, the director steps in—asserts himself as the important public—and demands/ suggests changes in accord with his own tastes. The performer may feel betrayed at this moment of intrusion. And the director may feel too powerful, having usurped the rights of the audience.

It is easier to be positive regarding point 7. Theater does not approach the finished state of a sonnet, a film, or even a well-turned letter. Each of these may be revised until the author is satisfied or feels he can't do better. Then he abandons his project —which means he publishes it, screens it, sends it, files it, or destroys it. Once abandoned, the project exists independent of its creator. Not so with theater. Theater is a group project, and part of the group is the audience. Theater incorporates into its structure the dynamics of change. Its authors include the audience, the writer, the performers, the director, the environmentalist. The authors of theater are always in the process of authoring it. Theater is the interaction between its "finished" components (text, mise-en-scène, score) and its "unfinished" components (audience, performers, director). The orthodox and environmental theater models of rehearsal-performance rhythms are:

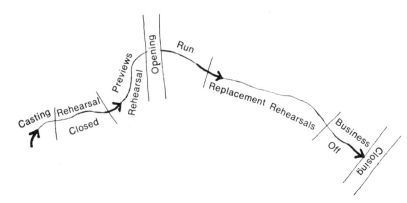

Orthodox. Rehearsals go up and down but generally up toward a finished product until things are *set* for the opening. After the opening the performance is *maintained* with as few changes as possible. After a while, the production begins to "run down," and it closes when audiences are too small to make the production commercially feasible. The audience is excluded from all rehearsals and included at all performances. The production is treated as a commercial object or "property."

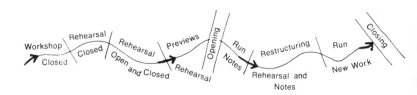

Environmental. The performance develops during its entire existence. Much of the developmental work is achieved during open rehearsals. Closed rehearsals exist side by side with both open rehearsals and performances. Even after the play opens there is restructuring, open and closed rehearsals. *The rehearsal process is coexistent with the life of the production.* Changes in the mise-en-scène are always happening —not only to make the play "better," but in recognition that the authors of the play are changing. Even during "regular performances" experiments are tried that may transform any performance into an open rehearsal. The play closes when the process of change no longer interests the performers and director. The moment of closing may coincide with an upsurge of attendance and audience interest. The life of the play, not its commercial viability, determines its run.

Some of the most radical changes in *Commune* were made in November, 1972, in Paris. The play was running down. The performers were bored with it; I was bored with it. The Parisian audience was indifferent. Watching a performance, I decided to suggest a complete change in structure—rearranging the events, dropping many scenes. The performers liked the ideas, and we rehearsed the changes the next afternoon and performed the new version at night. It was dismal. Technically things went along well, but the heart of the play was gone: most of its comedy, some songs, and enthusiasm. All the changes reinforced the indifference of the French audience: as if TPG were saying, "You think *this* is a drag, wait until you see how draggy it can really be!"

By the next afternoon everyone realized what we'd done. Instead of putting the play back to what it was, we changed the beginning—eliminated the March to Death Valley (dancing with the audience was archaic by 1972), and started with the Sharon Tate murders. The murder scene was repeated near the end of the play, as in all the earlier versions of *Commune*. The new start refreshed *Commune*'s structure, tightened it, and gave the audience a chance to decide whether or not the murders would be re-enacted. Out of about twenty remaining performances in France, the audience twice deliberately stopped the repetition of the murders. This had never happened before. It was the first thematically relevant, wholly conscious audience participation during the two years of playing *Commune*.

Mise-en-scène Meetings

Mise-en-scène meetings are more or less formal gatherings where every aspect of the production is up for discussion. This process goes on in rehearsals, of course. But there are times when it is good to concentrate all attention not on action but on argumentation. The performers—and anyone else connected to the production—meet the director on the director's turf: analysis, discussion, argument, thought. Also what is worked out is an overview, the production seen as a whole. Finally, at a mise meeting the director has a chance to run some ideas without committing everyone to working these out in action.

What goes on in a mise meeting is a free throwing around of ideas, feelings, opinions, and suggestions. A mise meeting is less concrete than a rehearsal, but it covers more ground. Associations arise that would otherwise not occur for reasons of logic or economy. A mise meeting is a stew, but it is also a trial, and what is being judged are the concepts the play comes from or points to. Decisions aren't made at mise meetings, if by decision one means choosing among alternatives. A few years back I liked people to vote on different choices (not that I always followed the outcome of the voting). Now I like the meetings to be as free as possible. I am training myself to listen more and talk less. Maybe I can convey the feel of a mise meeting by selecting from a notebook and a tape some conversation from the meeting of May 25, 1970. At that time we'd been working on *Commune* for about seven weeks.

JAYME. It's really about us. The slow motion race—I'm confused about how to get into it. Our own past histories mingling with the history of America? Maybe the scenes will help us—*The Tempest* people or the *Lear* people split off to form a colony.

STEVE. We could stretch out and enumerate each element in the Recapitulation. I don't understand how the Recap is relevant to the piece.

SPALDING. I don't know what the Recap is.

JOAN. It's rebirth.

STEVE. The Recap goes beyond *Dionysus*. It goes to and through and beyond the killing of the king.

SPALDING. The Recap is in real time; it's our own celebrate ourselves.

STEVE. It's about moving from one value system to another. About moving from a one-to-one exchange kind of living to a kind of electric life. The image of a spider web: It is three-dimensional and at every intersection there is a jewel of water and it glimmers to every other jewel. From individuation to killing the leader to a quantum jump which goes beyond the individual. Finding ways of making the jump—really a leap of faith—no way of knowing until we do it.

MIK. I don't really understand. The part about communes is getting a little clearer. We made up a story—Richard pushed Patricia off the mat—out of the Group—for some reason. Jim and I decided that what she had done was not that bad. What we ended up doing was trying to get the people away from Richard one at a time. Finally we killed the leader, but we also raped him. Steve played the leader.

JIM. I wondered what being in the Virginia Colony would

be like for me. What would it be like to not be able to move or breathe? Possibilities of the future—from love for possessions to an inner sense of what we have inside. Property is too important. Resolution of the play is a very personal awareness of our uniqueness—and celebration of that, which takes no space at all.

SPALDING. From the United States of America to united states of mind. But instead of being conscious of the metaphor, play the action and let the action be the metaphor.

JOAN. For me it starts with the breakup of the old Group and the need to get away from people. That was when I heard about Charlie Manson—about what it means to have a group of people—a fine line between something that gives you freedom and something that becomes fascistic. In *Makbeth* I was a servant and spent all my time getting people killed so that I could get power. I want to discover what my American roots are. I know I have a lot to say about utopias and America—I know it has to be articulated through my body. By metaphor, not indicating. From workshops, from relationships with Spalding and Jayme and Steve—it comes out in the Recap—it has to do with me being a woman—in the Recap I am the female prize for the leader. I'd be willing to offer myself as the guinea pig in things between men and women. I feel I am strong. The shape of the piece is going to come from us as people vis-à-vis each other. Out of that will come your throughline or whatever. I do want a story to be there. I have visions of people in a commune—incredibly strong-willed, fascistic, believing what they believe in, period. The story has to do with our making our own commune. We have to explore the things that are going around, astrology and things.

PATRIC. It's almost painful, this cerebral thing. I remember four years ago in California, Timothy Leary on a podium, fifty thousand people, two thirds of them freaked out on acid, Leary saying, "This is the Brave New World!" I myself am a product of progressive education, the commune kind of thing, screwed, every one of us, by the Establishment. And I look around and I thought about you, Linda [Ewing Gates, our voice teacher then], coming from Louisiana, and Joany from the hills of Scotland—the fact that there is a Performance Group, I don't want to make any value judgments, Liz looking like an eighteenth-century lady from New England, and Jayme like John Steinbeck from Oklahoma. The communes I've been in have all been in the country—but those kids on Sunset Strip, and those cops, are part of it, too. The whole Recap thing we do—like the last scene in *The Lord of the Flies*. Los Angeles couldn't exist anyplace else except in New York. But it's so beautiful, too. I'm very tied up with America. Not just Charles Manson, but Mel Lyman, too. I remember four years ago in the *Oracle* a picture of John. They said, "He's going to be very important—he's the Second Coming." I haven't heard. The *Oracle*'s gone now. People are very hip now. Like you can drive in a cab and people will hand you a joint from the next cab. Why are there so many fags in New York? It's connected with *Satyricon*. I haven't seen it yet. People ball, ski, and take acid, and a lot of kids shoot skag at my old school. They built there, the kids, the biggest tree house in the world and nobody ever fell out of it.

At this point Bruce White began to tell the story about his first astral projection. We took Bruce's story word for word into the play. (I don't know why we didn't take Patric's speech into the play, too. It's magnificent.)

This particular meeting went on for hours. Mise meetings usually last a long time. It takes time for themes to emerge, for everyone to shift modes so that the talk gets deep. The director can be a guide bringing people back to the play, to their own experiences in relationship to the play; he tries to help people who are withdrawing, or not speaking out of shyness. He keeps his own ideas to himself as long as he can, and after he does speak he allows for plenty of feedback. There is no limitation on subject matter. Tangents may be long and far-fetched, but good things can be brought back from distant places. Listening to a mise meeting afterward on tape you hear something chaotic, halting, tedious, sometimes explosive, irrelevant, and loaded with personal associations. The sense of chaos is deceptive. What is really happening is that things usually suppressed or translated directly into phsyicalizations during rehearsals are coming out verbally. Patient study reveals an organization of energies, a release to the surface of patterns of concern. After a mise meeting, rehearsals take on, if only temporarily, clarity and purpose.

After several mise meetings and many workshops, I could list by the end of June some basic themes/conflicts of *Commune:*

individuality	vs.	commune
given names	vs.	new names of our choice
work	vs.	play
finished	vs.	exercise
polished	vs.	process
mask	vs.	naked
talk	vs.	body-language
story	vs.	open structure

assault	vs.	exchange
separate	vs.	together
walls	vs.	contact
tragedy	vs.	celebration
there/then	vs.	here/now
domination	vs.	submission
ownership	vs.	sharing
keeping	vs.	giving
buying-selling	vs.	stealing-throwing away
myth/history/books	vs.	us/now/songs
painting	vs.	architecture
huddled masses	vs.	birds flying
Marlboro country	vs.	our country

As the work went on, I found that these antipathies were not so different as I thought: The old world kept finding its way back into the new. The story congealed around violence: Manson, My Lai. Every leap toward new values found us like the circus clown caught on his own suspenders. Except we weren't able to embody the farce. As in *Dionysus* the positive pole of the dialectic was felt in the way we worked together, not in the themes we expounded.

We kept trying to work through the contradictions in the themes. From late spring onward we thought of *Commune* as structured in four parts:

1. *A Day at the Ranch*. This takes place in real time, as the audience enters, a kind of after-supper "let's pretend to be in the Old West." A kid's game combining clichés, Spahn's ranch, old movies. Lots of images were tried, and most were rejected. Finally the progression became: welcoming, dozing, singing, riding horses, flirting, shooting. Then a sudden flash of the Tate murders. This is redeemed by another song: either "Bound for the Promised Land" or "Big Rock Candy Mountain."

2. *Exploration and Discovery*. This recapitulates the arrival of the first European settlers in America, their race across the new land—the fabled rat-race. Then the dropout culture, the communes, an alternative life-style: The Temptations of Clementine.

3. *The Belly of the Whale*. The commune turns sour as the contradictions in the alternative life-style dominate the play's action. All of America as a commune (the American Dream, El Dorado) turning sour. Flashes of the Tate murders; the My Lai massacre; the arrest, interrogation, torture, trial, conviction, and "crucifixion" of Manson. Fantasies of life in Death Valley. "The desert is heaven because nobody

else wants it." Finally a swift, but detailed reactualization
of the Tate murders followed by a press-conference-tour of
the Tate house conducted by Roman Polanski.

Actual names are never used in the production. The murders in
Commune are not photocopies of the murders in Beverly Hills.
They are done the way the Commune would act out the story
of the murders if the performers were the Commune. The murders
are not performed as an actualization of the past but as a story
told now: "Remember what happened last night because you
were there!"

> 4. *Possibilities*. This was to show an authentic new world:
> where America could begin again once Americans acknowl-
> edged history. The moral was to be simple: if Americans
> accept responsibility for the facts of American history, then
> the nation could go on in good faith. But as long as Ameri-
> cans believe that Manson is "crazy" and My Lai an event
> without precedent or root cause in "normal" American
> society, then the destructive round of American violence
> will play over and over. The difficulty was that we could not
> find the actions for possibiliies. We had no solutions.

Bruce White was eager for us to get to Possibilities. He found
it hard to perform without the redeeming qualities of Possibilities.
I had no idea where Possibilities would come from. We kept on
rehearsing through the New Paltz months, and on to Goddard.
Lado Kralj, a director from Lyubiana, Yugoslavia, joined the
Group as my assistant at the beginning of September. Because I
had no idea of what Possibilities were, I asked the performers
to freeze after the Polanski interview. After our first open rehearsal
at Goddard, Lado said: "The ending must stay as it is!" I
explained that the freeze was a stop-gap. "No, no," Lado insisted,
"you have no answers to the questions of the play, why pretend?
You are against pretending, yes? Throw the questions back to the
audience!" Reluctantly I accepted his judgment. Several times
during the winter we tried other endings: whispering our actual
names, then exchanging names with spectators; music; discussions.
Nothing was an improvement on the freeze, on its sense of imbalance, unfinished business. Sometimes the audience would wait
in silence with us—for up to ten minutes. Then in the summer
of 1971 we found what I now think is the correct ending for
Commune.

The dialogue is over, and there is a freeze for about ninety
seconds. Then Spalding leaves his place in the center of the Wave
and goes to the side, sits, takes out a penny whistle, and blows

a loud shriek—like a work-whistle ending a day at the factory. Then he begins to play music. Clementine goes to the tub and starts washing. Others join her, or return "stolen" articles to spectators, or go somewhere to remove their costumes. Slowly the play fades into the routines of performers divesting themselves of their roles, spectators preparing to go home. Invariably some spectators approach the performers, talk, bathe their feet in the tub, lie on the Wave. Possibilities begins where it must: with the resumption of everyday life.

Models, Patterns, Ikonography: The Music of Action

George Kubler rejects Aristotle's biological model of art and proposes instead

> a system of metaphors drawn from the physical sciences. . . . We are dealing in art with some kind of energy: with impulses, generating centers, and relay points; with increments and losses in transit; with resistance and transformers in the circuit. In short, the language of electrodynamics might have suited us better than the language of botany.[4]

Kubler's model looks like something Bela Lugosi might invent on the Late Show, but it gives a good sense of simultaneity, backward as well as forward motion, transformation, input-output-feedback, short-circuit, jumps, flashes, implosions-explosions, rapidity. What Kubler's model lacks is life—and life is exactly what Aristotle's model is.

I had Kubler's model in mind when I drew four models of *Makbeth* in my notebook on March 27, 1969. One of them looked like this:

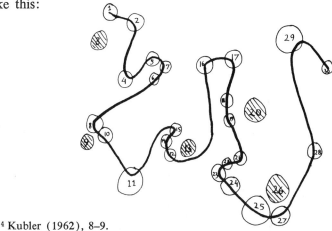

I meant this drawing to be both conceptual and actual. At that time I thought *Makbeth* would consist of *x* number of scenes, *y* of which would be played on any given night. Thus the performance would always keep an immediacy and an indeterminacy. I showed the drawings to the performers and to Rojo. That same day I wrote in my notebook that *Makbeth* should be made of "convulsive space, audience fragmentation, territorial space, comings and goings, ups and downs, opens and closeds, buildings and demolitions, audience pockets. There may be several scenes with the same action—simultaneous and fragmented—convulsive actions as well as convulsive space." Then I formulated what I called "first rules or parameters" of the mise-en-scène:

> For example:
>> Ten necessary scenes, three necessary spaces or routes.
>> Performance on any given night: twenty-five scenes played,
>>> seven spaces or routes used.
>>
>> Potential $\Big\}$ thirty scenes, ten spaces or routes.
>> Virtual

I saw *Makbeth* as a core of ten scenes that had to be played every night. These would embody the root story. The other twenty scenes would depend on nightly contingencies. Also there were three necessary spaces that had to be used each night; and seven additional spaces that could be used. I saw *Makbeth* combining theater, games, and electric circuitry.

This was not how the play was staged finally. But if I were to do the play again, I would attempt to realize this idea.

Rehearsals got rid of my plans, but some aspects of Kubler's scheme were kept. The Garage was divided into a number of connecting spaces. The performers, Rojo, and I mapped routes connecting these spaces. Epstein used the environment as drums and sounding boards for stampings, rappings, knockings, marchings, shufflings. As the mise evolved, rules were devised. The Dark Powers use all routes; the Makbeths are restricted in their movements. While Duncan rules, Malcolm and Macduff go where they please. When Makbeth has the crown, M. & M. are forced to sneak around the periphery, singing of their coming revenge —to the tune of "God Save the King." During most of the performance two or more scenes play simultaneously. The entire play takes a bare seventy minutes. The audience's attention is directed by more than sixty swift pulsations of light and dark, and "sound circuitry"—applications of Kubler's ideas. For example, just before Duncan is murdered, Lady Makbeth, standing at the center of the huge banquet table that dominates the space, is startled by a slight laugh from a Dark Power crouching near Duncan. Lady Makbeth's stifled cry is transformed into loud laughter by the other two Dark Powers carousing with Banquo (a woman) high in a corner. Their laughter is transformed into a sleepy/dreaming grunt by Duncan. He, in turn, being spied on by the giggling Malcolm and Macduff, is told to "shhhh!" All this while Makbeth makes his way as quietly as he can to Duncan. Thus:

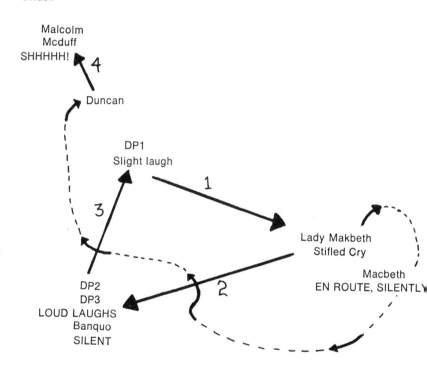

My intention in staging a scene such as this is to uncover several layers of action, irony, and meaning. I believe that these layers are arranged in somewhat of a spiral: at the bottom is the action, arresting in itself; a spectator need be aware of nothing else but Makbeth's movements through a not quiet space toward the uneasily sleeping Duncan. Above that is the laughter of the Dark Powers, seemingly unrelated to Makbeth's moves, but in the larger scheme a giggling at the fact that Makbeth will soon find himself "steep'd in blood so far" that he cannot turn back. And throughout the play—in the TPG version—the Dark Powers celebrate whenever any of the ruling class murders another. As one of them says:

> The rich warring against the rich, the great nobles tearing each other to pieces! O, I am well fed! Are these nobles fit to govern? No, not fit to live!

Lady Makbeth encourages Makbeth when they are together and suffers terrible fears and nightmares when she is alone. This will be her undoing: her inability to share who she is even with her closest comrade, Makbeth. These levels of action and irony —focusing the past and the future on the immediate—make up the meaning of the scene: The event *cannot* trammel up its consequences, blood murder begets blood murder. So it is in political life as it is in personal life. But even in the middle of the terror there is laughter—because look who's killing who: Duncan who executed his rebellious son, and more, is now under Makbeth's knife. A curse on all their class!

Ikonography is as important to a mise-en-scène as rhythms and patterns. A rhythm is movement in time; an ikon is a stop-action, a condensation of movement into an arrested moment, a gesture, an arrangement. In staging ikonographically it is most important to allow just enough time for the ikon to press itself on the awareness of the spectator. Too much time makes for the self-irony of a *tableau-vivant;* too little time means the audience won't have a chance for the image to sink in. Like a stop-action in a film—and much ikonography of contemporary theater owes a debt to the cinematographers—an ikon is a moment *taken out of time,* an opportunity for the audience to reflect and evaluate the scene: a version of Brecht's *V-effekt.* The following are examples of ikons from TPG productions:

> *Dionysus.* Just after the women kill Pentheus and the other men, they freeze. The grimaces of the murdering mothers are not different from the agonies of the murdered sons. It is hard to tell whose blood is whose. The whole grizzly scene is from Vietnam and Auschwitz. After a freeze of about five seconds the women drop the limbs of the men and rush into the audience bragging of "this great deed I have done."

> *Makbeth.* Malcolm, Macduff, and the Dark Powers advance on Dunsinane in short, loud leaps; after each leap the scene freezes. Makbeth sees a scene as much inside his head as

Photograph 40. Makbeth orders his men —Dark Powers—to kill Banquo, who is seen leaving through a trap-door immediately behind Makbeth. (*Frederick Eberstadt*)

Photograph 41. Makbeth awaits his guests for the famous banquet at which Banquo's ghost appears. (*Frederick Eberstadt*)

Photographs 42, 43, 44, 45. Ikonograph: details from *Makbeth:* The Dark Powe: spy on their masters. (*Frederick Ebe. stadt*)

Photographs 46 and 47.
Ikonographic details from
Commune: A coyote
watches as Clementine is
isolated in a circle of
suffering.

Photographs 48 and 49.
Ikonographic details
from *Commune:* a stop
and a start in the quest
for El Dorado by a blind
woman who is a version
of *Lear*'s Gloucester
(*Frederick Eberstadt*)

outside it. He sees his destiny rising incredibly not as a tide but coming in sudden, inexplicable bursts the exact nature of which he can't understand. From his point of view the final battle is a "tale told by an idiot." From the point of view of the Dark Powers it is a farce.

Commune. When Bruce speaks during the Tate murder scene, everyone else freezes in the act of screaming, killing, being killed. Bruce talks of the artist for whom time stops as he works on carving a "perfect staff." In the midst of the carnage someone is making a beautiful thing out of the agonies of the others. As Bruce finishes, the scene resumes: Knives are thrust, screams screamed, bodies drop.

The Tooth of Crime. Hoss is telling a story about how two of his friends were taunted into fighting the jocks from their own high school. The story is a big production number with full musical backup. At the moment before the fight itself is described, Hoss brings his arms down like a conductor ending a symphony, and all the music stops. Then Hoss says: "Then I saw it. This was a class war." The scene starts again with full backup and Hoss tells how he and his lower-class friends beat up their eight middle-class tormentors.

The function of ikonography is to direct the spectator's attention and stimulate his imagination.

A film is nothing other than a progression of ikons, stop-action shots that have the appearance of flow because of the rapidity with which they succeed each other. The theatrical stop-action shot is even more effective than in films because it is not "natural" to the medium. Life is not lived as a series of stop-actions accelerated to give the appearance of continuous motion. Life is lived continuously, and when the action is stopped, a definite wrench is felt. In film the frame is actually stopped—everything is absolutely frozen. In theater the performers' bodies still move, if slightly, breaths are drawn, hands tremble: there is a deterioration of illusion even in the ikonographic moment. In the ikonographic freeze the illusion of disillusion is itself disillusioned.

Ikonography is more than stop-action. It is a web of gestures not entirely natural to the situation that multiplies the points of view from which the action can be regarded. Each ikon is a comment on the action in the form of counterpoint. In *Makbeth,* for example, the Dark Powers are servants, lower-class people, soldiers; they are also gargoyles hanging over the action, eyes and ears spying, hands casting spells.

There is only one actual prop in *Makbeth*—a solid brass crown fashioned by Phil Phelan, the play's stage manager. The crown is worn by Duncan, Makbeth, and Malcolm; during the play everyone touches it: for the crown is the allpowerful mana/ anima of royalty. It is not a symbol. He who wears the crown is the Crown. Originally I planned a scene where the Dark Powers play catch with the crown, stealing it from Makbeth's head during the Banquet scene. For Duncan the crown is too heavy; his head is bent with its weight, it gives him a stiff neck. Makbeth is always adjusting the crown, reaching up and feeling it on his head. It is too big, too small, it falls off, it slides down over his forehead: almost a farce. "Now does he feel his title hang loose about him, like a giant's robe upon a dwarfish thief." Macduff fiercely snatches the crown from the dead Makbeth. Macduff is afraid of the crown, it is a hot potato. He thrusts it into Malcolm's stomach the way a quarterback stuffs the ball into the running back's gut. Or he offers it to Malcolm as if it were a Thanksgiving Day turkey on a platter. Either way Malcolm takes it hungrily. Malcolm never puts the crown on—he doesn't dare let it out of his hands/sight. Suddenly Malcolm bites into the crown; he want to eat it, get it inside him permanently, make it part of his body. Malcolm cracks his teeth on the indigestible crown.

The crown of *Makbeth* is both a rhythm and an ikon. By keeping one's eye on what happens to the crown, a spectator can understand the action of the play. The crown is what T. S. Eliot would call an objective correlative.

The thousands of ikonographic details of each production give the production its feel, its texture. It isn't possible for any spectator to take in all the planned details, no less the thousands of moments that crystalize through playing the play as one plays a game: from predetermined rules but without anticipation, simply in response to whatever is going on. Once the company is capable of generating ikons, the problem is not one of invention but of selection.

> The most articulate performances are always those which have been pared away. All that's nonessential, all that's accessory, all that's indulgent, all that's outside the center has been dropped, and what remains is a spare language of tasks which speak of life and nature.[5]

[5] Chaikin (1972), 64–65.

Ikons work on the performer as well as on the spectator. To a degree not examined enough performers are spectators for each other. This operates very strongly in rehearsals and is a source of the inward-flowing energies of a performance, what Stanislavski called "circles of attention." Also a performer can watch part of himself: He can become fascinated by what his hands are doing, for example. Ikons set off associations and accumulate details—these add up to the feel of a role. Not a role as a character ("myself as another") but as a language of tasks ("myself doing something").

All the time, the director listens/watches for poses, tones, rhythms, patterns, attractions, avoidances. These concrete languages are the substance of the mise-en-scène. My own work tends to be over-full at the start. I add images on images, cut very little, accumulate; marvel at the generative energies of the performers. The plays I direct are about twice as long at the start of their runs as at the end.

The Director

The director is the performer's Tiresias, Horatio, Sganarelle, Pylades: Friend, Servant, Sidekick, and Seer. This kind of character has dropped out of drama as the director has come into full force. Is it too fancy an idea to connect their going out to his coming in? The director functions as leader cum parent cum therapist cum colleague cum child: His roles during workshop and rehearsal are many, as long as he disappears during performance. But some contemporary directors—Grotowski, Chaikin, André Gregory, and I, for example—have a hard time becoming anonymous during performance. Grotowski is an *eminence grise,* Gregory laughs up a storm, Chaikin is shyly obvious, and I carry my big notebook. Up against the presence of the performers is the presence of the directors.

The performer is a doer, the director is a seer. The director is present, he sees, he says what he sees. But also he accomplishes many less mighty tasks, especially in a small group. These housekeeping duties are important because in doing them the director trains to respond in different ways to the myriad situations that come up in rehearsal and workshop. His responses are no more false than those of the performers. The director doesn't "play roles" in the orthodox sense.

> Each group requires more or less radical internal transformation of the persons who comprise it. Consider the meta-

morphoses that one man may go through in one day as he moves from one mode of sociality to another—family man, speck of crowd dust, functionary in the organization, friend. These are not simply different roles: each is a whole past and present and future, offering different options and constraints, different degrees of change or inertia, different kinds of closeness and distance, different sets of rights and obligations, different pledges and promises.[6]

The changes in the modes of sociality that most people experience among different groups the director experiences in the *one* group. The performers are masters of transformation, and the director learns to become a master adapter. The problem is to do this without, at the same time, becoming a schemer, an Odysseus, or a hypocrite.

I have been numb, unable to see. I have been distracted. I have seen things but lacked the courage to speak of them. I have manipulated people by not saying the kernel of what I've seen. I've been in terror of saying what I've felt. I have guarded my self-esteem and my public reputation, as well as my reputation within the Group. Worst of all I've lied to myself. There are ten reasons for not being present, one hundred reasons for not seeing, and one thousand reasons for not saying what one sees.

Lest the reader think that these things have little to do with directing, let me say that the fundamental life-feels of the director are what directing in a group is all about. The director's life-feels are communicated in the way tasks are distributed, the way time is ordered in workshops and rehearsals, the way individual needs are balanced against group needs when the two conflict, the way in which the director's fantasies are brought into the work, or kept out of it.

To be natural = to be function of all that is happening to you here and now = to learn = to change.

The Great Initiatory Wheel

When group work succeeds, it makes a Great Initiatory Wheel.

Personal: to be wholly who I am now . . . self-realization leads to
Group: to dissolve ego boundaries making works which are more than expressions of each person alone . . . collective creativity leads to

[6] Laing (1968), 96–97.

Social: to show an audience the possibility of becoming a community . . . solidarity leads to
Political: to reveal patterns in history, what has happened to peoples, classes, nations . . . consciousness leads to
Metaphysical: to demonstrate that human beings can bring about their own evolution . . . change leads to the
Personal: . . .

Self-realization leads to collective creativity leads to solidarity leads to consciousness leads to change leads to self-realization . . .

Group work is neither mine nor yours nor ours nor its. The director doesn't invent it any more than the sailor invents the wind. Theater exists in a place that is inside and outside, here and there, now and then, mine and yours, actual and fantasy. A place where performers are themselves and others, where deeds are real and symbolic, where the dead come back to life, the old grow young; where audiences are seated yet carried away, touched yet left alone, still yet moved. Where stories are immediate and distant, where space is concrete and abstract, time accelerated, distorted, and slowed. From where do theatrical events come? They are not the purely personal actions or fantasies of the performers; they are not objective events taken from everyday life; they are not fiction; they are not embodiments of the director's wishes; they are not realizations or interpretations of a text; they are not re-creations of earlier events. There is something of all these in a performance: a precarious arrangement of unstable elements, a juggling act. *Theater is situated between all the contending forces that give it life; and theater is itself a life-giver.*

Theater's existence is precarious. The underlying theme of all theater is to restore a balance that cannot be restored: a striving on a wheel. Imbalance is the root-motive of action, the reason why action is necessary. The imbalance of theater is not just in the story but in the relationship between performers and spectators, in the space, in the social occasion, in the entire incredibly complicated, lovely placement of mirrors that makes it impossible to separate theatrical image from theatrical object. Theater is a playing-with-playing. Even the heaviest tragedy has an irreducible kernel/core of the *lusory* = ludicrous, allusive, collusion, prelude, interlude, elusion, illusion, delusion, prolusory. From Latin *ludus* (a game) and *ludere* (to play). From Old Irish *loid* (a song). Also Middle Irish *laidim* (to exhort or admonish). And Greek *loidoros* (insulting). And Old Celtic *leut* (to be joyous).

Bibliography

Note: Dates refer to date of publication of edition cited in text. When I feel that it is important to know the date of original publication this original date is bracketed.

Aldena, Guillermo E. 1971. "Mesa del Nayar's Strange Holy Week." *National Geographic Magazine,* Vol. 139, No. 6, 780–794.

Arieti, Silvano, 1948a. "Autistic Thought." In *J. N. & M. Disease,* 288–303.

———. 1948b. "Special Logic of Schizophrenic and Other Types of Autistic Thought." *Psychiatry,* Vol. 11, November 1948, 325–338.

Arrowsmith, William. 1956. "Introduction to *Cyclops.*" In *Euripides II.* Chicago: University of Chicago Press. 2–8.

Artaud, Antonin. 1958 [1932–1938]. *The Theater and Its Double,* tr. Mary Caroline Richards. New York: Grove Press.

———. 1965 [1945]. "Symbolic Mountains," tr. Victor Corti. TDR, Vol. 9, No. 3, 94–98.

Barba, Eugenio, 1965. "Theatre Laboratory 13 Rzedow," tr. Simone Sanzenbach. TDR, Vol. 9, No. 3, 153–171.

Barber, Bernard, 1941. "Acculturation and Messianic Movements." *American Sociological Review.* Vol. 6, No. 5, 663–669.

Bateson, Gregory. 1958 [1936]. *Naven.* Stanford: Stanford University Press.

Beck, Julian. 1964. "How to Close a Theatre." TDR, Vol. 8, No. 3, 180–190.

———. 1972. *The Life of the Theatre.* San Francisco: City Lights Books.

Beck, Julian and Malina, Judith. 1969. "Containment is the Enemy," an interview with Richard Schechner. TDR, Vol. 13, No. 3, 24–44.

———. 1971. *Paradise Now.* "A Collective Creation of The Living Theatre Written Down by Judith Malina and Julian Beck." New York: Random House.

Beisser, Arnold R. 1970. "The Paradoxical Theory of Change." In *Gestalt Therapy Now,* eds. Joen Fagan and Irma Lee Shepherd. New York: Harper Colophon Books, 77–80.

Bentley, Eric. 1969. "An Interview with Eric Bentley." *Yale/Theatre.* II, Spring, 1969, 106–112.

———. 1972. *Theatre of War.* New York: Viking Press, Inc.

Berndt, Catherine H. 1959. "Ascription of Meaning in a Ceremonial Context in the Eastern Central Highlands of New Guinea." In *Anthropology in the South Seas,* 161–183.

Berndt, Ronald M. 1962. *Excess and Restraint*. Chicago: University of Chicago Press.

Berne, Eric. 1961. *Transactional Analysis in Psychotherapy*. New York: Grove Press.

———. 1964. *Games People Play*. New York: Grove Press.

Bettelheim, Bruno. 1962 [1954]. *Symbolic Wounds, Puberty Rites and the Envious Male*. New York: Collier Books.

———. 1967. *The Empty Fortress*. New York: The Free Press.

Birdwhistell, Ray L. 1970. *Kinesics and Context*. Philadelphia: University of Pennsylvania Press.

Boas, Franz. 1966 [1911, 1939]. *The Mind of Primitive Man*. New York: The Free Press.

Bongartz, Roy. 1970. "It's Called Earth Art—and Boulderdash." *New York Times Magazine,* February 1, 1970, 16 ff.

Brecht, Bertolt. 1964 [1918–1956]. *Brecht on Theatre,* tr. and ed. John Willett. New York: Hill & Wang.

Brecht, Stefan. 1969. "Revolution at the BAM." TDR, Vol. 13, No. 3, 46–73.

Brook, Peter. 1970. *The Empty Space*. New York: Atheneum.

Burke, Kenneth. 1961 [1941, 1957]. *The Philosophy of Literary Form*. Baton Rouge, La.: Louisiana State University Press.

———. 1962 [1945, 1950]. *A Grammar of Motives and A Rhetoric of Motives*. Cleveland: World Publishing Co.

Cage, John. 1966. *Silence*. Cambridge: M.I.T. Press.

———. 1967. *A Year From Monday*. Middletown, Connecticut: Wesleyan University Press.

———. 1969. *Notations*. New York: Something Else Press.

Campbell, Joseph. 1964. "Primitive Man as Metaphysician." In *Primitive Views of the World,* ed. Stanley Diamond. New York: Columbia University Press. 20–32.

Cassirer, Ernst. 1946. *Language and Myth,* tr. Susanne K. Langer. New York: Dover Publications.

Castaneda, Carlos. 1968. *The Teachings of Don Juan: A Yaqui Way of Knowledge*. New York: Ballantine Books, Inc.

———. 1971. *A Separate Reality*. New York: Simon & Schuster.

———. 1972. *Journey to Ixtlan*. New York: Simon & Schuster.

Chaikin, Joseph. 1972. *The Presence of the Actor*. New York: Atheneum.

Clark, Kenneth. 1956. *The Nude*. New York: Pantheon Books.

Close, Henry T. 1970. "Gross Exaggeration with a Schizophrenic Patient." In *Gestalt Therapy Now,* eds. Joen Fagan and Irma Lee Shepherd. New York: Harper Colophon Books, 194–196.

Cohn, Ruth C. 1970a. "Therapy in Groups: Psychoanalytic, Experiential, and Gestalt." In *Gestalt Therapy Now,* eds. Joen Fagan and Irma Lee Shepherd. New York: Harper Colophon Books, 130–139.

———. 1970b. "A Child with a Stomachache: Fusion of Psychoanalytic Concepts and Gestalt Techniques." In *Gestalt Therapy Now,* eds. Joen Fagan and Irma Lee Sheperd. New York: Harper Colophon Books, 197–203.

Cole, Toby and Chinoy, Helen Krich, eds. 1963 [1903–1960]. *Directors on Directing*. New York: Bobbs-Merrill.

Cooper, David. 1970. *The Death of the Family*. New York: Pantheon Books.

Croyden, Margaret. 1971. "Peter Brook Learns to Speak Orghast." *The New York Times,* Arts and Leisure Section, October 3, 1971, 1 ff.

Dent, Thomas C., Moses, Gilbert, and Schechner, Richard, eds. 1969. *The Free Southern Theater by The Free Southern Theater.* New York: Bobbs-Merrill.

Diamond, Stanley, ed. 1964. *Primitive Views of the World.* New York: Columbia University Press.

Draeger, Donn F., and Smith, Robert W. 1969. *Asian Fighting Arts.* Tokyo and Palo Alto: Kodansha International, Ltd.

Eliade, Mircea. 1965. *Rites and Symbols of Initiation,* tr. Willard R. Trask. New York: Harper & Row.

———. 1970 [1951]. *Shamanism: Archaic Techniques of Ecstasy,* tr. Willard R. Trask. Princeton: Princeton University Press.

Emenau, M. B. 1942. "Review of La Meri's *The Gesture Language of the Hindu Dance.*" *Journal of the American Oriental Society.* Vol. LXII, No. 149.

Enright, John B. 1970. "An Introduction to Gestalt Techniques." In *Gestalt Therapy Now,* eds. Joen Fagan and Irma Lee Shepherd. New York: Harper Colophon Books. 107–124.

Epstein, Paul. 1972a. "Music and Theater." *Performance.* Vol. 1, No. 2, 11–19.

———. 1972b. "Music and Theater: Part 2." *Performance,* Vol. 1, No. 4. 110–123.

Erikson, Erik H. 1959. *Identity and the Life Cycle. Psychological Issues,* Monograph 1. New York: International Universities Press.

Evans-Pritchard, E. E. 1960. "A Selection from *Nuer Religion.*" In *Anthropology of Folk Religion,* ed. Charles Leslie. New York: Random House. 53–99.

Fagan, Joen. 1970. "The Tasks of the Therapist." In *Gestalt Therapy Now,* eds. Joen Fagan and Irma Lee Shepherd. New York: Harper Colophon Books. 88–105.

Farb, Peter. 1969. *Man's Rise to Civilization.* New York: Avon Books.

Fergusson, Francis. 1949. *The Idea of a Theater.* Garden City: Doubleday.

———. 1961. "Introduction to Aristotle's *Poetics.*" In *Aristotle's Poetics.* New York: Hill & Wang.

Firth, Raymond. 1967. *Tikopia Ritual and Belief.* London: George Allen and Unwin.

Frankfort, Henri. 1948. *Kingship and the Gods.* Chicago: University of Chicago Press.

Freud, Sigmund. 1952 [1924]. *A General Introduction to Psychoanalysis,* tr. Joan Riviere. New York: Washington Square Press.

———. 1958 [1908–1923]. *On Creativity and the Unconscious.* New York: Harper & Row.

———. 1961 [1900]. *The Interpretation of Dreams,* tr. James Strachey. New York: John Wiley & Sons.

———. 1962a [1913]. *Totem and Taboo,* tr. James Strachey. New York: W. W. Norton.

———. 1962b [1930]. *Civilization and Its Discontents,* tr. James Strachey. New York: W. W. Norton.

———. 1963 [1905]. *Jokes and Their Relation to the Unconscious,* tr. James Strachey. New York: W. W. Norton.

Gardner, Robert and Heider, Karl G. 1968. *Gardens of War*. New York: Random House.

Genet, Jean. 1963 [1954]. "A Note on Theatre," tr. Bernard Frechtman. TDR, Vol. 7, No. 3, 37–41.

Giedion, S. 1962. *The Eternal Present: The Beginnings of Art*. New York: The Bollingen Foundation. (Distributor: Pantheon Books.)

———. 1964. *The Eternal Present: The Beginnings of Architecture*. New York: The Bollingen Foundation. (Distributor: Pantheon Books.)

Goffman, Erving, 1959. *The Presentation of Self in Everyday Life*. Garden City: Doubleday.

———. 1961. *Encounters*. Indianapolis: Bobbs-Merrill.

———. 1963a. *Stigma*. Englewood Cliffs: Prentice-Hall.

———. 1963b. *Behavior in Public Places*. Glencoe, Ill.: The Free Press.

———. 1967. *Interaction Ritual*. Garden City: Doubleday.

———. 1969. *Strategic Interaction*. Philadelphia: University of Pennsylvania Press.

———. 1971. *Relations in Public*. New York: Basic Books.

Gould, Richard A. 1969. *Yiwara: Foragers of the Australian Desert*. New York: Charles Schribner's Sons.

Grotowski, Jerzy. 1968a. *Towards a Poor Theatre*. Holstebro: Odin Teatrets Forlag.

———. 1968b. "Theatre and Ritual," tr. Malgorzata Ruska Munk. *Dialog*, No. 9, 1968. (In manuscript translation only.)

———. 1969. "Not Actor, Son of Man." Article developed by George Reavey from lecture given by Grotowski at the Brooklyn Academy on December 6, 1968. (In manuscript only.)

Haigh, A. E. 1907. *The Attic Theatre*. Oxford: Clarendon Press.

Hall, Edward T. 1969. *The Hidden Dimension*. Garden City: Doubleday.

———. 1970 [1959]. *The Silent Language*. Greenwich, Connecticut: Fawcett Publications.

Halprin, Ann. 1968 "Mutual Creation." *Tullane Drama Review*, Vol. 13, No. 1, 163–175.

Hanks, Jane Richardson. 1964. "Reflections on the Ontology of Rice." In *Primitive Views of the World*, ed. Stanley Diamond. New York: Columbia University Press. 151–154.

Hart, C. W. M. and Pilling, Arnold R. 1966. *The Tiwi of North Australia*. New York: Holt, Rinehart and Winston.

Hoffman, Abbie [FREE]. 1968. *Revolution for the Hell of It*. New York: The Dial Press.

———. 1969. *Woodstock Nation*. New York: Random House.

———. 1971. *Steal This Book*. New York: Pirate Editions.

Hogbin, Ian. 1965. *A Guadalcanal Society: The Kaoka Speakers*. New York: Holt, Rinehart and Winston.

Huizinga, Johan. 1955 [1938]. *Homo Ludens*. Boston: Beacon Press.

Isaac, Dan. 1971. "The Death of the Proscenium Stage." *The Antioch Review*, Vol. XXXI, No. 2, 235–253.

Kaplan, Donald M. 1968. "Theatre Architecture: A Derivation of the Primal Cavity." TDR, Vol. 12, No. 3, 105–116.

———. 1969. "In Stage Fright." TDR, Vol. 14, No. 1, 60–83.

———. 1971. "Gestures, Sensibilities, Scripts." *Performance*. Vol. 1, No. 1, 31–46.

Kaprow, Allan, 1966a. *Assemblages, Environments, & Happenings.* New York: Harry Abrams.

———. 1966b. *Some Recent Happenings.* Great Bear Pamphlet. New York: Something Else Press.

———. 1967. *Untitled Essay and Other Works.* Great Bear Pamphlet. New York: Something Else Press.

———. 1968a. "Extensions in Time and Space." Interview with Richard Schechner. TDR, Vol. 12, No. 3, 153–159.

———. 1968b. "Self-Service." TDR, Vol. 12, No. 3, 160–164.

———. 1970. *Days Off, A Calendar of Happenings.* New York: Museum of Modern Art.

Kempler, Walter. 1970. "Experiental Psychotherapy with Families." In *Gestalt Therapy Now,* eds. Joen Fagan and Irma Lee Shepherd. New York: Harper Colophon Books. 150–161.

Kerr, Walter. 1968. " 'Come Dance With Me.' 'Who, *Me*?' " *The New York Times,* Arts & Leisure Section. June 16, 1968, p. 1 ff.

Kirby, Michael. 1965a. *Happenings.* New York: Dutton.

———. 1965b. "The New Theatre," TDR, Vol. 10, No. 2, 23–43.

———. 1969. *The Art of Time.* New York: Dutton.

Kirby, Michael and Schechner, Richard. 1965. "An Interview with John Cage." TDR, Vol. 10, No. 2, 50–72.

Kohler, Wolfgang. 1970 [1947]. *Gestalt Psychology.* New York: Liveright.

Kris, Ernst. 1964 [1952]. *Psychoanalytic Explorations in Art.* New York: Schocken Books.

Kubler, George. 1962. *The Shape of Time.* New Haven: Yale University Press.

La Barre, Weston. 1972. *The Ghost Dance.* New York: Dell Publishing Co.

Laing, R. D. 1960. *The Divided Self.* Chicago: Quadrangle Books.

———. 1962, 1969. *The Self and Others.* New York: Pantheon.

———. 1967. *The Politics of Experience.* New York: Ballantine Books.

———. 1969, 1971. *The Politics of the Family.* New York: Pantheon.

Laing, R. D. and Esterson, A. 1964. *Sanity, Madness, and the Family.* New York: Basic Books.

Langer, Susanne K. 1953. *Feeling and Form.* New York: Charles Scribner's Sons.

Lederman, Janet. 1970. "Anger and the Rocking Chair." In *Gestalt Therapy Now,* eds. Joen Fagan and Irma Lee Shepherd. New York: Harper Colophon Books. 285–294.

Leslie, Charles, ed. 1960. *Anthropology of Folk Religion.* New York: Random House.

Levi-Strauss, Claude. 1963. "The Sorcerer and His Magic." In *Structural Anthropology.* New York: Basic Books. 167–185.

———. 1966. *The Savage Mind.* Chicago: University of Chicago Press.

———. 1969a [1949, 1967]. *The Elementary Structures of Kinship,* trs. J. H. Bell, J. R. von Sturmer, R. Needham, ed. Boston: Beacon Press.

———. 1969b [1964]. *The Raw and the Cooked,* trs. J. and D. Weightman. New York: Harper & Row.

Levitsky, Abraham and Perls, Frederick S. 1970. "The Rules and Games of Gestalt Therapy." In *Gestalt Therapy Now,* eds. Joen Fagan and Irma Lee Shepherd. New York: Harper Colophon Books. 140–149.

Lewis, I. M. 1971. *Ecstatic Religion.* London: Penguin Books.

Lindzey, Gardner. 1967. "Some Remarks Concerning Incest, the Incest Taboo, and Psychoanalytic Theory." In *American Psychologist,* Vol. 22, No. 12, 1051–1059.

Living Theatre, The. 1969a. "History Now." *Yale/Theatre* II, Spring 1969, 18–29.

———. 1969b. "The Living Theatre Raps." *Yale/Theatre* II, Spring 1969, 40–44.

———. 1969c. "The Last Discussion." *Yale/Theatre* II, Spring 1969, 45–52.

———. 1969d. "Meditations on the Life of the Theatre." *Yale/Theatre* II, Spring 1969, 117–127.

———. 1969e. "Flip Pages." *Yale/Theatre* II. Spring 1969.

———. 1969f. "*Paradise Now* Notes." TDR, Vol. 13, No. 3, 90–107.

———. 1971a. *Paradise Now.* New York: Vintage Books.

———. 1971b. *The Living Book of the Living Theatre.* Greenwich, Connecticut: New York Graphic Society.

Lommel, Andreas. 1967. *Shamanism: The Beginnings of Art,* tr. Michael Bullock. New York: McGraw-Hill.

Lorenz. 1959. "The Role of Aggression in Group Formation." In *Group Processes: 1957 Conference,* ed. B. Schaffner. New York: Macy Foundation.

———. 1967. *On Aggression.* New York: Bantam Books.

McDermott, Patrick. 1969. "Portrait of an Actor, Watching." TDR, Vol. 13, No. 3, 74–83.

McLuhan, Marshall. 1965. *Understanding Media.* New York: McGraw-Hill.

———. 1967. *The Medium is the Massage.* New York: Bantam Books.

Malinowski, Bronislaw. 1954 [1916–1925]. *Magic, Science, and Religion.* Garden City: Doubleday.

———. 1961 [1922]. *Argonauts of the Western Pacific.* New York: Dutton.

Marcuse, Herbert. 1962. *Eros and Civilization.* New York: Random House.

Marx, Leo. 1967. *The Machine in the Garden.* New York: Oxford University Press.

Maybury-Lewis, David. 1965. *The Savage and the Innocent.* New York: World Publishing Co.

Meyerhold, Vsevolod Emilevich. 1969 [1902–1938]. *Meyerhold on Theatre,* tr. and ed. Edward Braun. New York: Hill & Wang.

Morgan, Charles. 1961 [1933]. "The Nature of Dramatic Illusion." in *Reflections on Art,* ed. Susanne K. Langer. New York: Oxford University Press. 91–102.

Nadeau, Maurice. 1965. *The History of Surrealism,* tr. Richard Howard. New York: MacMillan.

Naranjo, Claudio. 1970. "Present-Centeredness: Technique, Prescription, and Ideal." In *Gestalt Therapy Now,* eds. Joen Fagan and Irma Lee Shepherd. New York: Harper Colophon Books. 47–69.

Oeasterley, W. O. E. 1923. *The Sacred Dance.* New York: Dance Horizons. (Reprint of the original, issued by Cambridge University Press.)

Oldenburg, Claes. 1967. *Store Days.* New York: Something Else Press.

Performance Group, The. 1970. *Dionysus in 69,* ed. Richard Schechner. New York: Farrar, Straus, & Giroux.

———. 1973. *Makbeth & Commune,* ed. Richard Schechner. New York: Drama Book Specialists Publishers.

Perls, Frederick S. 1970a. "Four Lectures." In *Gestalt Therapy Now,* eds.

Joen Fagan and Irma Lee Shepherd. New York: Harper Colophon Books. 14–38.

———. 1970b. "Dream Seminars." In *Gestalt Therapy Now,* eds. Joen Fagan and Irma Lee Shepherd. New York: Harper Colophon Books. 204–233.

Perls, Laura. 1970. "One Gestalt Therapist's Approach." In *Gestalt Therapy Now,* eds. Joen Fagan and Irma Lee Shepherd. New York: Harper Colophon Books. 125–129.

Piaget, Jean. 1962. *Play, Dreams, and Imitation in Childhood,* trs. C. Gattegno and F. M. Hodgson. New York: W. W. Norton.

——— 1967 [1948]. *The Child's Conception of Space,* trs. F. J. Langdon and J. L. Lunzer. New York: W. W. Norton.

Pickard-Cambridge, A. W. 1962. *Dithyramb, Tragedy, and Comedy.* 2nd ed., revised by T. B. L. Webster. Oxford: Clarendon Press.

Pospisil, Leopold. 1963. *The Kapauku Papuans.* New York: Holt, Rinehart and Winston.

Read, Kenneth E. 1965. *The High Valley.* New York: Charles Scribner's Sons.

Rhyne, Janie. 1970. "The Gestalt Art Experience." In *Gestalt Therapy Now,* eds. Joen Fagan and Irma Lee Shepherd. New York: Harper Colophon Books. 274–284.

Richards, M. C. 1970. *Centering.* Middletown, Connecticut: Wesleyan University Press.

Rogers, Carl. 1970. *Carl Rogers on Encounter Groups.* New York: Harper & Row.

Roheim, Géza. 1950. *Psychoanalysis and Anthropology.* New York: International Universities Press.

———. 1969 [1945]. *The Eternal Ones of the Dream.* New York: International Universities Press.

———. 1971 [1943]. *The Origin and Function of Culture.* Garden City: Doubleday.

Rostagno, Aldo. *We, The Living Theatre.* New York: Ballantine Books.

Rothenberg, Jerome, ed. 1968. *Technicians of the Sacred.* Garden City: Doubleday.

Rubin, Jerry. 1970. *Do It!* New York: Simon & Schuster.

Rubin, William S. 1968. *Dada, Surrealism, and Their Heritage.* New York: Museum of Modern Art.

Ruesch, Jorgen, and Bateson, Gregory. 1951. *Communication.* New York: W. W. Norton.

Sainer, Arthur, ed. 1973. *Radical Theatre Notebook.* New York: Avon Books.

Saulnier, Tony. 1963. *Headhunters of Papua.* New York: Crown Publishers.

Schechner, Richard. 1964. "Interviews with Judith Malina and Kenneth Brown." TDR, Vol. 8, No. 3, 207–219.

———. 1965. "Theatre Criticism." TDR, Vol. 9, No. 3, 13–24.

———. 1966a. "Approaches to Theory/Criticism." TDR, Vol. 10, No. 4, 20–53.

———. 1966b. "Is It What's Happening, Baby?" *The New York Times,* Arts & Leisure Section. June 12, 1966, p. 3 ff.

———. 1968. "Theatre & Revolution." *Salmagundi,* Vol. II, No. 1, 11–27.

———. 1969a. *Public Domain.* New York: Bobbs-Merrill.

————. 1969b. "Speculations on Radicalism, Sexuality, & Performance." TDR, Vol. 13, No. 4, 89–110.

————. 1969c. "The Playwright Out of Time." In *Genet/Ionesco: The Theatre of the Double,* ed. Kelly Morris. New York: Bantam Books. 183–212.

————. 1969d. "Notes Toward an Imaginary Production." Introduction to *Woyzeck* by Georg Büchner, tr. Henry J. Schmidt. New York: Avon Books. 11–23.

————. 1968e. "Want to Watch– Or Act?" *The New York Times,* Arts & Leisure Section. January 12, 1969, p. 1 ff.

————. 1970a. "Actuals: A Look into Performance Theory." In *The Rarer Action,* eds. Alan Cheuse and Richard Koffler. New Brunswick: Rutgers University Press. 97–138. (Also in *Theatre Quarterly,* Vol. 1, No. 2, 49–66.)

————. 1970b. "After the Blow Up in the Garage." *The New York Times,* Arts & Leisure Section. December 13, 1970, p. 1 ff.

————. 1971a. "Post-Proscenium." In *American Theatre 3.* New York: Charles Scribner's Sons. 24–33.

————. 1971b. "Incest and Culture: A Reflection on Claude Levi-Strauss." *The Psychoanalytic Review,* Vol. 58, No. 4, 563–572.

————. 1972. "Surrounded—But Not Afraid." *The New York Times,* Arts & Leisure Section, September 17, 1972, p. 5 ff.

————. *Ritual and Theatre.* London: Penguin Books. (Forthcoming.)

————. "A Structural Analysis of *The Bald Soprano* and *The Lesson.*" In *Ionesco: Twentieth Century Views,* ed. Rosette Lamont. Englewood Cliffs: Prentice-Hall. (Forthcoming.)

Schechner, Richard, and Rojo, Jerry N., and McNamara, Brooks. 1973. *Environmental Theatre Design.* New York: Drama Book Specialists/ Publishers.

Shepherd, Irma Lee. 1970. "Limitations and Cautions in the Gestalt Approach." In *Gestalt Therapy Now,* eds. Joen Fagan and Irma Lee Shepherd. New York: Harper Colophon Books. 234–238.

Schilder, Paul. 1950. *The Image and Appearance of the Human Body.* New York: International Universities Press.

Shirokogoroff, S. M. 1935. *Psychomental Complex of the Tungus.* London: Kegan, Paul, Trench, Trubner & Co.

Simkin, James. 1970. "Mary: A Session with a Passive Patient." In *Gestalt Therapy Now,* eds. Joen Fagan and Irma Lee Shepherd. New York: Harper Colophon Books. 162–168.

Slater, Philip E. 1966. *Microcosm.* New York: John Wiley & Sons.

————. 1970. *The Pursuit of Loneliness.* Boston: Beacon Press.

Southern, Richard. 1961. *The Seven Ages of Theatre.* New York: Hill & Wang.

Stanislavski, Konstantin. 1946 [1936]. *An Actor Prepares,* tr. Elizabeth Reynolds Hapgood. New York: Theatre Arts Books.

————. 1961 [1918–1922]. *Stanislavsky on the Art of the Stage,* tr. with an introduction by David Mgarshack. New York: Hill & Wang.

Suvin, Darko. 1970. "Reflections on Happenings." TDR, Vol. 14, No. 3, 125–144.

TDR. 1965. *Special Issue on Happenings,* eds. Michael Kirby and Richard Schechner. Vol. 10, No. 2.

————. 1968. *Special Issue on Architecture/Environment,* ed. Richard Schechner. Vol. 12, No. 3.

Turnbull, Colin M. 1962. *The Forest People.* Garden City: Doubleday.

Van Gennep, Arnold. 1960 [1908]. *The Rites of Passage,* trs. Monika B. Vizedom and Gabrielle L. Caffee. Chicago: The University of Chicago Press.

Veblen, Thorstein. 1967 [1899]. *The Theory of the Leisure Class.* New York: Viking Press.

Verzuh, Ron. 1972. "Review of *The Tooth of Crime*" *The Peak,* Vancouver: British Columbia. September 20, 1972, p. 17.

Wallen, Richard. 1970. "Gestalt Therapy and Gestalt Psychology." In *Gestalt Therapy Now,* eds. Joen Fagan and Irma Lee Shepherd. New York: Harper Colophon Books, 8–13.

Williams, F. E. 1940. *The Drama of the Orokolo.* Oxford: Clarendon Press.

Yale French Studies. 1966. *Special Issue on Structuralism.* Nos. 36–37.

————. 1968. *Special Issue on Game, Play, Literature.* No. 41.

Zegwaard, Gerard A. 1959. "Headhunting Practices of the Asmat of Netherlands New Guinea." *American Anthropologist,* Vol. 61, No. 6, 1020–1041.

Index

THE NEW RADICAL THEATER NOTEBOOK

by Arthur Sainer

The New Radical Theater Notebook is part ongoing history, part document, part working journal, part complaint and part blessing. It is a giant colloquium among the many of the people who changed the face of theater from the Sixties onward. And it is filled with photographs, drawings, odd little private notes and occasional flyers documenting the many-faceted movement that is sometimes lurching and sometimes speeding and sometimes trying to find its feet in these strange times. The book employs Sainer's long out-of-print, *Radical Theater Notebook*, as a jumping-off point, incorporating much of that early material, but then moves onward from the mid-Seventies to the present moment.

$15.95 paper
ISBN: 1-55783-168-8

THE END OF ACTING

A RADICAL VIEW
by Richard Hornby

"PASSIONATE...PROVOCATIVE...A clear, comprehensive book bound to be read with great interest by anyone concerned with the future of American acting."

—*Variety*

"Few theorists are this brave; even fewer are this able.'

—**William Oliver**
Criticism

"**A VAST AND LEARNED BOOK**....a blend of passionate conviction, deep understanding, scholarly erudition and a matured practical savvy. *The End of Acting* **SHOULD BE REQUIRED READING, FOR BOTH FACULTY AND STUDENTS, IN EVERY THEATRE TRAINING PROGRAM IN AMERICA.**"

—**Robert Scanlan**
Harvard Review

"A study that is both **STIMULATING AND HELPFUL** to actors and the informed reader and theatre-goer."

—**Wallace Fowlie**
The Sewanee Review

"**THEATRE LOVERS WILL FIND MUCH TO PONDER** in his zingy restatement of a central argument about American acting."

—*Publishers Weekly*

$21.95 • cloth
ISBN: 1-55783-100-9

DIRECTING THE ACTION

ACTING AND DIRECTING IN CONTEMPORARY THEATRE
by Charles Marowitz

"An energizing, uplifting work...Reading Morowitz on theatre is like reading heroic fiction in an age without heroes."

—Los Angeles Weekly

"A cogent and incisive collection of ideas, well formulated and clearly set forth; an important contribution on directing in postmodern theatre."

—Choice

"Consistently thought provoking...Sure to be controversial."

—Library Journal

"Stimulating, provocative, sometimes irascible, but always courageous."

—Robert Lewis

$12.95 . Paper
ISBN: 1-55783-072-X

❦APPLAUSE❦

IN SEARCH OF THEATER

by ERIC BENTLEY

Fɪʀsᴛ published in 1953, *In Search of Theater* is widely regarded as the standard portrait of the European and American theatre in the turbulent and seminal years following World War II. The book's influence contributed substantially to the rising reputations of such artists as Bertolt Brecht, Charles Chaplin and Martha Graham.

"The most erudite and intelligent living writer on the theatre."

—Ronald Bryden, *The New Statesman*

"Cᴇʀᴛᴀɪɴʟʏ Aᴍᴇʀɪᴄᴀ's ꜰᴏʀᴇᴍᴏsᴛ ᴛʜᴇᴀᴛʀᴇ ᴄʀɪᴛɪᴄ…"

—Irving Wardle, *The Times*

ISBN: 1-55783-111-4

RECYCLING SHAKESPEARE
by Charles Marowitz

Marowitz' irreverent approach to the bard is destined to outrage Shakesperean scholars across the globe. Marowitz rejects the notion that a "classic" is a sacrosanct entity fixed in time and bounded by its text. A living classic, according to Marowitz, should provoke lively response—even indignation!

In the same way that Shakespeare himnself continued to mediate and transform his own ideas and the shape they took, Marowitz gives us license to continue that meditation in productions extrapolated from Shakespeare's work. Shakespeare becomes the greatest of all catalysts who stimulates a constant re-formation of the fundamental questions of philosophy, history and meaning. Marowitz intoduces us to Shakespeare as an active contemporary collaborator who strives with us to yield a vibrant contemporary theatre.

paper • ISBN 1-55783-094-0

THE LIFE OF THE DRAMA

by ERIC BENTLEY

"The most adventurous critic in America."

—Kenneth Tynan

"Eric Bentley's radical new look at the grammar of theatre...is a work of exceptional virtue, and readers who find more in it to disagree with than I do will still, I think, want to call it CENTRAL, IN-DISPENSABLE...If you see any crucial interest in such topics as the death of Cordelia, Godot's non-arrival...THIS IS A BOOK TO BE READ AGAIN AND AGAIN."

—Frank Kermode, *The New York Review of Books*

"*The Life Of The Drama*...is a remarkable exploration of the roots and bases of dramatic art, THE MOST FAR REACHING AND REVELATORY WE HAVE HAD."

—Richard Gilman, *Book Week*

ISBN: 1-55783-110-6

THE COLLECTED WORKS OF HAROLD CLURMAN

Six Decades of Commentary on Theatre, Dance, Music, Film, Arts, Letters and Politics

edited by Marjorie Loggia and Glenn Young

For six decades, Harold Clurman illuminated our artistic, social and political awareness in thousands of reviews, essays and lectures. In 1930 he began a series of lectures at Steinway Hall that would lead to the creation of the Group Theater. His work appeared indefatigably in Tomorrow, The New Republic, The London Observer, The New York Times, The Nation, Stagebill, Show, Theatre Arts and New York Magazine.

This chronological epic offers the most comprehensive view of American theatre seen through the eyes of our most extraordinary critic–the largest collection of criticism by a dramatic critic ever published in the English language.

cloth•ISBN 1-55783-132-7